D1286995

THE MYTH OF SACRED PROSTITUTION IN ANTIQUITY

In this study, Stephanie Lynn Budin demonstrates that sacred prostitution, the sale of a person's body for sex in which some or all of the money earned was devoted to a deity or a temple, did not exist in the ancient world. Reconsidering the evidence from the ancient Near East, the Greco-Roman texts, and the early Christian authors, Budin shows that the majority of sources that have traditionally been understood as pertaining to sacred prostitution actually have nothing to do with this institution. The few texts that are usually invoked on this subject are, moreover, terribly misunderstood. Furthermore, contrary to many current hypotheses, the creation of the myth of sacred prostitution has nothing to do with notions of accusation or the construction of a decadent, Oriental "Other." Instead, the myth has come into being as a result of more than 2,000 years of misinterpretations, false assumptions, and faulty methodology. The study of sacred prostitution is, effectively, a historiographical reckoning.

Stephanie Lynn Budin received her Ph.D. in Ancient History from the University of Pennsylvania with concentrations in Greece and the ancient Near East. She is the author of *The Origin of Aphrodite* (2003) and numerous articles on ancient religion and iconography. She has delivered papers in Athens, Dublin, Jerusalem, London, Nicosia, Oldenburg, and Stockholm, as well as in various cities throughout the United States.

THE MYTH OF SACRED PROSTITUTION IN ANTIQUITY

STEPHANIE LYNN BUDIN

2008

CAMBRIDGE
UNIVERSITY PRESS

CAMBRIDGE UNIVERSITY PRESS
Cambridge, New York, Melbourne, Madrid, Cape Town, Singapore,
São Paulo, Delhi, Dubai, Tokyo

Cambridge University Press
32 Avenue of the Americas, New York, NY 10013-2473, USA

www.cambridge.org
Information on this title: www.cambridge.org/9780521178044

First published 2008
Reprinted 2009
First paperback edition 2010

Printed in the United States of America

A catalog record for this publication is available from the British Library.

Library of Congress Cataloging in Publication Data

Budin, Stephanie Lynn.
The Myth of sacred prostitution in antiquity / Stephanie Lynn Budin.
    p.   cm.
Includes bibliographical references and index.
ISBN 978-0-521-88090-9 (hardback)
1. Prostitution – History – To 1500.   2. Prostitution – Historiography.   3. Prostitution –
Religious aspects.   4. Literature, Ancient – History and criticism. I. Title.
        HQ113.B83   2008
306.7409182'20901 – dc22   2007026324

ISBN 978-0-521-88090-9 Hardback
ISBN 978-0-521-17804-4 Paperback

In Loving Memory of A. John Graham

δίδάσκαλος καὶ φίλος

CONTENTS

ACKNOWLEDGMENTS

A number of people helped me, through encouragement, feedback, and suggestions, to make this book better. To them I am truly grateful. Many thanks go out to Julia Assante, T. Corey Brennan, Michael Flower, Daniel A. Foxvog, David Greenberg, Thomas Harrison, Victor Hurowitz, Kimberly Huth, Thomas McGinn, Aislinn Melchior, Rosaria Munson, Beatrice Rehl, James Rushing, Johanna Stuckey, Jean MacIntosh Turfa, and the incredibly helpful staff at the Center for Advanced Judaic Studies in Philadelphia. My thanks also go to everyone at the Summer Session Office, Rutgers Camden, for time, compassion, and office supplies. I am, of course, solely responsible for whatever is erroneous in the pages that follow.

Additional thanks go to Sifu Rommie Revell for always providing me with something to punch during stressful times, and for never giving up on the rather hopeless endeavor of telling me to relax.

Finally, I send all gratitude and love to my husband Paul C. Butler, an eternal source of support and drawings. The images in Figures 7.1 and 7.2 are by him. He is very, very tired of hearing about sacred prostitution.

ABBREVIATIONS

AHR	*American Historical Review*
AJPhil	*American Journal of Philology*
AJSL	*American Journal of Semitic Languages and Literatures*
ArchClass	*Archeologia Classica*
AS	*Anatolian Studies*
BCH	*Bulletin de Correspondence Héllenique*
BDB	Brown-Driver-Briggs. *Hebrew and English Lexicon*
BICS	*Bulletin. Institute of Classical Studies. University of London*
BTB	*Biblical Theology Bulletin*
CAD	*Chicago Assyrian Dictionary*
CP	*Classical Philology*
CQ	*Classical Quarterly*
HTR	*Harvard Theological Review*
JA	*Journal Asiatique*
JANER	*Journal of Ancient Near Eastern Religion*
JAOS	*Journal of the American Oriental Society*
JESHO	*Journal of the Economic and Social History of the Orient*
LSJ	Liddell, Scott, and Jones. *Greek-English Lexicon*
MGR	*Miscellanea Greca e Romana*
RA	*Revue Assyriologique*
RB	*Revue Biblique*
Rend. Pont.	*Rendiconti. Pontificia Accademia Romana de Archeologia*
RHR	*Revue de l'Histoire des Religions*
RlA	*Reallexikon der Assyriologie*
UF	*Ugarit-Forschungen*
ZA	*Zeitschrift für Assyriologie*
ŽA	*Živa Antike*
ZPE	*Zeitschrift für Papyrologie und Epigraphik*

THE MYTH OF SACRED PROSTITUTION IN ANTIQUITY

CHAPTER ONE

INTRODUCTION

S ACRED PROSTITUTION NEVER EXISTED IN THE ANCIENT NEAR EAST
or Mediterranean. This book presents the evidence that leads to that
conclusion. It also reconsiders the various literary data that have given
rise to the sacred prostitution myth and offers new interpretations of what
these may have actually meant in their ancient contexts. I hope that this
will end a debate that has been present in various fields of academia for
about three decades now.

What is sacred prostitution, also known as cult, cultic, ritual, or temple
prostitution? There are, as one might imagine of a topic that has been
the object of study for centuries and the object of debate for decades,
a number of different answers to that question. If we were to approach
the topic from a classics perspective, we might come across the definition
in the second edition of the *Oxford Classical Dictionary*, where sacred
prostitution

> existed in two main forms. (1) The defloration of virgins before mar-
> riage was originally a threshold rite, whereby the dangerous task of
> having intercourse with a virgin was delegated to a foreigner, since
> intercourse was in many, if not all, cases limited to strangers . . . (2)
> regular temple prostitution, generally of slaves, such as existed in Baby-
> lonia, in the cult of Ma at Comana Pontica, of Aphrodite at Corinth,
> and perhaps at Eryx, and in Egypt.[1]

If we were researching the roles of cult prostitutes of the Old Testament
we would read in the *Anchor Bible Dictionary* that

> When speaking of cultic prostitution, scholars normally refer to reli-
> giously legitimated intercourse with strangers in or in the vicinity of

[1] *OCD*: 890.

I

the sanctuary. It had a ritual character and was organized or at least condoned by the priesthood, as a means to increase fecundity and fertility. There is, however, another, more restricted way in which one can speak of cultic prostitution. We may use the term to call attention to the fact that the money or the goods which the prostitutes received went to the temple funds.[2]

Looking more deeply into the possible Mesopotamian roots of this alleged practice, we might come across in the *Dictionary of the Ancient Near East* an entry on "Prostitution and Ritual Sex" that combines several different categories of sexual act. Extracting the material pertaining specifically to sacred prostitution, one reads,

> Prostitutes are mentioned together with various groups of women engaged in more or less religious activities. Inana/Ishtar was a protective goddess of prostitutes. Possibly prostitution was organized like other female activities (such as midwifery or wet nursing) and manipulated through the temple organization.[3]

Turning to New Testament studies, we would find in S. M. Baugh's article on "Cult Prostitution in New Testament Ephesus: A Reappraisal" a more focused description, identifying cult prostitution as

> union with a prostitute (whether with a female or a male makes no difference) for exchange of money or goods, which was sanctioned by the wardens of a deity whether in temple precincts or elsewhere as a sacred act of worship. In such cases, the prostitute had semi-official status as a cult functionary, either on a permanent or temporary basis, and the sexual union is usually interpreted to have been part of a fertility ritual. More generally, cult prostitution could simply refer to acts of prostitution where the money or goods received went to a temple and to its administrators. In this latter case, the prostitutes would be slaves owned by the temple.[4]

Four different definitions have brought up several different, although not always conflicting, notions of what sacred prostitution was. It was some manner of prenuptial defloration ritual. It was the prostitution of slaves for the economic benefit of the temples. It was the prostitution of permanent or temporary priests and priestesses as an act of worship.

---

[2] *ABD*: 5. 510.
[3] Bienkowski and Millard (eds.) 2000: 236.
[4] Baugh 1999: 444.

It was a fertility ritual. It was "women's work" managed by the temple organization.

At least part of these vagaries and variations in definition comes from the different sources for sacred prostitution in antiquity.[5] As we shall see in the upcoming chapters, some of the sources seem to refer to a professional class of sacred prostitutes (e.g., the cuneiform tablets), whereas others seem to refer to the occasional prostitution of women who are otherwise not prostitutes (e.g., Herodotos).

For the sake of clarity, I offer my own definition of sacred prostitution here. Sacred prostitution is the sale of a person's body for sexual purposes where some portion (if not all) of the money or goods received for this transaction belongs to a deity. In the Near East, this deity is usually understood as Ištar or Aštart; in Greece, it is usually Aphrodite. At least three separate types of sacred prostitution are recorded in the Classical sources. One is a once-in-a-lifetime prostitution and/or sale of virginity in honor of a goddess. So much is recorded in our earliest testimonial of such a practice, Herodotos 1.199. A second type of sacred prostitution involves women (and men?) who are professional prostitutes and who are owned by a deity or a deity's sanctuary. Finally, there are references to a temporary type of sacred prostitution, where the women (and men?) are either prostitutes for a limited period of time before being married, or only prostitute themselves during certain rituals.[6] Each of these three subdivisions, of course, has its own subdivisions, but this will do for a start.

What is ultimately important to remember, though, is that sacred prostitution did not exist. As such, *all* definitions are innately abstract to begin with. What I offer here is not so much a definition of a ritual or institution or practice that took place in the ancient world, but rather a sketch of an artificial conglomeration of ideas that have been pulled together over the centuries into the *image* of a ritual or institution or practice. In creating this definition, then, I have attempted to keep to the absolute basics, offering only the information provided by the Near Eastern and Classical "sources," while remaining cognizant that most of these "sources" had nothing to do either with sacred prostitution or with each other. I have eschewed the secondary interpretations that have emerged in the definitions and studies over the centuries, such as fertility ritual or rite of defloration, although, as seen above, these are quite prevalent in

[5] I use the term "antiquity" as a short form for the ancient Near East and Mediterranean.
[6] Budin 2006: 78–79.

the current literature. Furthermore, I have insisted on the aspect of economic exchange, the *sine qua non* of prostitution. As will become apparent
throughout this book, several authors who write about sacred prostitution are willing to dismiss this economic aspect, thus confusing sacred
prostitution with other categories of what might be termed sacred sex.

ORGANIZATION

I have taken a mostly philological approach to the problem of sacred
prostitution in antiquity. This is because sacred prostitution is ultimately
a literary construct. Although various icons and archaeological remains
have been drawn into the sacred prostitution debate, this is only because
the idea of sacred prostitution already existed. For example, as we shall see
in Chapter Nine, the remains of a series of rooms in Etruscan Pyrgi were
identified as a sacred brothel based on written testimonia that associated
the site with the cult of Phoenician Aštart and, independently, *scorta*
(whores, or possibly leather bags; no one knows for sure). Erotic scenes
in Mesopotamian art are commonly analyzed based on preconceived
notions of sacred prostitution, inevitably misconstruing their meanings.
Thus, to quote one of the primary scholars on the nonexistence of sacred
prostitution in Mesopotamia,

> Old Babylonian terracotta plaques with sexual scenes, according to
> current reasoning, depict sacred marriage, sacred prostitution, or just
> plain harlotry. They do not. Like thousands of other Old Babylonian
> terracotta plaques without sexual content, they are complex tools of
> domestic magic whose images are grounded in Sumerian folk tra-
> ditions... Women in Middle Assyrian lead erotica, occasionally in
> ménages à trois, must be female temple officiants offering themselves
> on altars in Ishtar's orgiastic cults.[7] Mistakenly assumed to have come
> from the Ishtar Temple at Assur, one erotic relief appeared as an illus-
> tration for "prostitution and ritual sex," an entry in a popularizing
> Mesopotamian dictionary. The truth is, such lead reliefs show foreign
> captives performing bizarre sexual acts for Assyrian viewers and thus
> carry strong political messages that equate sex and visual possession with
> territorial conquest.[8]

The archaeological and artistic "evidence" contribute to the myth of
sacred prostitution by offering the illusion of confirmation in alternate

---

[7] Sarcasm definitely implied.
[8] Assante 2003: 15.

media. But the understanding of these things as pertaining to sacred prostitution inevitably comes back to the literary sources. Thus, they do not so much provide confirmation as contribute to the vicious cycle that is sacred prostitution studies.

Although of differing genres, the written materials that pertain to sacred prostitution can be initially categorized into two main groups: implied references in the Near Eastern corpus and direct references in the Classical corpus. By "implied" I refer to the fact that many of the words identified as "sacred prostitute" in the ancient Near Eastern languages (Sumerian, Akkadian, Ugaritic, and Hebrew) are actually of uncertain definition. Thus, the study of sacred prostitution in these areas mainly boils down to a study of terminology. As the evidence presented in Chapter Two will show, there are no words for "sacred prostitute" in the ancient Near Eastern vocabularies, thus removing any indigenous evidence for this practice from the Near East.

By "direct" references in the Classical corpus I refer once again to the transparency of the vocabulary: The Greek and Roman texts that (supposedly) refer to sacred prostitution are understood to use more clearly defined words. There is no doubt that, in Greek, a *pornê* is a whore, whereas a *hetaira* might be understood as a more upper-class courtesan.[9] Likewise with the Roman *scortum* and *meretrix*, respectively.[10] *Porneuô* and its compounded forms refer to prostitution, as do the Latin *prostare* and *prostituare*. Theoretically, there should be no cause of confusion based on terminology in the study of the Classical sources. Of course, if you have to qualify something with the word "theoretically," you already know that this is not going to be the case.

Chapter Three provides a collection of the most commonly cited references to sacred prostitution in the Greco-Roman repertoire. These range in date from Pindar in the mid-fifth century BCE to Augustine in the fifth century CE. With two exceptions, the translations I have used in this chapter come from different Web sites or commonly consulted books.[11] The idea is to present to the reader the reasons that the myth of sacred prostitution appears as viable and prolific as it does – a quick perusal on the Web or in a local library presents multiple examples, all primary sources, of sacred prostitution throughout the ancient world.

---

[9] For more explicit definitions of these terms and how they relate to each other, see Davidson 1997: Chapter Three; Kurke 1999: Chapter Five; and Cohen 2006: *passim*.

[10] Adams 1983: *passim*.

[11] I offer my own translations in the relevant chapters of the book.

Chapters Four through Ten reexamine the texts in Greek and Latin that have given rise to the myth of sacred prostitution. Chapter Four analyzes what is in reality the oldest reference to sacred prostitution – Herodotos' *Histories*, Book 1, Chapter 199. I place Herodotos here, slightly out of chronological sequence in relation to Pindar, for two reasons. Herodotos picks up where Chapter Two leaves off, looking for sacred prostitution in the ancient Near East. Secondarily, as will become apparent, Pindar's fragment 122, typically cited as a reference to sacred prostitution, actually has nothing to do with it. He is therefore reserved for study in Chapter Six.

Chapter Five looks at two narratives that some scholars claim derived directly from Herodotos – Lucian's *De Dea Syria* §6 and the "Letter of Jeremiah" vv. 42–43. Once again, I subordinate chronology to cladistics, Lucian being one of the latest references to sacred prostitution in the repertoire and the dating of "Jeremiah" being still in debate. The close (or not) connections between these later two works and Herodotos will help to unravel to what extent the sacred prostitution myth might ultimately be brought back to the so-called "Father of History."

Once both Herodotos (et al.) and Pindar have been examined, the study moves on to one of the most important names in the generation of the sacred prostitution myth: Strabo. Strabo has provided more "examples" of sacred prostitution than any other author, and in many ways he, far more than Herodotos, might be regarded as the "Father of Sacred Prostitution." It is evident that Strabo made use of Herodotos in his *Geography*, and his *ethôn tôn para tois Assyriois* (customs among the Assyrians) is mostly based on the former's Babylonian *logos*. As such, it is not surprising to find references to the Herodotean Babylonian rite of Mylitta here. Likewise, although Strabo was certainly familiar with Pindar, it is clear that one of Pindar's later commentators – Khamaileon of Heraklea – provided critical data for Strabo's own understanding of the rites of Aphrodite in Corinth.

Beginning with Strabo's Corinth and continuing throughout the rest of Chapter Seven (and really the rest of the book), the study changes perspective somewhat. As stated above, Herodotos wrote the first narrative of sacred prostitution. It is explicit, describing the process by which women come to the temple, receive payment in exchange for sex, and leave having discharged their duty to the goddess. Lucian, following Herodotos, is likewise unambiguous. Although, as will be seen, Strabo expresses some doubt concerning Herodotos' Mylitta rite, he nevertheless passes on the account. In these cases, what is at issue is clearly sacred prostitution – the sale of a person's body for sexual purposes where some portion of the money received belongs to a deity. Once we get to Corinth (Pindar's and Strabo's), this ceases to be the case. Starting partially with Pindar and definitely with Strabo, the "transparency" of the Classical vocabulary comes under consideration. For example, is a "hierodule" a sacred prostitute? Several modern authors insist that she (sometimes he) certainly is, and hierodules form the basis of many of Strabo's perceived sacred prostitution accounts. What about the *hiera sômata* ("sacred bodies"); are they also sacred prostitutes, synonymous with the hierodules? What about a *hiera*, or a *pallakis*? Does the word *kataporneuô* inevitably refer to prostitution?

The answer to all of these questions is "no." As it turns out, Strabo seldom refers to sacred prostitution; I highly doubt he even had a clear conception of this idea. In reality, Strabo only discusses sacred prostitution twice – once pertaining to Babylon (plagiarized from Herodotos), and once in regard to the cult of Anaitis in Armenia. Except that the latter narrative goes on to give a description of the rite that is clearly not sacred prostitution as here defined, and it seems that Strabo was at a loss to explain the (to him) unusual nature of Armenian courtship rituals. In all other instances – Egypt, Comana, Corinth, Eryx – Strabo is discussing institutions entirely distinct from sacred prostitution. We simply misunderstood his vocabulary.

Similar problems emerge for other authors. Chapter Eight looks at three authors – Klearkhos of Soli, Pompeius Trogus/Justinus,[12] and Valerius Maximus – and the four contributions they made to the sacred prostitution debate. Once again, in all but one instance, the narratives from these authors actually have nothing to do with sacred prostitution. Here the problems can be boiled down to bad scholarship and, once again, vocabulary. The presence of sacred prostitution in Justinus' Cyprus or Valerius Maximus' Sicca depends very much on the definition of the word *quaestus*. At its most basic, the word refers to profit. It can, under specific circumstances, refer to the "wages of a harlot," insofar as prostitutes earn profits. The problem emerges when *quaestus* is automatically associated with prostitution merely because females are involved. In fact, most scholars working on the passages in question include the word "prostitution" in their translations in spite of the fact that all that is really presented is "profit." As such, there is a specter of prostitution,

---

[12] Taken together here as "joint authors" of sorts.

understood as sacred prostitution, in passages that have little or nothing to do with this practice.

Klearkhos can only be taken as a source for sacred prostitution provided the reader only reads *one* sentence from Book Four of his *Lives* and completely disregards the rest of the text. Apparently, this has not proven to be too much of a problem, either in the ancient scholarship or in the modern. Justinus seems to have been this careless, for it would appear to be just this misreading that generated the one actual account of sacred prostitution mentioned in this chapter – the *votum* of Epizephyrian Lokris. This mistake, embellished with literary leitmotifs, furnished one of the very few direct and detailed references to sacred prostitution in antiquity.

Chapter Nine is the only chapter that is primarily archaeological in character, investigating references to sacred prostitution in Etruria and pre-Roman Italy. Once again, though, the debate comes back into the realms of the literary, as the archaeological and epigraphic identifications and interpretations are made through the lens of the written materials. Chapter Ten considers the use of the accusation of sacred prostitution in early Christian rhetoric. As with Chapters Six, Seven, Eight, and Nine, it will quickly become apparent that very few (two, actually) of the texts used to construct the myth of sacred prostitution actually have anything to do with it. Instead, later scholars, already well familiar with the myth, read it into just about any passage that somehow involved religious ritual and sexuality – once again, what might be termed "sacred sex." Except that not even the "sacred sex" really existed, and all we are left with is a lot of hot air.

The final chapter – Last Myths – looks at what happened to the myth of sacred prostitution in modern times, by which I mean since the eighteenth century. A really good myth takes on a life of its own and, like most other life forms, is capable of reproduction. Sacred prostitution is no different, and this myth has generated a number of subordinate myths. Apart from the general myth that sacred prostitution existed, there are the myths that it was somehow implicated in ritual defloration or fertility. There is the myth that sacred prostitution, not being a historical reality, was invented by Herodotos, or possibly Sir James Frazer, or maybe the Victorians generally. Another myth suggests that sacred prostitution is a sign or a remnant of matriarchy; another that it induces mystic initiation and union with the Goddess. Divisions between "the academy," "popular culture," and "the New Age movement" break down here; almost all myths can be found in some guise in all of them.

DIVIDE AND CRUMBLE

One of the biggest problems in the study of ancient sacred prostitution is
that it crosses disciplines. On the one hand are the Classicists with their
Histories and *Geographies* telling them that sacred prostitution existed in
Babylon, Egypt, Phoenicia, and the like. On the other hand are the
Assyriologists, Egyptologists, and Biblical scholars, who do not necessarily find the same in their own sources. Which is, technically, odd, because
their sources happen to come from Babylon, Egypt, and Phoenicia. And
so a bit of a divide emerged in the study of sacred prostitution.[13] Originally the nascent Assyriologists of the nineteenth century were willing
to accept the Classical data and translate different cult titles as, possibly,
"sacred prostitute."[14] But over time, especially in the late twentieth century, this came to be challenged, and there is, at best, extreme ambiguity
in ancient Near Eastern studies over the existence of sacred prostitution,
with many scholars now in the camp that believes it never existed. In other
words, they looked at the new evidence (recently translated cuneiform
texts) in the places where the old evidence (Greco-Roman sources) told
them they would find sacred prostitutes, and they realized, eventually,
that none were there.

Nothing comparable happened in Classical studies. The Greco-Roman
sources said that there were sacred prostitutes "there," and most Classicists
were content to believe that "there" they were. If in doubt, they looked
at the translations and studies from the earlier twentieth century,[15] or
discussions of the ancient Near Eastern evidence as written by other
Classicists,[16] and were reaffirmed in their belief in ancient Near Eastern
sacred prostitution. Some Classicists were willing to entertain the notion

[13] There is rather little literature on sacred prostitution in Egyptology, just as the references
to Egyptian sacred prostitution are sparse. At best, there is ambiguity. To give two
typical examples, L. Manniche (1997: 12) notes that "In various places in the Middle
East, in Greece and in India there was a particular arrangement intended for the
pleasure of gods and men: temple prostitution. It is difficult to determine the extent to
which this had a place in Egypt." Likewise, Montserrat (1996: 125) claims that "Cultic
prostitution or *hierodouleia* was not an Egyptian tradition, although it might have gone
on at such places as the precinct of the foreign deity Astarte at Saqqara. However,
textual references to specifically Egyptian cultic prostitutes are highly ambiguous."
[14] See especially Chapter 11 on this development.
[15] The most common source used by Classicists that I have seen is J. Pritchard's *Ancient
Near Eastern Texts*, published in 1950.
[16] The most commonly cited such text is E. Yamauchi's 1973 publication "Cultic
Prostitution: A Case Study in Cultural Diffusion."

that, although Near Eastern sacred prostitution certainly did exist, it was never really adopted in the West, contrary to Pindar and Strabo.[17] A somewhat radical and definitely minority view is that sacred prostitution did exist in Greece, as per Pindar, but did not exist in Babylon; rather, this was a literary construct of Herodotos.[18] But very few Classical scholars actually doubt that sacred prostitution existed somewhere.

The clash between these two points of view became particularly vivid at a conference I attended in 2002. At the "Prostitution in the Ancient World" conference hosted by the University of Wisconsin, Madison, I delivered a paper entitled "Sacred Prostitution in the First Person" in which I tested some of Robert Oden's theories on sacred prostitution as accusation (see below). The core point of my paper, however, was that sacred prostitution never existed anywhere in the ancient world. Or, to quote one of the conference participants, a Classicist, "You mean, that it never existed *at all?*" Apparently, to make such a sweeping statement was simply going too far. A vehement debate ensued. On the one side was the sole Assyriologist taking part in the conference (it is interesting to note that a conference that intended to look at the issues of prostitution in the "ancient world" generally featured one Assyriologist, one Biblical scholar, and a host of Classicists). On the other side were two of the most highly renowned Classicists to publish on ancient prostitution.[19] No resolution could be achieved.

The point is, sacred prostitution crosses traditional dividing lines in academia, and for all the current enthusiasm about studying the ancient world as a whole, East meets West, this is still barely in the incunabula phase. As a result, the Classical scholars are slow to consult primary texts and recent publications pertaining to the ancient Near East. Alternatively, ancient Near Eastern scholars do not necessarily understand the full intricacies of Classical literature. They may be able to determine that sacred prostitution *is* a myth, but not how it came into being and evolved.

THE HYPOTHESIS OF ACCUSATION

It was just this divide between the Classical authors who invented the myth and the modern scholars who deny it that led to the most popular

---

[17] Pirenne-Delforge 1994: 125–126; Saffrey 1985: 368 and 373–374; Conzelmann 1967: *passim.*
[18] Kurke 1999: Chapter 6.
[19] Somehow, I got left out of the debate entirely.

theory concerning the nonexistence of ancient sacred prostitution. In 1987, in Chapter 5, "Religious Identity and the Sacred Prostitution Accusation," of his book *The Bible Without Theology*, R. A. Oden Jr. established what is one of the most important developments in the historiography of sacred prostitution. Trying to reconcile the abundant evidence for sacred prostitution coming from the Classical and Patristic authors with the apparent lack of sacred prostitutes in the eastern sources, Oden hypothesized that sacred prostitution was, in fact, a literary motif, used by one society to define itself through the denigration of an "Other."

> Perhaps sacred prostitution ought to be investigated as an *accusation* rather than a *reality*. Perhaps, then, this alleged practice belongs in the same category with cannibalism, sodomy, and abhorrent dietary and sexual practices generally – that is to say, in the category of charges that one society levels against others as part of that society's process of self-definition.... Viewed in this way, the accusation that other societies utilize religious personnel as part of sacred sexual rites surely tells us something about those who formulate and repeat the accusation. In the present case, it tells us something about ancient Israel, ancient Greece and Rome, early Christian tradition, and the modern theological tradition. But the accusation may tell us little or nothing about those religions against which the charge is leveled.[20]

Denial

Ultimately, I do not think that this theory is quite accurate, although it does work well with much of the early Christian rhetoric. Very few of the texts Oden understood to refer to sacred prostitution actually do. Those texts that do refer to it can be shown to be methodological mistakes or dependent, directly or otherwise, on Herodotos. And although there are those who do maintain that Herodotos' account was intended as accusation, I do not believe that this was the case. The only authors who use the sacred prostitution myth specifically as accusation are the early Christians, and they are few, and come at the end of a long line of development.

Nevertheless, Oden's hypothesis was, for me at least, invaluable, because it gave me a starting place from which to build.[21] It is confusing to read a dozen or so Classical sources that insist that sacred prostitution exists (see Chapter Three) and then to try to reconcile this with the fact that no local sources will offer any confirmation. The idea of accusation, though, makes sense of this predicament; it explains why "they"

---

[20] Oden 1987: 132–133. Emphases in original.
[21] And for this I thank Neal Walls, who first recommended the book to me.

always have sacred prostitutes "there" but "we" never do "here." My first attempt to confirm this hypothesis was in my paper, mentioned above, on "Sacred Prostitution in the First Person." In the end, I determined that there were, in fact, no references to sacred prostitution that claimed that "we" did it. Texts and inscriptions that referred to sacred prostitution in the here and now were either mistranslations or misattributions of the reference. (For example, Pindar did not refer to the prostitutes with whom he was drinking as sacred; Athenaios did, some 600 years later. It turns out that Athenaios did not think that they were sacred prostitutes either, but that is a matter for Chapter Six.)

With the absence of first-hand accounts, I went looking for whoever originally made the "accusation." At first I, like many before me, accused Herodotos. But this was inaccurate, and there was far more going on in his rite of Mylitta than mere accusation, including some remarkable sympathy and theology. Then Strabo looked guilty. But an examination of his texts revealed far less sacred prostitution than normally thought, and even he seemed shocked by references to the practice.

Then, as more and more of the evidence faded away under more careful scrutiny of the vocabulary and contexts, it became increasingly clear that not only was there no sacred prostitution in the ancient world, there was barely a historiography of it. Sacred prostitution was not an accusation; it was a methodological mistake, a huge misunderstanding.

But once that mistake achieved momentum, it became nearly impossible to stop. Every piece of "evidence" reaffirmed all the other pieces and made it easier to generate new pieces.[22] The division between disciplines has only helped this state of affairs, for, like a mouse, the myth always has someplace to hide. If we doubt the presence of sacred prostitutes in Greece or Italy, we can reassure ourselves that they are still lurking in Byblos.[23] If we doubt their presence in Babylon, we can consult new studies of Herodotos that show to a newer extent just how reliable and nonaccusational he was.[24] If we start to lose faith in Herodotos, we can consult a popular dictionary of things Near Eastern and see for ourselves pictures of men and women having sex on an altar – surely evidence of sacred prostitution.[25] The author may tell us that Herodotos'

---

[22] To offer just a couple of examples: Woodbury 1978, Gritz 1991, and La Regina 1997a.
[23] Conzelmann 1967.
[24] Dalley 2003: 189; Wilhelm 1990: *passim*.
[25] Black and Green (eds.) 1992: 152, fig. 124.

description was "imaginative," but Lucian's account came from "personal knowledge."[26]

This book is the study of a long-standing mistake, exacerbated by bad scholarship for some 2000+ years. Some of the bad scholarship is ancient, some is recent. All of it is understandable – simple errors that anyone could make. I certainly made all of them at some point in writing this book. Beyond the resolution of the sacred prostitution debate, I hope that this study of historiographic meltdown makes anyone who reads it aware of the utter fragility of the study of ancient history, how tenuous our link to the past is, and how strong the filters are through which we see it. If I sound less than entirely scholarly, authoritative, and commanding throughout the following pages, this is at least in part because I have read too many works that sounded scholarly, authoritative, and commanding that turned out to be entirely wrong. Please think of my sense of humor as an offering to the deities to avoid scholastic *hybris* and enjoy it accordingly.

---

[26] Bienkowski and Millard (eds.) 2000: 236. This article is just a reworking of the Black and Green article without the pictures.

CHAPTER TWO

THE ANCIENT NEAR EASTERN DATA

ANY CHAPTER OR ARTICLE ONE CARES TO LOOK AT REGARDING SACRED prostitution either suggests or states openly that the practice emerged in the ancient Near East (ANE). Thus S. Hooks, "[T]he existence of sacred prostitution in Israel and the ancient Near East is commonly accepted and made the starting point for the interpretation of numerous biblical and extra-biblical texts . . . "[1] As J. Assante noted, "Mesopotamia is believed to have been the home of 'the oldest profession' and to have originated sacred marriage rites and cult prostitution that later diffused into other cultures."[2] I. Haas wrote, "On the evidence of the Biblical passages that have stressed a licentiousness in polytheistic religions, it has been taken for granted that temple prostitution was practiced among the Semitic peoples in their fertility cults honouring mainly Baal or the goddess of love, especially in Babylonia and Phoenicia–Canaan, and that this practice penetrated the Israelite religion because of the influence that Canaanite culture exerted on it."[3] E. Ferguson, writing about Greco-Roman religion in the context of early Christianity, claimed that "Not only was prostitution a recognized institution, but through the influence of the fertility cults of Asia Minor, Syria, and Phoenicia it became part of the religious rites at certain temples."[4] As Hans Conzelmann published in 1967 concerning *sakrale Prostitution*, "Diese ist im semitischen Orient verbreitet."[5] In 1986 Gerda Lerner traced the origins of prostitution itself to fertility rites, and then sacred prostitution, which first emerged

---

[1] Hooks 1985: 4.
[2] Assante 2003: 14.
[3] Haase 1990: 95.
[4] Ferguson 1987: 52.
[5] Conzelmann 1967: 249–250.

in Mesopotamia. Both E. M. Yamauchi (1973) and Bonnie MacLachlan (1992) organize their studies of sacred prostitution and its diffusion east to west, starting with Mesopotamia before considering Egypt, Palestine, Cyprus, and finally the West (usually a West heavily influenced by Phoenician traders and colonists). A recent article on "A Brief History of Brothels" in Britain's *The Independent* claimed that

> The first recorded instances of women selling themselves for sex seem to be not in brothels but in temples. In Sumeria (*sic*), Babylonia and among the Phoenicians, prostitutes were those who had sex, not for gain, but as a religious ritual. Sex in the temple was supposed to confer special blessings on men and women alike. But that was very different to just doing it for money.[6]

Even our earliest Greek source for the so-called phenomenon – Herodotos 1.199 – locates the ritual in Babylon.[7] As such, any study of sacred prostitution must begin in the Near East.

As the evidence will show, for centuries there has been a mirage of sacred prostitution in the ancient Near East. Since the nineteenth century, terminology from the Bible and the cuneiform corpora has been translated as "sacred harlot" even though, as E. Fisher and S. Hooks have noted, even the earlier commentators "rightly realized . . . this interpretation stems more from the later statements of the classical historian than it does from biblical usage."[8] Seeking the sacred prostitutes supposedly described by Classical authors such as Herodotos and Strabo, Biblical scholars and early Assyriologists translated technical cultic terms in their texts as various types of sexual cult workers. This was especially so of the female cultic personnel, for whom, it would appear, the earliest Assyriologists could not fathom a religious role that did not somehow involve physical, and certainly sexual, services.[9] Once the definition of "sacred harlot" entered into the lexical materials, it became almost effortless to find countless references to various types of sacral-sex workers in the

---

[6] Published 21 January 2006. Accessed via http://news.independent.co.uk/uk/this_britain/article340078.ece

[7] On this passage M. Roth recently complained, "Although there is not a single modern piece of scholarship that gives any credence at all to any of Herodotus's other 'Babylonian customs' – whether wise or shameful – his story about the ritual defloration and sexual accessibility of common women in the sacred realm ('Babylonian sacred prostitution') remains stubbornly embedded as an accepted fact in the literature." Roth 2006: 22.

[8] Hooks 1985: 7, note 9; Fisher 1976: 225.

[9] Gruber 1986: 138. See also Assante 2003: 16.

Near Eastern texts.[10] These references then supported the classical references, suggesting that Herodotos and Strabo, *inter alia*, were accurate in their descriptions of Babylon, Lydia, Egypt, and the like. And so was born what Hooks termed "a pattern of reasoning that is circular and self-supporting with surprisingly little data to confirm it."[11]

As it turns out, none of the terminology originally translated as some form of "sacred prostitute" actually has that meaning. In many instances, the professional titles do refer to cult functionaries, but none of them have "prostitution" or even "sex" as an aspect of their job descriptions (so to speak). In the Biblical materials, the cult terminology is additionally complicated by its relationship with the rhetoric of apostasy, which is based on imagery of adultery and prostitution.

In spite of all the recent scholarship both redefining the original sacred prostitution vocabulary and analyzing the origins of the myth in the ancient Near East, there are still a surprising number of recent publications that maintain the presence of sacred prostitution in the ANE. To give just a few examples: Stephanie Dalley ends her 2003 article "Why Did Herodotus Not Mention the Hanging Gardens of Babylon?" with an appendix on "Items for which veracity of Herodotus and Ctesias has been challenged, but subsequent work by Assyriologists has shown the challenge to be ill-informed and wrong." Item #1 is "Herodotus on sacred prostitution."[12] Dennis Pardee, in his 2002 work on *Ritual and Cult at Ugarit*, while denying the presence of sacred prostitution in this Bronze Age Syrian city, nevertheless uses the argument that "Because prostitution was *not limited* in the ancient world *to the sacred variety* and because male sacred prostitution was *even rarer*, it appears unlikely from a historical perspective that such was the Israelite qadeš's role."[13] Edward Lipinski, in his 1995 book *Dieux et Déesses de l'Univers Phénicien et Punique* is quite emphatic that "La prostitution sacrée se pratiquait certainement dans certains sanctuaires phénciens et puniques."[14] And in his 2003 analysis of the Book of Genesis – *The Beginning of Wisdom: Reading Genesis* – Leon Kass

---

[10] Perhaps the most commonly consulted reference to ancient Near Eastern texts is J. B. Pritchard's *The Ancient Near Eastern Texts*. Here the scholar will find, *inter alia*, that in his famous law code Hammurapi decreed in §181 that, "If a father dedicated (his daughter) to a deity as a hierodule, a sacred prostitute, or a devotee and did not present a dowry to her..." (Pritchard 1958: 159).

[11] Hooks 1985: 2.

[12] Dalley 2003: 189.

[13] Pardee 2002: 240. Emphasis mine.

[14] Lipinski 1995: 486.

hierogamy as sacred sex

footnotes part of his analysis of the story of Judah and Tamar by noting that "The term is *qedeshah*, not as elsewhere *zonah*, 'whore' or 'harlot.' The former practiced ritual prostitution as part of pagan fertility rites."[15]

To put it another way, the myth of sacred prostitution is quite tendentious, and Mayer Gruber was quite apt in describing it as a computer virus "copied from book to book."[16] It is clear that more work is still needed on this issue in Near Eastern studies in spite of the excellent groundwork already accomplished.

MESOPOTAMIA

In keeping with tradition, I begin with Mesopotamia. I would like to start by removing from consideration two aspects that have clouded the study of ANE sacred prostitution: the Mesopotamian sacred marriage ceremony and male sacred prostitution.

The Sacred Marriage Ceremony[17]

What sacred prostitution and the sacred marriage ceremony have in common is a combination of sex and religion. However, a key defining feature of prostitution *per se* is its transactional nature. To quote J. Miner, prostitution is "the exchange of sex for something else of value."[18] There is no evidence for a transactional nature in the sacred marriage ceremony; as a result, it cannot be considered a type of sacred prostitution (although, as we shall see, this did not stop earlier scholars from defining the *entu* high priestess as a sacred prostitute for potentially taking part in this ritual). As E. J. Fisher himself put it quite correctly some 30 years ago, "ritual prostitution and ritual intercourse represent two quite different practices and should be rigorously distinguished . . . hierogamy, carried out in prescribed circumstances between prescribed personnel (priest and priestess) to represent the union of the god and his consort, is simply not the same thing as the whole-sale debauchery connoted by the term cultic prostitution."[19]

---

[15] Kass 2003: 534, note 37.
[16] Gruber 2005: 29.
[17] On this topic generally see Stukey 2005, Lapinkivi 2004, Westenholz 1995, Henshaw 1994, Cooper 1993, Frayne 1985, Hooks 1985, Cooper 1972–1975, Renger 1972–1975.
[18] Miner 2003: 30.
[19] Fisher 1976: 230. What I find particularly interesting in this regard is the way otherwise very meticulous and rigorous academics fall into the same methodological trap as the

MALE SACRED PROSTITUTES

There are three masculine titles that were once implicated in the study of sacred prostitution in Mesopotamia: the *assinnu* (*issinnu*), *kurgarrû*, and *kulu'u*.[20] As with the sacred marriage ritual, this is not because anything about their titles or functions pertained to the sale of sex in a cultic context, but because they were perceived to be sexually abnormal in some way in a cultic context, either being transvestites, homosexuals, castrati, or impotent.

Two methodological problems emerge. The first is that, like the sacred marriage ceremony, the conflation of sexuality and religion does not automatically relate to sacred prostitution. The *sine qua non* of prostitution, sacred or secular, is the exchange of sex for some other commodity. In the absence of actual prostitution in the roles of these male cult functionaries, sacred prostitution cannot be an issue.

Secondarily, there is no actual evidence for abnormal sexuality in the roles of these male cult functionaries; that is a myth as well. The idea that the *assinnu*, *kurgarrû*, and *kulu'u* were not normal "manly" men came from two texts. In one (*The Erra Epic* iv, line 56) the poet claims that in the city of Uruk, Ištar changed the *kurgarrû* and *assinnu* from men into women in order to teach the people piety.[21] In a Middle Babylonian letter a man is claimed to be *kulu'u la zikaru šû*, "a *kulu'u*, not a man."[22] Furthermore, in the Sumerian version of *Inana's Descent in the Underworld*, the god Ea creates a *kurgarrû* from the dirt beneath his finger nails to enter into the domain of the dead to rescue Inana. In the Akkadian version of this tale, it is an *assinnu* which he creates, except in a Middle Assyrian version, where the *assinnu* is replaced with a *kulu'u*.[23] Based on the preconceived notion that these functionaries were sexually unorthodox, it has been assumed that these males were able to enter the underworld because of their sexually ambivalent natures. According to B. Foster, "Male prostitutes or transvestites were devotees of Ishtar. It is not clear how such a person could avoid being held by the netherworld.

New Age authors (see Chapter 11). In both instances, the notions of transaction and especially payment are left out of the definition and understanding of sacred *prostitution*, thus completely blurring the lines between sacred sex and sacred prostitution.

[20] Hooks 1985: 3 and 26–28; Arnaud 1973: 113; *CAD*: kurgarrû: 558–559.

[21] *CAD*: kugarrû, 558: LÚ.KUR.GAR.RA LÚ *isinni ša ana šupluh niše Ištar zikrussunu uteru ana sinnišuti*. See also Henshaw 1994: 288–289.

[22] *CAD*: kulu'u, 529.

[23] Henshaw 1994: 288.

Perhaps a male in female costume 'partook of both worlds' or could pass anywhere as an itinerant entertainer."[24] S. Dalley suggests, "He may have been a boy castrated as an act of devotion. Such a practice is described by Lucian, *The Syrian Goddess*... In the Sumerian version of the story, two impotent creatures are sent down to the Underworld and they take a plant of life and water of life with them."[25]

However, the majority of the texts that pertain to these various functionaries show no sexual functions or peculiarities in their roles. The *assinnu*, who first appears in texts from Mari, originally appears to have been some manner of junior prophet for the goddess Annunitum.[26] In a later lexical list (Lu = ša IV) the *assinnu* appears between the ecstatics (perhaps referring back to his prophetic functions) and a list of singers and dancers.[27] In the majority of our extant texts, the *assinnu* is paired with the *kurgarrû* where both appear as singers, dancers, and cult actors.[28] In the later first millennium BCE the *kurgarrû* and the *assinnu* were listed together along with the *naratu* (female singers) on a pay list from the Rahim-Esu archive (BRM 1 99: 37–39), indicating that they held similar functions even into the Hellenistic period.[29] In some instances they may carry items associated with females, such as spindles; in others they carry and even dance with swords (utterly macho, of course!).[30] Very little is know about the *kulu'u* generally, other than that he was a member of Ištar's personnel.[31] There is no evidence that he was sexual, normally or abnormally, in any cultic context. Thus the author of the *kurgarrû* entry in the *CAD* ended his essay:

> The *kurgarrû*, *assinnu*, *kulu'u* and others were members of the temple personnel – most often mentioned in connection with Ištar – performing games, plays, dances and music as part of the ritual (of the great festivals). There is no evidence that they were eunuchs or homosexuals.[32]

[24] Foster 1995: 82, note 1.
[25] Dalley 1998 [1989]: 161, note 13.
[26] Fisher 1976: 228–229; Henshaw 1994: 284.
[27] Henshaw 1994: 286.
[28] *CAD* assinnu and kurgarrû; Henshaw 1994: 284–292; Hooks 1985: 26–28.
[29] Boiy 2004: 276 and 284. Their duty in this instance was to participate in the "ritual of the love lyrics."
[30] Henshaw 1994: 282–284.
[31] *CAD* kulu'u; Hooks 1985: 28. Henshaw's analysis of this functionary is quite speculative (Henshaw 1994: 299–300).
[32] *CAD* kurgarrû, 558–559.

It is a tribute to the methodological quagmire that is sacred prostitution studies that male cult functionaries with no known sexual roles and with no associations with prostitution whatsoever could, nevertheless, be identified as sacred prostitutes.

FEMALE SACRED PROSTITUTES

Unlike the Classical corpus, where words for "prostitute" are fairly well established (*pornê, hetaira, scortum, meretrix*), the Mesopotamian vocabularies are still really only in the incunabula phase, with the meanings of many words still in doubt. This can especially be so where words are titles that do not necessarily have exact equivalents in other languages. Consider, for a modern example, the Japanese term *nyataimori*. In the dictionaries this translates as "adorned body of a woman." Practically, it is the title given to women who serve as tables, allowing a primarily male clientele to eat sushi off of their naked bodies. In the absence of modern Japanese commentary, how long would it take, say, an American to figure out the true meaning of this term, and what is the likelihood that he or she would come up with some combination of "mannequin" and "waitress"?[33]

Until 1985, there were seven terms translated as female "cult prostitute" in the Mesopotamian repertoire: *entu/ugbabtum* (NIN.DINGIR),[34] *ištaritu* (NU.GIG), *kezertu* (MÍ.SUHUR.LÁ), *kulmašitu* (NU.BAR), *naditu* (LUKUR), *qadištu* (NU.GIG), and *šamhatu*.[35] However, since the work of Stephen Hooks in his 1985 dissertation *Sacred Prostitution in Israel and the Ancient Near East*, and 1998, with the publication of Julia Assante's "The kar.kid/*harimtu*, Prostitute or Single Woman? A Reconsideration of the Evidence" it has been clear that these words in the cuneiform corpus actually have no such meaning. The first three titles to be knocked out of the "sacred prostitute" category were *entu*, *naditu*, and *qadištu*.[36]

---

[33] Many thanks to Christopher Robinson for finding this term for me!

[34] Both the Akkadian terms *entu* and *ugbabtu* are translations of the single Sumerian term NIN.DINGIR, literally "Lady Deity." While the precise relationship between the *entu* and the *ugbabtu* remains unclear, it seems likely that the *ugbabtu*s were a high class of priestesses with an *entu* at their head. When the *entu*-priestess died, she was replaced with an *ugbabtu* who then became the *entu*. So much is evident in an Old Babylonian omen claiming that the *entum* will die and be replaced by an *ugbabtum*. (Henshaw 1994: 48; Jeyes 1983: 266; Batto 1974: 79.)

[35] Assante 1998: 39–45; Leick 1994: 148–149; Hooks 1985: 3. Words in italics are Akkadian, words in capitals are their Sumerian equivalents.

[36] Full studies of all of these terms have already been accomplished. This text is not meant to be exhaustive, but to provide enough information to be helpful for the study at

Entu / NIN.DINGIR

Entu, the female equivalent of the *en*-priest[37] and attested at least since the Akkadian Empire (2234–2112 BCE), might functionally be translated as "high priestess."[38] Traditionally, this office was reserved for the highest levels of society, usually a daughter or sister of the reigning monarch – thus Enheduanna, daughter of Sargon, *entu* of the moon-god Sîn at Ur.[39] Although the Lipit Ištar Law Code suggests that the NIN.DINGIR lived in her father's house, other data suggest that she had individual living quarters: the *gipar*, or the *gagûm* in Sippar (see below: *naditu*), or the *entu*-house in Babylonian texts.[40]

The sexual status of this figure is ambiguous. The majority of our evidence suggests that the *entu* was chaste. At the end of the *Atrahasis* legend, the god Enki declared (III.vii): "Establish *ugbabtu, entu, egisitu*-women/They shall be taboo, and thus control childbirth."[41] Line 84 of the Lipšur Litanies states that intercourse with a NIN.DINGIR is a great sin in need of absolution, falling into the same category as assault, murder, and adultery.[42] Section 127 of the Codex Hammurapi offers severe punishment for the man who accuses either the *entu* or the lawfully wedded wife of illicit sexual relations. Finally, the sexual conduct of the *entu* features in a number of omen texts. In all known cases, the sexual activity of the *entu* – be it having children, having sex *per anum* to avoid pregnancy, or contracting a venereal disease – leads to unfavorable consequences.[43] Thus, they are bad actions to the Mesopotamian mind.

The ambiguity arises from the common beliefs that (a) the *en*-functionary, be it male or female, functioned as the spouse of his/her deity; and that (b) the *entu* specifically took part in the sacred marriage ceremony with the king.[44] In the former instance, one would once again expect chastity on the part of the functionary, because sexual relations

---

hand. The reader is encouraged to look to Hooks 1985, Henshaw 1994, and Glassner 2002 for full commentary.

[37] It is interesting to note that the masculine equivalent has never been associated with prostitution.

[38] *CAD* entu: 172.

[39] Hooks 1985: 11.

[40] Henshaw 1994: 46.

[41] Dalley 1998[1989]: 35.

[42] Hooks 1985: 13.

[43] See Henshaw 1994: 48–49; Hooks 1985: 13; Jeyes 1983: 266 for full citations.

[44] Typically, the female functionary is implicated in sexual issues that are not considered relevant for the male equivalent.

with another human would constitute a form of adultery. The latter instance has proved more vexing. It must be noted that the literature of the "sacred marriage" does not necessarily imply a physical manifestation of a *hieros gamos* as part of a ritual, although this is commonly suggested.[45] According to this belief, the *hieros gamos* of Inana and Dumuzi is played out by mortals, the king playing the role of Inana's beloved – Dumuzi – while the *entu* plays the role of Inana. One possible result of this would be the conception and birth of the next king. However, because the *entu* is often the daughter of the king, this would entail an extraordinary degree of incest in the royal line. All in all, it is rather unlikely that a physical ritual accompanied the sacred marriage ceremony. In any event, for the reasons discussed at the beginning of this section, whether the *entu* did have purely theoretical sex with a divine spouse, or even sex with the king, it in no way implicates this functionary in any form of prostitution.

Naditu[46]

The role of the *naditu* first appeared in the Ur III period, although the majority of our information about them comes from the Old Babylonian period (1880–1550 BCE).[47] It was until recently understood that this cultic function died off in the second millennium BCE, but a recently discovered cuneiform text dating from Hellenistic Babylon (JCS 43–45 102–106) mentions one *naditu* priestess, indicating a much longer life for this priesthood than previously believed.[48] The institution existed in at least three different cities, where the *naditu*s were dedicated to a dominant male deity of the city: Šamaš and his consort Aya (as well as Marduk) in Sippar, Marduk in Babylon, Ninurta in Nippur.[49] The position of *naditu* often fell to members of the upper classes, who would dedicate an eldest daughter to *naditu*-hood to pray for the family. There are records of four princesses so dedicated: Ajalatum, daughter of Sumulael; a daughter of Sîn-muballit, Iltani, sister of Hammurapi; and Iltani, daughter of Samsuiluna.[50]

---

[45] See Frayne 1985: *passim*.
[46] For a full study on this cult functionary, see Harris 1964.
[47] Jeyes 1983: 260; Harris 1964: 135.
[48] Boiy 2004: 276–277.
[49] Colbow 2002: 86; Jeyes 1983: 261; Harris 1964: 116–122. Considering the tendency to link "sacred prostitutes" with Ištar, the frequent association of these women with male deities is particularly ironic.
[50] Jeyes 1983: 262 and 270.

Naditu linguistically means "woman who lies fallow,"[51] from the verb *nadû*, "of field 'fallow'; of building, city, region 'deserted, abandoned?'"[52] It is clear that the *naditu* was celibate. Those *naditu*s dedicated to Šamaš in Sippar were not permitted to marry, and they dwelled together in what is generally translated as a "cloister," the *gagûm*, a walled-off region by the temple where each *naditu* owned and ran her own house and land.[53] By contrast, the *naditu*s of Marduk could marry. However, they were not allowed to bear children, a fact emphasized in the Law Code of Hammurapi, where the *naditu* who marries is obliged to provide her husband with a second wife – the *šugitu* – to bear him heirs (*CH* 144–147).[54] Furthermore, the Ur-Utu archive of Sippar contained records of *naditu*s adopting heirs and bequeathing legacies to them in exchange for lifelong support.[55] In this instance, the *naditu* may have been adopting in the absence of a husband. All the evidence points to an emphatic lack of sexuality on the part of the *naditu*, making it highly unlikely that she was a prostitute of any kind.[56]

Qadištu/NU.GIG

This is one of the most important characters in the study of ancient Near Eastern sacred prostitution, as the title is cognate with the Biblical Hebrew *qedešâ*, also originally taken to mean "sacred prostitute." The radicals *qdš* in the Semitic languages mean "set apart" "holy," thus indicating some sacral function for this individual. Associations with prostitution come both from the Biblical evidence and from a Neo-Assyrian lexical list (*malku* = *šarru*) that equated the *qadištu* with the *šamhatu*, also originally taken to mean "prostitute" (see below).

The Sumerian equivalent of both the *qadištu* and the *ištaritu* (see below) is the NU.GIG, a title that could attach itself not only to human females, but to the goddess Inana/Ištar as well.[57] All the evidence points to the facts

---

[51] Harris 1964: 106, note. 2.
[52] Black et al. 2000: 230.
[53] Colbow 2002: 88; Jeyes 1983: 268–272; Harris 1964: 130–132.
[54] Henshaw 1994: 193–194; Harris 1964: 108.
[55] Colbow 2002: 87.
[56] Hooks 1985: 14–15. Glassner 2002: 159, "Une naditû est une femme d'affaires, de rang social aisé et qui ne peut en aucne façon être confondue avec une courtisane ou une prostituée."
[57] Glassner 2002: 152; Zgoll 1997: *passim*.

that (a) this person was a member of the uppermost echelons of society and (b) she could marry. The king of Ur Mesanepada was married to a NU.GIG, and the NU.GIG Gemešugalamma was a member of the royal family of Girsu, as the NU.GIG Ganezan was likewise a member of the prince's coterie.[58] In Tell ed-Der, Inana-mansum, the GALA.MAH (chief lamentation priest) of the goddess Annunitum was married to Ilša-hegalli, a NU.GIG.[59]

References to the *qadištu* exist since Old Babylonian/Old Assyrian times. Once again, as with the NU.GIG, she appears to be a female of high socioeconomic status with a fair amount of economic freedom.[60] Her functions are sufficiently diverse, as is her reputation, so that one must imagine that her role varied over its long duration in Mesopotamian history.

The *qadištu* is associated with the goddess Annunitum in Mari[61] and in Mesopotamia with the weather god Adad; she is linked with the delivery and nursing of infants, with purification rituals, and with sorcery.[62] The Middle Assyrian ritual text 154 refers to a cult ritual performed by (several?) *qadištu*s and a SANGA-priest – they are required to sing their songs before Adad, and they may partake of the leftover meat and beer from the deity's repast.[63]

The *qadištu*'s functions of purification may have been associated with her role as a midwife. So much may be inferred from a Standard Babylonian literary text referring to "the *naditu*s who with skill heal the foetus, the *qadištu*s who with water perform the purifications."[64] Concerning issues of childbirth and wet-nursing, the *Atrahasis* legend states, "let the midwife rejoice in the house of the *qadištu*-woman where the pregnant wife gives birth."[65] Furthermore, the *qadištu* could marry, as is evident in the Middle Assyrian law (*MAL* A 40) that specifies that she might wear a veil if married, but she must not veil herself in public if unwed.[66]

---

[58] Glassner 2002: 152–153.
[59] Colbow 2002: 86.
[60] Glassner 2002: 153.
[61] Batto 1974: 111.
[62] Westenholz 1989: 253–255; Gruber 1986: 146; Hooks 1985: 15. The sorcery aspect may be related to her function in purification, thus in a form of magic.
[63] Gruber 1986: 140–141.
[64] Westenholz 1989: 253 (KAR 321.7). See also Harris 1964: 135.
[65] Westenholz 1989: 252.
[66] Gruber 1986: 144.

Likewise, a late-second-millennium legal training exercise – *ana ittišu* (VII iii, 7–10) – records the case of a man who

Afterward he took a *qadištu* in from the street.
Because of his love for her, he married her even though she was a *qadištu*.
This *qadištu* took in a child from the street.
At the breast with human milk [she nursed him].[67]

Although the woman's status as "from the street" and "even though she was a *qadištu*" were originally used as arguments that this woman was a prostitute, it is now generally accepted that "in the street" means that the woman was without family, and "even though ... " either because she was not supposed to bear children on account of her office, or because her role as a cult functionary would detract her attentions from her husband.[68]

There is no evidence from the cuneiform corpus that would suggest that the *qadištu* is a prostitute of any kind.[69] J. J. Glassner comments that

La *qadištu* est donc une femme issue de l'élite sociale et qui dispose d'une certaine liberté qui lui permet de se mouvoir dans l'espace publique. Ce que l'on sait d'elle, malgré son charactère partiel, suffit à exclure la traduction "prostituée" trop systématiqement admise.[70]

J. G. Westenholz likewise notes that:

In the Old Babylonian legal system, the *qadištu*-woman appears together with other classes of women regulated by the codes: the *naditu*, *kulmašitu*, *ugbabtu* were women who were organized into special groups, each having a special relationship to a male deity, and whose sexuality was controlled by celibacy or marriage. These classes were opposed to the classes of women not regulated by the codes: the *harimtu*, *šamhatu*, and *kezertu* who has a special relationship to a female deity and whose sexuality was unregulated.[71]

In the light of such evidence, the *entu*, *naditu*, and *qadištu* are no longer regarded as sacred prostitutes. The 2000 publication of Black, George, and Postgate's *A Concise Dictionary of Akkadian* has these terms defined as "high priestess," "celibate priestess," and "a type of priestess," respectively.

---

[67] Westenholz 1989: 251.
[68] Hooks 1985: 17.
[69] *CAD* qadištu: 50, "There is no evidence of her being a prostitute."
[70] Glassner 2002: 153.
[71] Westenholz 1989: 251.

Ištaritu/NU.GIG[72]

Such evidence has still not entirely dispelled the specter of the sacred prostitute from the Mesopotamian vocabulary, for there remain the other four titles: the *ištaritu*, *kezertu*, *kulmašitu*, and *šamhatu*. The first of these – the *ištaritu* – is now only marginally considered to relate to sacred prostitution (Black et al. define the term as "a priestess, hierodule"). The Akkadian word has the same Sumerian equivalent as does *qadištu* – NU.GIG[73] – and what limited evidence exists about them suggests that they were functionaries dedicated to Ištar (see also the "Counsel of Wisdom" below). According to their entry in the *CAD*:

> The status of the *ištaritu* in OB, as well as that of the women of special status who are mentioned together with the *ištaritu* in the lists and lit. texts, such as the *qadištu*, *kulmašitu*, *amalitu*, etc., is not clear. The evidence indicates that they were dedicated to a god and that they had children, but the enumerations in lit. texts do not offer contexts that would allow a clearer specification.[74]

Harimtu/KAR.KID

For all of the remaining terms, the complicating factor, the reason they are associated with prostitution at all, is their association with the word *harimtu*/KAR.KID, until recently accepted as meaning "prostitute."[75] However, since the work of J. Assante, it is now more commonly recognized that these terms refer not to prostitutes, but to single women not under the authority of a father. That is to say, they are women whose lives and sexuality are not regulated by a male authority figure. These women certainly *may* have been prostitutes, or even merely promiscuous, but there is no clear evidence that they are necessarily professional prostitutes *per se*.[76] Thus, pertaining to the Sumerian KAR.KID, often

---

[72] See evidence on the NU.GIG above.

[73] Henshaw 1994: 213; *CAD* ištaritu: 271.

[74] *CAD* ištaritu: 271.

[75] The masculine equivalent *harmu* is not associated with prostitution, but is defined primarily as "lover" or "boyfriend," especially as regards the relationship between Tammuz and Ištar.

[76] Assante 1998: *passim*; see also Westenholz 1989: 251, quoted above. Some have argued that removing the meretricious meaning of *harimtu* leaves the Akkadian language without a specified word for "prostitute." This is a weak argument, as all languages are notorious for lacking words. There is, to the best of my knowledge, no word in

the (independent) owner of a tavern, Glassner claims: "la kar.kid peut être une séductrice dont la sexualité n'est pas bridée par les lois et les contraintes de la société. Rien ne permet, cependant, de l'assimiler à une prostituée."[77] The fact that a number of cult functionaries were associated with the term *harimtu* probably derives from the fact that the women in question were not prostitutes, but "independent" women, no longer functioning under the auspices of their fathers or of a husband. As Assante notes, the terms *harimtu*/KAR.KID do not appear in the cuneiform corpus as job titles, but as social designators.[78]

This new understanding of the *harimtu* dashed the last possibilities for sacred prostitution in Mesopotamia. For example, a fragmentary text, SMN 1670, from the Hurrian city of Nuzi and dated to c. 1400 records that one woman named Utubalti – who lived in *harimutu* – was dedicated (*ušelli*) by an unknown individual to the goddess Šauška-Ištar "*kîma naputi*" "as a pledge," presumably for a debt.[79] Taking *harimutu* as "prostitution," this tablet has been held up as definitive evidence for sacred prostitution in Mesopotamia, whereby Utubalti worked off the debt through prostitution at the temple.[80] However, according to the new understanding, Assante argues that the document merely indicates that this Utubalti was pledged to the temple to work off/stand as pledge of the contractor's debt, a legal stipulation in ancient Mesopotamia, where debt on one's own or another's body was common. The *ana harimutu* indicated that Utubalti was neither the wife nor daughter of the contractor.[81]

The associations between various (cult) titles and the *harimtu* are both literary and lexical. The *Erra Epic* (iv 52–53) refers to the city of Uruk as "the dwelling of An and Ištar, the city of *kezertu*s, *šamhatu*s, and *harimtu*s, whom Ištar deprived of husbands and called her own."[82] In a Late Babylonian version of *Gilgameš*, Ištar once again pulls together these women (VII v): "Ištar gathered together the *kezertu*s, the *šamhatu*s, and the *harimtu*s; she arranged weeping over the Bull of Heaven's

English for "to give someone something to drink," the liquid equivalent of "to feed." Ukranian is missing a verb "to be."

[77] Glassner 2002: 156.

[78] Assante 1998: 12.

[79] Wilhelm 1990: 517.

[80] *Ibid*: passim; Dalley 2003: 189.

[81] Assante 1998: 60–61.

[82] Foster 1993: 797. This is also the place, geographically and textually, where Ištar turned the *kugarrûs* and *assinnus* from men into women.

shoulder."[83] An early first-millennium "Counsel of Wisdom" advises
(ll. 72–74):

> Do not marry a *harimtu* who has countless husbands,
> An *ištaritu* who is dedicated to a god,
> A *kulmašitu* whose favors are many.[84]

The *šamhatu*, *harimtu*, *kezertu*, and KAR.KID all come together again on
a Neo-Assyrian lexical list (*malku = šarru*, 82–87):

$$ša - am - ha - tum = KAR.KID$$
$$ša - mu - uk - tum = MIN^{85}$$
$$ha - ar - ma - tum = MIN$$
$$ha - ri - im - tum = MIN$$
$$ka - az - ra - tum = MIN$$
$$ke - ez - re - tum = MIN^{86}$$

In the same series, variations of *šamhatu* are also equated with the terms
naditu and *qadištu*,[87] thus contributing to all of them being at one point
or another designated "sacred prostitute."

Kulmašitu

Of all of these titles, the easiest to remove from the list of potential sacred
prostitutes is the *kulmašitu*. The sole criterion on which her "promiscuity" is based is the piece of wisdom literature cited above, where her
"many favors" are seen as sexual. However, as Hooks has noted, the
actual translation of this line is fraught with difficulties. The problem
rests in the meaning of the signs KI.KAL-*ša* ("her?.?"). Normally, this is
taken as "favors," presumed sexual. However, one might also read them
as "barrenness" or possibly even *amati*, "spells." Thus, the *kulmašitu* is
a bad wife not because she is promiscuous, but because she is infertile,
or potentially magically dangerous.[88] Even if one were to read the signs
simply as "favors," there is no evidence that these are sexual. Rather, they
may be religious, and thus the text warns against marrying a woman with
copious religious duties. The same is suggested for the *ištaritu*.

---

[83] Dalley 1989: 82, adapted.
[84] Lambert 1992: 133.
[85] "Ditto."
[86] Kilmer 1963: 434.
[87] *Ibid*: 131–133.
[88] Hooks 1985: 22–23.

In all other respects, the *kulmašitu* appears to be a religious functionary.[89] So much is apparent in *Gilgameš* III iv, where her name appears
in a list of votaries; the above "Counsel of Wisdom," where she comes
after the *ištaritu*; and §181 of the Codex Hammurapi, which deals with
the inheritance rights of *naditu*s, *qadištu*s, and *kulmašitu*s dedicated by
their fathers to a deity.[90] Once again, there are no sexual components
attributed to her. She is not a sacred prostitute.

Kezertu and Šamhatu

To date, there is no clear understanding of what these two terms designate.
Both have been defined as prostitutes based on their association with the
harimtu in the literary and lexical lists, and sacred prostitutes specifically
based on their relationship with Ištar. The *kezertu*, defined in the *CAD* as a
prostitute, was also identified as a priestess based on one Old Babylonian
letter, wherein Hammurapi ordered that (the statue of) a goddess be
transported to Babylon accompanied by *kezretu*-women.[91]

A *kezertu* literally means "female with curled hair," and Finkelstein
once suggested that it might simply refer to a hairdresser.[92] Both the association with the *harimtu* and the description as one "whom Ištar deprived
of husbands" suggest that the *kezertu* is unmarried. However, Old Babylonian documents do indicate that she could marry,[93] and a text from Mari
reveals that one *kezertu* bore a child to Zimri-Lim, indicating that she
may have been either a courtesan or concubine.[94] Furthermore, a Middle Assyrian text refers to the DUMU.MEŠ.SAL.SUHUR.LÁ.MEŠ, the
sons of the *kezertu*s.[95] That the term designates a specific class of individuals is apparent in a distribution list from Mari (ARM VII 206) in which
the *kezertu*s are classed together with cleaning women, female scribes,
and professional singers.[96] Nevertheless, the term is probably not a professional title *per se*, for, Assante noted, the word might also function as a

---

[89] Her definition in the *CAD* is simply "a woman devotee of a deity."
[90] It is interesting to note that the translations for these terms in J. B. Pritchard's *The Ancient Near East*, for years the most commonly sought out text of ANE translations, are *hierodule*, sacred prostitute, and devotee, respectively. Pritchard 1958: 159.
[91] Batto 1974: 114.
[92] Assante 1998: 41–42.
[93] Henshaw 1994: 198; Hooks 1985: 23.
[94] Glassner 2002: 159.
[95] Assante 1998: 42; Henshaw 1994: 199; Hooks 1985: 23, with full citations.
[96] Henshaw 1994: 199; Batto 1974: 115.

personal name ("Curly"), and professional titles never doubled as names in the way that personal attributes did.[97] Male *kezru*s are also attested,[98] and both categories could be dedicated to a deity. One Neo-Assyrian contract (IM 56869) lists as a penalty to one who would contest the contract that s/he give "7 LÚ.SUHUR.LÁ.MEŠ ù 7 MÍ.SUHUR.LÁ.MEŠ *ana Ištar ašibat Arbail iddan*" "s/he gave 7 *kezru*s and 7 *kezretu*s to Ištar dwelling at Arbela." The function(s) of these individuals might be hinted at in a Sumerian-language document (CBS 10467) claiming that a girl "acted like a *kezertu* – sang songs and played games."[99] Furthermore, an OB letter from Mari, written by Zimri-Lim to one Malik-Akka mentions a "splendid young *kezertum*" to enter into Malik-Akka's retinue.[100] This might indicate that the *kezertu* belongs among the palace personnel or within the royal retinue.

It is possible that a *kezertu* (and *kezru*) functioned as some kind of entertainer who was responsible for "cheering up" a royal or religious environment. Glassner insists that they have some musical function, being professional musicians, singers, or dancers.[101] The closest equivalent would perhaps be the Japanese *geisha*. In typical Western practice, though, such a function was reduced to the mere or primarily sexual component of courtesan, and thus prostitute.[102]

A similar case might be made for the *šamhatu*. This is a term which could also be used as a personal name (see note 97), most famously in the case of Šamhat in the *Gilgameš Epic*. Once again, as professional titles seldom function as personal names, it is quite unlikely that *šamhatu* is a professional title, but rather a characteristic. Furthermore, as Assante notes, in the *Gilgameš Epic* the character is referred to as "Šamhat the *harimtu*," which would be rather redundant if both words meant "prostitute."[103] The word itself comes from the verb *šamahu* "to grow, flourish,

---

[97] Assante 1998: 42. Texts from Mari reveal Kezertum as well as a Šamhatum. (Glassner 2002: 160.)

[98] And, being male, have never been associated with prostitution of any kind.

[99] Roth 1983: 276.

[100] Batto 1974: 115–116.

[101] Glassner 2002: 159.

[102] This imagined sexual component then created its own "feedback" loops in the study of this title. For example, Gallery, in her 1980 study "Service Obligations of the *kezertu*-Women," argued that the women referred to in her texts were *kezertu*s because one of the stipulated "duties" was *harimutu*, originally taken to mean "prostitution," in spite of the fact that the term *kezertu* itself did not appear on the tablet. This was then used as further evidence for *kezertu*s being sacred prostitutes.

[103] Assante 1998: 41, no. 100.

be magnificent, to attain extraordinary beauty or stature."[104] The word
šamhat, then, is a feminine form that might be taken as "Beautiful" or even
"Voluptuous." The close connection between the *šamhatu*, the *kezertu*,
the *harimtu*, and Ištar as described above may indicate that all three types
of woman were independent and associated with beauty, laughter, and
general revelry. The lack of a comparable category in the modern vocabulary apparently facilitated a connection with sexuality, hence prostitution,
and then sacred prostitution.

AMATEUR CONSIDERATIONS

All of the above involve terms that have been taken to refer to some kind
of professional sacred prostitute. However, as discussed in Chapter 1,
some references to sacred prostitution do not involve a specialized class,
but rather a once-in-a-lifetime kind of sacred prostitution (Herodotos
1.199) or merely an occasional practice by normal women (Lucian, *de
Dea Syria* 6). Such women might not have had a specific terminology to
describe them, and thus one must question how one would, or would
not, find them in the textual record.

Some authors, such as Hooks, have looked at marriage clauses requir-
ing the virginity of brides as evidence that the "Herodotean" style of
sacred prostitution cannot be accurate, as, obviously, having "discharged
her duty" the Mesopotamian female in question would obviously no
longer be a virgin. This argument breaks down in two places. On the
one hand, there is no evidence before the early Christian period that the
women partaking in sacred prostitution were virgins; quite the contrary
in Herodotos specifically (see Chapter 4). There is therefore no reason
to assume that virginity was at issue with many of our early Classical references. Furthermore, it is currently not entirely evident that virginity is
always demanded in Mesopotamian marriage contracts. The words originally accepted as "virgin" were *batultu* and *nu'artu*.[105] These, however, are
age-group designations, and there is evidence to suggest that the *nu'artu*
at least need not be a virgin.[106] *Batultu* is generally defined as "adolescent,
nubile girl," just as the masculine equivalent – *batulu* – is "boy, young
man."[107] Although J. Cooper maintains that the *batultu* in the marriage
contracts is a "good girl" – "a young woman who has not been married

---

[104] Black et al. 2000: 352.
[105] Roth 1989: 6–7.
[106] *Ibid.*
[107] Black et al. 2000: 41.

previously and is sexually innocent, i.e. a virgin,"[108] he also notes that virginity, while prized, was not a prerequisite even for a first marriage. Only later Christian authors, who placed a high value on chastity, would emphasize the deflowering aspect of sacred prostitution (see Chapter 10).

Perhaps more helpful are references to adultery and (il)legitimacy in the cuneiform documents. Infidelity on the part of wives had been of great concern in Mesopotamian law since at least the time of Hammurapi, whose law code provides various stipulations on this account (CH 129–136). According to the Middle Assyrian Law Code, a woman caught in adultery might be killed (MAL 13–16), whereas ten Babylonian marriage contracts from the seventh and sixth centuries indicate that a wife caught in adultery "will die by the iron dagger."[109] One would have to accept that allowances were made for this one instance of "sacred" adultery, for which, once again, there is no evidence. Furthermore, issues of legitimacy were of extreme importance in the second and first millennia, especially as regards the equitable division of inheritances. Births occurring in previous marriages, or to a married couple before the signing of an official marriage contract, as well as after a contract was signed are all accounted for in our legal documentation.[110] The extreme concern shown by the legal documents over the legitimacy and parentage of children strongly argues against the notion that there was an entire potential class of bastards functioning invisibly in Mesopotamian society. In short, the concerns of the Mesopotamians as seen in their own written documents run contrary to the ethos and implications implied by an "amateur" style of sacred prostitution.

In the end, there is no evidence for sacred prostitution in Mesopotamia. All of the terms that had previously been held up as "sacred prostitute" have not only been shown not to have been prostitutes, but not necessarily even sexual, and occasionally downright chaste. Likewise, there is no evidence for common women functioning temporarily as sacred prostitutes, whereas it is clear that such an activity was very much against Mesopotamian values and culture. While some might contend that this is arguing *ex silencio*, one must admit that it is a deafening *silencio*, as E. J. Fisher noted back in 1976:

> If sacred prostitution was religious law and had such a central place in the ancient cult, one would expect that the law codes, the records of temple

---

[108] Cooper 2002: 93.
[109] Roth 1989: 15; Roth 1988: *passim*.
[110] Roth 1989: 15–18; Postgate 1992: 96–106.

administration, and the lists of temple personnel which we now have in some abundance would make fairly explicit if not frequent mention of it. If there existed a special class of sacred persons whose function was < <to submit to promiscuous lewdness, especially for hire> >, one could reasonably expect a body of law to regulate a practice so essential to the prosperity of land and nation. As we shall see, however, such is not the case with the evidence we have.[111]

CANAAN AND ISRAEL

The Biblical Evidence[112]

The usual "culprit" when looking for sacred prostitutes in ancient Israel and Canaan is the *qadeš* (m.)/*qedeša* (f.). Both are defined in *BDB* as "temple-prostitute," whereas the usual translations in modern Bibles are "temple -," "cult -," or "sacred prostitute," with the additional modifier of "male" inserted in the case of the *qedešîm* (pl. of *qadeš*). The association with some aspect of holiness is easy enough to understand – the radicals qdš in the Semitic languages refer to something that is "set apart," often in a manner suggesting consecration, and thus "holy" or "sacrosanct" (see *qadištu* above). Based on the meaning of the radicals and comparison with its cognate *qadištu*, as well as the actual uses of these titles in the Hebrew Bible, it appears that the *qedešîm*/*qedešôt* were cult functionaries, priests and priestesses, although clearly *not* Biblically approved Levitical priests in the cult of YHWH.[113] So much is attested in the Biblical passages.

Before proceeding to these, however, a methodological issue must be addressed: Is the title *qedeša* merely the feminine form of the masculine *qadeš*, or do these two words have entirely different meanings? The usual suggestion, per *BDB*, is that these words are simply the masculine and feminine forms of the same title. However, Mayer Gruber, in two articles, has suggested that the words *qadeš* and *qedeša* represent two completely different concepts. The male form denotes a Canaanite cult functionary, whereas the female form refers to a secular prostitute. In this instance, the radicals that conferred the notion of holiness onto the male – the priest – conveyed a meaning of "separated, set apart" onto the woman,

[111] Fisher 1976: 226.
[112] Unless otherwise stated, all translations come from the NRSV, adapted.
[113] Milgrom 1990: 479.

separated as in profane, thus a prostitute.[114] As such, the _qedešâ_ would be the equivalent of the more common word for prostitute in Hebrew, the _zônâ_.[115]

I believe that there are two flaws with this argument. Although it is true that the _qedešîm_ and _qedešôt_ seldom appear together in the Biblical texts, they do appear together in a parallel construction in Deuteronomy 23, suggesting that the author saw these two titles as a "matched set." Furthermore, as I shall show, there is no reason to define the _qedešâ_ as a prostitute, secular or sacred. As a result, the logical translation of the title is "female cult functionary," or "votaress," or simply "priestess," as is the case with the male.

Canaanite Priests[116]

In Deuteronomy 23:17, the Deuteronomist commands that "None of the daughters of Israel shall be a _qedešâ_; none of the sons of Israel shall be a _qadeš_." Whatever this title refers to, YHWH does _not_ approve either for females or for males.

This becomes increasing clear in the narratives of 1 and 2 Kings, where the _qedešîm_ appear in references to the apostasy and reformations of the Hebrew people. In 1 Kings 14:22–24, the people of Judah "did what was evil in the sight of the LORD," for they "built for themselves high places, pillars, and sacred poles; there were also _qedešîm_ in the land. They committed all the abominations of the nations that the LORD drove out before the people of Israel." Later, when Asa attempted to reform this wayward people in 1 Kings 15:12–13, "He put away the _qedešîm_ out of the land, and he removed all the idols that his ancestors had made. He also removed his mother Maacah from being queen mother, because she had made an abominable image for Asherah. . . ." Even later, when Jehoshaphat continued the reforms of Asa in 1 Kings 22:46, "The remnant of the _qedešîm_ who were still in the land in the days of his father Asa, he exterminated."

Something very similar occurs in 2 Kings 23: 6–8, when the great reformer Josiah "brought out the image of Asherah from the house of the LORD, outside Jerusalem . . . He broke down the houses of the _qedešîm_ that were in the house of the LORD, where the women did weaving for

---

[114] Gruber 1986: _passim_; Gruber 2005: 28.
[115] For extensive studies of this word and its meanings, see Hooks 1985: 65–151; Bird 1997: 219–236 (with references); and Bird 2006: 41–44.
[116] For a full study of the male _qedešîm_, see Bird 1997a: _passim_.

Asherah. He brought all the priests out of the towns of Judah, and defiled the high places where the priests had made offerings . . . ."[117]

In each instance (with the exception of the rather undetailed Deuteronomy 23), the *qedešîm* are listed together with cult items or practices that are recognized as being antithetical to the proper worship of YHWH. They are associated with the high places (*bammôt*), with the pillars and sacred poles (*ašerîm*), and with the cult of the goddess Asherah, in terms both of her idols (1 Kings 15:13, 2 Kings 23:6) and of her other cult functionaries (2 Kings 23:7). It would certainly seem, then, that the *qedešîm* are cult functionaries, probably of Asherah.[118] They appear when non-Yahwistic cults proliferate in Israel/Judah, and especially when attributes of Asherah's cults are mentioned.

The *qedešôt* appear less frequently in the Bible; there are only three references to them – Genesis 38, Deuteronomy 23:17 (mentioned above), and Hosea 4:14. This last reference suggests that, like their male counterparts, the *qedešôt* were also non-Yahwistic cult functionaries. Here Hosea complains:

> I shall not punish your daughters when they play the whore,
> nor your daughters-in-law when they commit adultery,
> for the men themselves go aside with whores and sacrifice
>   with the *qedešôt*,
> thus a people without understanding comes to ruin.

That the *qedešôt* engage in sacrificial rituals argues that they served some kind of cultic function, just like the *qedešîm*. There is good reason, then, to suggest that the *qedešâ* is a cult functionary of some sort.

Why, then, did the notion of "sacred prostitute" emerge, even to the point that some, such as Gruber, would argue that they not only are prostitutes, they are purely secular prostitutes?[119] There are three reasons – proximity, rhetoric, and a single literary narrative.

Proximity – Deuteronomy 23

Deuteronomy 23:17 is followed, of course, by 23:18: "You shall not bring the wages of a prostitute (*zônâ*) nor the wages of a dog into the house

---

[117] A final reference to the *qedešîm* appears in Job 36:14, where they are simply designated as a group of unrighteous people.

[118] For an alternate, non-meretricious, non-Asheran analysis, see Bird 1997a: 74–75.

[119] See also Tigay 1996: Excursus 22.

of the LORD your God in payment for any vow." The usual assumption is that these two verses are related. The *qedešâ* of verse 17 reflects the *zônâ* of verse 18, whereas the *qadeš* likewise foreshadows the "dog" (male prostitute) of the next verse.[120] Although it is possible that verses 17 and 18 were meant to be seen as a dyad, an exact correspondence between titles (*qedešâ/zônâ*, *qadeš/keleb*) is not necessarily at issue. On the one hand, the relationship between them may be nothing more than similar references to unacceptable professions – foreign cult functionary and prostitute. On the other hand, there may be a conceptual dividing line between verses 17 and 18. Deuteronomy 23:15–16 is a regulation pertaining to the liberation of escaped slaves. Deuteronomy 23:19–20 deals with the interest that might be charged on loans, whereas verses 21–23 deal with the making of vows, and verses 24–25 pertain to making use of one's neighbor's garden goods. One could argue that the passage on slaves (marginal in the society) is followed by another passage dealing with a marginal occupation, followed by two passages pertaining to money, with verse 21 picking up on the earlier theme of making vows in verse 18.[121]

Rhetoric – Apostasy as "Whoring"

There are five or six places in the Hebrew Bible where Israelites worshipping deities other than YHWH are referred to as whoring,[122] carrying over a metaphor established as early as the writing of Hosea that the land of Israel itself, when unfaithful to YHWH, is like an adulterous wife cheating on her husband.[123] In Exodus 34:15–16, YHWH orders:

> You shall not make a covenant with the inhabitants of the land for when they prostitute (וזנו) themselves to their gods and sacrifice to their gods, someone among them will invite you, and you will eat of the sacrifice. And you will take wives from among their daughters for your sons, and their daughters who prostitute (וזנו) themselves to their gods will make your sons also prostitute (והזנו) themselves to their gods.

In Leviticus 20:5 YHWH condemns "all who follow them in prostituting (כלהזנים . . . לזנות) themselves to [the deity] Molech." In Deuteronomy 31:16, YHWH tells Moses that after his death, "this people will begin to

---

[120] Hooks 1985: 170 and 195, note 95. On the *keleb* as a male prostitute, see Burns 2000: *passim.*

[121] Fisher 1976: 233–234.

[122] Keil 2001: 791.

[123] Bird 2006: 52–55.

prostitute (וזנה) themselves to the foreign gods in their midst, the gods of the land into which they are going. . . . " Judges 2:13 relates how the Israelites begin to worship Baal and the Aštorôth, described in Judges 2:17 as prostituting (זנו) after other deities. Judges 8:33 related how after the death of Gideon, "the Israelites relapsed and prostituted (ויזנו) themselves with the Baals, making Baal-berith their god."

An additional reference is often attributed to the Baal Peor incident, Numbers 25:1–2. Here the sons of Israel went whoring with the women of Moab (לזנות אלבנות מואב), who then invited the Israelites to come worship the Moabite god Baal Peor. C.F. Keil claims that this deity was "a Moabitish *Priapus*, in honour of whom women and virgins prostituted themselves," thus once again bringing up the specter of sacred prostitution. However, there is no reference to prostitution (sale of sex) in this context. Furthermore, the "whoring" of the sons of Israel occurs before the apostasy, paving the way for it, and thus in this instance the whoring seems to refer to actual sex, although, ultimately, a sex leading to religious impropriety. As Milgrom noted, this rare example of a form of the verb *zanâ* with a masculine subject "probably connotes Israel's religious defection as a result of cohabitation and intermarriage with Moabite women."[124]

In every example, a form of the verb *zanâ* is present; there are no references to the radicals qdš in any form. In five instances, what we have is an extended metaphor whereby the land of Israel is the wife of YHWH. If she (or her sons) worships another deity, she is committing adultery and/or "playing the harlot," two of the nuances contained in the verb *zanâ*. The issue of religiosity is present, but the sexuality implied by the verb is entirely symbolic. Or, in the case of the Baal Peor incident, the sexuality is present, but is a cause of, not in combination with, apostasy.

There is one place in the Hebrew Bible where the *qedešôt* are brought into this rhetoric: Hosea 4:14 (see above). This passage occurs in the midst of a lengthy tirade about the apostasy of the Israelites, making extensive use of the "whoring" rhetoric just described. In point of fact P. Bird has argued that this metaphor was originally created by Hosea, and it is a dominant and on-going motif in his book.[125] The presence of the *qedešôt* in a passage filled with sexual imagery (although all based on the verb *zanâ*) referring to men who are "whoring" away from YHWH led

---

[124] Milgrom 1990: 212.
[125] Bird 1997: 225–236; Bird 2006: 49–52.

prostitutes veil their faces

to the notion that the men (possibly even priests) were literally having sex with "cult prostitutes" (the *qedešôt*) as a form of apostasy. But this is merely a misunderstanding of the imagery. The men are whoring away from YHWH in their worship of other deities, a "whoring" not only intensified by references to more concrete examples of actual physical whoring – *zenûnîm* – in the beginning of verse 14, but shown to be related in that "what the men do has consequences on their daughters' behavior."[126] This apostatic whoring is done with the cult functionaries of the other deities – they sacrifice with *qedešôt*. Nothing in the verse suggests that the men are having sex with the *qedešôt*, nor is there any reason to believe that any form of sacral sex is a part of the rituals here discussed. So, yes, the men are whoring with the *qedešôt*, but the "whoring" is symbolic, sex is not implied, and the *qedešôt* themselves are not having sex, merely sacrificing. They are priestesses, not prostitutes, after all.

Narrative – Genesis 38

Outside of the rhetoric of whoring, there is one place where there appears to be an equation of the *qedešâ* with the *zônâ* – Genesis 38, the story of Tamar and Judah, where the word *zônâ* is set in semidirect apposition to *qedešâ*, thus causing the latter word to look like a synonym for the former.

In this narrative, Judah, son of Jacob, has left his family, has taken up with an Adullamite/Canaanite friend – Hirah – and has married a Canaanite woman – the unnamed daughter of Shua. With her he has three sons: Er, Onan, and Shela. The first he marries to the woman Tamar; but because Er was evil in the eyes of God, Er dies before siring children with Tamar. Per the custom of levirate marriage, Judah then marries Tamar to his next son Onan. He, however, not wishing to sire a child for his dead brother, "spilled his seed onto the ground." Being naughty in the eyes of God, he also died. Fearing for the life of his last son, but still bound by the levirate custom, Judah sent Tamar to her father's home promising to marry her to the youngest son when he came of age. Which, in the end, he did not do.

Later, Judah's wife died. After a period of mourning, Judah goes off to Timnah for the sheep-shearing. Tamar hears of this, changes out of her mourning clothes, dons a veil, and places herself by the city gate where her father-in-law will see her. Which he did, "and took her to be a prostitute (*zônâ*), for she had veiled her face" (ויחשב לזונה כי כסתה פניה).

---

[126] Bird 1997: 232.

Judah propositioned Tamar in disguise, settling on a fee of one kid. Until he could make payment, he gave the "*zônâ*" his signet, cord, and walking staff.[127] Later, he sent his friend Hirah to bring a kid to the woman. When Hirah arrived, he asked the locals where was the *qedešâ* at Enaim by the roadside (איה הקדשה הוא בעינים עלהדרך), and they replied that they had seen no *qedešâ*. Hirah reported this to Judah, who then simply considered the matter finished, for continuing would make them laughing-stocks.

Three months later Tamar was found to be pregnant. This was reported to Judah as "Your daughter-in-law Tamar has played the whore; moreover, she is pregnant from her whorings" (תמר כלתך וגם הנה הרה לזנונים זנתה). Judah demanded that Tamar be taken out and burned. In response, Tamar presented the signet, cord, and staff given to her by the sire — Judah. Judah proclaimed that Tamar was "more righteous/more in the right" (צדקה ממני) than he was and her life was spared.

Tamar gave birth to twin sons, somewhat reflecting the earlier story of Esau and Jacob. At first one — Zerah — stuck out his hand from the birth canal, and the midwife tied a red cord upon his wrist to mark him as the first-born. Then he pulled the hand back in, and the other son — Perez — was actually born first.

The fact that Hirah goes to pay a *zônâ* and calls her by the term *qedešâ* helped to give rise to the notion that a *qedešâ* must be some manner of prostitute, and since the radicals of the word pertain to holiness (see above), this, logically, implied a sacred prostitute. Such is the translation to be found in many modern editions. There are, however, other, far preferable reasons that the word *qedešâ* is set in opposition to *zônâ* in this text. These might be considered on two levels. On the one hand there are arguments that Hirah was either using a commonly accepted euphemism when approaching the men at Enaim or attempting to lie about what he was looking for. On the other hand, and far more important in my opinion, is the *contrast* of the words *zônâ* and *qedešâ* as the first in a series of contrasts that dominate the narrative in Genesis 38:12–30.

We must begin by accepting that Hirah's use of the word *qedešâ* makes sense in its context, although this certainly does not mean that we must accept a translation of "sacred prostitute." We must also understand that there are three levels of ethnic identity to be accounted for in this

---

[127] The signet and cord have a certain yonic symbolism, as the staff has phallic imagery, which, as the story goes on to show, together lead to fertility and impregnation. The fact that the combination of signet/cord and staff yields one kid is a pun really only available in English, unfortunately.

passage.[128] Hirah is a Canaanite speaking to other Canaanites. The story, however, was written by a Hebrew for a Hebrew audience (and then is read by us, the modern audience). Thus, we see how Hebrews conceive of Canaanites interacting, which removes us at least one step from what might be termed an accurate depiction. This aspect of being a doubly removed "ethnic outsider" leaves the modern audience at a disadvantage when considering the most common option of understanding Hirah's choice of words – euphemism. Both Hooks and Bird have argued that in Genesis 38:21 the word *qedešâ* functions as a Canaanite euphemism for prostitute.[129] To quote Bird:

> Hirah . . . uses a euphemism – comparable to our substitution of the term "courtesan" for the cruder expression "whore" (a substitution of court language in the latter instance, cult language in the former). Here we have an example . . . of a common contrast between private, or "plain," speech (which may also be described as coarse) and public, or polite, speech (which may also be described as elevated). Such an interchange of terms does not require that the two have identical meanings, especially since euphemism is a characteristic feature of biblical Hebrew usage in describing sexual acts and organs. A foot or a hand is not a phallus, though both terms are used with that meaning. And a *qedešâ* . . . is not a prostitute[.][130]

Another possible explanation for Hirah's choice of wording is that he was actually trying to hide the fact that he was looking for a prostitute by claiming to look for a priestess.[131] In this instance, Hirah is humiliated at the thought of walking around town, carrying a goat, looking for a hooker. When questioning the locals, then, "he is denying the affair and pretending to take the kid to the קדשה for a sacrifice, as in Hos 4:14."[132]

In either instance, we must accept that the use of the word *qedešâ* makes sense to the intended audience. The word-choice is significant, for it highlights a motif running through the text starting at Gen. 38:12 – the contrast between whoring and holiness. This contrast is first presented in the scenes discussed above: Judah takes Tamar for a *zônâ* when seeing her sitting by the side of the road; Hirah asks for the *qedešâ* at Enaim.

---

[128] Westenholz 1989: 246.
[129] Hooks 1985: 168–169; Bird 1997: 207–208.
[130] Bird 1997: 207–208. For more on sexual euphemisms in Biblical and Mesopotamian literature, see Paul 2002: *passim* and citations in note 1.
[131] Hooks 1985: 167; Westenholz 1989: 248.
[132] Westenholz 1989: 248.

Here, the most common word for prostitute is contrasted, certainly in a humorous fashion, with a word that translates directly, based on its radicals, to "holy woman," usually translated as "votary" or, here, "priestess." It is significant to note here that Hirah's word-choice occurs later in the narrative, specifically once Tamar has gone home and re-donned her widow's garments. The woman who looked like a *zônâ* when Judah saw her is now back to looking like, and in fact being, a good, righteous woman, right when Hirah uses the word *qedešâ* to describe her. This, I believe, serves to highlight Tamar's moral character in the narrative, especially in contrast to Judah's.

Later, Judah finds out that Tamar is pregnant through "whoring." Once again, forms of the verb *zanâ* are used (see above). This accusation, however, is rectified when Tamar is able to prove that her "whoring" was actually the fulfillment of her semireligious duty to her dead husband(s): she conceived by one of their closest male relatives to provide offspring and a continued family line for them. Even Judah, who formerly condemned her to be burned, must confess that she is "more righteous" than he is. Here there is a variation on the contrast presented earlier in the narrative. Before, we saw the contrast between a whore and a holy woman, one representing Tamar's temporary external appearance and one her true inner nature. Here, we see the contrast between a whore and a righteous woman, one representing Tamar's perceived sin and one, once again, revealing her true inner nature.

Finally, Tamar gives birth to twin sons. This serves the triple effect of (a) reflecting back on the story of Esau and Jacob, two generations earlier; (b) providing heirs for both dead husbands, Er and Onan; and (c) showing God's approval of Tamar by making her extra fertile the one time she will get to have sex in the Bible (Judah, recognizing that he has committed incest, refrains from having additional relations with Tamar, Gen. 38: 26). What is of interest is how the sons are born.

Zerah begins to emerge first, and the midwife ties a crimson thread onto his hand to mark him as the firstborn. But then Perez forces his way out first, "usurping" his brother's right.[133] This reflects on the story of Esau "the Red" and Jacob, where the second son usurps the rights of his brother.[134] However, the crimson thread does not just call to mind Esau; it also once again brings up the matter of prostitution. The crimson cord, as evidenced in the story of Rahab in Joshua 2:18, might signal a

---

[133] There is, to the best of my knowledge, no *possible* way for this to happen in reality.
[134] Kass 2003: 537, note 42.

prostitute or her residence.[135] In Tamar's story, we see that an image of prostitution – a crimson cord – is made manifest only to be usurped later by an image of holiness and righteousness, in this instance Perez, ancestor of King David.

In three instances, notions of prostitution are shown to carry false messages: Tamar is not a *zonâ*, she did not "play the harlot," and Zerah is not the first born. In three instances, the initial reference to prostitution is contrasted with a word or name that refers to holiness or righteousness – *qedeŝâ*, *tsadqâ*, Perez. In the deeper meaning of the narrative, then, Hirah *must* refer to Tamar as a *qedeŝâ* to fulfill the on-going parallelism that gives added meaning to the story. A *qedeŝâ* is not intended as a synonym for *zônâ* (except possibly euphemistically, as discussed above); it is a *contrast* in line with the dominant set of parallel contrasts (whore – holy) running through the narrative.

For all of the above reasons, there has been a mistaken impression that the *qedeŝîm* and *qedeŝôt* were male and female sacred prostitutes. But this is not the case. References to sexuality as pertaining to these figures are purely symbolic and appear only when Israel is being chastised for "whoring" away from YHWH. As the *qedeŝîm* and *qedeŝôt* were, apparently, functionaries for other deities, their presence in such rhetorical passages is hardly surprising. Likewise, while Hirah may have gone looking for a *zonâ* and called her a *qedeŝâ* instead, this does not mean that the two words were synonymous. If anything, there is a contrast between the words that not only heightens the humorous effect of the passage, but also commences an ongoing parallel of opposites running through the narrative. There are no sacred prostitutes in the Bible.

CONFUSING THINGS FURTHER – THE SEPTUAGINT AND VULGATE

The redactors of the Hebrew Bible did have it easy in one respect: Even if they had no idea what a *qedeŝâ* was, all they were really required to do was write out the word in the appropriate places. Such was not the case for the Hellenistic authors of the Septuagint and St. Jerome in the fourth century CE, all of whom had to have some understanding of what the Hebrew text said in order to translate it appropriately into Greek and Latin.[136] When it came to the *qedŝîm*/*qedeŝôt*, they were clearly at a loss. The Septuagint presents no fewer than four different translations of the

---

[135] Bird 1997: 213.
[136] Westenholz 1989: 248–249; Gruber 1986: 135, note. 8; Boswell 1980: 99.

words *qedešîm/qedešôt*. In Gen. 38 both Judah and Hirah refer to the unrec-
ognized Tamar as a *pornê*, making no distinction between the Hebrew
zonâ and *qedešâ*. Deut. 23:17 demands that "there shall not be a *pornê*
among the daughters of Israel, nor a *porneuôn* ("whoring one") among
the sons. There shall not be a *telesphoros* among the daughters of Israel, nor
a *teliskomenos* among the sons." While the basic translations offered for
the words *telesphoros* and *teliskomenos* are "idolatress" and "initiated person," respectively, an alternate meaning for the word *telesphoros* is given
in nineteenth-century English as "sodomitess or harlot."[137] The Septuagint thus offers an extended version of the verse from what is given
in the Hebrew (and Latin) text, offering both *pornê/porneuôn* and *tele-
sphoros/teliskomenos* for the Hebrew *qadeš/qedešâ*. Likewise in Hosea 4:14,
God chastised the Jews for mingling together "with the *pornôn*, and sacrificing with the *tetelesmenôn*." The *qedešôt* are thus whores *and* initiated
ones. In 3 Kings 15:12, Asa "removed *tas teletas* from the land," thus not
only making the *qedešîm* "initiated ones" as well, but also female. The
translator of 4 Kings 23:7 was clearly at a loss, for he or she simply records
that the king "cast down the house of the *kadêsim* who were in the house
of the LORD."

It is evident that the translators of the Septuagint had a vague understanding of the terms *qedešîm/qedešôt*. In most instances there is some
combination of the concepts of "prostitute/fornicator" and "initiate"
involved, thus combining the ideas of illicit sexuality and religious person. The latter understanding is closer to the original meaning of the
words, certainly: functionaries in the cult of Asherah. The notions of
"whore" and "fornicator" probably emerged through the euphemistic
usage of the word *qedešâ* in Gen. 38 and the close relationship between
the words *qedešîm/qedešôt* and the rhetoric of fornicating apostasy as discussed above.

The *qedešîm/qedešôt* experienced yet a further development in the
fourth century CE when Jerome, having an even worse grasp of what
they were, put them into Latin.

Gen. 38:21–22

Ubi est *mulier* quæ sedebat in bivio? Respondentibus cunctis: Non fuit
in loco ista *meretrix*. Reversus est ad Judam, et dixit ei: Non inveni

---

[137] Brenton 2005 [1851]: 262.

eam: sed et homines loci illius dixerunt mihi, numquam sedisse ibi *scortum*.

Deut. 23:17

Non erit *meretrix* de filiabus Israël, nec *scortator* de filiis Israël.

1 Kings 22:46

Sed et reliquias *effeminatorum* qui remanserant in diebus Asa patris eius, abstulit de terra.

2 Kings 23:7

Destruxit quoque ædiculas *effeminatorum* quæ erant in domo Domini . . .

Hosea 4:14

Non visitabo super filias vestras cum fuerint fornicatæ,
et super sponsas vestras cum adulteraverint,
quoniam ipsi cum *meretricibus* conversabantur,
et cum *effeminatis* sacrificabant. . . .

For Jerome, the *qedešôt* were, quite simply, prostitutes of some kind. The words he used for them are *meretrix* ("prostitute"), *scortum* ("whore"), or simply, in Gen. 38, *mulier* ("woman"). Concerning the *qedešîm*, however, the translator seemed a tad more confused. In Deut. 17 he is content to call them *scortator* – one who makes use of *scorta* (whores), and thus what might be deemed a "whoremonger" of sorts. In 1 and 2 Kings and Hosea, however, Jerome takes these men to be *effeminati* – "effeminate" men, almost certainly referring not to eunuchs, but to (passive) homosexuals – those men who accept the "female" position in sexual intercourse.[138] Whatever Jerome might have meant by these so-called *effeminati*, the word *qadeš* came to be translated into the English language as "sodomite" (read: homosexual). This at least until the turn of the

---

[138] Boswell 1980: 99.

twentieth century, when the newly emergent discipline of Assyriology transformed the "whores" and "sodomites" of the Old Testament[139] into female and male cult prostitutes.[140]

UGARIT AND PHOENICIA

For chronological reasons, Bronze Age Ugarit really should come before the Biblical materials. Furthermore, it is generally accepted in the modern literature that any sacred prostitution apparent in ancient Israel leaked over from Canaanite neighbors. Thus Hooks: "The supposition is rife in scholarly literature that the practice of sacred prostitution developed in ancient Israel as a direct result of contact with the fertility cults of Canaan."[141]

However, the chain of evidence works in the reverse direction. Cultic titles from the Ugaritic and Phoenician corpora came to be translated as "sacred prostitute" often through comparison with Biblical cognates. As such, it is easier to deal with the Canaanite/Phoenician materials once the Mesopotamian and Biblical materials have already been considered.

There are five titles that have been translated as "sacred prostitute" in the Canaanite corpora (the first from Bronze Age Ugarit, the latter four from Iron Age Phoenicia and colonies)[142]: qdšm[143], klbm, grm, 'enšt, and 'lmt.[144] The first is based on comparisons with the Mesopotamian qadištu and the Biblical qedešâ, whereas the second (literally "dog") is based on the reference to "wages of a dog" in Deuteronomy 23 (see above).

If the Mesopotamian qadištu and the Biblical qedeš(â) were sacred prostitutes, as was originally believed, then it would be logical that their Canaanite cognate, the qdšm (pl.), would also be sacred prostitutes. As the evidence above has already shown, this is not the case. Furthermore, there is nothing in the Ugaritic texts that would suggest that there was anything sexual, much less meretricious, about the duties of these cult

---

[139] I use the term "Old Testament" to encompass the Hebrew Bible, Septuagint, and Vulgate.

[140] Actually, the translations are "cult prostitute" for females and "male cult prostitute" for males. Apparently Biblical cult prostitutes are naturally understood to be female unless otherwise noted. For the influence of early Assyriology on the development of the sacred prostitution myth, see Chapter 11.

[141] Hooks 1985: 36. See also Haase 1990: 95, quoted above.

[142] Delcor 1979: 161–163; Hooks 1985: 38; Lipinski 1995: 487.

[143] "...who were probably male cultic prostitutes." Yamauchi 1973: 219.

[144] ". .littéralement <<filles nubiles>>." Lipinski 1995: 487.

functionaries. Although references to them are sparse, in five administrative tablets they appear immediately after the *khnm* (priests), "who usually comprise the same number and are accorded the same privileges."[145] In UT 63:3 these two groups each provide nine men and a donkey,[146] and in UT 81 they get identical units of metals,[147] whereas in UT 113:73 they together provide one archer for the city.[148] In the one instance where something might be learned about their actual cult functions – KTU 1.112 (RS 24.256) – they serve as singers in cult liturgy.[149] As with the Biblical materials, it would appear that the Canaanite *qdšm* are a variety of cult functionary, possibly to be translated as a type of priest or cantor.

The *klbm*, "dogs," appear on a personnel record from the temple of Aštart at Kition (Cyprus) dating from the fourth century BCE (*CIS* I, 86). Here, in addition to sacrificers, artisans, and even barbers, are listed on line 15 the *klbm* of the temple.[150] According to Delcor: "Pour ce qui concerne notre text de Kition, KLB a pris en phénicien le sens particulier de 'prostitué sacré' mâle attesté en hébreu uniquement en Dt 23, 18–19 [LXX version] où il fait sans doute allusion à la pratique cananéenne."[151] Although Deuteronomy 23 may indicate a parallel between the *keleb* and the *zônâ*, it is, as Hook claimed, "quite a leap of reasoning which produces

---

[145] Westenholz 1989: 249.

[146] UT 63:

> *khnm . tš*
> *bnšm . w . hmr*
> *qdšm . tš*
> *bnšm . w . hmr*

[147] UT 81: 1–2:

> *khnm* 3 GUR ZÌ-KAL-KAL 6 GÍN KU[BABBAR 6]
> *qdšm* 3 6 6

[148] UT 113: 72–73 and colophon:

> *khnm*
> *qdšm*
> . . . .
> tu[p]-pu sabê^MEŠ ša ^GI[^Š qašá]ti^MEŠ

[149] Westenholz 1989: 249; Pardee 2002:239. RS 24.256: 21: [*w*] *qdš . yšr . b hmš* (*ibid*: 37).

[150] Delcor 1979: *passim*, esp. 161.

[151] *Ibid*: 162.

a conclusion that they were sacred prostitutes."[152] Furthermore, there is no reason to assume that the Phoenician conception of the "dog" must be the equivalent of the Biblical, or that the "dogs" in question must be human, rather than just, well, dogs. It is only by presupposing the notion of sacred prostitution that one would come to the conclusion that the Canaanite *klbm* are male sacred prostitutes.

The *grm*, which follow the *klbm* on the tablet from Kition, line 15, are considered to be the younger versions of the *klbm*, based on the Hebrew cognate *gur* referring to an animal's young. As such, the *grm* were taken as junior-level male sacred prostitutes.[153] Once again, there is no evidence for these individuals being professionally sexual, or even human, as was the case with the *klbm* before them. In both instances, M. Heltzer has suggested that these titles refer to actual canines – dogs and puppies – associated with the temples.[154] Their "pay" as listed on the personnel list may simply refer to the funds needed to maintain them.

Very little is known about the *'enšt*, the "pleasant/sociable woman,"[155] although based purely on the meaning of their name they would appear to be the Canaanite cognates of the Mesopotamian *kezertu* (see above). The *'lmt* who appear on line B9 of the Kition inscription also show up in Palmyra (*CIS* II, 3913, II, 125–126).[156] They are certainly related to cult to judge from their appearance on the Kition tablet, but, once again, there is no reason to assume that their functions were sexual and paid for. "In truth there is no text of Canaanite origin which depicts the *'lmt* in the role of a sacred harlot."[157]

CONCLUSION

There were no sacred prostitutes in the ancient Near East.

---

[152] Hooks 1985: 39.
[153] Delcor 1979: 163.
[154] Heltzer 1987: 312–313.
[155] Hooks 1985: 39.
[156] Lipinski 1995: 487.
[157] Hooks 1985: 39.

CHAPTER THREE

THE SO-CALLED "EVIDENCE"

T HERE IS NO EVIDENCE FOR SACRED PROSTITUTION IN THE ANCIENT
Near East, and thus it is not possible to argue that the supposed
practice came from there. Nevertheless, there are numerous texts in the
Classical corpus, including Greek, Roman, and early Christian, that have
been taken as evidence for the existence of sacred prostitution in antiquity,
including its origin in the Near East. What follows is a gathering of the
most important of these texts. A number of points must be kept in mind
when considering what follows.

It is nearly impossible to pull together a complete list of texts pertaining
to sacred prostitution, as every scholar dealing with the issue will have a
different sense of what texts actually discuss or allude to the phenomenon.
In some cases, as with Herodotos 1.199 (Chapter Four), the reference
seems quite overt. In other instances, as with the Simonides epigram
(Chapter Six), the reference is more implied than direct. And with others,
such as the Tralles inscriptions (Chapter Seven), the reference is entirely
inferred. What I have chosen to include here is the more blatant examples,
where there is at least a word or description that might summon images
of sacred prostitution. The more inferred examples (and, as I shall show
throughout this work, even the majority of the supposed references to
sacred prostitution here are actually inferred) appear throughout the book
in their appropriate chapters.

For the most part, these are not my own translations; those will come
later, along with the Greek and Latin texts themselves. What follows
is some of the more popular translations available in the English language, coming from sources such as the Loeb Classical Library, the Perseus
Project, Penguin editions, and the World Wide Web. My purpose here
is to allow the reader to see what the most common and accessible

48

translations of the "sacred prostitution texts" are, and how the biases of translation augment the illusion that sacred prostitution actually existed.

PROBLEMS OF TRANSLATION AND INTERPRETATION

The matter of translation is a crucial one. Belief in sacred prostitution not only mucked up matters of vocabulary in the ancient Near East, as we saw in the previous chapter; it also is of considerable relevance in the classical materials as well. The more any individual translator has accepted the notion of sacred prostitution, the more he or she has been inclined to color translations to highlight the sexual content of the various passages. Consider the following example. In Chapter 12.516a–b of his *Deipnosophistai*, Athenaios, a third century CE author, quotes a fourth century BCE Peripatetic philosopher named Klearkhos of Soloi as saying

οὐ μόνον δὲ Λυδῶν γυναῖκες ἄφετοι οὖσαι τοῖς ἐντυχοῦσιν, ἀλλὰ καὶ Λοκρῶν τῶν Ἐπιζεφυρίων, ἔτι δὲ τῶν περὶ Κύπρον καὶ πάντων ἁπλῶς τῶν ἑταιρισμῷ τὰς ἑαυτῶν κόρας ἀφοσιούντων.

Gulick, in his translation of this passage in the Loeb edition, has this as follows:

But it is not merely the women of Lydia who were allowed free range among all comers, but also those of the Western Locrians, also those of Cyprus and of all tribes in general which dedicated their daughters to prostitution.[1]

Even more intense is J. Karageorghis in her work on Cypriot Aphrodite, translating as follows:

But not only the women among the Lydians are free to make love to any man, but also the women among Locrians..., even those among the Cypriots and generally all those who dedicate their daughters to sacred prostitution.[2]

A more exacting translation, in my opinion, would be

Not only the women of the Lydians are free to those present, but also those of the Epizephyrian Lokrians, and those about Cyprus, and simply of all those expiating their own girls by "companionship."[3]

[1] Gulick 1927, Vol. 5: 321.
[2] J. Karageorghis 2005: 52.
[3] For more on this passage, see Chapter 8.

The word *hetairismos* only appears twice in ancient Greek, in this instance and in a first century CE regulation of prices (*misthôtas*) from Egypt. The word in the inscription denotes a trade associated with women,[4] and its relationship to one of the most common words for an up-scale prostitute – *hetaira* – strongly suggests that the word refers to prostitution. Nevertheless, because the masculine form *hetairos* means simply "companion," there is a vaguely euphemistic ring to the feminine form, which I have chosen to maintain in this translation, indicating the euphemistic quality with quotation marks. Although "prostitution" as Gulick has it is an adequate translation, Karageorghis's "sacred prostitution" certainly goes too far.

The verb *aphosioô* is a more difficult matter. Normally it means either "to sanctify" or "to expiate." Apparently the lexicographers did not think that this meaning made sense in this instance, for the *LSJ* translates the word in this one usage as "to devote, dedicate." Such a translation solidifies notions of sacred prostitution, insofar as one might "dedicate" in a religious fashion (**hosios*) a girl to "companionship." What it does not do is take into account the alternate meanings or tones intended by the author. For example, in at least two of the instances cited – Lydia and Western Lokris – the nonstandard "companionship" of the women served to purge or get revenge for someone's anger, and thus the meaning of "to expiate" is logical. This passage will be dealt with further in Chapter 8, but hopefully it has here highlighted the importance of translation and preconceived notions in the generation and maintenance of the sacred prostitution myth.

THE CLASSICAL EVIDENCE

Pindar, fr. 122, fifth century BCE:[5]

O Queen of Cyprus, hither to thy sanctuary
Xenophon hath brought a troupe of one hundred girls to browse
Gladdened as he is by his vows now fulfilled.
. . .
Young girls who welcome many strangers with your hospitality,
ministrants of Persuasion in rich Corinth –
who on the altar send up in smoke the auburn tears of fresh frankincense
the many times that ye fly in thought up

---

[4] *OGI* 674, line 17: γυναικῶν πρὸς ἑταιρισμὸν δραχμὰς ἑκατὸν ὀκτώ.
[5] Gulick 1927, Vol. 6: 99.

to the Mother of the Loves, heavenly Aphroditê;
upon you, my children, free from reproach she hath bestowed,
the right to cull the fruit of soft beauty in your desired embraces.
When Necessity required it, all things are fair. . .

. . .

And yet I wonder what the lords of the Isthmus will say of me,
seeing that I have devised such a prelude as this to a glee with honeyed
    words,
linking myself with common women.

Simonides, *Epigram* 14 Page, FGE, fifth century BCE:[6]

These women were dedicated to pray to Cypris with heaven's blessing,
for the Greeks and their fair-fighting fellow citizens.
For the divine Aphroditê willed it not that the citadel of Greece
should be betrayed into the hands of Persian bowmen.

Herodotos, *Histories* I.99, fifth century BCE:[7]

There is one custom amongst these people which is wholly shameful:
every woman who is a native of the country must once in her life go
and sit in the temple of Aphrodite and there give herself to a strange
man. Many of the rich women, who are too proud to mix with the rest,
drive to the temple in covered carriages with a whole host of servants
following behind, and there wait; most, however, sit in the precinct of
the temple with a band of plaited string round their heads – and a great
crowd they are, what with some sitting there, others arriving, other
going away – and through them all gangways are marked off running
in every direction for the men to pass along and make their choice.
Once a woman has taken her seat she is not allowed to go home until
a man has thrown a silver coin into her lap and taken her outside to
lie with her. As he throws the coin, the man has to say, "In the name
of the goddess Mylitta" – that being the Assyrian name for Aphrodite.
The value of the coin is of no consequence; once thrown it becomes
sacred, and the law forbids that it should ever be refused. The woman
has no privilege of choice – she must go with the first man who throws
her the money. When she has lain with him, her duty to the goddess is
discharged and she may go home, after which it will be impossible to
seduce her by any offer, however large. Tall, handsome women soon
manage to get home again, but the ugly ones stay a long time before
they can fulfill the conditions which the law demands, some of them,

---

[6] *Ibid*: 97.
[7] De Sélincourt 1972: 121–122.

indeed, as much as three or four years. There is a custom similar to this in parts of Cyprus.

Letter of Jeremiah 6.42–43, late fourth c. BCE, or possibly as late as 70 CE:[8]

And their women, girt with cords, sit by the roads, burning chaff for incense; and whenever one of them is drawn aside by some passer-by who lies with her, she mocks her neighbor who has not been dignified as she has, and has not had her cord broken.

Klearkhos, *apud* Athenaios, fr. 6, fourth c. BCE (see above):

But it is not merely the women of Lydia who were allowed free range among all comers, but also those of the Western Locrians, also those of Cyprus and of all tribes in general which dedicated their daughters to prostitution.

Strabo, *Geography* 16.1.20, first century BCE–first century CE:[9]

And in accordance with a certain oracle all the Babylonian women have a custom of having intercourse with a foreigner, the women going to a temple of Aphrodite with a great retinue and crowd; and each woman is wreathed with a cord round her head. The man who approaches a woman takes her far away from the sacred precinct, places a fair amount of money upon her lap, and then has intercourse with her; the money is considered sacred to Aphrodite.

Strabo, *Geography* 6.2.6, first century BCE–first century CE:[10]

Eryx, a lofty hill, is also inhabited. It has a temple of Aphrodite that is held in exceptional honor, and in early times was full of female temple-slaves, who had been dedicated in fulfillment of vows not only by the people of Sicily but also by many people from abroad; but at the present time, just as the settlement itself, so the temple is in want of men, and the multitude of temple-slaves has disappeared.

Strabo, *Geography* 8.6.20, first century BCE–first century CE:[11]

And the temple of Aphroditê was so rich that it owned more than a thousand temple-slaves, courtesans, whom both men and women had dedicated to the goddess. And therefore it was also on account of

---

[8] Translation accessed via http://www.usccb.org/nab/bible/baruch/baruch6.htm
[9] Jones 1917, Vol. 7: 227.
[10] Accessed via the Perseus Project.
[11] Jones 1917, Vol. 4: 191.

these women that the city was crowded with people and grew rich; for instance, the ship-captains freely squandered their money, and hence the proverb: "Not for every man is the voyage to Corinth."

Strabo, *Geography* 11.14.16, first century BCE–first century CE:[12]

Now the sacred rites of the Persians, one and all, are held in honor by both the Medes and the Armenians; but those of Anaïtis are held in exceptional honor by the Armenians, who have built temples in her honor in different places, and especially in Acilisene. Here they dedicate to her service male and female slaves. This, indeed, is not a remarkable thing; but the most illustrious men of the tribe actually consecrate to her their daughters while maidens; and it is the custom for these first to be prostituted in the temple of the goddess for a long time and after this to be given in marriage; and no one disdains to live in wedlock with such a woman. Something of this kind is told also by Herodotus in his account of the Lydian women, who, one and all, he says, prostitute themselves. And they are so kindly disposed to their paramours that they not only entertain them hospitably but also exchange presents with them, often giving more than they receive, inasmuch as the girls from wealthy homes are supplied with means. However, they do not admit any man that comes along, but preferably those of equal rank with themselves.

Strabo, *Geography* 12.3.36, first century BCE–first century CE:[13]

Now Comana is a populous city and is a notable emporium for the people from Armenia; and at the times of the "exoduses" of the goddess people assemble there from everywhere, from both the cities and the country, men together with women, to attend the festival. And there are certain others, also, who in accordance with a vow are always residing there, performing sacrifices in honor of the goddess. And the inhabitants live in luxury, and all their property is planted with vines; and there is a multitude of women who make gain from their persons, most of whom are dedicated to the goddess, for in a way the city is a lesser Corinth for there too, on account of the multitude of courtesans, who were sacred to Aphrodite, outsiders resorted in great numbers and kept holiday. And the merchants and soldiers who went there squandered all their money so that the following proverb arose in reference to them: Not for every man is the voyage to Corinth.

[12] Accessed via the Perseus Project.
[13] Accessed via the Perseus Project.

Strabo, *Geography* 17.1.46, first century BCE–first century CE:[14]

> But to Zeus, whom they hold in highest honour, they dedicate a maiden
> of greatest beauty and most illustrious family (such maidens are called
> "pallades" by the Greeks); and she prostitutes herself, and cohabits with
> whatever men she wishes until the natural cleansing of her body takes
> place; and after her cleansing she is given in marriage, after the time of
> her prostitution, a rite of mourning is celebrated for her.

Justinus, *Epitoma Historiarum Philippicarum Pompei Trogi* 18.5.4, first century CE:[15]

> It was a custom in Cyprus to send young girls down to the sea-shore on
> specific days before their marriage to earn money for their dowry by
> prostitution, and to offer Venus libations for the preservation of their
> virtue in the future.

Justinus, *Epitoma Historiarum Philippicarum Pompei Trogi* 21.3, first century CE:[16]

> Once, when the Locrians were hard-pressed by the war with Leophron,
> tyrant of Rhegium, they had made a vow to prostitute their unmar-
> ried women on the festival of Venus if they were victorious. This vow
> had gone unfulfilled, and now the Locrians were fighting an unsuc-
> cessful war with the Lucanians. Dionysius called them to a meet-
> ing and urged them to send their wives and daughters to the tem-
> ple of Venus dressed in all their finery. From these women a hundred
> would be selected by lot to discharge the communal vow and, to sat-
> isfy the religious requirements, spend a month on show in a brothel,
> but all the men would have previously sworn not to touch any of
> them.

Valerius Maximus, *Factorum et Dictorum Memorabilium* 2.6.15, first century CE:[17]

> There is a temple of Venus at Sicca, where respectable ladies got
> together, and then they go off to make money and amass a dowry by
> degrading their bodies. It is, of course, by means of such dishonorable
> unions that they intend to enter the honorable union of marriage.

---

[14] Jones 1917, Vol. 8: 125.
[15] Yardley and Devlin 1994: 157.
[16] *Ibid*: 169–170.
[17] Walker 2004: 60–61.

Lucian of Samosata, *De Dea Syria* 6, second century CE:[18]

And they [the women of Byblos] shave their heads like the Egyptians when the Apis-bull dies. Of the women, those who do not wish to shave their heads pay the following fine. They put their beauty on sale for a single day; the market is open to strangers alone, and their fee becomes forfeit to Aphrodite.

Athenaios, *Deipnosophistai* 13.573e, c. 200 CE:[19]

Even private citizens vow to the goddess that, if those things for which they make petition are fulfilled, they will dedicate courtesans to Aphrodite. Such, then, being the custom concerning the goddess, Xenophon of Corinth, when he went to Olympia to take part in the games, vowed that he would dedicate courtesans to the goddess if he won.

Dedication to Zeus from Tralles, second–third century CE:[20]

> Good Fortune
> L. Aurelia Aimilia
> from an ancestry of
> *pallakides* and those
> with unwashed feet,
> daughter of L. Aur.
> Secundus Se[i]us[21]
> having been a
> *pallakê* and
> according to an oracle
> to Zeus.

Dedication to Zeus from Tralles, second–third century CE:[22]

> Meltine Moskha,
> *pallakê*, of the mother
> Paulina, of
> Valerianus Philtate,
> who was a *pallakê*

[18] Lightfoot 2003: 251.
[19] Gulick 1927, Vol. 6: 99.
[20] Translation my own.
[21] Robert 1970, [1937], 406 has [i] (?)-. The family name Seius is attested in the Roman prosopography, possibly of Etruscan origin. See Schulze 1904, 93.
[22] Translation my own.

> consecutively during two
> five-year periods,
> from an ancestry of
> *pallakides*. To Zeus.

Lactantius, *The Divine Institutes*, 1.17.10, third–fourth century CE:[23]

As it says in the Sacred History, [Venus] started prostitution, and promoted it on Cyprus as a way the women could make money from public hire of their bodies: she required it of them to avoid herself being seen as the only wicked woman, with a gross appetite for men.

Athanasius, *Against the Nations* 26, fourth century CE:[24]

In times past women displayed themselves in front of idols in Phoenicia, offering the price of their bodies to the local gods, and believing that by prostitution they conciliated their goddess and incurred her favor through these practices.

Eusebius, *Life of Constantine*, 3.55, fourth century CE:[25]

This was a grove and temple, not situated in the midst of any city, nor in any public place, as for splendor of effect is generally the case, but apart from the beaten and frequented road, at Aphaca, on part of the summit of Mount Lebanon, and dedicated to the foul demon known by the name of Venus. It was a school of wickedness for all the votaries of impurity, and such as destroyed their bodies with effeminacy. Here men undeserving of the name forgot the dignity of their sex, and propitiated the demon by their effeminate conduct; here too unlawful commerce of women and adulterous intercourse, with other horrible and infamous practices, were perpetrated in this temple as in a place beyond the scope and restraint of law.

Eusebius, *Life of Constantine*, 3.58.1–2, fourth century CE:[26]

We may instance the Phoenician city Heliopolis, in which those who dignify licentious pleasure with a distinguishing title of honor, had permitted their wives and daughters to commit shameless fornication.

---

[23] Translation from Bowen and Garnsey 2003: 99.
[24] Translation from Thomson 1971: 69.
[25] Translation from http://www.fordham.edu/halsall/basis/vita-constantine.html
[26] Translation from http://www.fordham.edu/halsall/basis/vita-constantine.html

St. Augustine, *City of God* 4.10, fourth–fifth century CE:[27]

> To her [Harlot Venus] also the Phoenicians offered a gift by prostituting their daughters before they united them to husbands.

Socrates, *Ecclesiastical History* 1.18.7, fifth century CE:[28]

> [Constantine] also directed that another church should be constructed in Heliopolis in Phoenicia, for this reason. Who originally legislated for the inhabitants of Heliopolis I am unable to state, but his character and morals may be judged of from the [practice of that] city; for the laws of the country ordered the women among them to be common, and therefore the children born there were of doubtful descent, so that there was no distinction of fathers and their offspring. Their virgins also were presented for prostitution to the strangers who resorted thither.

Sozomen, *Ecclesiastical History* 5.10.7, fifth century CE:[29]

> I am convinced that the citizens of Heliopolis perpetrated this barbarity against the holy virgins on account of the prohibition of the ancient custom of yielding up virgins to prostitution with any chance comer before being united in marriage to their betrothed. This custom was prohibited by a law enacted by Constantine, after he had destroyed the temple of Venus at Heliopolis, and erected a church upon its ruins.

---

[27] Translation by Marcus Dods in *Augustine*. Great Books of the Western World, vol. 18. University of Chicago Press. 1952.

[28] Translation from http://www.ccel.org/fathers2/NPNF2-02/Npnf2-02-06.htm#P 173-39581

[29] Translation from http://www.ccel.org/fathers2/NPNF2-02/Npnf2-02-23.htm#P 3744-1642748

CHAPTER FOUR

HERODOTOS

(*Histories* 1.199) The most shameful of the customs among the Babylonians is this: It is necessary for every local woman to sit in the sanctuary of Aphrodite once in life to "mingle" with a foreign man.[1] But many

[1] I agree with Powell (1977: 235) that the appropriate translation of the various forms of *xeinos* in Chapter 1.199 should be taken as "foreign(er)" and not merely "stranger/unknown man." The reason for this is the *categorical* use of the term. If we were to take *xeinos* to mean "stranger," that is, a man unknown to the woman being bought, rather than a foreigner, we would have to concede that this is an extremely *relative* meaning for the word. The extent to which any man is *xeinos* would be dependent on his relationship with any of the women at the sanctuary. At any given time, then, the full category of shoppers (so to speak) are men who may or may not be *xeinoi* to the various women about the sanctuary. The category of *xeinoi* would be a subsection of the category of male buyers. However, in line two, Herodotos mentions that there are passages through which the *xeinoi* passing through might chose their women, and in line three once again Herodotos uses the word in the plural to designate the group of males doing the buying. If *xeinos* meant merely "stranger/unknown man," we would expect the word *andres*, the complete category of shoppers, where each *anêr* may or may not be *xeinos* to the various women. This is not the case, a fact that becomes apparent in, for example, de Sélincourt's translation, where he must tweak his translation and refer to the gangways "for the *men* to pass along" rather than Herodotos' *xeinoi* (my emphasis). The *xeinoi* form a category coterminous with the full category of shoppers. There is no sense of relativity. If all the men are equally *xeinoi* to all the women, mere acquaintance cannot be at issue. Thus I find the translation "foreigners" more logical, being a more absolute translation (at least *vis-à-vis* a group of women specifically designated as Babylonian) and more comfortably forming a concrete category into which all the male shoppers might belong. A possible supporting datum might be found in Lucian's *De Dea Syria* 6. Here, in a work generally accepted as being based on Herodotos (see Chapter 5), Lucian refers to the one-day sacred prostitution of those women refusing to shave their heads for Adonis, and that the prostitution "market" is open only to *xeinoisi*, inevitably taken as "foreigners." Once again, I would argue that it is the categorical use of the word – in contrast to a strictly relative use as implied by the translation "stranger" – that

do not deign to mingle with the others, thinking highly of themselves because of their wealth, and they set themselves before the sanctuary having arrived in covered chariots, with many a maidservant in tow. But the majority act thus: In the *temenos* of Aphrodite many women sit wearing a garland of string about their heads. Some come forward, others remain in the background. They have straight passages in all directions through the women, by which the foreigners passing through might make their selection. Once a woman sits there, she may not return home before someone of the foreigners tossing silver into her lap should mingle with her outside the sanctuary. And in tossing he must say thus: "I summon you by the goddess Mylitta." The Assyrians call Aphrodite Mylitta. The silver is of any amount, for it may not be rejected: This is not their sacred custom, for the money becomes sacred. The woman follows the first man who tossed her silver, nor may she reject anyone. When she should have mingled, having discharged her obligation to the goddess, she leaves for home, and after this time you might not take her, offering gifts no matter how great. Those who are attractive and tall go home quickly, while those homely in these respects wait about a long time, being unable to fulfill the law; some among them wait about for three or four years. And in some areas of Cyprus the custom is similar to this.

ὁ δὲ δὴ αἴσχιστος τῶν νόμων ἐστὶ τοῖσι Βαβυλωνίοσι ὅδε. δεῖ πᾶσαν γυναῖκα ἐπιχωρίην ἱζομένην ἐς ἱρὸν Ἀφροδίτης ἅπαξ ἐν τῇ ζόῃ μειχθῆναι ἀνδρὶ ξείνῳ. πολλαὶ δὲ καὶ οὐκ ἀξιεύμεναι ἀναμίσγεσθαι τῇσι ἄλλῃσι οἷα πλούτῳ ὑπερφρονέουσαι, ἐπὶ ζευγέων ἐν καμάρῃσι ἐλάσασαι πρὸς τὸ ἱρὸν ἑστᾶσι, θεραπηίη δέ σφι ὄπισθε ἕπεται πολλή. αἱ δὲ πλεῦνες ποιεῦσι ὧδε· ἐν τεμένεϊ Ἀφροδίτης κατέαται στέφανον περὶ τῇσι κεφαλῇσι ἔχουσαι θώμιγγος πολλαὶ γυναῖκες. αἱ μὲν γὰρ προσέρχονται, αἱ δὲ ἀπέρχονται. σχοινοτενέες δὲ διέξοδοι πάντα τρόπον ὁδῶν ἔχουσι διὰ τῶν γυναικῶν, δίων οἱ ξεῖνοι διεξιόντες ἐκλέγονται. ἔνθα ἐπεὰν ἵζηται γυνή, οὐ πρότερον ἀπαλλάσσεται ἐς τὰ οἰκία ἤ τίς οἱ ξείνων ἀργύριον ἐμβαλὼν ἐς τὰ γούνατα μειχθῇ ἔξω τοῦ ἱροῦ. ἐμβαλόντα δὲ δεῖ εἰπεῖν τοσόνδε· Ἐπικαλέω τοι τὴν θεὸν Μύλιττα. Μύλιττα δὲ καλέουσι τὴν Ἀφροδίτην Ἀσσύριοι. τὸ δὲ ἀργύριον μέγαθός ἐστι ὅσον ὤν· οὐ γὰρ μὴ ἀπώσηται· οὐ γὰρ οἱ θέμις ἐστί· γίνεται γὰρ ἱρὸν τοῦτο τὸ ἀργύριον. τῷ δὲ πρώτῳ ἐμβαλόντι ἕπεται οὐδὲ ἀποδοκιμᾷ οὐδένα. ἐπεὰν δὲ μειχθῇ,

prompts this reading. Furthermore, if Lucian is indeed imitating Herodotos here, it would appear that Lucian himself understood Herodotos to be referring to foreigners in this context.

ἀποσιωσαμένη τῇ θεῷ ἀπαλλάσσεται ἐς τὰ οἰκία, καὶ τὠπὸ τούτου
οὐκ οὕτω μέγα τί οἱ δώσεις ὥς μιν λάμψεαι. ὅσαι μέν νυν εἴδεός τε
ἐπαμμέναι εἰσὶ καὶ μεγάθεος, ταχὺ ἀπαλλάσσονται, ὅσαι δὲ ἄμορφοι
αὐτέων εἰσί, χρόνον πολλὸν προσμένουσι οὐ δυνάμεναι τὸν νόμον
ἐκπλῆσαι. καὶ γὰρ τριέτεα καὶ τετραέτεα μετεξέτεραι χρόνον μένουσι.
ἐνιαχῇ δὲ καὶ τῆς Κύπρου ἐστὶ παραπλήσιος τούτῳ νόμος.

THIS QUOTATION FROM THE HISTORIES OF THE FIFTH-CENTURY Greek
historian Herodotos is the earliest reference to the institution of sacred
prostitution in the ancient world. According to Herodotos, all Babylonian
women, once in their lives, have sex with a foreigner in honor of the
goddess Mylitta, identified by Herodotos as Aphrodite, the Greek goddess
of sexual pleasure and love.[2] The money they make for the sale of their
bodies is considered to be sacred – *themis*.

The importance of this quotation is inestimable. As the previous chapters have indicated, there are no references to sacred prostitution in the
ancient Near Eastern corpus. This passage from Herodotos, then, serves
as the first reference to this mythic institution – one of the myth's foun-
dations, in point of fact. As such, it is imperative to understand how
Herodotos' notion of the Babylonian women's prostitution came about,
what the story's origins are, and why it came into being.

HERODOTOS THE HISTORIOGRAPHER

This issue, though, is complicated by two main factors. One is the unique
and rather ambiguous nature of Herodotos' *Histories* in the history of historiography, oral literature, and philosophy. As has been discussed in detail
in numerous recent publications on the "childless Father of History,"
Herodotos stands at a turning point in the evolution of what we might
now term historiography, where the *histor* brought together the, for him,
recently emerging disciplines of ethnography and natural sciences and
combined them with the age-old tradition of epic poetry and other forms
of oral literature.[3] What resulted was a complicated narrative that on the
surface appears to be partially an extensive ethnography of greater or lesser

[2] See the Appendix on the name of this goddess.
[3] An *extremely* abbreviated list: Brock 2003; Harrison 2003; Munson 2001; Gould 2000
[1989]; Thomas 2000; Thomas 1992; Lateiner 1989; Murray 2001 [1987]; Fornara
1971. More generally: Bakker, de Jong, and van Wees 2002; Luraghi 2001; Boedeker
1987.

levels of reliability combined with a general history of Greece and the Near East leading up to the story of the Persian Invasions of 490–479 BCE. The casual nature of Herodotos' style, especially in contrast to Thucydides, has raised countless questions concerning the veracity of Herodotos' narrative, the accuracy – or even existence – of his sources, the possibility of unity within his narrative, and what that unifying theme might have been.

To what extent historians have accepted anything Herodotos reported has varied greatly over the centuries.[4] Ktesias, Manethon, and especially Plutarch accused Herodotos of being a liar (or at least inaccurate), not to mention a "barbarian-lover" (*De malignitate Herodoti* 12 857 A). Strabo (*Geography* 2.6.3) reproached Herodotos for his *philomuthia* while simultaneously adopting several of his eastern *nomoi*, including sacred prostitution, as did, perhaps, the author of "The Letter of Jeremiah."[5] To quote Momigliano: "Dionysius is in fact the only ancient writer who never said anything unpleasant about Herodotus."[6]

Modern critics have, for the most part, been easier on Herodotos. Extensive archaeological excavations, as well as the translation of several of the relevant languages, have shown many of Herodotos' accounts to have been correct, especially as concerns the Babylonian *logos*.[7] Nevertheless, problems and debates remain. That at least *some* of Herodotos' accounts are made up seems inescapable. This is perhaps most clear in Book 3.79–83, wherein Herodotos recounts the debate held by three Persians on the best form of government: democracy, oligarchy, or monarchy. That Herodotos had access to this "transcript" seems unlikely to extremes, whereas the arguments proffered read far more like Greek political debates of the sixth and fifth centuries than any Near Eastern treatise on proper government.[8] Clearly, then, Herodotos inserted an artificial dialogue to further the didactic (?) aims of his narrative, rather then to present the

---

[4] For a full account of the "Rezeptionsgeschichte Herodots." see Wilhelm 1990 and Hartog 1988: 297–309.

[5] Dalley 2003: 171; Wilhelm 1990: 506; Hartog 1988: 303.

[6] In Lateiner 1988: 7. That would be Dionysios of *Halikarnassos*, which may explain the sympathy.

[7] See especially Dalley 2003: *passim*, MacGinnis 1986: *passim*.

[8] Or, as Munson put it: " . . . Herodotus' particulars often appear . . . to have less to do with the construction of the national identity of a foreign people than with projecting onto a faraway setting pieces of a problematic that is entirely Greek." Munson 2001: 13. See also Nagy 1990: 325.

"truth." How often he did this, though, is quite difficult to determine. To quote Gould:

> We have to allow for the presence side by side within his text of things as they are – precisely observed, measured, counted and recorded – with things imagined in terms of a prescriptive order, whether that order is narrative or moral. The problem for the modern reader of Herodotus is to determine where one begins and the other ends, or even to know whether the distinction makes sense in the face of a perception of the worlds so finely meshed.[9]

How to determine when Herodotos "made thing up," then, is still at issue, a fact clearest in the on-going debates concerning the nature of Herodotos' sources. It is now generally accepted that Herodotos worked primarily from an oral tradition, recording narratives he heard throughout his travels in Europe and Asia. It is therefore impossible to go back and check his sources, and the focus now is more on the extent to which we must be grateful to Herodotos for being, in some cases, the only one to record these oral traditions for posterity. Nevertheless, this is not entirely comforting for the historian trying to determine the veracity of any particular Herodotean chapter or the nature, validity, or trustworthiness of any professed "source." Furthermore, recent scholarship has placed the source debate squarely within the discourse of Herodotos' rhetoric. That is to say, Herodotos' references to his sources are intimately involved in the *histor's* desire to convince his hearers of the veracity of his report. Thus, whether Herodotos had any actual informants, whether or not he cited them, and why, becomes less a historical issue and more a matter of style and persuasion. This has led some scholars, notably Fehling, to suggest that Herodotos actually made up his sources along with his narratives, once again casting Herodotos into the "Liar's School" of historiography.[10]

In a more sympathetic tone, N. Luraghi has argued that the presence or lack of declared sources in Herodotos' narrative relates more to the expectations of his audience than any desire on Herodotos' part to "put one over" on the Greeks. Thus, although Herodotos clearly had various types of observation in play in the acquisition of his data, notably *akouê* (hearing), autopsy (seeing), and *gnomê* (opinion, recording local traditions), his recorded sources "represented knowledge in the way in which it would usually be conceived and experienced by his audience," and

[9] Gould 2000 [1989]: 106.
[10] Fehling 1989: *passim.*

furthermore such localized traditions must inevitably account for variations and degrees of reliability in the narratives themselves.[11] As such, citing sources in Herodotos becomes an inquiry into epistemology generally.

This in itself seems to be supported by yet another on-going debate in the field of Herodotean studies: the extent to which Herodotos himself believed what he said. Herodotos claimed that he presented in his *Histories* all the things he heard and saw in his travels, whether he agreed with what he heard or not (7.152.3). This is particularly evident in his inquiries concerning the "backwards" flooding of the Nile River (Book 2. 18–24), where the *histor* provides four possible hypotheses to explain why the Nile floods right when all other rivers are at their lowest, ending with his own opinion on the matter. In some instances, such as the one just mentioned, Herodotos lays claim to his own opinion. In other places, though, his thoughts are more difficult to discern. This is particularly evident in the debate over Herodotos' use of the word *legetai* – "it is said." According to D. Lateiner, Herodotos specifically introduces a narrative with this verb when he is not wholly convinced of the data he is presenting.

> Λέγεται, "it is said," separates the historian from a report...He employs this convenience for 1) what he has not seen and deems most unlikely, 2) what is divine or miraculous...3) what seems best or worst or otherwise superlative, and 4) when more than one account of a given event is current and no secure resolution is discernable. These four categories represent what he does not know, what he cannot know, and what cannot be known by anyone.[12]

By contrast, T. Harrison argues that no such simple techniques can be employed to determine Herodotos' levels of credulity, and that Herodotos' own opinions might only be surmised on a careful case-by-case basis.[13] Thus, not only is it difficult to determine whether Herodotos was reporting the truth, but it is likewise unnerving to determine if he *thought* he was reporting the truth, much less when.

Complicating this notion further is *how* Herodotos presented his data, especially his ethnographic materials. To one extent or another, Herodotos presented foreign *nomoi* in such a way as to be specifically comprehensible to his Greek audience. "[T]he *Histories* is a Greek book for Greeks about Greeks and others – and it makes Greek sense of the

---

[11] Luraghi 2001: 160.
[12] Lateiner 1989: 22.
[13] Harrison 2000: 25–30.

others."[14] Herodotos typically achieves this by presenting foreign *nomoi* as variations of Greek practice. For F. Hartog, all the foreign *nomoi* are inversions of "normal" Greek practice, so that if the Greeks do X, the barbarians do some manner of $-X$ (see especially 2.35–36). That is to say, he presented, construed, or even created foreign *nomoi* as direct inverses of typical Greek practice, and barbarians are constructed as the non-Greek "Other." Furthermore, an important aspect of Hartog's hypothesis is that he sees in Herodotos the explicit idea that the foreign *nomoi*, being different, are also somehow inferior. The "Other," then, is an inferior "Other."[15]

R. Munson takes a different approach to Herodotos' foreign "translations." Quite contrary to Hartog, and in keeping with a strong idea of relativism in the *Histories*, she sees Herodotos as presenting the foreign *nomoi* as valid variations on Greek traditional norms. The *Histories* serve to indicate that there really is no "Other," nor is there necessarily a "Same," because the Greeks themselves have variations in their customs, and thus all *nomoi* are variations on general human existence.

> Although he represents otherness according to culturally determined – one might say, unconscious and inevitable – patterns of thought, he devalues its familiar implications through a series of concomitant strategies. He occasionally sets up the other as a model of what the Greeks would consider appropriate behavior; he complicates knowledge to both confirm and confuse ideological stereotypes; or he counterbalances his representation of difference with indications of unexpected similarities between his ethnographic subjects, other groups of barbarians, and different groups of Greeks.[16]

What is fairly consistent in all studies of Herodotos' ethnographies is that foreign *nomoi* are inevitably presented from a Greek perspective in a way that is meaningful and comprehensible to a specifically Greek audience.[17] This in itself has complicated issues of Herodotos' "truthfulness" by introducing into the debate questions concerning to what extent Herodotos was even writing about "foreigners" and to what extent he was simply projecting Greek notions and concerns onto a constructed "Other."[18]

---

[14] Redfield 2002 [1985]: 30.
[15] Hartog 1988: Chapter 5, *inter alia*.
[16] Munson 2001: 8. See also Thomas 2000: Chapter 4; Romm 1998: Chapter VII.
[17] Just as all encounters with the new and unknown must be translated through a filter of the known and familiar.
[18] Or, following Munson, a constructed "Same."

The unified nature of the *Histories* is another issue that has been subjected to lengthy debate.[19] Earlier scholars had viewed this work as a two-part endeavor: Herodotos started out writing an ethnography in the spirit of his predecessor Hekataios and later on wound up writing a history of the Persian Wars. As such, the ethnographies of the first four books of the *Histories* were only artificially tacked onto the historical books at the end. More recently, the general consensus is that the *Histories* is a unified work, held together by a number of important themes that pervade the text. Different scholars have focused on different unifying themes within Herodotos' chapters, none of which are mutually exclusive and all of which are equally viable. To give but a few examples, John Gould boils down the *Histories* to a long investigation of systems of debt and reciprocity. "Herodotus' model of a world which is structured spatially and socially by patterns of reciprocity, tending outwards from the norm of a central *ego* (which may be either individual or group – city, culture, people) and held together by a criss-crossing network of obligations, is the key to understanding his work as a proto-historian."[20] For his own part, Donald Lateiner sees the *Histories* as "a synthesis of recent world events that demonstrates the value of political independence, a hardy way of life, and moral courage."[21] Rosaria Munson, Rosalind Thomas, and James Romm see Herodotos as advocating the Pindarian notion that "*Nomos* (custom) is King." Thus Herodotos argues against the idea that the Greek way of life is inherently superior to that of the barbarians, and says that all cultures are inherently "valid."[22] Continuing in this vein, Thomas also seeds significant in Herodotos the idea that human fortunes wax and wane, and that, as Solon said to Croesus in the first book of the *Histories*, no man should consider himself fortunate until he is dead.[23] Harrison agrees, noting man's ultimate impotence in the face of fate:

> He is buffeted by chance reversals beyond control or foresight. He is also subject to fate. Herodotus' sense of fatalism cuts across all the forms of divine intervention, . . . it colours his entire understanding of causation.[24]

---

[19] See especially Lateiner 1988: 3–5.

[20] Gould 2000 [1989]: 110. For a full reciprocity-based analysis of Herodotos 1.196 and 1.199, see Kurke 1999: Chapter 6.

[21] Lateiner 1989: 17.

[22] Munson 2001: 170–172; Thomas 2000: Chapter 4.

[23] Thomas 2000: Chapter 4; see also Harrison 2000: 28.

[24] Harrison 2000: 223.

THE UNIQUENESS OF CHAPTER 1.199

Herodotos is complicated. If this were not enough, there is the second problem present in dealing with Herodotos' sacred prostitution narrative, and this is that Chapter 1.199 is itself unique. It is a unique passage in a unique text.

One of the first difficulties in assessing Chapter 1.199 is the fact that Herodotos gives us no information concerning how he derived his knowledge of sacred prostitution specifically, or the customs of Babylon more generally. As stated above, the issue of sources in Herodotos is already problematic, but it cannot be denied that Herodotos generally does present some explanation of how he came by his materials, whether that be in all honesty or as a means of persuasion. We have nothing of the sort for the Babylonian *logos*. At no point does Herodotos state that he had been to the city himself, a fact further complicated in recent years by Stephanie Dalley's argument that Herodotos may have been describing not Babylon, but Nineveh.[25] There is no statement of *akouê, gnomê*, or autopsy. We do not even have a *legetai*. In short, the modern reader is left completely in the dark about how Herodotos learned of this Babylonian cult of Mylitta. Furthermore, as stated in Chapter Two, this so-called institution is clearly not of Near Eastern origin, nor is there a distinct word for "prostitute" in the Mesopotamian vocabulary. This strongly argues against an indigenous, Mesopotamian origin for this custom: The source for Chapter 1.199 cannot be local. However, the notion of sacred prostitution also did not exist in Greece at this time, especially of the nature described in Chapter 1.199 (even a misreading of Pindar, fragment 122, yields a completely different institution; see Chapters 6 and 7). In the end, I suggest that this is one of the very few instances where one might argue that Herodotos did in fact construct his data for the sake of effect.

Another unique aspect of Chapter 1.199 is the fact that it, along with its "companion" Chapter 1.196, bride auction,[26] is an unqualified superlative (*aiskhistos − sophôtatos*). As M. Bloomer has noted, superlative claims in Herodotos occasion certain narrative structures, both qualifying the superlative ("that we know of . . . "), and legitimizing it (e.g., "The historian justifies the claim that that this tomb is a *megiston ergon* by giving

---

[25] Dalley 2003: 178–188.
[26] Griffiths 2001: 165–168.

measurements and by mentioning his autopsy"[27]). In the case of Chapter 1.199 (and 1.196), there is no qualifying information: Herodotos never tells us either why this *is* the most shameful custom (or 1.196 the wisest), or why he *thinks* it so.

Finally, and perhaps the most unique aspect of Chapter 1.199, is Herodotos' use of the word *aiskhistos* – "most shameful." As stated above, an appreciation for the relativity of *nomos* is a dominant theme running through the *Histories*. Herodotos tends to take a very neutral approach in his ethnographies, presenting foreign *nomoi* with the dispassionate distance of a trained anthropologist. The disdain perceived by such scholars as Hartog is subtle, if present at all, and Herodotos does not even offer disparaging vocabulary when referring to such practices as polygamy and cannibalism. At best, he might liken his subjects to "animals" or "cattle," (e.g., 3.97), but it is left to the reader to decide if this is a good or a bad thing.[28] And yet, in the midst of all this cultural diversity and relativity, Herodotos finds one thing, and one thing only, throughout his foreign *nomoi* to condemn thoroughly, and this is the sacred prostitution of the Babylonians.[29]

Altogether, the oddities of Chapter 1.199 shine out like a beacon. In spite of all the recent findings showing that Herodotos did present accurate information in his *Histories*, this chapter still stands out as being a fabrication, both for the lack of corroborating evidence in Mesopotamia itself, and for the unique qualities mentioned above. Herodotos seems deliberately to be drawing attention to this part of the Babylonian *logos*, and in the absence of historical corroborating evidence, we must surmise that Herodotos had an alternate purpose for this chapter – symbolic, didactic, or both.

ISSUES OF SEXUALITY AND INVERSION

If one is to claim that Chapter 1.199 is, in fact, a fabrication, the next issue is to ask *how* Herodotos devised the institution of sacred prostitution. The description the *histor* gives is extremely detailed; it is unlikely that he merely garbled or misunderstood a description he received (or saw,

[27] Bloomer 1993: 39–40.
[28] Concerning the debate on ethics, naturalness, and animals in Herodotos, see Thomas 2000: 3, 129–130.
[29] Munson 2001: 139, 171; Romm 1998: 99; Lateiner 1989: 138.

or heard about) of an existing custom. Fortunately, Chapter 1.199 is not completely unique. Its "construction," if one might use the term, makes use of a number of techniques and foci present throughout the *Histories*. Of particular relevance here are Herodotos' use of inversion in the presentation of foreign *nomoi*, as discussed above, and his interest in barbarian women and sexual moeurs.

As noted by S. Pembroke, Rosellini and Saïd, and C. Dewald, Herodotos often made use of women and sexual practices when rendering pictures of non-Greeks. Cases could be extreme when looking at the so-called "edges of the Earth," that is, when Herodotos described far-distant societies such as the Scythians, Libyans, or Indians.[30] For example, when discussing the northern Agathyrsi, Herodotos notes (4.104) that "They have their women in common, so that they may all be brothers and, as members of a single family, be able to live together without jealousy or hatred." Sauromatian women (4.117) "have a law which forbids a girl to marry until she has killed an enemy in battle; some of their women, unable to fulfill this condition, grow old and die spinsters." The Adyrmakhidai (4.168) "are the only Libyans . . . who take girls about to be married to see the king. Any girl who catches his fancy leaves him a virgin no longer." Farther west on the North African coast are the Nasamones (4.171): "Each of them has a number of wives which they use in common, like the Massagetai – when a man wants to lie with a woman, he puts up a pole to indicate his intentions. It is the custom at a man's first marriage to give a party at which the bride is enjoyed by each of the guests in turn." Concerning those who live by Lake Tritonis in northern Africa (4.180), "The women of the tribe are common property; there are no married couples living together, and intercourse is casual." Concerning the Indians generally, Herodotos claims that they all "copulate in the open like cattle" (3.97).[31]

So much for women on the edges. Similar practices might be found even closer to home. According to Herodotos (1.93), "Working-class girls in Lydia prostitute themselves without exception to gather money for their dowries, and they continue this practice until marriage. They

[30] See Romm 1992: *passim* for a full treatment of this subject in Classical authors generally. Nippel 2002 [1996]: 282–83; Redfield 2002 [1985]: 40, "We place the fabulous beyond the edges of the known world . . . not only because they are beyond our knowledge, but because, as we move towards the edges, we encounter more extreme conditions and therefore atypical forms, both natural and cultural."

[31] Translations by de Sélincourt 1972.

choose their own husbands." Herodotos then goes on to note that "Apart from the fact that they prostitute their daughters, the Lydian way of life is not unlike our own." Although the Thracians to the north do not necessarily practice prostitution (5.6), "they do not guard their young girls, and they allow them to have intercourse with whomever they wish."

It is worth noting here that a common motif, both "far" and "near," is the matter of women being held in common by communities. The Agathyrsi, Nasamones, Massagetai, and "Tritonians" all have their women in common, whether they have a marriage institution or not. The commonality of Lydian women comes from their self-prostitution before marriage. This contrasts strongly with the Greek ideal, which is to keep married women faithful and sexually inaccessible.[32]

This contrast once again brings up the notion of inversion in the *Histories*. Such inversions might be blatant or quite subtle. They might portray the subjects of investigation as pointedly non-Greek (as emphasized by Hartog) or quite similar to the Greeks in many respects (as emphasized by Munson). The most clear-cut example of the presentation of an "Other" through opposition or inversion appears in Chapters 2.35–36, where Herodotos claims that the Egyptian *nomoi* run contrary to those of everyone else:

> Among them the women go to market and keep shop, while the men stay home and weave. Other people weave pushing the woof upwards, but the Egyptians downwards. Men bear loads on their heads, women on their shoulders. Women pee standing up, men sitting down. They ease themselves inside their homes, but eat outdoors – claiming that shameful necessities ought to be done in hiding, unshameful in the open.... The priests of the deities in other places grow long hair, but in Egypt they shave. For other peoples it is customary in times of mourning to shave the heads of those most closely involved, but the Egyptians, upon a death, let the hairs on their heads and chins grow, shaving afterwards. They knead grain with their feet, clay with their hands.... In writing or calculating, instead of going, like the Greeks, left to right, the Egyptians go right to left.

A more subtle example, one that emphasizes how similar foreign and Greek *nomoi* might be, and one that will be of extreme importance in this

[32] Lateiner 1989: 136.

study of Chapter 1.199, is the Babylonian bride auction of Chapter 1.196. Here Herodotos claims that the wisest of the Babylonian customs was that

> Once a year the following is done in each village. When the maidens (*parthenoi*) are of age to marry, they lead them all together into one place with a crowd of men standing around them. Standing them up one-by-one, the herald sells them, starting with the most beautiful among them, and whenever she has been sold – fetching a lot of gold – then he puts the next most beautiful up for sale. They are sold for the purpose of cohabitation (= marriage). Many prosperous Babylonians who were of marriageable intent would contend with each other to buy the prettiest girls; but those of the common folk who sought marriage – those who had no need for good looks – they instead would receive money as well as the uglier maidens. For indeed, as the herald finished selling off the prettiest of the *parthenoi*, he would stand up the ugliest, or if some one of them were crippled, and he would put her up for "sale"; whoever wanted the least gold for her got to take her home. The gold came from the pretty maidens, and thus the pretty ones provided a marriage for the ugly and crippled ones. It was not permitted for anyone to give away his own daughter in marriage according to his own designs, nor could one lead away a purchased maiden without providing a guarantee: He had to provide a guarantee that he would marry her so as to take her away. If the couple should not get along, the custom permitted the return of the money. Anyone who wanted could even come from a different village to buy a wife.

Herodotos then goes on to say that this custom had since gone out of practice, and that now the poorer Babylonians all prostitute their daughters.

The inversions from Greek practice are quite evident, with the most obvious being the notion of a bride-auction at all. There is the fathers' inability to choose husbands for their daughters and thus regulate systems of familial alliance and acquisition. The bride-price went not to the bride, but to the auctioneer, and thence to the poorer husbands. Furthermore, contrary to Greek practice, a girl was valued exclusively for her physical appearance, not for her family. The nobility of blood was replaced by a nobility of aesthetic appeal.

Nevertheless, there are also evident a number of similarities to Greek practice, the most obvious of which is the institution of marriage at all. The practices of both bride-price and dowry are present, although here in Babylon they are mutually exclusive: Pretty girls eventuate a bride-price, ugly girls a dowry. Laws existed both to protect the honor of the new bride and to protect the execution of the custom. Ideally this ritual took place in the closed society of the village, but men could travel to other villages to buy a wife. In this we see a reflection of Greek practice, where local marriage was an accepted, if not preferred, norm, especially in Athens, but extranational marriages were common for the social élite (save in Athens post-451). In Babylon, those who could afford to travel could also afford a handsome bride, as well as a bride-price, whereas the poor folk remained at home with local wives, subsidized by the state. As both Leslie Kurke and Rosalind Thomas have noted, Herodotos' description may be related to the theories of Phaleas of Chalcedon (*apud* Aristotle, *Politics* II, 1266a39–65), who sought to equalize disparities of wealth through a strict regulation of dowries.[33] In such a case, not only would the foreign practice be related to the Greek, but also it would serve as a Greek ideal.

Herodotos created the narrative of Babylonian sacred prostitution as an inversion of Greek sacred and sexual moeurs. In structure, it reflects a variation on standard Greek practice, with its primary interest in the sexuality of Babylonian women. As such, although unique, Chapter 1.199 follows along with typical Herodotean forms of presentation. The model of the inversion particular to Chapter 1.199, I argue, is Greek women's ritual.

Consider the typical Greek women's ritual, as enacted by married, citizen women, such as the Thesmophoria.[34] Here, once a year as regulated by local religious calendars, women came together for a three-day ritual in honor of Demeter and Korê, leaving behind husband and children. Because religious calendars in Greece were established and approved by males, this gave some masculine ("responsible?") control over the event. The women celebrated this ritual in temporary sacred space walled off to protect the goings-ons from potentially prying male eyes; so much is made evident in Aristophanes' *Thesmophoriazousai*. Each of the three days has a defined name, ritual, and purpose. The women celebrate together under the direction of preselected *arkhousai*, or female officiants, and it is generally understood that the Thesmophoria served partially as a feminine family-reunion time, when woman separated from each other through patrilocal marriage could gather together again. During this all-female ritual, the women are chaste (not necessarily sober, according to Aristophanes, but chaste). In fact, many elements of the Thesmophoria relate

---

[33] Thomas 2000: 129; Kurke 1999: 240–242.

[34] For a full description of the Thesmophoria with up-to-date references, see Dillon 2001: 110–120.

to a denial of sexuality: separation from husbands, exclusion of males, the drinking of pennyroyal, seen in ancient times as an antiaphrodisiac and possibly a type of birth control, as were the branches the women sat on the second day of the ritual (the *nesteia*, or fasting).[35] All of this was seen, ultimately, to promote good will with the goddesses and to enhance the fertility of the land, and possibly the women's bodies as well, building up critical amounts of unused fertility, as it were. When the festival was done, after the Kalligeneia, the women went home to their families and, supposedly, extrapotent fields.

The Babylonian custom described by Herodotos is similar to these rituals in some ways. It involved all the *gynaikes* of the region, regardless of class, leaving their families behind and coming together to perform a sacred ritual at the temple, once again, in sacred space. As with Greek tradition, sex could not take place in this sacred space ("outside the sanctuary"), hardly a shocking fact when we consider that, according to Herodotos, the Babylonians considered sex to be polluting, husbands and wives fumigating themselves after sex as related in Chapter 1.198. We can see, then, that a certain sympathy existed between Greek and Babylonian moeurs, making the eventual Babylonian aberrations that much more appalling to a Greek audience.

For consider the antithetical differences between Greek custom as evidenced in rituals such as the Thesmophoria, and the sacred prostitution of Chapter 1.199. Unlike Greek custom, the sacred prostitution does not occur according to a regulated calendar. It seems that women just show up whenever. Likewise, there is no clear pattern to the ritual, or set number of days. Women must remain at the temple until a man pays them for sex, and, as Herodotos notes, this can take up to four years for the ugly ones, whereas the pretty ones can go home quickly. Although the *gynaikes* do leave husbands and family to come to sacred space, they are not hidden from prying male eyes. Quite to the contrary, they are set out on display, with roads running among them. Unlike the Greek women's rituals, women are not in charge of this sacred prostitution. Men choose the women they prefer. Thus, not only are women not in charge of their own dedications to the goddess, but in contrast to the female-bonding/women's reunion seen in the Greek practice, women are set up in competition with each other. Every women present at the temple of Mylitta is one more women who might keep you from discharging your duty and getting home to your family. There is also a clear

---

[35] Nixon 1997: 85–88.

class issue involved, as Herodotos specifically mentions that the wealthy do not feel that they should be so debased as to mingle with the others. Women cannot even control the amount of money they receive. Women are specifically *not* chaste for this ritual; having sex is its *raison d'être*. But, because one cannot have sex in the sanctuary, one must leave the sacred space to fulfill the ritual. A religious ritual that cannot be performed on religious ground must have seemed inherently flawed to the Greeks. Furthermore, just as abstinence functioned in promoting fertility in Greek eyes, the sex required of the Babylonian women must have had an antithetical effect, thus decreasing or bastardizing the fertility of field and body. The women are of necessity having sex with foreigners; any fertility of their bodies in this context would corrupt the citizen body as a whole, especially by Greek standards.

And so we can see that "the most shameful" custom among the Babylonians is an inversion of Greek custom. The women's ritual is not regulated by calendar; thus there is no formal structure, and no overarching male control. There is no Babylonian control at all, really: The citizen men have no say whatsoever in the ritual; the women are at the mercy of foreign men. The women Greek society most chose to hide, even more so than their *parthenoi*,[36] are set out on display specifically for foreign men (not to mention everyone else passing by the temple). Rather than a bonding retreat, the women are in competition with one another, not likely to build civic goodwill among the citizen matrons. The core of the ritual – sex with a foreigner in honor of Aphrodite – cannot even be performed at the sanctuary. Rather than being a fertility ritual, fertility is a clear disadvantage for all involved in this rite. In all aspects, the Babylonian ritual of sacred prostitution is an inverse of Greek ideals:[37]

---

[36] For example, the restriction on *gynaikes*, but NOT *parthenoi*, for attendance at the Olympic games. See Scanlon 1996: *passim*.

[37] In point of fact, the Greek ritual Babylonian sacred prostitution most closely resembles is the Adonia. Even though this ritual did occur at a specific time, July, it was not on any religious calendar, and took place in spite of being "unorthodox." Women of all classes and categories (matron, *parthenos*, *hetaira*, etc.) gathered together on rooftops, celebrating and drinking, quite possibly in the company of male admirers, as some romances had the male and female protagonists consummate their love under the auspices of the Adonia. Even here, though, we have the notion of women in charge and enjoying each others' company, a far cry from Chapter 1.199. For a full structuralist contrast between the Thesmophoria and the Adonia, see Detienne 1994 [1972]: 78–82.

Thesmophoria	1.199
Women	Women
Sacred Space	Sacred Space
Once a Year	Whenever
Three Days	However Long
Hidden	Full View
Female Officiants	Men In Charge
Female "Bonding"	Female Competition
Chastity	Sex for Sale
Fertilizing	Polluting/Bastardizing

Furthermore, let us consider *who* actually practiced this sacred prostitution. Herodotos uses the word *gynaikas* in line 20, and *gynaikes* in line 27. The word *gynê* is used 373 times in Herodotos, 199 times meaning "woman," 128 times meaning wife.[38] As with other languages that do not have separate words for "woman" and "wife" (French = "femme"), distinction in translation is usually determined by the presence of a possessive form: "a woman" *versus* "my wife." As such, the *gynaikes* of Chapter 1.199 would first appear to be just plain women, not necessarily wives. However, other arguments suggest that Herodotos had married women, even mothers, in mind, and that this implication would come across to his Greek audience. To begin, at least some of the women performing the ritual *must* be married, for Herodotos is quite specific when referring to unmarried girls, using the term *parthenos*, as he does in Chapter 1.196. That he says *gynaikes*, not *parthenoi*, suggests that at least some of the women in 1.199 are married.[39]

Likewise, there is a certain continuum established in Chapters 1.196 through 199. In 1.196, Herodotos describes the old custom of bride-auction, referring to the unmarried girls as *parthenoi*. In Chapter 1.198, man and wife (*gynaiki, gynê*) perform a postcoital ritual of fumigation. Finally, there is the reference to the sacred prostitution of Chapter 1.199, performed by *gynaikes*. The continuum seems to take us from marriage (196) to sexual intercourse (198) to prostitution (199). Herodotos uses a linkage of associations to insinuate that the women selling themselves for

---

[38] Powell 1977: 71. If we follow the even more specific vocabulary of Demand and Garland, we might even consider that the *gynaikes* of 1.199 were not merely married, but also mothers. Demand 1994: 17; Garland 1990: 243: "A woman was a *gunê* from the birth of her first child until her death."

[39] And thus I argue that the 1.199 ritual should not be seen as ritual defloration or sale of virginity *per se*, as is commonly assumed. See also Beard and Henderson 1998: 63–64.

Mylitta are married women, possibly mothers. Thus, what we have here is not merely sacred prostitution, but sacred adultery.[40]

This aspect adds further complications and inversions to the ritual as seen through Greek eyes. Once again, the women most in need of being kept hidden – fertile, married women – are put on display for a foreign, male viewing audience. Note that in Greece even the *parthenoi* are allowed certain opportunities to display themselves publicly, especially at religious and athletic events. By contrast, married women usually take part in their own rituals (such as the Thesmophoria, Haloa, Skira, etc.), and are forbidden access to the athletic events, occasionally under pain of death, as at Olympia.[41] One reason offered for the idealized sequestering of married women is fear of adultery. In "The Murder of Eratosthenes," to give one example, Euphiletos specifically mentions that his wife met her lover when he saw her at her mother-in-law's funeral. Thus: woman outside = woman with potential for corruption. Such an equation certainly manifests itself in the Babylonian ritual, where women wait out of doors in a religious context precisely for the purpose of extramarital sex.

Then there is the religiosocial corruption that inevitably *must* result, in Greek eyes, from this ritual. According to Greek law, a "convicted" adulteress must be divorced and may no longer take part in religious rituals. To cite two Athenian references, one attributed to the laws of Solon in the sixth century,

> Aes. 1.183: And Solon, the most famous of law-givers, has written in ancient and solemn manner.... For the woman who is taken in the act of adultery he does not allow to adorn herself, nor even to attend the public sacrifices, lest by mingling with innocent women she corrupt them.[42]

> [Dem] 59.87: When he has caught the adulterer, it shall not be lawful for the one who has caught him to continue living with his wife, and if he does so, he shall lose his civic rights and it shall not be lawful for

---

[40] I am admittedly using a modern understanding of the term adultery here – a married woman engaging in extramarital sex. While it is true that the Greeks were concerned about any citizen female, married or not, engaging in fornication (*moikheia*), there was a generally greater concern *vis-à-vis* married women, as they brought with them a higher potential for introducing both bastards and thieves into the paternal household. It is this worry that is emphasized in the 1.199 ritual; thus the emphasis on a specific subcategory of Greek *moikheia*.

[41] Herodotos notes a similar contrast in relative freedoms between Thracian girls (*parthenoi*) and women (*gynaikes*) in 5.6.

[42] Adams 1988 [1917]: 141.

the woman who is taken in adultery to attend public sacrifices; and
if she does attend them, she may be made to suffer any punishment
whatsoever, short of death, and that with impunity.[43]

The barring from sacrifices results at least partially from the woman's
inherent and irremovable impurity (*miasma*) through adultery.[44] And so
Chapter 1.199 brings up another irony by Greek standards: The required
ritual, once fulfilled, either precludes women from taking part in further
religious rituals, or necessitates that women's rituals henceforth are as
impure as their participants.

An additional complication arises regarding reproduction. Once the
woman discharges her duty, as Herodotos informs us, she goes home. If
she is married and then has sex with her own husband, there is no way to
determine an eventual child's sire. Thus, the ritual can introduce foreign,
bastard children into the Babylonian population, a notion anathema to
both Babylonian and Greek ideology. If the couple refrains from sex until
after pregnancy can be determined, the ritual disrupts a married couple's
sex life, infringing not only upon Hera's domain but also, ironically, upon
Aphrodite's, in whose honor the ritual supposedly takes place. Once
again, a ritual that ultimately dishonors the goddess it is meant to honor
would appear to a Greek as essentially flawed.

THE IMPLICATIONS OF CHAPTER 1.199

ETHNICITY AND IDENTITY

On a superficial level, then, we might understand Chapter 1.199 as a
Herodotean creation based on inversion, not an historical reality at all.
However, as stated above, Chapter 1.199 is a unique entry in the *Histories*;
Herodotos' use of the word *aiskhistos* alone sets off this so-called ritual
for special attention. The next question we must ask ourselves, then, is
what Herodotos is trying to say with Chapter 1.199; what is the deeper,
poetic meaning of sacred prostitution? To answer this question we must
first consider the various repercussions of the 1.199 ritual as understood
by a fifth-century Greek before delving into the deeper, philosophical
ramifications.

Already discussed are the issues of *miasma* (ritual impurity) and bastardy.
Another issue, although of debatable importance for Herodotos, is the

[43] Trans. Perseus Project.
[44] Parker 1996: 74–75, no. 4.

ethnic integrity of the Babylonians, what might even be dubbed the "foreign bastardy" of the Babylonians.

The issue of foreign bastardy, I believe, is one that Herodotos would see as especially critical for the Babylonians. During their rebellion against the Persians, the Babylonians (3.150) "herded together and strangled all the women of the city – each man exempting only his mother and one other woman from his household to bake his bread." Later, when Darius had retaken the city (3.159): "in order to prevent the race from dying out, [he] compelled the neighboring peoples each to send a certain number of women to Babylon . . . It is from these that the present inhabitants are descended." Hence, the Babylonian blood was already "thinned out." Herodotos states that the current Babylonians, those who perform the sacred prostitution ritual, were descendants of the foreign women brought in by Darius to keep the Babylonian *ethnos* alive.

Technically, Darius' plan would work. According to Herodotos' Athenians, "ethnicity" is determined by "the community of blood and language, temples, and [a] common way of life" (8.144). Nevertheless, common blood or ancestry was perhaps the least important of these and could even be mythologically "corrected" if necessary.[45] Herodotos gives at least one example of an ethnic population relocating, marrying foreign women, and engendering new children with them without losing their original ethnicity in Book 2.29. Here the Egyptian "Deserters" flee to Ethiopia. When the Pharaoh tries to lure them back by referring to the men's wives and children, one of the soldiers points to his genitals and claims that wherever *those* go, there will be wives and children. The men settle in Ethiopia, and "the result of their living there was that the Ethiopians learned Egyptian manners and became more civilized." Thus, a group of men can settle in a foreign country with foreign wives and nevertheless impose their own culture upon their new surroundings.

The situation in Babylon is complicated by the fact that the Babylonian women are still functionally breeding, once in their lives, with foreign men. The initial introduction of foreign women into the Babylonian population is exacerbated by the sacred prostitution ritual, whereby Babylonian blood is continually "thinned."

How Herodotos perceived this lack of ethnic integrity is a matter of debate. On the one hand, it might be contrasted to notions of autochthony prevalent in Herodotos' Greek milieu. If we consider that the Athenians constituted a major, although not exclusive, share of

---

[45] Sourvinou-Inwood 2003: 140 and 144; Hall 2002 [1992]: 144–147.

Herodotos' audience, the importance of autochthony and its relation to character come strongly to the fore. According to Athenian ideology, only the autochthonous can truly love their land as a parent, and so fight bravely in that parent's defense. Thus, autochthony is related to bravery. On a political level, the equal parentage of all citizens leads inevitably to democracy (*isonomia* and *parrhesia*, equality and freedom of speech). By contrast, "other states, which are necessarily non-autochthonous and made up of mixed peoples, must be inegalitarian."[46] The continued influx of foreign bastards after the initial introduction of foreign women into Babylon suggests that city is filled with "immigrants, a motley rabble tainted with foreign blood,"[47] thus bringing into question the Babylonians' potential for bravery, and highlighting their servile nature, being inevitable slaves to a monarchial regime (a recurring theme in Herodotos regarding Asia).

What is problematic in this analysis is that such notions of autochthony run contrary to the prevailing themes in Herodotos, such as the dominance of *nomos* and the instability of the human condition. Autochthony implies that ethnic qualities are innate, and thus not culture-based nor mutable. Of course, we might recognize that Herodotos did undermine a number of Greek conceptions concerning the meaning and effects of autochthony as it related to a Greek population, especially the Athenians. This is especially evident in Books 1.56–58 and 8.44. In the former, Herodotos recounts how the indigenous population of Greece comprised the semimythical Pelasgians, a non-Greek population. The Athenians, being autochthonous, and thus indigenous, were a part of this group. Only later, with the arrival of the Dorian Greeks, did the Athenians Hellenize, adopting the Greek language. In the latter Herodotos records that the Athenians used to be a Pelasgian people called Kranai; later, under the reign of Kekrops, called Kekropidai; then Athenians under the reign of Erekhtheus; and finally Ionians when Ion, son of Xuthus, was their general. These narratives preserve both local tradition and Herodotos' aims. The equation between Pelasgians and Athenians maintains the Athenian claim of autochthony.[48] The change of language, and thus ethnicity, and title highlights Herodotos' notions of changeability and the rule of *nomos*. Herodotos might then go on to show that the

---

[46] Ogden 1996: 169. See also Thomas 2000: 117–122.
[47] Parker 1987: 195.
[48] For a full treatment of the Pelasgians, the Athenians, and autochthony, see Sourvinou-Inwood 2003: *passim*.

fine qualities of the Athenians, including their military prowess, might be linked to their democratic institutions, *nomos*-based in his view, even if autochthony-based in theirs.[49]

Autochthony does not imply continuity and cannot be credited with the noble or ignoble behavior of a population. Neither, then, can foreign bastardy. And I believe that it is here that Herodotos is playing with the expectations of his Greek audience. It is clear that foreign bastardy, as presented in Chapter 1.199, has some strongly negative associations. The ethnic miscegenation of the Babylonians is highlighted in a passage that Herodotos uniquely qualifies with the word *aiskhistos*. Miasma and bastardy generally are inherently at issue, and, as I shall discuss below, notions of effeminacy and defeat. A Greek audience sensitive to notions of autochthony certainly would be expected to perceive this association. However, just as autochthony cannot be a *cause* of good qualities for the Athenians, foreign bastardy cannot be a *cause* of negative qualities for the Babylonians. It is the "most shameful" *nomos*, the ritual in honor of Mylitta, that continues the ethnic miscegenation (and whatever negative qualities the Greeks would have associated with it), not the miscegenation that impels the *nomos*. Once again, Herodotos maintains his notion of "*Nomos* as King," contrasting it with the autochthony-oriented expectations of his Greek audience,[50] while simultaneously privileging custom, religion, and language over blood in the creation of ethnic identity.

FEMININE AND MASCULINE

Additional implications for the sacred prostitution of Chapter 1.199 might be derived by considering it next to its "companion" chapter, the bride auction of Chapter 1.196 (translated above). That these two chapters form a linked pair has long been noted, both for their related content — the regulation of sexuality among Babylonian women — and for their reciprocal superlatives — *aiskhistos* and *sophôtatos*.[51] Likewise, both chapters appear to be fabrications, as, once again, there is no evidence for bride auction as narrated by Herodotos in Mesopotamian history. Finally, as

---

[49] Thomas 2000: 118.

[50] Once again recalling Munson's statement that much of Herodotos' discussion on Greeks and barbarians is "based on a dialectic between traditional notions of the Greeks, on the one hand, and Herodotus' overt disruption of these notions, on the other." Munson 2001: 8.

[51] Bloomer 1993: 43; Kurke 1999: Chapter 7; Griffiths 2001: 165–168.

in Chapter 1.199, Herodotos never does justify his use of superlatives in Chapter 1.196.

I believe that the reason for the moral evaluations for both rituals – sacred prostitution and bride auction – has to do with the social/personal qualities each ritual implies. Specifically, I think it possible to engender the two rituals, with the sacred prostitution of Chapter 1.199 coming across as specifically unregulated, thus feminine, and thus negative and "shameful," whereas the bride auction is, by contrast, orderly and democratic, thus masculine, and thus positive and "wise."

Consider once again some of the defining characteristics of the sacred prostitution ritual. It is not calendrically regulated or controlled. There is no set time limit; the women must sit by passively waiting to be chosen. The female participants have no control over with whom they have sex, nor over the amount of money they receive for it. The ritual has a very high potential for introducing foreign bastards into the citizen family. Put simply, Chapter 1.199 reflects standard Greek male perceptions and paranoia about the Female.

As Anne Carson noted in her work "Putting Her in Her Place: Women, Dirt, and Desire,"

> [Women] are intimate with formlessness and the unbounded in their alliance with the wet, the wild, and raw nature. They are, as individuals, comparatively formless themselves, without firm control of personal boundaries. They are, as social entities, units of danger, moving across boundaries of family and *oikos*, in marriage, prostitution, or adultery. They are, as psychological entities, unstable compounds of deceit and desire, prone to leakage.
>
> In sum, the female body, the female psyche, the female social life, and the female moral life are penetrable, porous, mutable, and subject to defilement all the time.[52]

The image of the "leaky," boundless female is reflected in the nonregulated quality of the 1.199 ritual: no clear start time, end time, or duration.

Likewise, Greek men understood women to be lacking in *sophrosynê*, self-control or temperance.[53] This "lack of self-control" is reflected in the

---

[52] Carson 1990: 159.
[53] See Plato, *The Laws*, §6.780e, "[T]he female sex . . . which in any case is inclined to be secretive and crafty, because of its weakness . . . a woman's natural potential for virtue is inferior to a man's, so she is proportionately a greater danger, perhaps even twice as great." (Trans. T. J. Saunders, in Lefkowitz and Fant [eds.] 1992: 47.)

Babylonian women's inability to control with whom they had sex in the ritual, or how much money they acquired for it. Perhaps the greatest fear that Greek men had about their women was the women's potential for bringing bastard children into the *oikos*. Ritual 1.199 almost guarantees that most, if not all, Babylonian women will bring at least one such foreign bastard into the paternal estate.

These last considerations are bolstered when we contrast this "most shameful custom" with the Babylonians' "wisest custom": the bride auction. This function took place once a year. The girls were organized, ranging from most to least pretty, and sold accordingly. A guarantee of marriage was legally required. No man could marry his daughter separately, but all had to take part in the custom. Here we see the "masculine"[54] traits of order (calendar), organization (beauty scale), rationality (price scale), legality (guarantee), and democracy (all men subject to

---

[54] The notion of masculinity, to be an *anêr* and to express *andreia*, changed considerably from the age of Homer to the age of the polis. Originally to be an *anêr* involved exclusively physicality – bravery in battle and the leaving behind of a beautiful, masculine corpse. (Bassi 2003: 26, 33–34.) In the later Archaic and early Classical periods, the need for physical, especially military prowess continued as part of the definition of *andreia*, although once the fighting style changed from a heroic mano-a-mano to the organized and communal phalanx, the ability to maintain order to defend one's fellow soldier must have tweaked the notion of military *andreia* to include an ability to maintain *taxis*. But at the same time, new, more "ethical" attributes came to the fore; so much is still evident in Plato's *Lakhes*. Amusingly, such attributes tend to be discussed in the negative – both Thucydides and Plato discuss the inversion of manly ideals during periods of *stasis*. Thus, in his *History* Thucydides argues that the partisans in stasis claim, "Rash daring was considered 'partisan' manliness, cautious hesitation was considered specious cowardice, moderation was considered a disguise for a lack of manliness, and comprehensive intelligence was considered a complete inability to act" (*ibid*: 28). Likewise in his *Republic* (560d8), Plato/Sokrates complains that those who corrupt the mind of the young "call insubordination 'erudition,' disorder 'freedom,' extravagance 'magnificence,' and uninhibitedness '*andreia*'" (Sluiter and Rosen 2003: 10). During "normal" times, then, it is clear that the masculine virtues included caution, moderation, intelligence, order, and *sophrosynê*. These are the same ideals that, in a more physical fashion, Iskhomakhos attempts to instill in his wife in Xenophon's fifth century *Oikonomikos*, thus symbolically turning her not only into a "man," but a "good citizen" (Murnaghan 1988: *passim*). Finally, as Bassi notes in her study of the evolution of manliness in ancient Greece, by the fifth century the notion had transferred from the individual male to an attribute of the polis which reared its men (Bassi 2003: 47–49). The description of the city of Athens as presented in the Periclean Funeral Oration might then be seen as a testament of Athens' *andreia*. Once again, notions of courage, deliberation, and moderation are present (§39–40), as well as the virtues of equality (both political and legal) and democracy (§37).

---

the same tradition).[55] But, as Herodotos noted, *this* tradition was no longer in place. Poor families now prostitute their daughters, while all women/wives inevitably prostitute themselves for Mylitta. In short, the masculine disappeared, leaving only the feminine in its wake; the democratic disappeared, leaving chaos.[56]

CONQUEST AND RAPE

The notion of femininity is closely associated with military defeat in Herodotos, either as a precondition for it or as a result of it. The latter is best exemplified in Book 1 after the defeat of Lydia. After a rebellion on the part of Sardis, Croesus offers Cyrus advice as to how to control the Lydians humanely (1.56): "Keep them from bearing weapons. Make them wear tunics under their cloaks, and high boots, and tell them to teach their sons to play zither and harp, and to start shopkeeping. If you do that, my lord, you will soon see them turn into women instead of men, and there will not be any more danger of their rebelling against you." The former is presented in Chapter 2.103, where in the course of his campaigns, Sesostris placed the symbol of female genitalia upon the victory stele over those peoples who did not fight valiantly to defend their homeland. More generally, in Chapter 8.88, while Queen Artemisia is (apparently, to Xerxes at least) defeating her foes in battle while the rest of his fleet is floundering, Xerxes exclaims "My men have turned into women, my women into men!"[57]

Furthermore, there is a rape motif inherent in Herodotos' sacred prostitution ritual. Although the act is both sacred (*themis*) and paid for, the lack of volition in the ritual and sexual act is strongly implied in Herodotos' text. This is clearest with the wealthy women who do not deign to mingle with the other women. The use of the related verbs *meikhênai/anamisgesthai* so close together gives a slight sense of continuity to the feelings of these wealthy women – they do not deign to "mingle" with commoners of either sex, sexually or socially. The humiliation of the ugly women is also emphasized with presumed exaggeration, as Herodotos notes that some of the less lovely Babylonians must wait

---

[55] Munson 2001: 139. Issues of regulation vs. nonregulation in a specifically economic sense are explored in detail by Kurke 1999: Chapter 6.

[56] *Ibid.* That Near Eastern populations were not automatically antithetical to democracy is discussed in Thomas 2000: 114–117.

[57] On Herodotean concepts of gender, ethnicity, and *andreia* generally, see Harrell 2003: *passim.*

about the sanctuary for up to four years to fulfill their sacred duty. Third, Herodotos mentions quite explicitly that the Babylonian women must have sex with the first man who tosses them money, "nor may they reject anyone," once again emphasizing a lack of volition. Finally, Herodotos is very clear in noting the overall faithfulness of the Babylonian women apart from the ritual – "When she should have mingled, having discharged her obligation to the goddess, she leaves for home, and after this time you might not take her, offering gifts no matter how great." There is no direct reference to rape in the 1.199 narrative, nothing that would merit such words as *hybris* or *bia*. But the lack of volition in the sexual act is clearly implied, a sexual act outside of marriage, where such a lack of volition might simply be chalked up to "wifely duty."[58] Here, the reticence is implied four times, encompassing the rich, the ugly, and the women generally. For its clear lack of extramarital willing participation, one must infer a rape motif, however subtle, in the text.

These concepts – defeat, effeminization, and rape – are long-enduring and long-entwined in Greek ideology, present as early as Homer's portrayal of Andromakhê[59] and possibly even evident in the iconography of the red figure Eurymedon Vase, where it is a male Persian soldier potentially being anally raped (and thus effeminized) by a Greek.[60] To be defeated implies effeminization and rape, and *vice versa*.

THE TRAGEDY OF THE DEFEATED

The sacred prostitution ritual reflects this ideology, where, on a symbolic level, all Babylonian women being penetrated by foreign men serves as a reflection for the conquered status of Babylon itself, conquered, effeminized, and symbolically "raped" by Persia. This in itself implies a double feminization on the part of the Babylonians. For it was the Persians whom the Greeks, and especially the Athenians, typically portrayed as the exceptionally effeminate "Other," both in literature and in art.[61] What could one say, then, about a society defeated and symbolically raped by the quintessential, Asian feminine? Two possibilities come to mind.

On the one hand, a possible disdain for the Babylonians might be inferred from Chapter 1.199. For what we have here is not merely rape:

---

[58] Harrison 2002 [1997]: 197.
[59] E. Hall 1993: 110–113.
[60] Although see Davidson 1997: 170–182 for alternate theories.
[61] E. Hall 1993: *passim*.

It is involuntary sex with foreign men for pay in honor of a deity. The fact that the women receive pay for their "services," even though they have no control over the amount of that pay, implies a certain complicity in the rape motif. That is, the Babylonians accept their defeated, passive, penetrated status, and actually "sell out" to their penetrating conquerors. That the penetration/rape is cast as a religious ritual suggests that Babylon's conquered status derives from divine mandate, or at least meets with divine approval. The gods require that Babylon be a conquered nation.

This contrasts well with the Greeks' own experience with Persian aggression. In contrast to the Babylonians, the Greeks held off the Persians, and did not submit to conquest, or to the rape of Greek women by foreigners, and clearly the Greek victory was through the will of the deities.[62]

However, a more sympathetic tone must surely be perceived. The Babylonians put up a noble defense against the Persians, twice as a matter of fact (1.191; 3.158–159), suggesting that the Babylonians were not innately nor originally as effeminate as they became *after* conquest. This correlates nicely with the case of the Lydians.[63] Before the Persian conquest, Herodotos notes that (1.79) "there were no stouter or more courageous fighters in Asia that the Lydians; they were cavalry men, excellent horsemen, and they fought with long spear." After conquest, they became zither-playing shopkeepers. Chapter 1.199, then, could be seen as a "tragedy of the defeated," a description of what could happen to even a noble race when conquered, as exemplified by the literal subjugation and prostitution of its women. To quote Lateiner:

> [W]omen in the *Histories* suggest the vulnerability of a culture to external enemies or internal stress. So the capture of Lemnian or Carian females and their subjugation to conquering males marks the end of their group's ethnic identity, and the rapid success of the Persians leads to various abuses to (and sometimes by) the women of their élite.[64]

To this list should surely be added the women of Babylon. That the deities condoned, even demanded, this ritual reflects back on Herodotos'

---

[62] Consider, for example, Chapter 8.13, where Herodotos at least partially credits the Greek victory at Salamis to a sea storm, thus, Poseidon.

[63] Harrell 2003: 78–80.

[64] Lateiner 1989: 139.

notions of the vicissitudes of fate and fortune.[65] The Babylonians were just as victimized as anyone else.

That the sacred prostitution ritual is linked with notions of defeat on the one hand, and the kind of ethnic heterogeneity discussed above concerning foreign bastardy on the other, is emphasized in who, specifically, practiced this ritual: Babylon and parts of Cyprus. For, as Herodotos notes at the end of Chapter 1.199, this practice of sacred prostitution existed in certain parts of Cyprus as well. And so we must ask ourselves, what in Herodotos' mind linked Babylon and Cyprus so that they would *both* have ritualistic prostitution in honor of Aphrodite?

Cyprus actually plays a rather minimal role in the *Histories*. According to Herodotos, the island received the cult of Aphrodite Ourania from the temple/cult at Ashkalon (1.105); it practiced, like Babylon, sacred prostitution (1.199); it had the tradition of the "Linus" song, as did Egypt (2.80); the island paid tribute to Egypt before being conquered by Persia (2.182); it gave services to Persia after conquest and paid the Great King 500 talents as tribute (3.19, 5.50); the Cypriots, with the exception of Amathus, revolted against Persia (5.104 ff.); and, finally, the ethnic composition of the island was a bit of a mishmash, being composed, according to Herodotos, of Greeks, Phoenicians, and Ethiopians (7.90).[66]

Of these, the most frequently attributed common denominator between Cyprus and Babylon is the cult of Aphrodite/Aštart/Mylitta, Mylitta being the Assyrian name and Aštart, presumably, the Cypro-Phoenician name for Aphrodite. Thus, a common cult to a common goddess yielded a common ritual, no doubt spread from Babylon to Cyprus by way of Ashkalon. However, the correlations between Aphrodite, Aštart, and any of the Near Eastern goddesses are not as

---

[65] Harrison 2000: 223.

[66] This last statement is rather indicative of the accuracy, and inaccuracy, of Herodotos. By the fifth century Cyprus had been colonized by the Greeks and the Phoenicians, who divided up the island into a series of small kingdoms. Only the region of Amathus remained indigenous Eteocypriot into the fourth century and the Ptolemaic conquests. Herodotos seems to have confused the Eteocypriots with the Ethiopians. That Amathus was, in fact, Eteocypriot is confirmed in the archaeology, which shows a relocation from Cypriot Paphos at the time of the arrival of the first Achaean settlers. Eteocypriot remained the language of inscriptions until the fourth century. I thus find Petit's hypothesis unlikely, that the Amathusians as Ethiopians claimed kin with Persia through the mythical marriage of Perseus and Andromeda, only claiming indigenous/autochthonous origins later in the fourth century through Athenian influence (Petit 2004: 15–16.)

direct as generally perceived. Herodotos betrays no knowledge of Aštart at all, whereas he associated Aphrodite not only with Mylitta, but also Egyptian Hathor, Arabic Alilat,[67] and even Scythian Argimpasa as well. There is no common cult between Babylon, Ashkalon, and Cyprus, even Phoenician Cyprus, much less Scythia! If Herodotos were to find common elements in the Near Eastern "Aphrodite" cults, we would expect to find more of them.

There are two other elements that, to my mind, are more likely to have produced a common sacred prostitution element in Babylon and (parts of) Cyprus: Both regions engaged in rebellions against Persia after conquest, and both regions were typified as ethnically heterogeneous. The ethnic heterogeneity of Cyprus has been mentioned above: Herodotos claims that ethnic groups of three separate continents inhabit the island. The ethnic heterogeneity of the Babylonians was discussed above. Both Babylon and Cyprus rebelled against Persia after their initial conquest. Herodotos recounts the rebellion, siege, and eventual defeat of Babylon in Book 3.150–158. The Cypriot rebellion occurs in Book 5.104 and following. It is particularly noteworthy in this instance that there are only three times in the *Histories* when the Cypriots are not spoken of as a single unit: when Herodotos lists their ethnic origins, when he notes that Amathus refused to join in with the other Cypriots in the revolt, and when he claimed that the sacred prostitution ritual occurred in *some* parts of Cyprus.

Both Babylon and Cyprus were doubly defeated, conquered once by Persia, and a second time after an unsuccessful rebellion. If, as I suggest, the sacred prostitution ritual of Chapter 1.199 has symbolic associations with defeat, it may be this doubly defeated status, combined, perhaps, with associations with an Aphrodite cult, that led Herodotos to attribute the sacred prostitution concept to both regions. Additionally, by the time the *Histories* were written, both Babylon and Cyprus were well, and one might even say comfortably, ensconced in the Persian Empire. Those conquered and "raped" had come to terms with their captors. Furthermore, as an inevitable foreign element *must* be introduced into whatever

---

[67] This in itself is probably a misunderstanding on the part of Herodotos. Later texts indicate that the Jahili Arabs did worship three goddesses – Manat, al'Uzza, and al-Lhat. The last, probably Herodotos' Alilat, is the queen deity, more likely to be associated with Hera, whereas it was al-Uzza who was syncretized with Aphrodite as the Venus deity. Budin 2004: 128–129.

community practices this ritual, the ritual itself may be, consciously or subconsciously, associated with regions marked by ethnic heterogeneity, and thus with Babylon and Cyprus.

CONCLUSIONS

In the end, the sacred prostitution Herodotos describes in Chapter 1.199 is not real. Rather than a historical reality, it is an almost poetic description of the current, conquered state of Babylon that pulls together a number of important themes running throughout the *Histories*.

In form, the sacred prostitution of Mylitta's cult is an inversion of Greek women's rituals. Certain immediate associations with this ritual are notions of religious impurity, known as *miasma* to the Greeks, and issues of bastardy. Deeper themes are matters of ethnic miscegenation and heterogeneity, and how these may have related to Greek concepts of autochthony; effeminization and rape; and finally conquest and defeat.

When considered together, all of these notions reinforce the themes, both dominant and subtle, running throughout Herodotos' text. Quite explicitly, Chapter 1.199 combines notions of foreign women, "barbarian" sexuality, and issues of exchange into one neat ritual – or two, if we consider the sacred prostitution alongside the bride auction. Herodotos places the Babylonians on a midrange between the wholly communal sexuality of the "Barbarians" living at the edges of the world, such as the Libyans and Indians, and the strict monogamy practiced by the Greeks. Like the Lydians and Thracians, the Babylonians have a partial commonality of women. While the Lydian women share themselves through prostitution before marriage, Babylonian women share themselves through prostitution once in life, probably after marriage. Unlike the Lydian and Thracian women, the commonality of the Babylonian women is not wholly voluntary. It is not Greek monogamy, nor is it the animalistic sexuality of those on the edge; it is a form of religiously mandated rape.

Issues of exchange are made manifest through both practices, 1.199 and 1.196. In the latter, there is a clear correlation between the worth of a bride as determined by her looks and the amount of money either paid or received for her. The system is fair (assuming you are not one of the brides, I suppose), orderly, democratic, masculine, and thus quite "wise." By contrast, although there is a correlation between beauty and time in the 1.199 ritual, there is no clear correlation between value and money, and thus the system of economics is thrown out of whack. If we are to follow Gould's hypothesis that systems of debt and reciprocity are of dominant importance in Herodotos, 1.199 shows a society whose economically unregulated *nomoi* lead to chaos.

That chaos is expressed through a women's ritual is especially telling. According to Lateiner: "Powerless women and children convey human frailty, loss, the situation of the victim, the demands of *nomos* in preserving the *oikos* or family, and social values under siege."[68] The fact that Babylon went from a period exemplified by the practice of bride auction to a period exemplified by universal prostitution reveals that the city and its culture have gone through a period of considerable decline, almost certainly the result of defeat at the hands of the Persians. So much proves for Herodotos the truth in his opening narrative (1.5): "For most of those [cities] which were once great are now small, and those which were once small are great in my own day. Knowing, thus, that human fortune never abides long in the same place, I shall give both equal attention." Chapter 1.199, then, manifests in a symbolic way the theme of instability in Herodotos, a theme that Thomas claims to be particularly strong in Book 1 and that serves as a warning for the Greeks in Book 8.[69]

This warning is hardly frivolous. The fact that the Babylonian bride auction could actually be seen as a Greek ideal, as per Phaleas of Chalcedon, as well as the fact that both cultures recognize the polluting properties of sex (1.198), shows a commonality between Greek and Babylonian ideologies. If the Babylonians could be turned from practitioners of a Greek ideal to a "most shameful" custom, it is certainly possible that the same might occur to the Greeks themselves. Herodotos presents the almost paradoxical idea that, although no society is free from the rigors of Fortune, it is nevertheless the responsibility of all societies to avoid the path to decline. This is manifest in Book 1 in the person of Croesus, who deemed himself (too) happy, tested fate, and lost an empire. The idea is echoed at the very end of the *Histories* (9.121):

> "Soft countries," said Cyrus, "breed soft men. It is not natural that any one place produces simultaneously good fruits and good soldiers as well." The Persians had to admit that this was true and that Cyrus was wiser then they were. So they left him and chose instead to live in a harsh land and to rule others than to cultivate rich fields and be others' subjects.[70]

[68] Lateiner 1989: 137.
[69] Thomas 2000: 113.
[70] Trans. de Sélincourt 1972: 624.

Although Croesus was subject to fate – *moira* – he also had a hand in his own demise, thus manifesting the Greek ideology that humans take an active part in their own destinies. At the end of the *Histories*, the Persians actively chose to avoid the same fate for themselves, choosing to eschew physical comfort for the greater perk of political ascendance. Later, as we and Herodotos' later audience well know, the Persians changed their minds, opting for comfort, its concomitant effeminacy, and defeat at the hands of the Greeks. As Herodotos wrote his *Histories*, the Greeks themselves were in a period of instability, with the Athenians in particular playing a role similar to those of both Croesus *and* Cyrus. The threat of effeminacy thus hung doubly over the heads of the Greeks. Would they choose empire and luxury – the Persian effeminacy – or defeat and rape – the Lydian version? Either way, the threat was palpable in Herodotos' world. The image of all local women penetrated by foreigners, desecrated, yet compliant, accepting money for their services as demanded by the gods, must ultimately have served as a harsh lesson on the vicissitudes of fortune and divinity and the wages of war and defeat for its Greek audience.

HERODOTOS 1.199: LINE-BY-LINE ANALYSIS

The most shameful of the customs among the Babylonians is this:

Herodotos signals his disapproval of a foreign custom, quite unique in the Histories.

It is necessary for every local woman to sit in the sanctuary of Aphrodite once in life to "mingle" with a foreign man.

Statement of ritual and introduction of "foreign bastardy" motif.

But many do not deign to mingle with the others, thinking highly of themselves because of their wealth, and they set themselves before the sanctuary having arrived in covered chariots, with many a maidservant in tow.

First implication of a lack of volition in the ritual as well as interacting with members of other classes.

But the majority act thus: In the *temenos* of Aphrodite many women sit wearing a garland of string about their heads. Some come forward, others remain in the background.

There is a lack of organization among the women indicating the unregulated nature of the ritual.

They have straight passages in all directions through the women, by which the foreigners passing through might make their selection.

Wives and mothers who, by Greek ideals, are to remain hidden are put on display for foreigners and the community.

Once a woman sits there, she may not return home before someone of the foreigners tossing silver into her lap should mingle with her outside the sanctuary.

Lack of female agency and, once again, the unregulated nature of the ritual in the lack of a clear terminus time. Once again, themes of foreign bastardy, and the irrational nature of the ritual — it cannot be performed in sacred space.

And in tossing he must say thus: "I summon you by the goddess Mylitta." The Assyrians call Aphrodite Mylitta.

Herodotos reveals his knowledge of Assyrian divine names.

The silver is of any amount, for it may not be rejected: This is not their sacred custom, for the money is sacred.

The ritual's inability to correlate money received for "goods and services" provided.

The woman follows the first man who tossed her silver, nor may she reject anyone.

Once again the lack of volition on the part of the Babylonian women.

When she should have mingled, having discharged her obligation to the goddess, she leaves for home, and after this time you might not take her, offering gifts no matter how great.

The lack of volition on the part of the Babylonian women and their fidelity otherwise.

Those who are attractive and tall go home quickly, while those homely in these respects wait about a long time, being unable to fulfill the law; some among them wait about for three or four years.

The inverted economy of the ritual — value in terms of beauty does not translate into more money, but rather less time in fulfilling the ritual. This section also emphasizes the unregulated quality of the ritual.

And in some areas of Cyprus the custom is similar to this.

Cyprus shares the implications of sacred prostitution, including defeat, ethnic heterogeneity, and possibly a cult of Aphrodite.

APPENDIX: MYLITTA AND MULISSU

In 1979 Stephanie Dalley published an article showing that, contrary to currently prevailing opinion, Herodotos' use of the name Mylitta for Aphrodite was actually reasonably correct. The Mesopotamian name in question was an EME-SAL dialectical variation of the name of the goddess Ninlil, written as a logogram but known to be pronounced as Mulliltu(m) in the Old Babylonian period (1750–1590 BCE).[71] Later, due to linguistic changes between the Old Babylonian and Neo-Assyrian dialects of Akkadian, the name mutated from Mulliltum to Mulissu or even Mulešsu,[72] which form Dalley claimed was used by both Assyrians and Babylonians in Herodotos' day.[73]

Over the centuries Ninlil came to be conflated with other Mesopotamian goddesses, including Ištar, the Mesopotamian goddess of sex and war.[74] As such, it seemed perfectly reasonable that Herodotos would attribute a documented Mesopotamian divine name – Mulissu – associated with the Mesopotamian goddess of sex to Aphrodite.

The remaining problem is one of linguistics. Quite simply, Herodotos would never transliterate Mylitta for Mulissu. Writing in the Ionic dialect, Herodotos would not translate the /s/ phoneme of the Akkadian form into a double-*tau*, as one might expect for the Attic dialect. Furthermore, we would expect not only a *Mylissa form, but even the more thoroughly Ionic form of *Mylissê, ending with an Ionic *eta* instead of the *alpha* (as is seen with Herodotos' Athenaiê for Athena, Herê for Hera, and, of course, Aphroditê herself).

This problem might now be resolved, for more recent discoveries have attested to the presence of a Mul(l)itta variation in the Neo-Babylonian prosopography.[75] R. Zadok discovered a woman named Mullittu-silim in tablet BM 29356, a Late Babylonian document datable to the years 24–29 of the reign of Darius I (498–493 BCE).[76] This Babylonian form might be contrasted with the Assyrian variation seen in the name Ú-bar-^{d}mul-le-šú (Ubar-Mullešsu) documented in BM 59699 datable to 539 BCE.[77]

---

[71] Dalley 1979: *passim*; Parpola 1980: 177 ff.; MacGinnis 1986: 77–78; Müller-Kessler and Kessler 1999: 71; Dalley 2003: 173–174.

[72] Dalley 1979: 177; *RlA* "Ninlil" 452; Stol 1995: 1138.

[73] Dalley 1979: 177–178.

[74] *RlA* "Ninlil": §3.1.15.

[75] Hämeen-Anttila and Rollinger 2001: 92–93.

[76] Zadok 1997.

[77] Zadok 1998.

Likewise, Müller–Kessler and Kessler have discovered the "Mulita" (*mwlyt*) form in several late (third to second century BCE) Mandaean cylinder seals, often associated with the goddess Ištar. In the first century BCE, then, it becomes increasingly clear that there was a goddess known by the name or title Mul(l)itta in the region of Babylon and that this goddess could be closely connected with the Mesopotamian goddess of sex.

The presence of the final *alpha* is far less troubling. The double-*tau* ending of Mylitta, especially if Herodotos knew of the possible double-*sigma* variant, is strongly reminiscent of other words in the Greek vocabulary which vary between double-*sigma* and double-*tau*, all of which display mixed Attic fronting. Herodotos, consciously or not, may have categorized Mylitta with such words as *glossa/glotta* or *thalassa/thalatta*. Unfortunately, in the absence of any case other than the nominative, it is impossible to verify this hypothesis.

Once again, Herodotos seems to have gotten it right. Or, at least, mostly. Herodotos claimed that "the Assyrians call Aphrodite 'Mylitta.'" Actually, the Assyrians call Aphrodite Mulissu; the Babylonians call Aphrodite Mulittu. This in itself might provide further information concerning from whom Herodotos received his information about Babylon. Although Stephanie Dalley does make a good argument that Herodotos may have been describing not Babylon but Nineveh, it is evident that in this case at least he got his information from a southerner.

CHAPTER FIVE

IN THE FOOTSTEPS OF HERODOTOS: LUCIAN AND "JEREMIAH"

Herodotus, like all Greeks, wrote about "barbarians" with the intention of proving the superiority of Greeks, and allegations of cannibalism and sexual licentiousness abound. In his descriptions of barbarian sexual mores, he may also have been trying to show the horrible results that could follow if proper women were not kept as guarded and secluded as they were in Greece. All the later Roman and Christian allegations of sexual initiation ultimately derive from this one passage in Herodotus.[1]

S UCH A TESTIMONIAL, ALTHOUGH PERHAPS JUST A BIT OVERSTATED, is not uncommon among modern scholars who see in ancient references to sacred prostitution not historical accuracy but accusation. As one of the earliest authors to write clearly and directly (apparently) about the perceived ancient custom, Herodotos gets a lot of flak for supposedly denigrating his eastern neighbors, and even more so for getting the "sacred prostitution ball" rolling. It was Herodotos, many claim, who created the entire myth. Thus J. G. Westenholz notes that "Such allegations first appear in the work of Herodotus (*Hist.* 1.199) whose view of Mesopotamian culture was considerably biased and whose speculations have been elaborated by Strabo in his *Geography* (16.1.20), and by other classical authors."[2] Oden, in his analysis of the literary sources for sacred prostitution, concludes, "What appears to be a list of more than a dozen sources may in fact be a list of a couple of sources, perhaps even and ultimately a single source: Herodotus."[3] F. Glinister mentions in her own work on sacred prostitution (or the lack thereof) in Italy that

[1] Frymer-Kensky 1992: 200.
[2] Westenholz 1989: 261.
[3] Oden 1987: 146.

"Virtually every reference [to sacred prostitution] in the ancient sources can be shown to go back to Herodotus' original report on Babylonian temple prostitution (1.199), itself set in 'once-upon-a-time' territory, and for which the copious contemporary Near Eastern documents provide no support."[4] R. A. Henshaw, in his 1994 study of Mesopotamian cultic functionaries, lists the following ancient authors as influenced by Herodotos' 1.199 account: The author of the "Epistle of Jeremiah," the author of the "Testament of Judah 12.1," Strabo, Lucian of Samosata, Eusebius, Sozomen, and the author of 2 Maccabes 6.4.[5]

This modern accusation of accusation is not accurate. As Chapter 4 showed, the metaphorical description of Babylonian sacred prostitution probably had more to do with warning, sympathy, and a testimonial to fickle fortune than a desire on Herodotos' part to denigrate or otherwise vilify the Babylonians. Furthermore, as we shall see, there were other ancient authors who, in their own, inadvertent ways, contributed to the myth of sacred prostitution, including Pindar and, most especially, Strabo. Herodotos cannot really be singled out for blame.

Nevertheless, Herodotos' narrative about Babylonian sacred prostitution did have an impact on the literature. Ancient authors (and quite a few modern ones) did incorporate Herodotos' story into their own works, and these later authors then went on to become yet further fodder for the growing sacred prostitution myth. The next step in unraveling that myth, then, is looking at how Herodotos' account went on to generate children and grandchildren of its own. This chapter will consider two authors of such accounts: Lucian of Samosata and the author of the "Letter of Jeremiah." Strabo will be dealt with in Chapter 7. Athanasius will be considered in Chapter 10 with other aspects of early Christian sexual rhetoric.

LUCIAN'S *SYRIAN GODDESS*, 6

They shave their heads [for Adonis], just like the Egyptians when Apis dies. Of the women, as many as do not wish to shave perform this penalty: For a single day they stand for the sale of their beauty. The market is open to foreigners only and the payment becomes a penalty to Aphrodite.

καὶ τὰς κεφαλὰς ξύρονται ὅκως Αἰγύπτοι ἀποθανόντος Ἄπιος. γυναικῶν δὲ ὁκόσαι οὐκ ἐθέλουσιν ξύρεσθαι, τοιήνδε ζημίην

---

[4] Glinister 2000: 31.
[5] Henshaw 1994: 226–227.

ἐκτελέουσιν· ἐν μιῆ ἡμέρῃ ἐπὶ πρήσει τῆς ὥρης ἵστανται· ἡ δὲ ἀγορὴ μούνοισι ξείνοισι παρακέαται, καὶ ὁ μισθὸς ἐς τὴν Ἀφροδίτην θωιὴ γίγνεται.

So wrote the author of *Peri tês Theou Syrias* in what is generally accepted to have been the second century CE. This quotation is extremely important for the study of ancient sacred prostitution for two reasons. On the one hand, it is the only source for sacred prostitution occurring in the very ancient city of Byblos.[6] Perhaps more importantly, though, once the notion of the Biblical *qedešîm/qedešôt* is removed from the equation (see Chapter 2), it is the oldest testimony for the practice of sacred prostitution at all in the Levant. Its accuracy thus winds up implicating not only the Syrians, but also the Phoenicians and their various colonies. Determining its accuracy is thus a rather important matter to say the least.

Inconveniently, the issue of Byblian religion, and certainly sacred prostitution, in Lucian's day is complicated by the fact that the best source we have for it is Lucian himself, and nobody knows to what extent to take him seriously, or even if "he" is actually Lucian, or even if "he" lived in Lucian's day at all.[7] If, as many claim, Lucian did write the *Syrian Goddess*, then certainly it must be satire,[8] not to be taken seriously at all. If, rather, it was written by another author, almost certainly a pious Hellenized Syrian (as the author himself claims to be at the incipit of the piece – *graphô de Assyrios eôn*), then the data provided in the work should be taken at face value and as accurate.[9] The problem with these hypotheses is that they turn the analysis of the *Syrian Goddess* into a zero-sum game: either it is all false and parody (the Lucian-author theory), or it is all correct (the alternate-author theory). And, since some of the data have proven to be verifiable, the only logical result is that the *Syrian Goddess* is a non-Lucianic work that should be accepted as fact. To quote Lucinda Dirven, "On the basis of this evidence it must be concluded that a great deal of the information provided by DS on Hieropolitan religion is accurate. *We may therefore presume that those elements for which there is no external confirmation are essentially trustworthy as well.*"[10]

---

[6] Assuming that "sale of one's beauty" might be taken as a euphemism for prostitution.

[7] See Polanski 1998, especially for the suggestion that the *Syrian Goddess* was actually composed in the fourth century CE.

[8] Oden 1977: 16–24.

[9] Dirven 1997, 163.

[10] *Ibid*. Italics mine.

Such a hypothesis founders at two points. As J. L. Lightfoot has argued in her masterful work on the *Syrian Goddess*, all the stylistic and historic evidence points toward Lucian of Samosata as the author of the piece.[11] The fact that this work is unusual does not preclude the curmudgeonly satirist as the author, just as the comedic tone of *The Hand of Ethelberta* does not preclude Thomas Hardy as having written it. Furthermore, just because some data are accurate in the piece does not mean that all are, either intentionally or otherwise. As already discussed in Chapter 4, Herodotos' *Histories* are filled with accurate historical and ethnographic details, occasionally punctuated by a trip into poetic, metaphoric, or fantastic literature.

Reference to Herodotos is not random here, for the most widely accepted aspect of the *Syrian Goddess*, whoever the author, is that the work relies very heavily on Herodotos' *Histories* as its model for language, organization, and content.[12] Therefore, just as the "Father of History" could occasionally play loosely with historical accuracy, so too could his protegé. To quote Lightfoot:

> The fact that *DDS* is Herodotean literary pastiche has implications for its truth-value and historical worth which are far more complex that the (over-simple) question whether it is heir to a Herodotean tradition of lying-literature. One could imagine a spectrum, at one extreme of which there would be details which are pure literary fictions, merely inspired by Herodotos . . . , with no correspondence in reality; and at the other, there would be real, actual, tangible things. But the greatest length of this spectrum would be occupied by things which are indeed there, yet owe their very mention to the fact that Herodotean ethnography had created an expectation that they would be there.[13]

Lightfoot's full Herodotean–Lucianic spectrum appears in paragraph 6 of the *Syrian Goddess*, where Lucian ranges from (apparent) accuracy to pure Herodotean fabrication: the reference to sacred prostitution. Even more so, Lucian very much modeled paragraph 6 on the Herodotean technique of inversion, whereby the rites and traditions of the "Other" are presented as a kind of inverse of expected Greek practice (see Chapter 4).

[11] Lightfoot 2003: 195. See especially Chapter 2 for a very full discussion of this problem and its resolution.
[12] Lightfoot 2003: Chapter 2, *inter alia*, especially pp. 195–198. I could not even begin to summarize her level of detail here. See also Dirven 1997: 157, 164; Oden 1977: 20.
[13] Lightfoot 2003: 214–215.

As such, not only is the reference to Byblian sacred prostitution a tip of the nib to Herodotos, but it appears precisely where it does to round out Lucian's mimicry of the Father of History. For Byblos then, as for Babylon, paragraph 6 shows cultural/cultic inversion followed by invention.

The passage about sacred prostitution marks the end of the first paragraph of Lucian's description of the temple and rites of Aphrodite and Adonis in ancient Byblos. The preceding narrative describes in detail the Byblian rites of mourning for Adonis, functionally the Syrian equivalent of the Greek Adonia:

> They say that the affair of Adonis and the boar took place in their country, and in memory of the sad event they beat their breasts each year and lament and perform the rites, and there is much mourning throughout the country. After they have finished beating their breasts and lamenting, they first make offerings to Adonis as to the dead, and afterwards, on the next day, they claim that he lives and send him into the air.[14]

The following paragraph (7) offers an alternate interpretation of the Byblian ritual, whereby some Byblians claim that the rites of mourning are actually for the Egyptian deity Osiris rather than Adonis, as that god is buried in their land. Paragraph 8 continues with the Byblian Adonis theme, describing how once a year the local river turns red with the flowing blood of Adonis, thus signaling the commencement of the Byblian "Adonia." In strong Herodotean fashion, Lucian winds up this paragraph with an alternate, more "logical" reason for the reddening of the waters: wind blows red dirt into the water up-stream.

The initial information in paragraph 6, then, refers to the death and ritualistic mourning offered in honor of the demigod Adonis in the temple of Byblian Aphrodite. According to Lucian, throughout the country (*ana tên khôrên*) they (no gender indicated) beat their breasts and make lament, and then offer sacrifices. On the following day, they proclaim that Adonis lives and send him into the air (whatever that means).

Although this description shows certain parallels with Biblical references to Adonis's Mesopotamian cognate Tammuz (see especially Ezekiel 8:14), it is a rather odd reflection of the Adonia rites carried out in Greece. Initially, in the Archaic Age, there did appear to be some accord between the Byblian and Greek mourning, as expressed in our earliest reference

[14] *Ibid*: 251.

to the "Occidental" mourning for Adonis – Sappho. In one of her lyrics the poet writes:

> Delicate Adonis is dying!
> O Kytherea, what shall we do?
> Beat your breasts, girls!
> Tear your dresses!

The beating of breasts correlates well with Lucian's description; the tearing of clothes could be seen as a parallel for the Byblian lamentation.

But, as time moves on, the Greek Adonia acquire, in addition to the original lamentation, a far more festive air. According to the comic poets of the Classical age through the second century CE, the Greek Adonia were unofficial rites, tolerated but not publicly recognized, celebrated in private houses and apparently on private rooftops, mainly by women of all social standings but especially concubines and courtesans, along with their lovers.[15] As early as the fifth century BCE, Aristophanes in his *Lysistrata* relates how the women were worshipping Adonis on the rooftops . . . dancing and yelling "Poor young Adonis!" . . . getting drunk and saying, "Beat your breasts for Adonis!"[16] In the fourth century, Menander's *Samia* is set around the all-night revelry of the Adonia where citizen wife and foreign *hetaira* celebrate together with much *paideia*, just as Diphilos's comedies associate the rite/festival with obscene jokes (*Theseus* = PCG F49) and references to prostitutes as celebrants (*Painter* = F42).

In the third century BCE Theokritos in *Idyll XV* reveals that the Adonia were "celebrated" in Alexandria with a formal lament of the demi-god. However, the dirge of the female singer, passing from the joyful marriage to the sorrowful funeral of Adonis, contrasts strongly with the humorous antics of the crowd making their way to the celebrations. Once again, the mournful quality of the rite is undercut by its execution.

In Lucian's own day, the sophist Alkiphron provided the following narrative in the voice of Megara writing to another woman named Bakkhis:

> We are going to arrange a banquet to celebrate Adonis at the house of Thessalia's lover. It is she who is going to be responsible for providing "Aphrodite's Lover." Remember to bring a little garden and a statuette with you. And also bring along your Adonis whom you smother with kisses. We shall get drunk with all our lovers.[17]

---

[15] Detienne [1977] 1994: 65.
[16] Henderson 1996: 56, lines 390–397.
[17] Detienne 1985: 65.

The "little garden" refers to the so-called "Gardens of Adonis" (*kêpoi Adônidos*), which were prevalent in the hero's cult in Greece. These were shallow pots sown with quick-growing herbs such as fennel and lettuce.[18] After allowing the plants to grow quickly but rather precariously, the women allowed the plants to wither and die as part of the Adonia ritual. Several Athenian vase paintings depict this scene, showing a woman climbing (up to the roof?) upon a ladder while holding a shallow dish. The "statuette" is probably a small effigy of Adonis. The origin of both concepts is to be sought not in Syria and the cult of Adonis, but in Egypt and the cult of Osiris. Part of the ritual mourning and honoring of Osiris, the Egyptian deity associated with death and afterlife, was the creation of small images of the god known as "Osiris Beds," composed of organic substances and sown with seeds.[19] Thus the mummy of Osiris promotes the sprouting of new life. The fact that Lucian himself suggests in paragraph 7 of the *Syrian Goddess* that even some Byblians themselves believe their rites to Adonis are actually directed to Osiris emphasizes the close connection between the rituals and paraphernalia of these two deities. Nevertheless, these Osirianic implements appearing in the Greek rites have no place in the Byblian rites mentioned in paragraph 6.

The mournful quality of the western Adonia reappears in the literature centuries after Lucian. According to Ammianus Marcellinus, writing in the mid-fourth century CE, when the Emperor Julian visited Antioch in 362 he arrived "on those days when the annual cycle was completed and they were celebrating in the ancient fashion the rites (*ritu veteri*) of Adonis, the lover of Venus . . . on all sides were heard mournful wailings and tearful cries" (*ululabiles undique planctus et lugubres sonus audiebantur*).[20] Even in the absence of the comedic genre, this does not sound like the drunken cries of "Woe to Adonis" as mentioned in Aristophanes. The reference to the "ancient fashion" and the setting in Syria itself may indicate that, although the Adonia had become festive rites in the West, they maintained their funerary character in the Levant (including, of course, Byblos).

Nevertheless, what is important here is that Lucian was writing during the long period when the Adonia were revelrous, even erotic, in nature, in the West, in contrast to the mournful quality present in the Byblian ritual. Thus, the Greek and Byblian rites contrast.

[18] Winkler 1990: 189–190.
[19] Mettinger 2001: 170–171. Functionally, it's an Osiris Chia Pet.
[20] *Ibid*: 116–117.

The issue of actual death is also an important distinction between the two rites of Adonis. By Greek standards, Adonis was a hero, not a deity. He was mortal, and his death was permanent.[21] By contrast, on the second day of the Byblian ritual the people declared that Adonis lived. There is thus a notion of resurrection in the Near Eastern ideology that is not present in the Greek.

The end result of this is that the rites to Adonis described by Lucian show an interesting inverse of the Adonia as experienced by Lucian's Greek-reading audience. As such, Lucian replicated the Herodotean practice of ethnography as inversion while simultaneously presenting accurate information. Quite simply, he takes the true (and possibly even similar) and presents it as the different and spectacular.[22] Thus, to compare the Byblian and Greek Adonia:

Byblian	Greek
Beating Breasts	Beating Breasts
Lamentation	Tearing Clothing
Ungendered	Women Mainly
Official	Unofficial
Rite at Temple and throughout the Land	Mourning in Private Homes and on Rooftops
Death Offering to Adonis	"Gardens of Adonis" and Figurines
Resurrection	Early and Permanent Death
Sending Adonis into the Air	Casting Away of "Gardens"[23]

Lucian's adherence to the Herodotean prototype in paragraph 6 does not end here, however, for following this description come two additional oddities: the ritualistic cutting of hair and the rite of sacred prostitution.

---

[21] *Ibid*: 113–16 with full notation.

[22] Lightfoot notes a similar technique when Lucian is describing the pilgrimage made by various visitors to the Holy City of Hierapolis. A number of the practices mentioned, such as wearing a garland and staying at the house of a functional *proxenos*, have Greek parallels, but Lucian deliberately attempts to make the narration of paragraphs 55–57 of his *Syrian Goddess sound* exotic through use of vocabulary and juxtaposition. To quote Lightfoot on this topic: "some features of this account of pilgrimage are distinctly un-Greek, *and others are at least presented as if they were*. Vocabulary, content, and literary positioning – in the wake of Herodotus and his own ethnography of Egyptian πανηγύρεις – work together to create a picture of a set of exotic cultural practices." Lightfoot 2003: 520 (emphasis mine).

[23] One could offer an additional inversion specifically with the dirge in Theokritos XV: Here the rite goes from joyous to mournful, *hieros gamos* to funeral. In Lucian, the progression is from mournful funeral to joyous resurrection.

In and of itself the cutting of hair as a sign of mourning for the dead is hardly strange or unusual to a Greek audience. Herodotos himself mentions in Book 2.36 of his *Histories* that one of the backward things about the Egyptians is that during periods of mourning they allow their hair to grow long, the inverse (naturally) of what everybody else does. Reference to the shaving of the head in a time of mourning would thus, at first glance, seem quite natural to a Greek.

Except... Except that Lucian compares this ritual to an Egyptian ritual, whereby the Egyptians *shave* their heads to mourn the death of the bull-deity Apis. This runs contrary to what Herodotos told us (and Lucian certainly had read) about the Egyptians: that during periods of mourning they let their hair and beards grow long.[24] Furthermore, Lucian mentions this rite of mourning *after* he has already revealed that Adonis "lives" and his resurrection has been celebrated. Although the reference to shaving could certainly be an afterthought, its placement after the resurrection has a jarring effect, giving the impression that something is slightly out of whack. We had a similar experience in Herodotos 1.199. Here, contrary to the historian's usually dispassionate and impartial manner of presenting foreign *nomoi*, he calls the sacred prostitution of the Babylonian women *aiskhistos*. Both references to sacred prostitution, then, the Herodotean and the Lucianic, are preceded by narration that indicates that something is not quite right.

In one fell swoop Lucian calls to mind Herodotos while conjuring feelings of unease, once again like Herodotos in his Babylonian *logos*. Then Lucian presents a description of sacred prostitution that strongly mirrors the description offered by Herodotos in his own work. The so-called "rite" takes place in the latter in **Babyl**on, in the former in **Byblos**.

---

[24] In reality, it seems that neither author got it quite right. Although it is true that Egyptian priests did remove their hair for the sake of ritual purity (Sauneron 2000: 36–37), there is no evidence that they let their hair grow long in times of mourning. By contrast, there is no evidence that the nonpriestly Egyptians regularly shaved their heads (Shaw and Nicholson 1995: 117–118). Quite contrary to Herodotos, the Egyptians could cut off a lock or two of hair to mourn a death, but, once again, there is no reference to actual shaving, as per Lucian (*ibid*). Likewise, although the Egyptians did formally mourn the death of the Apis bull, there is no reference to shaving the head. The fullest description of the formal mourning of the Apis bull was given by Psamtik III, who claimed to have fasted completely from food and water for four days, and to have observed minor fasting for an additional 70 days (Meeks and Favard-Meeks 1996: 139). No shaving is mentioned. Lucian's reference to this "rite," then, had more to do with calling to mind Herodotos, and even contradicting him, then expressing any aspect of actual Egyptian cult practice.

Both are oriented around a temple and cult of Aphrodite[25] (and one of only two references to Aphrodite's cult specifically in Lucian). The participants in both rituals are women (*gynaika/gynaikes* in Herodotos, *gynaikôn* in Lucian) and both have an immediate reference to lack of volition (*pollai de kai ouk axieumenai anamisgesthai* for Herodotos, *hokosai ouk ethelousin xuresthai* in Lucian). Both authors note that only foreigners (*xeinoi/xeinoisi*) have access to the women for sale, and both mention that the fee earned for the prostitution becomes sacred (*ginetai gar hiron touto to argyrion* in Herodotos, *ho misthos es tên Aphroditên thôiê gignetai* for Lucian).

What, then, is the likelihood that Lucian's account of Byblian sacred prostitution is pure literary fabrication, indebted primarily to Herodotos? It is already clear that the entire *Syrian Goddess* is heavily predicated upon Herodotos in terms of dialect, vocabulary, organization, points of interest, and emphasis. Lucian certainly knew Herodotos' 1.199 narrative. There is no reference to sacred prostitution in Byblos other than Lucian's paragraph 6. What is more, there is no other known reference to sacred prostitution in the Levant before Lucian.[26] Lucian, then, is our sole source of evidence for a practice that looks very much like a nonexistent practice as described by Lucian's own historiographic model.

Finally, outright lies (or at least exaggeration) occur in other places in the *Syrian Goddess*. The best example is Lucian's account of the phallic pillars located outside of the temple of Atargatis in Hierapolis. In paragraph 28 Lucian claims that these pillars were some 300 *orgyiai* tall, roughly 1,800 feet.[27] This is a bit extreme. Furthermore, twice a year a man would climb up one of these pillars to sit there for a week in order to pray for the Syrian people, who would call up to him to ask for blessings. Although columns in front of temples have excellent parallels in the Near East (consider the bronze pillars before Solomon's temple in Jerusalem, constructed by Phoenicians, and the temple of Milqart in Tyre, with columns of, according to Herodotos at least, emerald and gold), the

---

[25] A Greek *interpretatio* of the Baalat Gubal, the "Lady of Byblos" revered in the city since the Bronze Age. On her history, cult, and iconography, see Bonnet 1996: 19–30. On the syncretism with Aphrodite, see Budin 2004: *passim*. The Baalat Gubal is most commonly associated with either Egyptian Hathor or Phoenician Aštart, neither of whom, the evidence will show, has any other associations with sacred prostitution.

[26] Lipinski's (1995: 97–99) suggestion that the "cellules" surrounding the sanctuary of Adonis at Dura Europos belonged to the sacred prostitutes seems a tad far-fetched and not well argued. On additional interpretations of architecture as sacred brothels, see Chapter 9.

[27] Lightfoot 2003: 367.

height Lucian gives is not feasible, especially if someone sitting at the top is having conversations with those below. If Lucian can make up such a detail, we should not be surprised to find him fabricating others, especially with such an excellent and comparable Herodotean precedent. All told, the argument that Lucian's description of Byblian sacred prostitution is pure fabrication is very strong. The above arguments, then, combined with the overall hypothesis of this book that *none* of the evidence for sacred prostitution in the ancient world is real, make, I believe, a very strong case that Lucian is here simply having a peck of fun with both Herodotos and his readers.

Lucian's description of sacred prostitution in Byblos is an homage to Herodotos. The account presented at the end of paragraph 6 of the *Syrian Goddess* is fictional, based on a prototype invented by Herodotos some 500 years earlier. The shock value of the preceding narrative, the vocabulary, the particulars, and even the homophony of the locations where the two narratives occur all support the notion that Lucian's sacred prostitution merely drifted up in Herodotos' wake.

THE *LETTER OF JEREMIAH*, VERSE 43

Verse 43 of the Apocryphal *Letter of Jeremiah* recounts about Chaldean (Babylonian) women that

> And the women, surrounded by cords, sit in the streets burning bran. Whenever someone of them, being drawn off, sleeps with someone of the passers-by, she humiliates her neighbor, because she [the neighbor] was not as worthy as she herself and did not have her cord torn.

> Αἱ δὲ γυναῖκες περιθέμεναι σχοινία, ἐν ταῖς ὁδοῖς ἐγκάθηνται, θυμιῶσαι τὰ πίτυρα· ὅταν δέ τις αὐτῶν ἐφελκυσθεῖσα ὑπό τινος τῶν παραπορευομένων κοιμηθῇ, τὴν πλησίον ὀνειδίζει, ὅτι οὐκ ἠξίωται ὥσπερ καὶ αὐτὴ, οὔτε τὸ σχοινίον αὐτῆς διερράγη.

This passage is frequently analyzed in reference to Herodotos. C. A. Moore's discussion of it in the *Anchor Bible Commentary* is as follows:

> 43. The practice described here is reminiscent of but not identical with the one described in Herodotus 1.199 ... [passage quoted here]. ... Strabo (born ca. 63 B.C.) described a similar practice (*Geography* XVI ch. 1); his account, however, seems to be dependent upon Herodotus. ... The Epistle, however, is not. In the custom described in the Epistle there is no mention of all women being required to prostitute themselves or of their having to be in the temple precinct. On

the other hand, in Herodotus there is no mention of the women burning bran.... The head cords mentioned in Herodotus do not resemble in form or function the cords (*schoinia*) in the Epistle. Nor does the Epistle indicate whether it was a once and for all act (so Herodotus) or a repeatable rite. In any case, all forms of prostitution, but especially sacred prostitution, were rejected by the biblical writers....[28]

In this instance, according to Moore, Herodotos' account merely helps to fill out information about a rite that nevertheless existed in its own right in Babylon, and to which the author of the "Letter" was an independent witness. B. Metzger likewise understood the sacred prostitution referred to in the "Letter" as an actual fact, once again supported by the later evidence of the classical authors: "The licentious fertility rites which were associated with this deity [Tammuz], to which Herodotus, Strabo, and Lucian make reference, are alluded to in verse 43."[29]

On the reverse side are those scholars who do not believe in the existence of sacred prostitution. For them, the debate is more to what extent the author of the "Letter" was or was not dependent upon Herodotos in the creation of the Chaldean sacred prostitution narrative, or even if sacred prostitution was at issue at all for "Jeremiah." In his study of this question S. Hooks wrote,

> Though this account has been compared to Herodotus there are many differences. In Herodotus the women are said to sit in the temple of Mylitta, while in pseudo-Jeremiah there is no mention of a temple or a goddess and the women sit by the side of the streets. In Herodotus' account every woman is said to submit to a single act of intercourse with the proceeds dedicated to the goddess. In pseudo-Jeremiah the participants are simply called "women" with no indication that it is to be a single act or any description of the proceeds or their use. In Herodotus the patron must be stranger, while in pseudo-Jeremiah he is simply a "passer-by." While both Herodotus and pseudo-Jeremiah do mention "cords," in Herodotus the term is used only the sense of "rope-drawn passageways" while in pseudo-Jeremiah each woman is said to have cords "around" them which are "broken" in the process of their being "drawn away." And so we see that other than the fact that they both ascribe lewd sexual acts to the citizens of Babylon these accounts have very little in common.[30]

---

[28] Moore 1977: 348.
[29] Metzger 1963: 97.
[30] Hooks 1985: 34–35, Greek portions omitted.

By contrast, R. Henshaw notes simply that "The dependence of this passage on Her I, 199 is strong."[31]

Before considering the complex relationship between "Jeremiah" and Herodotos, though, a couple of points need to be considered. First of all, there is nothing in verse 43 that pertains to religion – there are no temples, sanctuaries, priests, deities, or idols. The only word that produces a vaguely sanctimonious feel to the passage is the verb *thumiô*, "to burn," which often is used in reference to the burning of incense on an altar. Here, what is being burnt is bran, and there is no reference to an altar or a deity to receive such an offering. As such, there is nothing specifically sacred about this passage.

Furthermore, nothing in this verse pertains to prostitution. Although the women mentioned "sleep" (*koimêthêi*) with the passers-by, there is no reference to a monetary exchange, or even to money. Prostitution, then, is not at issue. These two facts considered, we must recognize that verse 43 does not, technically, relate to sacred prostitution, and is not, therefore, evidence of any kind for that so-called institution.

Not that this has slowed anyone down in recognizing it as such. Both Moore's and Metzger's takes on this verse were mentioned above. G. W. E. Nickelsburg, in his history of Jewish literature from the fourth century BCE through the second century CE, although not implicating Herodotos here in any way, nevertheless understands this passage as yet one more aspect of the degeneracy of pagan religion, and specifically sacred prostitution: "Thus, from a Jewish point of view the touching of sacrifices by women in a state of ritual impurity, the service of women at cultic meals, and cultic prostitution (vv. 29, 30, 43) speak for themselves."[32] Even Oden places this text second to Herodotos chronologically in the history of sacred prostitution texts, although pointing out that it has been far less influential than either Herodotos or Strabo.[33]

For some reason, then, there is a tendency to see verse 43 as relating to sacred prostitution in spite of the complete absence of religiosity or actual prostitution present in the verse. It is, I believe, that first point that has caused all the confusion.

The "Letter of Jeremiah" is a poetic invective against pagan/non-Jewish religions. It is based primarily on, and gets its name from, two passages in the Book of Jeremiah: an epistle written by the prophet Jeremiah to

[31] Henshaw 1994: 227.
[32] Nickelsburg 1981: 37.
[33] Oden 1987: 190, no. 32.

the exiles in Babylon during the Babylonian captivity of the mid sixth century BCE (Jeremiah 29) and an invective against idolatry in Jeremiah 10: 2–16. The portions of the "Letter" that condemn idol worship have close parallels to Jeremiah 10. Jeremiah 10:4 notes that it is the craftsman who adorns the idols with gold and silver, a theme mentioned several times in the "Letter" (vv. 8, 24, 30, 39, 51, 55, 58, 70, 72). Jeremiah 10:5 mentions that idols are dumb like a scarecrow in a plot of cucumbers, a verse repeated in the "Letter," v. 71, where "Jeremiah" points out that idols give no more protection than a scarecrow in a plot of cucumbers. Jeremiah 10:9 refers to the idols as dressed up in cloths of purple, an observation echoed in "Letter" v. 12. In Jeremiah vv. 14–15 the author notes that idols are merely made by humans, with no breath and no actual power, just as the "Letter" vv. 45–6 related that idols are simply the products of craftsmen, who themselves are not protected by their own creations. Finally, both Jeremiah 10:13 and "Letter" 61–63 contrast these false, dumb idols with the true God who controls both earth and weather. Clearly, the primary inspiration for the "Letter of Jeremiah" is Jeremiah, although there are similar references, possibly preludes to both, in Psalms 115:3–8, 135: 6–7 and 15–17, and Isaiah 44:9–20.[34]

However, there is a second theme also running through the "Letter," which is the general debauchery and immorality of the Chaldean cultic personnel. Thus in vv. 9–11 "Jeremiah" points out that the priests often steal the gold and silver from the idols, sometimes even giving it to prostitutes in the sanctuary.[35] Verse 28 relates how the priests sell the meat from the sacrifices to buy things for themselves, while their wives take the offerings for personal use rather than helping the poor and needy. Furthermore, such offerings might be touched by menstruating women and those who have recently given birth, both ritually unclean by Jewish standards (Leviticus 15:19–30). Verses 31–33 relate how the pagan priests disgrace themselves by acting out full-scale mourning in the temples while stealing clothing from the idols to dress their wives and children, and verses 37–38 add that these larcenous priests do not help the orphans or the needy. So, basically, not only are idols not deities, but pagan cultic personnel are simply disgraceful.

Finally, even the benighted people themselves show the impotence of their idols. Verses 41–42 relate that, when a person is mute, the Chaldeans

---

[34] Moore 1977: 319–323.
[35] This passage is not held up as an example of sacred prostitution, but rather an example of how the sanctuary is being profaned by having prostitutes in it.

summon the god Bel in his temple to cure him. Which, of course, he cannot do, being nonexistent by Jewish standards, but the people are still incapable of recognizing the falsity of their ways.

Every verse in the "Letter of Jeremiah" pertains to one of the above themes, either showing the impotence of idols, the corruption of the priesthood, or the general stupidity of the pagans in their religious beliefs. Except one: verse 43. Verse 43 stands out as the only passage that does not pertain to religion in any way in the entire "Letter of Jeremiah." It is an anomaly. And this is where Herodotos comes into play.

The influence of Herodotos on verse 43 may have entered in in two places. On the one hand, the author of the "Letter" may have known about Herodotos' Babylonian *logos*, and thus his reference to the sacred prostitution of the Babylonian women at the temple of Mylitta. A reference to this supposed practice would then qualify verse 43 as religious in nature, even in the absence of any reference to religion in the verse itself. That is, there is nothing specifically religious in verse 43, in stark contrast to the rest of the "Letter." A preconceived notion of some manner of religious sexual aberration as expressed in Herodotos might have left "Jeremiah" predisposed to including such damning material here, even when leaving out much of the specifically religious material.

On the other hand, it is possible that no reference to Herodotos was intended or even necessarily known by the author of the "Letter." However, in an attempt to get verse 43 to fit in with the rest of the text, modern scholars invoked Herodotos' 1.199 narrative to place religiosity *into* verse 43. That is to say, we looked to Herodotos to make sense of "Jeremiah," much as the drunken man looks for his keys not where he dropped them, but where the light is better. Herodotos is thus inevitably relevant to the study of the "Letter" because someone, either "Jeremiah" or we ourselves, made him relevant.

What is the likelihood that it was "Jeremiah" who invoked Herodotos, either intentionally or simply through a memory of that earlier author's work? It is certainly possible. The usual earliest date offered for the "Letter of Jeremiah" is 317 BCE, that being a rough estimate of the seven generations since the beginning of the Babylonian Captivity mentioned by the author of the "Letter." A *terminus ante quem* is established by a reference to the "Letter" in 2 Maccabees 2:2, dated to c. 100 BCE.[36] In either event, the "Letter" was written after the conquests of Alexander in the Near East, and thus during a period when Hellenism was making

[36] Nickelsburg 1981: 38.

broad inroads into the Levant. Even before the conquests of Alexander there were interactions and contacts between Greece and Palestine, dating well back into the Bronze Age, and as M. Hengel has argued, the Hellenization of the Jews started in the Classical age before the rise of the Hellenistic kingdoms.[37] We should not be surprised, then, to find a Jew of the late fourth century versed in Greek letters, including Herodotos.

As stated above, the majority of the text of the "Letter" has precedents in the Book of Jeremiah, as well as Isaiah and even the Psalms. By contrast, it is the invective against the cultic personnel that is original in "Jeremiah," and it is here that we might most profitably look for "Jeremiah's" sources of information and inspiration. While there are certainly close cognates to the "sins" described from Greek society, there are also explicit parallels from Mesopotamia. As such, although Greek influence is certainly possible, it is hardly necessary. Let us consider some of these cognates and parallels.

According to "Jeremiah," the priests steal gold from the deities and spend it on themselves (vv. 10–11). This might be seen as a somewhat inflammatory reference to using temple properties in secular economic transactions. One text from Hellenistic Babylon, CT 49 160, records how one Bel-ab-usir asked the officials of the Esagil temple to lease him the revenues from sacral properties for the period of one year, in exchange for which he would pay a monthly "rent" to the god's treasury.[38] This could be interpreted by non-disinterested parties as "selling off" the deities' gold. A more precise example of such an accusation comes from Classical Athens. The statue of Athena Promakhos in the Parthenon, as Thucydides tells us (2.13.5), was made with removable gold plates for clothing in case the city should ever have to borrow money from the goddess. Which they did: From the years 433 to 427 BCE the city under Kallias borrowed money from Athena's temple at 6% interest.[39]

According to "Jeremiah," the priests sell the sacrifices made to the gods and spend the money on themselves, while their wives take the meat from the sacrifices and prepare it for themselves (vv. 28). To give but one contemporary example from Babylon, cuneiform document ABC 13b: 9 records that the *kalû* priest of the Esagil temple, along with the *šatammu* high priest/high functionary, received a portion of the sacrifice offered on

---

[37] Hengel 2001: 11.
[38] Boiy 2004: 275.
[39] Meiggs and Lewis 1989: No. 58 (51): Financial decrees moved by Kallias: 434–433 BC.

8 Nisannu by the orders of King Seleukos III himself.[40] Two other texts from the Esagil archives (BM 78948 and 132271) mention that the wives and daughters of the *kalû* priests also receive rations from the sanctuaries.[41] In Greece, specific portions of sacrificial victims were designated as part of the priests' or priestesses' payment, which they could use or sell at their discretion. Typically this was the sacrificial animal's skin, which was sold to benefit the priest(ess) or sanctuary.[42] The priest(ess) could also take part in the sacrificial meal, which would implicate him/her in "preparing the meat."

According to "Jeremiah," women in states of impurity could approach and touch the altars and sacrifices (vv. 29 and 31). This in itself may simply be conservative Jewish horror at the notion of priestesses generally. Both Mesopotamia and Greece had full complements of female cult functionaries (see Chapter 2 for a partial listing of some Mesopotamian priestesses).[43] The extent to which they did or did not advertise their menstrual states is hardly known.

According to "Jeremiah," the priests of foreign gods act out formal, and apparently disgraceful, mourning in the temples. Rites of mourning for Dumuzi/Tammuz/Adonis were prevalent in both the Near East and Greece well into the first millennium BCE. Formalized rites of mourning for Dumuzi are attested as late as the Neo-Assyrian period in Mesopotamia (SAA 3: no. 38, rev. 3–19 and SAA 10: no. 19).[44] Less formal rites, as enacted by women at the entrance to the temple in Jersusalem, were condemned by Ezekiel (8:14) and analyzed by Origen.[45] On such (informal) rites as attested in Greece as early as the writings of Sappho, see above (Lucian). Although the various aspects of the Adonia rituals were never fully admitted into "legitimate" Greek religion, such rites of mourning and celebration are attested in Greece well into the Roman period.[46]

Finally, according to "Jeremiah," the Chaldean priests stole apparel from the gods to clothe their own families (v. 33). Although I know of no such direct cases of fashion-theft in Mesopotamia, one document

---

[40] Boiy 2004: 269.
[41] *Ibid*: 236 and 268.
[42] Burkert 1983: 7 with references.
[43] See also Boiy 2004: 264ff. for Babylonian cultic personnel in the Hellenistic period.
[44] Mettinger 2001: 193–194.
[45] *Ibid*: 129.
[46] Detienne [1977] 1994: 65.

from the Rahim-Esu archive (*Iraq* 43 143: 15) does mention 10 shekels of silver spent for the clothing of the female cult singer ᶠGigitu.[47] In Greece, the dedication of humans' clothing to the statues of goddesses (such as in *Iliad* 6: 271–273, 293–295) may have led to notions of idols and humans sharing clothing.[48]

It is not entirely possible to judge if "Jeremiah" got his data from East or West, if not both. The fact that the author is resurrecting well-known diatribes against idolatry just as the Hellenistic regimes are establishing themselves in Palestine does suggest that it was Western paganism that was on "Jeremiah's" mind, even if he based his rhetoric on earlier, eastern models.

How, then, might we understand verse 43 in this quintessentially Hellenistic, East–West mishmash of a text? A purely Eastern/Babylonian interpretation is certainly possible. Perhaps what we see here a reference to the Babylonian *harimtu*s, those liberated women under neither paternal nor husbandly authority and thus free both to work for themselves and to have sex with whomever they please. Their location "in the streets" (*en tais hodois*) reflects the *harimtu*s and even *qadištu*s "from the streets" in the Mesopotamian corpus, that is, women without established families.[49] In this instance, "Jeremiah" is complaining about the sexual liberty of (some) Chaldean women, which those impotent idols do nothing to suppress. This hypothesis, completely independent from Herodotos and Greeks generally, is certainly tenable.

However, there are a number of similarities between Herodotos 1.199 and "Letter" verse 43 that argue for some connection. In both texts the subject is the women (*gynaikes*) of Babylon. These *gynaikes* sit (*kateatai/ enkathêntai*)[50] surrounded by cords (*skhoinotenees/perithemenai skhoinia*) until they have euphemistic sex (to "mingle" in Herodotos, to "sleep" in "Jeremiah") with a man passing through the cordoned area (*skhoinotenees diexodoi . . . di'ôn oi xenoi diexiontes/ paraproeuomenôn*). The prettier women, as stated in Herodotos and vaunted in "Jeremiah," go through the cords before their less lovely/less worthy neighbors.

What about the differences? Herodotos tells us that every woman must go once in life to perform this meretricious action for Mylitta at her

---

[47] Boiy 2004: 276.
[48] On the dedication of clothing in Greek sanctuaries and its use by idols and mortal cult personnel generally, see Lightfoot 2003: 333–334.
[49] See Chapter 2 for more on these terms and offices.
[50] Herodotean term, and then "Jeremiah's."

sanctuary, and that they only "mingle" with foreign men. Why would "Jeremiah" leave out such details, especially when they would more neatly relate Verse 43 to the topic of religious corruption?

Part of the answer is that such details work against "Jeremiah's" over-arching theme in the "Letter," that is, the impotence of the pagan deities and the corruption of their believers. If a pagan goddess such as Mylitta could demand and receive such a sacrifice from the full female popula-tion of Babylon, then that goddess would hardly be impotent; she would receive her rites. Furthermore, if the sex with passers-by is done under the auspices of a goddess, the action goes from "lewdness," as it is called, to piety, a quality "Jeremiah" does not admit the pagans have.

What about the difference between the foreigners of Herodotos and the passers-by of "Jeremiah"? Here one really has to ask oneself: What meaning does "foreigner" have in Hellenistic Babylon, a city inhabited by no less than Amorites, Arameans, Chaldeans (however one under-stands them), Jews, Persians, and now Greeks, not to mention whatever mercenaries and resident aliens, to use a modern expression, lived and worked in that most cosmopolitan city? The foreigners of Herodotos' rhetoric have little meaning in "Jeremiah's" world.

Finally, why not mention women around the temple of Mylitta/Ištar, if this would contribute to the desecration of pagan religious practice? Possibly because, as established in Chapter 2, there is no evidence from Mesopotamia for droves of sexually active women hanging out around any Mesopotamian temples, in Babylon or elsewhere. For "Jeremiah's" invective to be credible, he cannot make any blatantly, provably inaccurate statements. If there were no sexually active women around the Babylonian temples, he cannot put them there; he can merely make reference to women "in the streets." And if there were a number of disreputable women burning bran in the streets of Babylon, adding such a detail strengthened the argument by adding a touch of credibility.

While it is impossible to prove in either direction, there is a good argument to be made that "Jeremiah" did know of Herodotos 1.199, and that, consciously or subconsciously, he included the historiographer's account in his religious diatribe. Whether this is the case or not, it is obvious that Herodotos influenced modern perceptions of *The Letter of Jeremiah*, for we never would have related verse 43 to sacred prostitution, or prostitution at all, without Herodotos as a conceptual "middleman." To one extent or another, "Jeremiah" is directly dependent on Herodotos in the sacred prostitution debate. What he is not is evidence for actual sacred prostitution.

CHAPTER SIX

PINDAR FRAGMENT 122

Young women visited by many, attendants
of Persuasion in wealthy Corinth,
who burn the fresh, amber drops of frankincense
often fluttering in thought to the mother of loves,
Ouranian Aphrodite.

To you without blame she granted,
O children, on lovely beds
to have plucked the fruit of soft youth.
With necessity all is lovely

. . .

But I wonder what the masters of the Isthmos will say of me
finding such a beginning to a honey-minded *skolion*
a companion to shared women.
We reveal gold by a pure touchstone.

. . .

O Mistress of Cyprus, here to your grove
the hundred-limbed herd of grazing girls
Xenophon brought, delighting in his prayers fulfilled.

πολύξεναι νεάνιδες ἀμφίπολοι
Πειθοῦς ἐν ἀφνειῷ Κορίνθῳ,
αἵ τε τὰς χλωρᾶς λιβάνου ξανθὰ δάκρη
θυμιᾶτε, πολλάκι ματέρ' Ἐρώτων
οὐρανίαν πτάμεναι
νόημα ποττὰν Ἀφροδίταν·

ὑμῖν ἄνευθεν ἐπαγορίας ἔπορεν,
ὦ παῖδες, ἐρατειναῖς ἐν εὐναῖς
μαλθακᾶς ὥρας ἀπὸ καρπὸν δρέπεσθαι.
σὺν δ' ἀνάγκᾳ πᾶν καλόν.

. . .

ἀλλὰ θαυμάζω τί με λεξοῦντι Ἰσθμοῦ
δεσπόται τοιάνδε μελίφρονος ἀρχὰν εὑρόμενον σκολίου,
ξυνάορον ξυναῖς γυναιξί.
ἐδιδέάξαμεν χρυσὸν καθαρᾷ βασσάνῳ.

. . .

ὦ Κύπρου δέσποινα, τεὸν δεῦτ' ἐς ἄλσος
φορβάδων κορᾶν ἀγέλαν ἑκατόγγυιον Ξενοφῶν τελέαις
ἐπήγαγ' εὐχωλαῖς ἰανθείς.

S UCH IS THE ORDER OF THE LINES OF POETRY IN PINDAR'S *SKOLION*,
although Athenaios places the last verse first in his *Deipnosophistai*.
The third century CE Alexandrian author introduces this fragment with
the following explanation:

> Even private citizens vow to the goddess that, if those things for which
> they make petition are fulfilled, they will even bring courtesans to
> Aphrodite. Such, then, being the custom concerning the goddess,
> Xenophon of Corinth, when he went to Olympia to take part in the
> games, vowed that he would bring courtesans to the goddess if he won.
> And so Pindar first wrote the *enkomion* for him, of which the beginning
> is "Praising the thrice-victorious-house at Olympia," and later he sang
> the *skolion* at the sacrifice, the beginning of which was dedicated to the
> prostitutes who joined in when Xenophon was present and sacrificing
> to Aphrodite.

> καὶ οἱ ἰδιῶται δὲ κατεύχονται τῇ θεῷ τελεσθέντων περὶ ὧν ἂν
> ποιῶνται τὴν δέησιν ἀπάξειν αὐτῇ καὶ τὰς ἑταίρας. ὑπάρχοντος
> οὖν τοῦ τοιούτου νομίμου περὶ τὴν θεὸν Ξενοφῶν ὁ Κορίνθιος ἐξιὼν
> εἰς Ὀλυμπίαν ἐπὶ τὸν ἀγῶνα καὶ αὐτὸς ἐπάξειν[1] ἑταίρας εὔξατο
> τῇ θεῷ νικήσας. Πίνδαρός τε τὸ μὲν πρῶτον ἔγραψεν εἰς αὐτὸν
> ἐγκώμιον οὗ ἡ ἀρχὴ "τρισολυμπιονίκαν ἐπαινέων οἶκον," ὕστερον
> δὲ καὶ σκόλιον τὸ παρὰ τὴν θυσίαν ᾆσθέν, ἐν ᾧ τὴν ἀρχὴν εὐθέως
> πεποίηται πρὸς τὰς ἑταίρας αἳ παραγενομένου τοῦ Ξενοφῶντος καὶ
> θύοντος τῇ Ἀφροδίτῃ συνέθυσαν.

Based on this fragment, its introduction by Athenaios, and apparently
corroborating evidence by Strabo (8.6.20; see Chapter 7), it has been
accepted for some 2,000 years that there was a professional class of sacred
prostitutes dedicated to Aphrodite who plied their trade in the city of
Corinth. There is some debate as to the "sacredness" of their status. J. B.

---

[1] On the use of *apagô* or *epagô* in this context, see below, p. X.

Salmon interpreted their functions in a primarily secular light, claiming that: "The anonymous women who served Aphrodite probably usually performed the hectic task of satisfying the desires of numerous ordinary Corinthians and others."[2] Following Strabo's attestation that the women dedicated to Aphrodite were *hierodoulai-hetairai*, "sacred slaves" as well as courtesans, others have suggested that the prostitutes in question may have served some religious functions as well as sexual. Thus, L. Kurke has suggested that "According to the most plausible reconstruction, Xenophon made a thanks-offering to Aphrodite, assisted by the hierodules, then adjourned with his guests to a banquet, attended by the hierodules – now turned *hetairai* – as a normal part of the entertainment. . . . It is probably safe to say that we can reconstruct more of the details of this particular performance than we can of almost any other Pindaric song context."[3]

To date, the commentary on this fragment has fallen into two distinct categories. On the one hand are those scholars, such as van Groningen, Salmon, and Kurke, who accept that Pindar was referring to sacred prostitution in this text. Thus, much of the analysis done on this text is predicated upon the reality of the institution. On the other hand are those scholars, such as H. Conzelmann, H. D. Saffrey, C. Calame, V. Pirenne-Delforge, and M. Beard and J. Henderson, who argue that sacred prostitution did not exist, and that frag. 122 is not evidence for the institution. In contrast to the former category, however, these latter authors have not, I believe, offered satisfactory alternate interpretations of the poem. For Conzelmann and Saffrey, for example, the notion of Corinthian sacred prostitution is merely a myth, an abusive miscommunication by Strabo or his source.[4] This notion, however, is predicated on the idea that sacred prostitution did exist in the east, and that it was simply inappropriately applied to Corinth. As sacred prostitution did not exist in the Near East either, this hypothesis cannot work. For Calame and Beard and Henderson, the concept of Corinthian sacred prostitution is a misunderstanding, accidentally conflating the wives of Corinth with the city's famous courtesans.[5] For Calame, this hypothesis is at least partially based on the suggestion that Greek women did not take part in sacrifices, and thus the only women present at Xenophon's supposed ritual must have been the city prostitutes. As J. B. Connelly has recently

---

[2] Salmon 1997 [1984]: 400.
[3] Kurke 1996: 50.
[4] Conzelmann 1967: *passim*; Saffrey 1985: 374.
[5] Calame 1989: 110–111; Beard and Henderson 1998: 73.

and thoroughly argued, though, Greek women most certainly did take part in sacrificial ritual, undercutting Calame's argument.[6]

There is nothing in Pindar's poem that refers to sacred prostitution. Rather than evidence for sacred prostitution in Corinth, Pindar's frag. 122 is indicative of the misunderstandings and circular reasoning that have typified this long-standing misconception. In order to understand how this poem came to be misinterpreted as evidence for sacred prostitution, let us first consider the text unfettered from its later commentary. Once able to appreciate the text on its own merits, we might examine the later accretions.

CONTEXT

The poem refers to a man named Xenophon and the city of Corinth. This would most logically be the Olympian victor of 464 BCE to whom *Olympian* 13 is also addressed. As Pindar himself tells us, frag. 122 is a *skolion*, the one extant use of that word in the Pindaric corpus.[7] The meaning of this word changed between the days of Pindar and those of his later scholiasts, such that this fragment and other apparent Pindaric *skolia* were redefined as *enkomia*, as frag. 122 is often dubbed in the modern scholarship (e.g., Lefkowitz 1991: 93; Race 1997: 351–353). Originally, however, the term *skolion* applied to three different types of drinking songs that were performed during the *symposion* – a paean sung by the *symposion* guests, simple stanzas sung individually, and finally songs sung to self-accompaniment on the lyre (the most difficult of the three).[8] Although during the period immediately preceding and including Pindar, the last of these literally lyric compositions could be original compositions (as frag. 122 is an original work), the trend later came to involve singing the works of the "Great Masters" such as Simonides, Alkaios, Sappho, and, of course, Pindar. Eventually, even this trend was displaced, as the nonlyric stanzas of Athenian drama came to replace the lyric verses, and self-accompaniment on the lyre was replaced with nonsung recitation.[9]

The fact that frag. 122 is a (self-declared) *skolion* of the mid-fifth century indicates that it was recited or sung at a *symposion*, a structured drinking

---

[6] Connelly 2007: 179–190.
[7] Slater 1969: 466.
[8] Harvey 1955: 162; Nagy 1990: 107
[9] Harvey 1955: 162–163; Nagy 1990: 107.

party attended by upper-class male citizens (the *hetaireia, andres, philoi,*[10] or *esloi*[11]) who were entertained by each others' conversation and singing. The only females who attended the *symposia* were various categories of prostitutes, be they flute-players, dancing girls, or "companions" – *hetairai*. E. Pellizer's succinct description of the Greek *symposion* adumbrates well the occasion of Pindar's frag. 122:

> The association of friends in the *symposion* . . . establishes a series of ritual acts regulated by a very precise set of norms, which range from libation to purification and to prayers directed to various specific deities, and from the consumption (regulated by appropriate restrictions) of wine and other foods to the performing of or the listening to songs or instrumental music, to watching dances and mimes, and finally to contests between the actual participants in the gathering. . . . The sympotic gathering in addition has the aim of being a specific celebration of certain occasions (for example victories in theatrical or sporting competitions), and therefore it has a precise social function as an organization of its time, intended to highlight, by means of collective consensus, exceptional moments in the life of the group which is meeting together, or of one of the members of it. Finally, it is undeniable that the *symposion* is a social activity of a ludic nature, which also has the aim of providing gratification for the participants.[12]

The performing of songs is evident in the *skolion* itself, whereas the sympotic nature of the genre intimates the consumption of wine. That frag. 122 was recited in the context of a celebration is evident in the name of the *skolion*'s eventual addressee: Xenophon of Corinth. This places the *symposion* in question in the context of an athletic victory celebration. "Gratification for the participants" might be inferred from the presence of the "young women visited by many," the ultimate subject of this chapter.

However, although frag. 122 might be defined as a drinking song, we cannot automatically assume a clearcut set of themes, words, associations, or attitudes inherent in the piece. As stated above, frag. 122 is the only extant work of Pindar self-identified as, or even using the word, *skolion*. Other Pindar fragments identified by van Groningen as *skolia* are so classified based on their apparently lighthearted nature; "Les scolies de Pindare se distinguent, si nous pouvons nous fier à ce qui en subsiste, par l'absence de toute gravité. Ils sont destinés à des fêtes joyeuses et le ton

---

[10] Schmitt-Pantel 1990: 15 and 23.
[11] Hubbard 1985: 157.
[12] Pellizer 1990: 177–178.

est léger et enjoué."[13] The problem with this methodology is twofold –
it assumes lightheartedness on the part of a *skolion* and seriousness for
anything else.

That a *skolion* could be serious, even one of the sources for the art
of historiography as developed by Herodotos and Thucydides, is evident
as early as the quintessential symposiastic poet himself, Anakreon, who
complained (frag. 116),

> I do not like him who, drinking wine by the full *krater*,
> speaks of strife and tearful war,
> but whoever calls to mind lovely cheer, mingling
> the Muses and the shining gifts of Aphrodite . . .

Likewise, as late as Pseudo-Aristotle's *Athenian Constitution*, the author
cites a *skolion* as evidence about the failed coup culminating at Leipsydrion
(*Ath. Pol.* § 19).[14] Sympotic *skolia* in the day of Pindar, then, need not
have been exclusively lighthearted and/or sensual.

Furthermore, certain themes or words deemed "skoliastic" by van
Groningen are paralleled in odes known to be *epinikia*. To give an example
we might compare frag. 123 (identified by van Groningen as a *skolion*),
dedicated to Theoxenos of Tenedos, with the first eight lines of *Isthmian*
2, technically dedicated to Xenocrates of Akragas although addressing
Thrasyboulos of Akragas:

> *Frag. 123*
> One should cull love, my heart,
> As appropriate during youth,
> But whoever has seen those rays
> Flashing from Theoxenos' eyes
> And is not flooded with desire
> Has a black heart forged of adamant of steel
>
> With a cold flame, and is dishonoured
> By bright-eyed Aphrodite,
> Or toils compulsively for money,
> Or with womanly courage,
> Is carried in service to an utterly cold path.
> But I, because of her, melt like the wax
> Of holy bees by the sun's heat, whenever I look
> Upon the new-limbed youth of boys.

[13] Van Groningen 1960: 15.
[14] Rösler 1990: 231.

So, after all, in Tenedos
Persuasion and Grace dwell
In the son of Hagesilas. [15]

Isthmian 2, ll. 1–8
Thrasyboulos, the men of days gone by who rode the
chariot of the gold-headbanded Muses took the
   resonant lyre and deftly
sent the arrows of mellifluous poetry at boys
or any handsome one whose summery mien
pressed its suit on Aphrodite Lovely-throne.

The Muse then neither cared for gain nor worked for hire,
and honey-toned Terpsikhore did not
   vend soft and sweetly subtle
songs or set them up as silver-plated. [16]

Both texts refer to Aphrodite and thus to notions of sexual pleasure
and desire. This sexual desire is in both instances directed generally to
youths, frag. 123 beginning with the necessity of "culling" love, *Isthmian
2* referring to the men of old who were inspired to poetry by "boys,"
the "handsome" and "lovely-throned Aphrodite." More specifically, the
desirable youths are narrowed down to Theoxenos in frag. 123 and presumably Thrasyboulos in *Isthmian 2*, a possibility strengthened by Pindar's
frag. 124ab, another so-called *skolion* dedicated to this same Thrasyboulos.
Both texts begin with a statement of desire that is immediately followed
by a negative reference to money. Pindar compares the greedy to one who
does not properly acknowledge Aphrodite's calling in frag. 123, whereas
he appears to contrast "poetry-for-hire" with love-inspired poetry in
Isthmian 2.

If only the first ten lines of *Isthmian 2* survived, the fragment could
have been classified not as an *epinikion*, but as a *skolion* per comparison
with frag. 123. That the distinctions between genres need not be hard
and fast might be attributed to the fact that at this period poetry was not
so much defined by its genre as by its occasion. [17] The *skolion* is a *skolion*
because it is (originally) sung at a *symposion*, regardless of the theme or
nature of the piece. An *epinikion* is an *epinikion* because it is (originally)
sung in honor of a victor at a celebration. Thus, a *skolion* might be serious,
and lightheartedness might typify alternate genres in Pindar. What this

---

[15] Race 1997: 355.
[16] Swanson 1974: 185.
[17] Nagy 1990: 362.

boils down to is the idea that we cannot automatically assume a playful, nonserious intent in frag. 122, nor is such a tone necessarily precluded.

An additional issue of concern in frag. 122 is the presence of prostitutes. Because, once again, the self-declared identity of the poem as a *skolion* indicates, during the mid-fifth century, that the context of the original performance was the *symposion*, and because the only women traditionally in attendance at such events (or, if you are Sokrates, pointedly excluded) were prostitutes, the use of the word *skolion* suggests that the women addressed in the text are prostitutes of some kind.

However, Pindar never directly refers to prostitution in this work; words such as *hetaira* or *porneuein* do not appear. Instead, Pindar addresses the objects of his *skolion* as *neanides* (young women), *amphipoloi* (attendants), *paides* (children), *gynaixin* (women), and *korân* (girls). That prostitutes are implied must be inferred from the context of the poem. Likewise, the fact that Pindar will openly discuss that these women have their "fruit" "plucked" implies the prostitutes who entertain at the *symposia*. Pindar seems to emphasize their "public" roles in the first line of the poem, both calling them "much visited" (*polyxenai*) and using a term which has nuances of "much welcoming" (*amphipoloi*) within the poem's first three words. This would seem to hint at prostitution. Finally, and perhaps most importantly, Pindar refers to these women as "shared" – *xynais*. Pindar thus uses extreme euphemism in this text, a notable issue considering the fact that prostitutes would not necessarily be an inappropriate topic in the context of a *symposion*.

The context of the original recitation of frag. 122, then, is a drinking party in Corinth, apparently celebrating in some way the double Olympic victory of Xenophon of Corinth in 464, attended by (some of) Corinth's male aristocratic élite, possibly other *xenoi* including Pindar himself, and about 25 prostitutes, assuming four limbs per girl.

TEXT

Fragment 122 as we have it preserved exhibits ring composition.[18] Of a postulated five stanzas, the first, second, and fifth are concerned primarily with the "young women." The lost fourth stanza probably was as well (see below). In the third stanza Pindar talks about himself (assuming, as is customary here, that he is truly speaking in the first person), specifically musing on the relationship between himself and his audience. The

---

[18] Race 1986: 30.

structure of the *skolion*, then, is that of four stanzas — 1, 2, 4, and 5 — about prostitutes framing a central stanza about the *hetaireia*, including the poet.

The dominant themes of the poem can be somewhat divided into those pertaining to the prostitutes and those pertaining to the men, although Pindar, with his typical flair, deftly interweaves these. The points of significance concerning the prostitutes are notions of sacrifice, sex, and orientalism. For the men of the *skolion*, Pindar focuses on divinity, *xenia*, and humor.

WELCOME

The first word of the poem sets the stage for all the themes that follow — *polyxenai*, an adjective loaded with multivalent meanings.[19] This word is typically translated as "visited by many" in this fragment, giving a passive sense when associated with women, thus emphasizing their roles as sexual commodities. When applied to men in other contexts, the word takes on an active sense, rendering "much welcoming." Here the word calls to mind the idea of great *xenia*, an attribute of Pindar's host Xenophon exemplified through his *symposion* and especially through his acquisition of the prostitutes to entertain there.

This feminine adjective also reflects the last word in our first line — *amphipoloi*, "attendants." Both words encircle the object of the stanza's address, the young women (*neanides*). Although as a substantive adjective *amphipolos* has the meaning of "attendant" or "handmaid" (*Olympian* 6.32; *Paian* 6.117), as a simple adjective it might also mean "much visited" as in *Olympian* 1.93. There is thus a certain redundancy in the opening line, with the young women in question being dubbed "much visited" and "much welcoming." This redundancy places extra emphasis on both their role as prostitutes and the idea of *xenia* in the text.

Furthermore, I believe that Pindar may have had a slight play on words in mind here, contrasting the word *polyxenai* with the name of their host Xenophon. Thus, as appropriate for ring composition, the *polyxenai* opening the *skolion* are reflected at the end by Xenophon, rejoicing in his prayers fulfilled.

Finally, the adjective *polyxenai* brings to mind Polyxena, the Trojan princess sacrificed to Akhilleus at the close of the Trojan War.[20] In this

---

[19] Kurke 1996: 59–60.
[20] *Ibid*: 60.

one allusion the themes of sacrifice, sex, and orientalism are introduced at the very start of the poem. Here Pindar presents a notion not only of sacrifice, but specifically of the sacrifice of a young, desirable girl so as to be a bride, or, perhaps better stated, a sexual partner for an illustrious hero. In this, Xenophon's "much visited" prostitutes reflect the sacrificial victim, just as the companions at the *symposion*, the "lords of the Isthmos," play the part of Akhilleus, the illustrious, semidivine hero soon to receive sexual access to the victim. The sacrificial nature of the word leads automatically into the domain of the sexual, the second theme of the *skolion*.

One must remember also that Polyxena was a *Trojan* princess, and thus emerges the third theme running through fragment 122 – orientalism. Beyond the ethnic identity of our eponymous heroine, the term *polyxenos* itself refers to foreignness, a foreignness that is welcomed through the establishment of the *xenia* relationship. An ideal location for the expression of such bonds is, of course, the *symposion*, characterized by commensality and much (*poly-*) *xenia* expressed between host and guests (*xenoi*). The orientalism, then, pulls us once again back to notions of *xenia*.

SACRIFICE

This opening word thus sets the stage for the dominant concepts running through Pindar's text. The most important of these is the notion of sacrifice, already present in allusion to the sacrificial Polyxena.[21] Two different aspects of sacrifice emerge between the first and last stanzas of the poem. The first strophe reflects a bloodless sacrifice, the burning of incense – "who burn the fresh, amber drops of frankincense." Such a sacrifice is eminently appropriate in this context for two reasons. The first is that the deity invoked in the song is Aphrodite, and, as W. Burkert notes, sacrifices of incense were especially associated with her and Adonis:

> Incense offerings and altars are associated particularly with the cult of Aphrodite and of Adonis; appropriately, the first mention of frankincense is found in that poem by Sappho which conjures up the epiphany of the goddess Aphrodite in her grove[22] of apple trees and roses between quivering branches and incense-burning altars. The use of frankincense

[21] There is no automatic relationship between the *symposion* and sacrificial ritual, even though the singing of hymns was a traditional part of the festivities. See Schmitt-Pantel 1990: 17.

[22] *Also*, just as in the last stanza of the *skolion* under consideration.

is later customary everywhere; to strew a granule of frankincense in the flames is the most widespread, simplest, and also cheapest act of offering.[23]

The offering of bloodless, vegetal sacrifices was especially typical of Aphrodite's most ancient temple in Paphos, where Aphrodite was the "Mistress of Cyprus," as Pindar calls her in the poem's final stanza.

Second, mention of frankincense conjures up images of the exotic east, thus calling to mind the tendency towards Orientalism prevalent throughout the text. Like *polyxenai*, then, one choice word pulls together multiple themes.

Although the prostitutes are burning these amber drops, it is not the frankincense that Pindar claims rises heavenwards to the heavenly mother of loves, but the prostitutes themselves. This is evident in the following line of the poem, where Pindar says that the prostitutes "flutter (present active participle, feminine plural nominative) in thought to Aphrodite." It is the prostitutes, not the smoke, who waft upwards, thus conflating the sacrificial incense with the sacrificing prostitutes. The same idea appears in line three. Here, two separate accusatives compliment the verb *thumiate* (the standard verb for the burning of incense specifically[24]) – *tas khlôras*, a feminine accusative plural; and *xantha dakrê*, neuter accusative plurals. *Libanou* in the genitive appears between the two. The most logical reading (assuming logic applies to the reading of Pindaric poetry) is that the prostitutes "burn the amber drops of frankincense." The contrasting gender of *tas khlôras* makes it extremely difficult to determine how these words fit into the translation, and most translators simply throw them in with the *libanou* or the *dakrê* – thus "*fresh, amber tears of (fresh) incense.*"[25] However, if we take *tas khlôras* as a substantive agreeing with the only other feminine plural in the stanza, the "fresh, young" things sacrificed would be the prostitutes themselves, who, we remember, "flutter" heavenward to Aphrodite. I would argue, then, that Pindar's purpose in this stanza is to conflate the idea of sacrifice and sacrificer, introducing the notion that the prostitutes will end up being the sacrificial victims.

[23] Burkert 1985: 62.
[24] *Ibid*; Detienne [1977] 1997: 38.
[25] Van Groningen found this line particularly frustrating, both grammatically and conceptually. " . . . on s'étonne de voir Pindare ajouter à ces deux substantifs des épithètes désignant l'une et l'autre la couleur et, par consequent, synonymes . . ., ce qui n'est point son habitude: il est toujours à la recherché de la veriété" (Van Groningen 1960: 25).

This is played out most forcefully in the final stanza of the *skolion*. Here the sacrificial imagery goes from one of incense to one of animals, with the prostitutes being emphatically "bestialized" in the final lines.

Let us begin with the line where Pindar claims that "Xenophon [brought] the hundred-limbed (*hekatogguion*) herd (*agelan*) of grazing (*phorbadôn*) girls." The hundred-limbed quality calls to mind that most impressive of ancient Greek sacrifices, the hecatomb. Thus, the postulated earlier thanksgiving sacrifice made by Xenophon (as related by Athenaios) is here reflected in vocabulary that implies perhaps an even greater "sacrifice," this time of female flesh.

The word *agelan* appears six times in the extant works of Pindar. In all but two cases, the word is modified by the name of an animal (or the word "wild animal" *thêron*) in the genitive plural. Thus we have herds of cows and bulls in *Pythian* 4, a herd of wild animals in *Dithyramb* 2, and a herd of lions in frag. 239.[26] Quite to the contrary, in frag. 112, Pindar refers to a herd of maidens (*parthenôn*), similar to our herd of girls (*korân*) in frag. 122. The maidens in frag. 112 are specifically referred to as Spartan – *Lakaina*, and use of the word here calls to mind the Spartan educational system, where boys at least were divided up into age-groups called *agela* for public education. Mention of a *parthenôn agela* in this instance may thus function at least partially as an ethnic indicator.

However, one should also keep in mind that it was not uncommon throughout Greece to refer to the wild, untamed nature of young girls who were specifically tamed – *damazô* "of animals, to tame, break in, to bring under the yoke; ... of maidens, to make subject to a husband"[27] – by marriage and/or sexual domination. Such an ideology is most explicitly exemplified by Anakreon in his "ode" to a Thracian filly:

> My Thracian filly, why do you glare with disdain
> and then shun me absolutely as if I knew
>   nothing of this art.
> I tell you I could bridle you with tight straps,
> seize the reins and gallop you around the posts
>   of the pleasant course.
> But you prefer to graze on the calm meadow,
> or frisk and gambol gaily – having no manly
>   rider to break you in.[28]

[26] Slater 1969: 4.
[27] LSJ.
[28] Barnstone 1988: 123.

To call the girls a herd, then, not only "bestializes" them, it calls to mind their youth, their related wildness, and their apparent need to be tamed/sexually dominated by men.

The herd is described as "grazing" (*phorbadôn*). This word is particularly interesting for its simultaneous active and middle voice connotations and its implications for the distinction between human and animal. On the one hand, the adjective *phorbas* might refer to one who gives food or pasturage to another, a transitive sense. On the other hand, it may refer to an animal that grazes with the herd, intransitive. Pindar has already made it clear that he is discussing a "herd" in this text, and thus the intransitive sense is immanently logical. In this instance, considering the sympotic context of the poem, the term "grazing" appears to be a euphemism for sexual activity, possibly an oblique reference to fellatio.

However, if the overarching theme is one of sacrifice, with the girls being the victims of that sacrifice, then there may also be a subtly implied transitive meaning for *phorbadôn*. Just as at the sacrifice the sacrificial victim later serves as a meal for the participants, so might we consider the future "consumption" of the hundred-limbed herd that "feeds" the *hetaireia*.

This hundred-limbed herd is brought to an *alsos*, specifically the *alsos* of the Mistress of Cyprus. The most basic meaning for *alsos* is "grove," later coming to have connotations of a specifically sacred grove, and then eventually referring to an outdoor sanctuary. Slater, in his *Lexicon to Pindar*, defines it as "*precinct, sanctuary, domain.*"[29] Pindar himself uses this word some sixteen times in his extant corpus, usually referring to the sanctuary of a named deity (Zeus, Demeter) and often accompanied by an adjective relating to sanctity (*theôn, hagnon, polyhymnetôi*). In at least one instance – *Pythian* 5, 89 – the wooded sense is made evident, as "Aristoteles also planted greater groves of the deities."

Like the word *polyxenai*, then, the word *alsos* has multiple meanings and connotations, all exploited simultaneously by Pindar. At its most basic level, the notion of a grove contributes to the bestialization of the prostitutes, as they are brought to a "grove" to "graze." The fact that a grove so-called might also be interpreted as a sanctuary contributes to the sacrificial imagery running throughout the text – Xenophon brings the pseudo-hecatomb to the "sanctuary" of Aphrodite. Such has been the standard understanding of this text in the past. However, once again, we know without a doubt that the poem in question is a *skolion*, and we know that

[29] Slater 1969: 35.

a *skolion* in Pindar's day was not sung at a sanctuary but in the context of the *symposion*. If Pindar refers to the "here" where he is singing his *skolion*, it cannot, categorically, be a sanctuary or a grove, and thus the understanding is that the poem was sung at the feast *after* the ritual (or, perhaps better, the drinking party after the feast after the sacrifice).[30] The *alsos*, not a sanctuary or grove, is most likely a euphemism for the *andrôn*, the men's room in which the *symposion* took place, a locus of drinking and sexual revelry, thus easily taken as a euphemism for a "grove/sanctuary of Aphrodite." Thus the word *alsos* serves two related functions: It contributes to the bestialization of the prostitutes while contributing to the overall sacral imagery within the poem.

All this effort to render the girls as animals rounds out the sacrificial imagery presented at the beginning and end of the text. In the poem's first stanza a bloodless sacrifice of incense takes place, although, as discussed above, in the end it is the girls themselves who theoretically waft heavenward. In the last stanza, the imagery is of an animal sacrifice in a grove-sanctuary, where the victims are a herd of girls filling out a full hecatomb with their 100 limbs. The main difference between the two stanzas, other than the type of sacrifice, is the prostitutes' active versus passive participation in the rites. In the opening stanza it is the prostitutes themselves who perform the (self-) sacrifice. In our final lines the girls are presented as mainly passive, "grazing" as Xenophon leads them to the *alsos*.

Who, then, is the recipient of the sacrifice? On one level it is, of course, Aphrodite, to whom the *skolion* serves as a hymn and a dedication.[31] However, as Kurke has written, the text creates strong parallels between the goddess and the *hetaireia* participating at the *symposion*.[32] This is most evident in the parallel use of titles applied to Aphrodite and the men. Aphrodite, in the final stanza of the poem, is addressed as the "Mistress of Cyprus," "*Kyprou Despoina*." In the midst of the third stanza Pindar refers to the *symposion* participants as "Masters of the Isthmos," "*Isthmou despotai*." Just as the goddess is the Mistress, so are the participants the masters, the like titles placing them, for the context of the poem, on a common footing. Furthermore, as Kurke noted, the word for rejoicing applied to Xenophon at the end of the poem (*iantheis*), is a word Pindar usually uses for deities (e.g., *Olympian* 2, 13; *Olympian* 7, 43). Xenophon

[30] Kurke 1996: 50.
[31] Schmitz 1970: 71, n. 50.
[32] Kurke 1996: 57.

then takes on some measure of divine identity within the text. The men at the *symposion*, likened to deities, receive the sacrifice of the shared women's bodies and sexuality.

SEX

The second dominant theme running through Pindar's poem is sex. We have already considered the sexual implications of the first word of the poem – *polyxenai* – which on at least one level serves as reference to Polyxena, who was offered up as a sexual sacrifice to Akhilleus. Notions of sex and desire continue in the first stanza primarily through references to Aphrodite, goddess of sexual pleasure and recipient of the skoliastic hymn in question. She is mentioned by name at the end of the last line of the stanza. In the previous line, Pindar describes the goddess with the epithet "Mother of Loves" or "Desires," emphasizing Aphrodite's erotic connotations (as opposed to, say, geographic connotations, as in *Olympian* 7, where Aphrodite is presented as the mother of Rhodes). This epithet "Mother of Loves" may be seen to compensate for the nonerotic character of the other two epithets Pindar uses of Aphrodite in this text – "Ourania" and "Mistress of Cyprus." More on these below.

The erotic imagery becomes stronger in what remains of the second stanza. Working still with subtlety and euphemism, Pindar claims that the prostitutes – here "children" – were granted the boon by Aphrodite to have youth "plucked" or "culled" on "lovely beds." The word I translate here as "lovely" is *erateinais*, containing within it the morpheme *era(t)-* pertaining to matters of love and desire in the Greek vocabulary (*eramai* – to be in love with; *erasmios* – lovely, desired; *erastês* – lover; *eratos* – lovely, charming; *eraô* – to love; *eromenos* – beloved). However, *erateinos* might also mean "welcome" in the Homeric vocabulary, and thus the "lovely" beds might also be "welcome" or "welcoming" beds, hinting back to the original epithet of the prostitutes themselves – "welcoming many." Concepts of eroticism and *xenia* are thus mixed in this one word.

What the children are doing on these lovely beds is also couched in a Pindaric euphemism. The word is *apo* – *drepesthai*, separated by the object of the infinitive *karpon*, "fruit," and translated as either "plucked" or "culled." The expression is used one other time in the extant Pindaric corpus in *Pythian* 9, when Pindar claims that a host of suitors were caused to "want to pluck the flowering fruit of Hebê golden-crowned" in their desire for the daughter of Antaeus. Pindar uses a similar expression when referring to his beloved Theoxenos in frag. 123 (see above). Here the poet claims that "One ought to pluck (*drepesthai*) loves, Heart, as appropriate in youth." To "pluck" youth/Hebe or love or fruit "in youth," then, is to desire or actually to have sex.

The one word in this stanza that has caused considerable debate is the third word in the first line, being taken either as (*aneu*) *epagorias* "without blame"[33] or *apagorias*, "without possibility of refusal."[34] To use the latter word makes blatant the status of the prostitutes in question – they have no control over the use of their bodies or sexuality. Furthermore, such a notion seems to be supported by the expression, probably a *gnomê*,[35] further along in the strophe – "With necessity all is lovely." The usual understanding is that Pindar is referring to the prostitutes' lack of volition in their sex lives, and why this, for them, should not be seen as a cause for shame.[36] However, a similar and enlightening reference to the relationship between "necessity" (*ananka*) and sex appears at the beginning of *Nemean* 8. Here Pindar claims that (1–4)

> Queen of youth, crier of Aphrodite's
> never-dying loves, when you
> inform the glance of maidens or youths,
> you stroke the boys with hands of sweet
> raw need (*anankas*), but not the girls.[37]

Sexual need or erotic necessity affects boys but not girls (*parthenoi*). This brings up the possibility that Pindar's gnomic statement pertains not to the prostitutes, but to the men at the *symposion*. It is they who need not feel shame at the sexual indulgences in which they are about to partake, as they are in the literal grip of sexual necessity. Although the lacuna following this statement makes it impossible to know this for certain, the fact that the *anankai* might involve the men rather than the women weakens the argument that the *gnomê* supports the *apagorias* reading.

Furthermore, if Pindar were to describe the prostitutes as having "no possibility of refusal," it would run contrary to the overarching ethos of the poem. Pindar pointedly avoids any direct references to prostitution within this text. Once again, words such as *hetaira*, *porneuô*, and even *ergastis* do not appear. Nor is there a direct reference to sex, merely the

---

[33] Van Groningen 1960: 33.
[34] Kurke 1996: 54–55.
[35] In the absence of any verb it is impossible to determine if this would be understood as a gnomic aorist.
[36] Norwood 1945: 20.
[37] Swanson 1974: 161, adapted.

"plucking" of "fruit." It would be jarring for Pindar suddenly to make such a blatant reference to the status of the prostitutes at this point.

Likewise, to say that the prostitutes have "no possibility of refusal" runs contrary to the sacrificial imagery in the text. The prostitutes are the sacrifice. Aphrodite and, more pointedly, the "Masters of the Isthmos" are the recipients. As was standard in the sacrifice of large animals in ancient Greece, an indication of willingness was required from the victim. Thus water was poured onto the heads of bulls so that they would nod and assent to being sacrificed for the deity.[38] To say that the prostitutes had no ability to refuse not only emphasizes their occupation in a way that Pindar has expressly avoided up to this point, but sullies the sacrificial imagery by suggesting that an improper sacrifice is being made – the victims have not and could not offer their assent.

By contrast, to say that they might have their "fruit" "plucked" without blame brings one back to the ethos of the *symposion* generally. To quote O. Murray, "The symposion became in many respects a place apart from the normal rules of society, with its own strict code of honour in the *pistis* there created, and its own willingness to establish conventions fundamentally opposed to those within the *polis* as a whole."[39]

A separate set of behavioral codes applies in the *symposion*, and this includes the sexual acts of the participants. Just as the *symposion* guests might drink to excess or take part in an excessive, unregulated sexuality, so too might the prostitutes engage in acts of delight on soft, lovely beds without blame or reproach.

The closest Pindar ever comes to expressing the true status and occupation of the women attending this *symposion* is the word *xynais* – "shared" – in the third stanza. It here becomes clear that prostitution must be at issue, for no other women in archaic or classical Greece could be so described. Once again, it seems almost odd that Pindar would stray from his use of euphemism in the description of the sympotic activities, using such a strong word.

However, in the context of the *symposion* specifically, the term takes on connotations significant in establishing the community of the *hetaireia*. For *xynos* means something which is held in common by a community. This could be the full community of the Greeks, as in *Olympian* 3, 18 or *Pythian* 9, 94; or the community of an individual family, as the lineage of Herakles in *Olympian* 7, 21; or even the community of drinkers at

---

[38] Burkert 1985: 56.
[39] Murray 1990: 7.

the *symposion*, as in frag. 124ab, 2. The idea of goods held in common is especially important in this last context, for notions of equality and commensality are dominant themes in the *symposion*. Here, according to the iconography, each participant received identical portions of food, drink, and even furniture, thus being, in the words of P. Schmitt-Pantel, "a way of underlining their *homoiotes*, their equality and identity...a sign and reminder of the equality of distribution and sharing prevalent at the banquet."[40] The "shared women" also take part in this ritual commensality. By being "shared" within the context of the *symposion*, they distinguish the privileged participants as those who have access to the hundred-limbed herd, while simultaneously emphasizing their equality and camaraderie by expressing what this group holds in common. The *hetaireia* shares its privileges.

This stanza marks the first point in the extant poem in which the prostitutes are being objectified. In the first stanza the women are active, burning sacrifices to heavenly Aphrodite. Likewise in the second stanza they are addressed with a vocative "O" clause, a common motif in sympotic poetry, although usually addressed to men.[41] We see a transition in this third stanza. Pindar begins to refer to himself here, and the prostitutes are set firmly into the third person. They cease being sentient beings worthy of address and begin their metamorphosis into animals, commodities shared among the *hetaireia*. The specific commodity was, of course, the prostitutes' sexuality.

In the last strophe of the fragment sexuality is once again manifest in an address to Aphrodite – here the Mistress of Cyprus – and in the reference to "grazing" discussed above. The theme of sex is strongest in the poem's second stanza, where Pindar is pointedly addressing the girls and describing exactly what their function at the *symposion* is. If ring composition does mark the poem as a whole, then we might have expected the missing penultimate stanza to refer to sexuality as well, probably showing the *hetaireia* as the active participants in an act where the prostitutes themselves have now become passive objects. But this must remain in the realms of speculation.

One final note of particular interest is what is missing from the poem's sacral–sexual imagery. To wit, there are no references to flowing or stabbing in the extant lines of poetry.[42]

---

[40] Schmitt-Pantel 1990: 18.
[41] Pellizer 1990: 179.
[42] Assuming that these were not the topics of the missing strophe.

Notions of flowing wine and flowing blood would be expected in a poem combining images of animal sacrifice with a sympotic occasion, an occasion emphasized by reference to the poem as a *skolion* within the text. Likewise, multiple forms of penetration would be expected, both the stabbing of the sacrificial animals and the parallel imagery of phallic penetration of the prostitutes. But there is no flowing wine, no stabbing or penetrating of victims, no consequent flowing liquids, be they alcoholic, sanguine, or sexual. This suggests that the "sacrifice," at all levels, is only in preliminary stages, and that the action, which is immanent, has not yet actually taken place.

So much is implied at the opening of our text, where the prostitutes burn drops of frankincense to Aphrodite. Although bloodless sacrifices of such spices are typical especially of Aphrodite's eastern cults (see above), they might also serve as prelude to a blood sacrifice, serving to form a link between humans and the deities, and to cover the stench of the sacrifice.[43] The frankincense has been burnt, the grazing hundred-limbed herd has been led in, but the blood component of the sacrifice has not yet been accomplished. Or, on another level, the preliminaries of the *symposion* have taken place, the prostitutes have been led in, but the orgy has not yet begun. Pindar's use of accomplished sacrifice by active prostitutes and an unaccomplished sacrifice of passive prostitutes sets the *skolion* in a moment of prelude just before the ludic aspects of the *symposion* begin.

ORIENTALISM

The third theme running through frag. 122 is Orientalism. Once again, this theme is first introduced in the opening word of the poem – *polyxenai*, with its oblique references to "much *xenia*" and a specifically Trojan princess. A second reference to things eastern and exotic is the mention of frankincense (*libanou*) in line three. As Herodotos tells us (3.106–7), the Greeks understood frankincense to come from Arabia, the burning and exotic land of spices to the east. Furthermore, as discussed above, an incense sacrifice was especially associated with the cults of Adonis and Cypriot Aphrodite.[44] Thus the use of *libanon* not only reinforces the identity of the deities being invoked, but casts Aphrodite specifically in an eastern guise.

[43] Detienne 1994 [1972]: 38.
[44] Burkert 1985: 62.

If use of frankincense were not enough to conjure Aphrodite's eastern persona, two epithets Pindar uses of her intensify this imagery – Ourania and Mistress of Cyprus. Neither epithet is particularly typical of Aphrodite's cults in Corinth, where she is more commonly revered as Melainis and Epaktia or Epilimenia.[45] Furthermore, for those heavily influenced by Platonic ideologies and myths, it would seem particularly odd to summon the goddess by the title Ourania in a poem that is so strongly associated with sexuality; one might expect a more physically eroticized Pandemos in this regard. However, Ourania is the epithet of Aphrodite most consistently associated with the goddess's supposed eastern origins and connections.[46] This is first apparent in Herodotos, Book 1.105, where the *histor* claims,

> Then [the Skythians], heading back again, appeared in the city Ashkalon of Syria; the majority of the Skythians passed by unharmed, but some of them, seizing the sanctuary of Aphrodite Ourania, plundered it. This is the sanctuary, as I discovered through inquiry, [that is] the oldest of all the sanctuaries of this goddess; for the sanctuary of Cyprus originated there, as the Cypriots themselves say, and as for the one amongst the Kytherians, the Phoenicians are its founders, who are from Syria too.

Later Pausanias was to support this idea, saying (1.14.7),

> Nearby is a sanctuary of Aphrodite Ourania. It was established that the first people to revere Ourania were the Assyrians, and after the Assyrians the Paphians of Cyprus and those of the Phoenicians who dwell in Ashkalon in Palestine; Kytherians worship her having so learned from the Phoenicians.

Ourania, then, combines two notions of importance in Pindar's text. On the one hand it establishes Aphrodite's celestial orientation, the place to which both burnt frankincense and prostitutes flutter. On the other hand, it calls to mind the goddess's eastern connections.[47]

This is also the case with Pindar's second epithet – Mistress of Cyprus. Here even more clearly Pindar establishes the goddess's eastern connections, tying her to the land that, since the days of Homer and Hesiod,

---

[45] Pirenne-Delforge 1994: 96–98.
[46] *Ibid*: 437–439.
[47] The epithet might also call to mind the Hesiodic tale of Aphrodite's birth from the severed genitals of Ouranos. However, I cannot imagine that references to castration were desired or welcomed at a *symposion*.

was seen to be her original home.[48] In both epithets, then, as well as the reference to frankincense, Pindar gives his *skolion* an Oriental flavor that runs throughout the text, from line 3 of the first strophe to the divine address of the final stanza.

What, then, is the purpose of these three themes? Why did Pindar choose to construct a *skolion* around the notions of sacrifice, sex, and exoticism? That Pindar chose to highlight the "oriental" in this context might be ascribed to the exotic, Oriental nature of Corinth itself. A poem for an oriental city could logically have an oriental theme.

However, this assumes a prejudice on the part of the Greeks that may not have in fact existed.[49] The ancient Greeks from the days of Homer (*Catalog of Ships*) through to Pindar himself described Corinth as "wealthy" (*aphneios*), not exotic. The city grew rich on typical Greek industries, pottery and trade, cashing in on its fortuitous placement at the isthmus (Thucydides 1.13.5). The city did not medize, nor did it support a number of exotic or "Oriental" cults, certainly nowhere as many as did Delos in the coming centuries. Although there was particular reverence to Aphrodite on the city's acropolis, she was not worshipped by any foreign epithets, merely "Dark" Aphrodite and "She by the Marshes" (see above). In truth, most understandings of the "exotic and Oriental" nature of Corinth come from references to the supposed institution of sacred prostitution practiced there, an institution understood to have been imported from the East.[50] If we accept that sacred prostitution did not exist, as I argue, and concede that Corinth may have had more prostitutes than usual, perhaps because of its prolific maritime commerce, then there is little on which to base the city's long-claimed Oriental affiliations.

Rather, references to Orientalism in Pindar's text may derive from a play on words. Specifically, Pindar was working his "foreign-voiced" patron into the text by incorporating the theme of Xenophon's name into the poem.

There are at least two other instances where Pindar structures a poem or its themes around the name of a patron or honorand. In *Isthmian 8*

---

[48] Pirenne-Delforge 1994: 310–318.

[49] *Ibid*: 121–124. It is interesting to note that in the early Archaic Age it was the sanctuaries of Hera at Perachora and Samos that had the largest number of "oriental" votives, 75% coming from Phoenicia, Egypt, and the "Orient" at Perachora, 60% coming from Egypt, Phoenica, Syria, Assyria, Babylon, Persia, and Urartu at Samos. If elements of an "oriental" cult are to be sought, they should be sought here before bringing either Aphrodite or Corinth into the picture. See Kilian-Dirlmeier 1985: *passim*.

[50] Salmon 1997 [1984]: 397–400.

Pindar deals with the "glories of men," a reference back to the honorand Kleandros, "he who has the glories of men," and whose name is the initial word of the *epinikion*.[51] Likewise, in *Pythian* 6, technically dedicated to Xenokrates of Akragas but addressed to his son and charioteer Thrasyboulos, Pindar uses the contrast in the son's name (*thrasy-* "rash"; *boulos* "counsel") to refer to a mythical exploit of the hero Antilokhos, who learned from his father how to balance looseness and restraint to win a chariot race (and who also, for the record, died saving his father's life).[52] In the case of frag. 122, the honorand's (if we might call him that in the context of a *skolion*) name is Xenophon, "foreign-voiced." Notions of foreignness might then serve throughout the text to call him to mind.

CRISIS?

It was perhaps Corinth's reputation for its prostitutes (Strabo 8.6.20), as well as the occasion of the poem, that instigated the second of Pindar's themes – sex. That Pindar chose such an appropriate sympotic theme for his *skolion* really should be no cause for wonder. A *symposion* in the city of the goddess of sexual pleasure may have been too much a temptation for the poet, who oriented his *skolion* not around the aristocratic *hetaireia*, as with frag. 123, but those *hetairai* so emblematic of the city. Pindar even gives the impression of one "embarrassed" by his inability to resist such a diversion from normal[53] practice, wondering what the "Masters of the Isthmos will say" of him, commencing (and ending!) the song with such a profane topic.

This apparent embarrassment has been the subject of considerable speculation. According to several analyses of this poem, at the core of frag. 122 lies Pindar's extreme insecurity regarding his status vis-à-vis the prostitutes. G. Norwood wrote concerning the phrase "with necessity all is lovely" that "Those words are applied to the courtesans, but Pindar may well have his own embarrassment also in mind: the reflexion that he writes for pay comes upon him at other times too, but not (we may believe) with such pungency."[54] Likewise, as argued by J. Svenbro and L. Kurke, "the encomiastic poet of the fifth century BCE confronted a

---

[51] Nagy 1990: 205.
[52] *Ibid*: 207–214.
[53] Although I would argue that determining what counts as "normal" for a Pindar *skolion* must be speculative in the absence of the majority of the data.
[54] Norwood 1945: 20.

dilemma in his work: composing on commission, he lacked the autarky of his poetic predecessors."[55] In short, Pindar lives in a time unlike the good old days when, as Pindar recounts in *Isthmian 2*, poets were inspired to "mellifluous" poetry by "boys/ or any handsome one whose summery mien/ pressed its suit on Aphrodite lovely-throne." Now does the Muse "work for hire" and Terpsikhorê vend — what has been called Pindar's "mercenary Muse."[56] Feeling himself to be one who sells what ought to be inspired by love and given in friendship, like the prostitutes, Pindar's ultimate aim in frag. 122 is to show that he is a separate category from the prostitutes and a full-fledged member of the *symposion's hetaireia*.[57]

Pindar's status, and that of the entire *hetaireia* of which he is a member, is further threatened, according to this analysis, by the fact that the women are specifically *sacred* prostitutes and thus have a special link with the divine denied to the men.

> Their special link to the goddess . . . generates a certain anxiety on the part of the citizen males, and it is this anxiety that Pindar's ode manages and transforms. First, the poet merges the hierodules' sacred and sexual roles in lines which emphasize not only the women's beauty, but also their complete lack of autonomy. Then he progressively effaces their sacral status entirely, while constructing a direct relation between the "masters of the Isthmus" and the "mistress of Cyprus," now nearly equal in power and freedom.[58]

By turning the prostitutes into a sacrifice, Pindar denies their own supposed power while intensifying that of the *hetaireia*, of which he is emphatically a member, identifying himself ultimately not with the hundred-limbed herd, but with the masters of the Isthmos.[59]

There are a number of problems with these theories, the most serious of which is predicating an analysis on the notion of sacred prostitution. If these are merely ordinary prostitutes, as I claim they are, there can be no anxiety over access to the divine, which Pindar is supposedly trying to appropriate.[60] Our context, if not the poetry as well, is quite secular.

---

[55] Kurke 1996: 53.
[56] Woodbury 1968: *passim*; Nagy 1990: 340.
[57] Kurke 1996: 54–56.
[58] *Ibid*: 58.
[59] Hubbard 1985: 157.
[60] Kurke herself notes, "If the attendant women were simple prostitutes, I doubt Pindar's ode would perform its strange turn. His identification with the women and subsequent distancing is necessitated by the fact that they are *temple* prostitutes, whose sacred status gives them a special link to the goddess" (Kurke 1996: 58).

The notion of Pindar's "mercenary Muse" is also doubtful. While in Athens specifically work for pay was considered servile, the antithesis of *andreia*, and only fit for slaves,[61] the pay epinician poets such as Pindar received for their compositions was all part of the great chain of honor and *xenia* running amidst athletic victors and their communities.[62] This chain begins with athletes competing at festivals that functioned on some early level as funerary games for dead heroes, and thus the athletes bestow honor, or *kleos*, upon their heroic ancestors.

> The religious ideology, clearly attested in Pindar's praise poetry, is matched by the religious ideology of the poetry: each ordeal of each victorious athlete, compensating for the proto-ordeal of the hero who struggled and died, demands compensation of its own in the form of song offered as praise for the athlete. And the song in turn demands compensation from the victorious athlete and his family, to be offered to the composer of the song.[63]

The concept of Pindar's reciprocal *xenia*, *philos*, and *kharis* with his patrons is a recurring motif throughout his odes, emphasizing his reciprocal and equality-based relationship with his poetic patrons. It strikes me as unlikely that Pindar would choose this one poem in which to have a public identity crisis.

DIVINITY, XENIA, AND HUMOR

It might instead be better to see Pindar's reference to his "embarrassment" as a poetic device. What remains of this stanza is highly transitional in nature (although coming between two lacunae it is difficult to determine between what and what exactly). Pindar's references to the first person, as Lefkowitz has shown, serve two purposes when referring to the poet – transitions in the text, and *kairos* statements, where the poet comments upon the appropriateness of his poetry in terms of themes, length, and intensity.[64] The stanza also contains a gnomic statement – "We reveal gold by a pure touchstone" – and gnomic statements likewise function as transitional devices.[65]

---

[61] Cohen 2002: 100–103.
[62] Hubbard 1985: 161–162.
[63] Nagy 1990: 151 and 188.
[64] Lefkowitz 1991: 55.
[65] Hubbard 1985: 143.

This particular *gnomê* is not exclusive to frag. 122. Pindar makes similar statements in *Pythian* 10, *Nemean* 8, and *Paian* 14. In *Pythian* 10, 67–68 Pindar states that "Integrity of mind/ is proved, like gold by touchstone, by a test."[66] In *Nemean* 8, 20–21, Pindar claims that "Many tales are told in many ways; to coin new ones and test them by touchstone is indeed perilous." In both cases, what appears to be at issue is honesty and sincerity.[67] In such a way, this *gnomê* might, like a first-person statement, function as a *kairos* statement, wherein Pindar establishes his sincerity to the *symposion* audience. The fact that Pindar speaks of "shared women" should not imply that he is not focused on more important matters, such as the glory of Xenophon and the camaraderie of the *hetaireia*, or that his praise derives from the material "gift" he received from his host, rather than from genuine *xenia*. Sex is present, but it does not overshadow *kharis* and *philia*.

The need for such a note of sincerity in the middle of the poem might be necessitated by the interplay of seriousness and playfulness running through the text. The aim of the first theme in the poem – sacrifice – is to heroize, if not actually deify, the *hetaireia*, placing them on par with Akhilleus and the Mistress of Cyprus. However, to bestow so much *kleos* upon a group of mortals is certainly to speak *para kairos*, with hubris. Pindar curbs the hubris by offering the reminder that this song is just a *skolion*, the men simple revelers, the poet somewhat awkward and embarrassed, and that there is no need for the deities to take their comments in this context too seriously.

As stated above, the use of sacrificial imagery has the result of deifying the *hetaireia*. The *Isthmou despotai* are paralleled with the *Kyprou despoina*. Certainly this serves to aggrandize the phenomenal *xenia* shown by Xenophon to his guests; he not only makes them welcomed guests, he makes them, and Pindar, and himself, heroes and gods. And yet it would seem here that Pindar speaks *para kairon*, for such human claims to excessive *eudaimonia* inevitably end badly in the works of Pindar. The perfect foil for such behavior is Pindar's Tantalos, who in *Olympian* 1 offered an excessive feast to his companions, serving them divine ambrosia and nectar; in short, serving them like deities. Such behavior was *para kairon*, and the man was duly punished.

---

[66] Swanson 1974: 120.

[67] There is too little of *Paian* 14 to determine how the reference to gold and touchstone was used. However, Rutherford suggests, based on Pindaric comparanda, that the ultimate meaning here was to show that the song had "lasting value" and, "signifying, like a seal, its provenance and guaranteeing its authenticity" (Rutherford 2001: 410).

More generally, Pindar makes explicit reference for his need not to speak *para kairon* for fear that excessive mention of human happiness will trigger the envy of the deities.[68] This is especially evident in *Nemean* 8, where the poet says (23–28),

> At the starting line I lightly stand and draw my breath
> before my race of words; for verbal novelties
>   are rife: experiments
> in poetry are always full of risk. Words whet envy's appetite, and
> envy always nibbles at good men and never tries to trim the bad:
> It fed upon the son of Telamon, spitting him on his own sword.[69]

And yet in frag. 122 there seems to be no fear of speaking *para kairon*, of equating men with gods. Once again, I must draw attention to the conspicuous use of the word *skolion* in the text. Whether festive, ribald, or completely serious, the fact that this poem is a *skolion* means that it was originally recited in the context of the *symposion*. As discussed above, the *symposion* was its own little world, a separate reality governed by its own set of rules, laws, and logic.[70] This separate reality may have palliated the potential hubris in the deification of the *hetaireia* – what deity could begrudge a group of drinkers a momentary sense of divine *kharis*, especially when they were prepared to share the divine prerogatives? The conspicuous use of the word *skolion* and Pindar's feigned embarrassment undercut the potential *para kairon* nature of the poem's sentiments, thus extolling Xenophon's *xenia* literally to the skies while nevertheless keeping the praise safe. Pindar offers a sense of frivolity, but nevertheless attests to his ultimate sentiments with the gnomic "gold."

Thus there is a strong interplay between religiosity and playfulness in the song. By conflating the *symposion* with a sacrifice through the use of the euphemisms mentioned above, Pindar gives a sanctimonious air to the *skolion*. But such an air must inevitably be tongue-in-cheek, for the locus of the poem is, clearly, the *symposion*; the receivers of the "sacrifice" are drinking men; and Pindar himself reinforces all of this by specifically referring to his song as a *skolion*, the only time he does so, thus counteracting the sacral imagery.[71] The contrast of sacral imagery with

---

[68] Lefkowitz 1991: 26.
[69] Swanson 1974: 162.
[70] Murray 1990: 7.
[71] One might perhaps consider a modern example of a bartender performing a "wedding" during the course of a night of drinking. After going through the traditional vows,

the actual presence of prostitutes then takes on a humorous air, deflecting any possible *phthonos*, human or divine.

The conflation of sacrificial and sexual imageries, with a sprinkling of Orientalism for flavor, achieves a noble aim on the part of Pindar. It allows him to talk of the joys of the *symposion*, the xenia and generosity of his host, the extreme nobility – even divinity – of his companions, and his own sincerity in a way that did not tempt fate.

On "Bringing"

The final issue to be addressed is the wording, meanings, and potential ambiguities of the final lines of the last stanza. The most problematic word is what, exactly, Xenophon is doing with those prostitutes[72] – is the verb *epagô* or *apagô*? This uncertainty is reflected in the wording of Athenaios' commentary, where it is uncertain if the text should be read *apaxein autêi kai tas hetairas* or *epaxein autêi kai tas hetairas*. On a basic level, both words simply mean "to bring." Typically, the *apagô* reading is preferred, with its connotations of "paying what is owed" or "rendering service or honor."[73] This gives a sense of "paying" courtesans to Aphrodite in return for her assistance, and thus the word is often translated as "render" – "they will even render courtesans to her."[74]

By contrast, *epagô* has connotations of introduction, invitation, and even supply. Because, as arguments below will show, Athenaios' commentary, as received from Khamaileon, is based upon the poetic text itself and not on independent ethnographic data, whatever word Pindar used in the final stanza must be the same word used in the commentary. What, then, would Pindar claim Xenophon was doing with the prostitutes in this context? As the above analysis has shown, the prostitutes were "sacrificial victims" to the erotic desires of the semidivine Masters of the Isthmos. The wording of the final stanza of the *skolion* implies directional movement – *deut' es alsos*. Either word, in the most basic meaning of "to bring," would work. However, connotations of "payment" only make sense if one accepts the notion of sacred prostitution, that one

---

and thus establishing the genre, he solemnizes the ritual by the power vested in him by the liquor control board and Jack's House of Tequila.

[72] Other than "culling" their "fruit."

[73] LSJ.

[74] Gulick 1927, Vol. 6: 99.

could permanently give or dedicate these prostitutes to Aphrodite. Furthermore, there is no recipient of the *apagag'*, as one would expect if payment or dedication were being rendered. Merely a place – *alsos* – is indicated. Furthermore, while one might argue that the prostitutes will, in fact, "render service or honor" to the *symposion* guests, they are not the subject of the verb; Xenophon is. And although one could argue that it is he who is honoring his semidivine guests with the "sacrifice," this would also place Xenophon outside the category of the recipients, which is unlikely.

If instead we take the word as *epagô*, not only is Xenophon "bringing in" prostitutes to the party, but also there are highly ambivalent connotations of invitation and supply. To invite the prostitutes to the party reflects their human status and autonomy in the opening stanza of the poem, when the girls actively offer sacrifices to Aphrodite. However, to "supply" prostitutes dehumanizes them, turning them into so many more comestibles or party favors (which, as argued above, they pretty much were). *Epagô* is therefore a better choice in this context, as it offers a fuller range of meanings concomitant with Pindar's overall imagery within the text.[75] To use *apagô*, though, opens the door to alternate readings with connotations of permanence, which then might be invoked as evidence for the practice of sacred prostitution. The ambiguity in reading thus opens the door for misunderstandings, which then are employed as evidence in the argument for sacred prostitution.

This ambiguity is emphasized by the structure of the final lines of the poem. Pindar refers to Xenophon's "rejoicing in prayers fulfilled" in a clause crossed with the reference to Xenophon's "bringing the hundred-limbed herd," with Xenophon's name serving as the subject of both clauses. This may have given the impression that the "bringing" of the prostitutes was, in fact, the fulfillment of the prayers, as I argue below some later commentators may have thought. But in the end we must accept that we, the modern reading audience, have no idea what those prayers were, and there is a very strong probability that Pindar's early commentators were likewise in the dark.[76] The conflation of the two clauses may hint at Xenophon's vows, but there are far more likely resolutions to this

---

[75] As Slater notes in his lexicon, the word *apagô* only appears once in Pindar's extant works, and that in the middle voice. *Epagô* shows up five times in the active. Slater 1969: 60 and 182.

[76] Lefkowitz 1991: 93–94, 149, 204; Hamilton 2003: *passim*.

verbal puzzle than sacred prostitution, including the sacrifice or *symposion* itself, or possibly even manumission for the prostitutes in question (see Chapter 7).[77]

In the end, there is no need to assume that the prostitutes who are the focus of the text are sacred, or that there is any reference to a dedication to Aphrodite in the poem. Although the poem addresses Aphrodite, there is nothing in the text that affirms that the prostitutes were a dedication of any sort to this goddess. The sacrifice is symbolic, just as the *alsos* is not really a grove or sanctuary, and the prostitutes are not really a herd. If Xenophon led a herd of prostitutes to an *alsos*, the *alsos* was an *andrôn*, the recipients mere mortals, and the overall tone festive and tongue-in-cheek.

PERSIANS, PROSTITUTES, AND PERPLEXITY: SIMONIDES' CORINTHIAN EPIGRAM AND THE ROLE OF KHAMAILEON[78]

If Pindar was not writing about a dedication of sacred prostitutes, where did this notion come from, how did it develop, and when? Our main source of information on this derives from Athenaios, although, as with the commentary on Pindar himself, a fair amount of analysis is necessary to derive useful information from this source. The revealing passage is actually a cross between a red herring and a tangent in the study of sacred prostitution. I hope that the reader will find the following apparent digression meaningful in the end. Referring to the prostitutes of Corinth, Athenaios recounted (13.573c–d),

> It is an old custom in Corinth, as even Khamaileon of Heraklea relates in his *On Pindar*, that whenever the city prays to Aphrodite about major events, they include as many courtesans as possible, and they offer prayers to the goddess, and later are present at the sacrifices. And when, then, the Persians led their army against Greece, as both Theopompos relates and Timaios in the seventh [book], the Corinthian courtesans prayed for the salvation of the Greeks, having gone to the temple of Aphrodite. And on this account Simonides – when they dedicated the *pinax* of the Corinthian women to the goddess which even still remains, and depicting separately the courtesans who at that time made the

---

[77] Pirenne-Delforge 1994: 124.
[78] On this epigram and its relation to Pindar and sacred prostitution, see Budin 2008.

supplication and who were later present [at the sacrifice] – composed the following epigram:

These ones, for the sake of the Greeks and straight-fighting citizens,
stood to pray to Kypris divine[79];
For holy Aphrodite did not contrive to betray
a Greek acropolis to bow-toting Persians.

νόμιμόν ἐστιν ἀρχαῖον ἐν Κορίνθῳ, ὡς καὶ Χαμαιλέων ὁ Ἡρακλεώτης ἱστορεῖ ἐν τῷ περὶ Πινδάρου, ὅταν ἡ πόλις εὔχεται περὶ μεγάλων τῇ Ἀφροδίτῃ, συμπαραλαμβάνεσθαι πρὸς ἱκετείαν τὰς ἑταίρας ὡς πλείστας, καὶ ταύτας προσεύχεσθαι τῇ θεῷ καὶ ὕστερον ἐπὶ τοῖς ἱεροῖς παρεῖναι. καὶ ὅτε δὴ ἐπὶ τὴν Ἑλλάδα τὴν στρατείαν ἦγεν ὁ Πέρσης, ὡς καὶ Θεόπομπος ἱστορεῖ καὶ Τίμαιος ἐν τῇ ἑβδόμῃ, αἱ Κορίνθιαι ἑταῖραι εὔξαντο ὑπὲρ τῆς τῶν Ἑλλήνων σωτηρίας εἰς τὸν τῆς Ἀφροδίτης ἐλθοῦσαι νεών. διὸ καὶ Σιμωνίδης ἀναθέντων τῶν Κορινθίων πίνακα τῇ θεῷ τὸν ἔτι καὶ νῦν διαμένοντα καὶ τὰς ἑταίρας ἰδίᾳ γραψάντων τὰς τότε ποιησαμένας τὴν ἱκετείαν καὶ ὕστερον παρούσας συνέθηκε τόδε τὸ ἐπίγραμμα·

Αἵδ' ὑπὲρ Ἑλλήνων τε καὶ εὐθυμάχων πολιητᾶν
ἔσταθεν εὔχεσθαι Κύπριδι δαιμονίᾳ.
Οὐ γὰρ τοξοφόροισιν ἐμήσατο δῖ' Ἀφροδίτα
Πέρσαις Ἑλλάνων ἀκρόπολιν προδόμεν.

It has long been argued that prostitutes praying to Aphrodite are evidence for sacred prostitution, and that their prayers were invoked due to their especially close relationship with the goddess.[80] This in turn has been used as supporting evidence for the Corinthian sacred prostitution supposedly present in Pindar's poem.[81] However, there are two other versions of this story, one preserved in Plutarch's "On the Malice of Herodotos" and the second in a scholion on Pindar's *Olympian* 13.[82]

---

[79] There is an on-going debate about the case and use of the word *daimoniai* here. The typical usage is that the word is feminine dative singular and modifies the epithet Kypris. Page 1981: 211 argues to the contrary that the adjective *daimonios* could not be applied to a deity, and has suggested instead that the word be emended to read "*daimonia*" = δαιμόνιον εὐχήν. In contrast, Brown 1991: *passim* suggests that *daimonai* is a feminine nominative plural describing the *haid'* at the beginning of the epigram. The females in question are "*daimoniai*" because they are sacred prostitutes, thus "sacred" because dedicated to Aphrodite (8–9).

[80] Wilamowitz-Moellendorff 1889: 4–5; Van Groningen 1956: 15–16; 19, 22; Kurke 1996: 64–65.

[81] A thousand pardons for the horrible alliteration.

[82] Pirenne-Delforge 1994: 106–109.

Neither refers to prostitutes. According to Plutarch (*De Malig. Herod.* 871 a–b),

> And in truth of the Greeks only the Corinthian women offered that fair and divine prayer, that the goddess should cast desire at their men to fight the barbarians. It was not credible that those about Herodotos were ignorant of this, nor even the remotest Karian! For the matter was made famous, and Simonides composed the epigram when bronze images were set up in the temple of Aphrodite, which they say Medea built (some say she did it so as to stop <loving> her husband, others say so as to get the goddess to make Jason stop loving Thetis). The epigram is as follows:

> > These ones, for the sake of the Greeks and straight-fighting citizens,
> > stood having prayed to Kypris divine;
> > For holy Aphrodite was not intending to betray
> > a Greek acropolis to bow-toting Medes.

> Καὶ μὴν ὅτι μόναι τῶν Ἑλληνίδων αἱ Κορίνθιαι γυναῖκες εὔξαντο τὴν καλὴν ἐκείνην καὶ δαιμόνιον εὐχήν, ἔρωτα τοῖς ἀνδράσι τῆς πρὸς τοὺς βαρβάρους μάχης ἐμβαλεῖν τὴν θεόν, οὐχ ὅπως <τοὺς> περὶ τὸν Ἡρόδοτον ἀγνοῆσαι πιθανὸν ἦν, ἀλλ'οὐδὲ τὸν ἔσχατον Καρῶν· διεβοήθη γὰρ τὸ πρᾶγμα καὶ Σιμωνίδης ἐποίησεν ἐπί-γραμμα, χαλκῶν εἰκόνων ἀνασταθεισῶν ἐν τῷ ναῷ τῆς Ἀφροδίτης ὃν ἱδρύσασθαι Μήδειαν λέγουσιν, οἱ μὲν αὐτὴν παυσαμένην <ἐρῶσαν> τοῦ ἀνδρός, οἱ δ'ἐπὶ τῷ τὸν Ἰάσονα τῆς Θέτιδος ἐρῶντα παῦσαι τὴν θεόν. Τὸ δ'ἐπίγραμμα τοῦτ'ἔστιν·

> > Αἵδ' ὑπὲρ Ἑλλάνων τε καὶ ἰθυμάχων πολιητᾶν
> > ἐστάθεν εὐξάμεναι Κύπριδι δαιμονίᾳ.
> > Οὐ γὰρ τοξοφόροισιν ἐμήδετο δῖ' Ἀφροδίτα
> > Μήδοισ'Ἑλλάνων ἀκρόπολιν προδόμεν.

The scholion to Pindar's *Ol.* 13 (Drachmann 32b = FGrHist 115, F 285b) tells how during the Persian invasion of Greece,

> ... during which, for the salvation of the Greek army, the Corinthians performed nobly, and Theopompos says even their wives, entering into the sanctuary of Aphrodite (which they say Medea built at Hera's command), prayed to Aphrodite to cast desire to fight the Medes for the sake of Greece upon their husbands. And even now they say the inscription is there, on the left hand going into the temple:

> > These ones, for the sake of the Greeks and close-fighting citizens,
> > stood praying to Kypris divine;

For holy Aphrodite did not wish to give
a Greek acropolis to bow-toting Medes.

...ἐν οἷς ὑπὲρ τῆς τῶν Ἑλλήνων σωτηρίας ἠνδραγάθησαν οἱ
Κορίνθιοι, Θεόπομπος δέ φησι καὶ τὰς γυναῖκας αὐτῶν εὔξασθαι
τῇ Ἀφροδίτῃ ἔρωτα ἐμπεσεῖν τοῖς ἀνδράσιν αὐτῶν μάχεσθαι ὑπὲρ
τῆς Ἑλλάδος τοῖς Μήδοις, εἰσελθούσας εἰς τὸ ἱερὸν τῆς Ἀφροδίτης,
ὅπερ ἱδρύσασθαι τὴν Μήδειαν λέγουσιν Ἥρας προστάξασης. εἶναι
δὲ καὶ νῦν ἀναγεγραμμένον ἐλεγεῖον εἰσιόντι εἰς τὸν ναὸν ἀριστερᾶς
χειρός·

Αἵδ' ὑπὲρ Ἑλλάνων τε καὶ ἀγχεμάχων πολιητᾶν
ἔστασαν εὐχόμεναι Κύπριδι δαιμονίᾳ.
Οὐ γὰρ τοξοφόροισιν ἐβούλετο δῖ' Ἀφροδίτα
Μήδοις Ἑλλάνων ἀκρόπολιν δόμεναι.

All three versions of this story claim that women went to the sanctuary of Aphrodite to pray on behalf of the Greeks during the Persian invasions. Plutarch gives no sources; the Pindaric scholion mentions Theopompos; Athenaios uses Khamaileon. M. Boas, when he
first analyzed the epigram in 1905, argued that Ephoros was the primary source for the epigram and its presumed narratives; Theopompos
took the narrative from him and passed it directly along to the Pindar
scholiast. The Theopompan version then combined with a hypotheti-
cal version from Timaios that together influenced Plutarch, Khamaileon,
and thus Athenaios.[83] D. Page has argued that Theopompos was the
original source for this anecdote, thus informing both the scholiast and
Plutarch.[84] Page, heavily relying on Boaz, placed the three versions into
two separate groups. The version as presented by the scholiast was the
"original" version of the epigram (and, less importantly for Page, the
anecdote). Plutarch's and Athenaios' versions were later derivatives. This
division, argued Page, was evident first of all in the different tenses used
for the women's praying – present for the former, aorist for the latter two.
Likewise, although the two latter authors attribute the epigram specifically to Simonides, the scholiast gives no poet's name, although he does
give the impression of having seen the actual dedication himself – "to
the left of the entrance" indicating autopsy. Because, as Page argued, it
would not really be possible to attribute any epigram to Simonides in the

---

[83] Boas 1905: 71.
[84] Page 1981: 208–210; Van Groningen 1956: 14.

Classical period, only later, more "adventurous" authors would claim him as poet.[85]

I would argue this case differently. I think it quite evident that Plutarch's and the scholiast's accounts fall into one category, and that it is Athenaios' that is wholly distinct. It is true that all three versions have inconsistencies, especially concerning whether we have straight-fighting (*euthymakhôn / ithymakhôn*), or close-fighting citizens (*agkhemakhôn*); or whether Aphrodite did not intend/contrive (*emêdeto* [imperfect]/ *emêsato* [aorist]) or wish (*ebouleto*) to betray the Greeks.[86] Far more important, however, is the identification of the enemy. Both Plutarch and the scholiast note that the archers are Medes; Athenaios takes them as Persians. Plutarch and the scholiast say that it was the wives of the Corinthians who prayed to Aphrodite; Athenaios claims it was the prostitutes. Specifically, the Corinthian wives prayed to Aphrodite to cast a desire to fight upon their husbands. No such reference is given in Athenaios. Finally, the two former authors make a point of saying that the sanctuary was founded/built by Medea (a detail that Page claims was "irrelevant"[87]), a fact missing from Athenaios.

It is clear that Athenaios' version of both the epigram and its surrounding story is quite different from the other two. Evidently, he had a different source, whom he himself identifies as Khamaileon (although Page suggests that Khamaileon got the version from Timaios).[88] We have two versions, then, of an anecdote relating how the women (be they wives or courtesans) of Corinth once went to the sanctuary of Aphrodite to pray for the salvation of Greece during the Persian invasions. We might dub these the Theopompan (scholion and Plutarch) and Khamaileonic (Athenaios) versions. An analysis of both versions allows us to determine how the different originators thought of this event, the meaning of the characters involved, and how the epigram was to be understood as a product of its cultural and historical background.

The epigram alone is not especially helpful. The referent is an unidentified *haid'*; we do not even know to whom the epigram was dedicated, other than a group of females. We do not know *where* they stood to pray/praying; the poem gives no indication of space.[89] All we can say is

---

[85] Page 1981: 210.
[86] Palumbo Stracca 1985: 61–62.
[87] Page 1981: 208, n. 2.
[88] *Ibid*: 209.
[89] It is generally assumed that the women fled to Aphrodite's sanctuary on Acrocorinth, but we have no specific reference to back up this assumption, and other sanctuaries

that some unknown females prayed to Aphrodite during a specific military encounter. Basically, the epigram is a caption with the captioned illustration missing. I believe it was in the absence of this kind of information (who? where? etc.) that stories emerged to fill in the perceived gaps, stories either heard or invented by Theopompos and Khamaileon. As we shall see, they had very different takes on the events at hand.

The Theopompan version has two details of particular interest. One is the author's attempt to reconcile Aphrodite, goddess of love and sex, as the recipient of prayers with the militaristic setting of the poem. Even more interesting are the references to Medea, both directly in reference to her foundation of the sanctuary, and reflected in the reference to the Medes in the final line of the epigram.

That Aphrodite had militaristic aspects of her persona appears in brief glimpses throughout her cult. The goddess herself emerged on Cyprus partially through the influence of Near Eastern goddesses associated both with sexuality and warfare, such as Ištar and Išhara.[90] At three Greek sanctuaries — Kythera, Sparta, and Corinth — the statue of the goddess was described as "armed" (*hoplismenê*). Aphrodite was the paramour of Ares, god of war; the wife of Hephaistos, maker of weapons; and a general instigator of militarism herself, for example, the Trojan War. Although her militaristic aspects seem to have been downplayed when the cult reached Greece, the fact that she could be portrayed armed suggests that at at least some early sites a militaristic aspect was maintained. At Corinth, this may have been due to contacts with Near Eastern, specifically Phoenician, traders, whose own chief goddess Aštart — identified by the Greeks as Aphrodite[91] — had a strongly militant character. Based on the origins of Aphrodite, then, and possibly on continual external influences, there is a reason that some Greeks would have understood a military aspect to Aphrodite's persona. In the actual, obscure history of this Corinthian event, this might explain why the women prayed to Aphrodite.

A militaristic Aphrodite was not, however, the norm, and depictions of Aphrodite armed or belligerent went very much against her standard depiction, as portrayed in Book Five of the *Iliad*, as one who went crying to her mother Dione when she was hurt in battle. Later, Roman

of the goddess are known in Corinth. See Pirenne-Delforge 1994: 93–104, Williams 1986: *passim*.

[90] Budin 2003a: 27–28, 79–80, 276–277.

[91] It is important to note here that it was not specifically Aštart whom the Greeks identified as Aphrodite, but any prominent Near Eastern goddess. See Budin 2004: *passim*.

depictions of "armed" Aphrodite/Venus showed the goddess nude, admiring herself in the mirror of Ares' shield, while little erotes "played" with the war god's weapons.[92] Quintilian, in his *Inst. Orat.*, 2.4.26, likewise posed the "stumper" question to Roman schoolboys as to why the statue of Aphrodite in Sparta was armed. Clearly, seeking help from Aphrodite on military matters was generally considered weird.

Theopompos, however, came up with an ingenious solution. As a goddess of love and sex, Aphrodite could cast a *desire* (*erôta*) to fight upon the husbands of the Corinthian women. Aphrodite being the expert in matters of desire, the prayer now "makes sense."[93]

Calling the enemy archers "Medes" in the Theopompan versions of the epigram reflects references to Medea in the origin tale of the sanctuary itself. Contrary to Page's notion that this detail was "irrelevant," I think that Medea is an especially important character in this account, a point emphasized by the fact that there is no other known reference to Medea as a founder of a sanctuary of Aphrodite in Corinth.[94] Whoever constructed the surrounding tale for the epigram either invented the details himself, or took it from an exceptionally local tradition.

Medea serves three important functions in the anecdote, both as it pertains to history and as it is used as a foil for the epigram – she is a powerful wife, she is the eponymous "mother" of the Medes, and her story manifests how Aphrodite is an aid to the Greeks against eastern barbarians.

Medea was the powerful "witch"[95] from Kolkhis who, through the machinations of Aphrodite, fell in love with the hero Jason, and who used her magical powers to assist her lover–husband in his quest for the golden fleece. She used her knowledge of magic to protect him from fire-breathing bulls and against earth-sown soldiers; so much seems to date back to the earliest elements of her mythology.[96] Medea, although

---

[92] Michaelides 2002: 358–360.

[93] Amusingly, Page claims that "The word ἐρῶτα in Theompompus . . . is then especially appropriate" when considering Wilamowitz's suggestion that it was in fact the city's *hetairai* who were doing the praying (Page 1981: 209). However, reference to the casting of *erôta* does NOT appear in the one version of the story that actually implicates *hetairai*, only those referring to wives. See also Dillon 2001: 201.

[94] Medea is far more commonly associated with Hera's sanctuary at near-by Perachora. For Medea's relationship with both the sanctuary and its goddess, see especially Johnston 1997: *passim*.

[95] On Medea as "witch" see Griffiths 2006, 41–47.

[96] Graf 1997: *passim*.

dangerous, is nevertheless a powerful wife with a great potential for help-ing her husband in times of need.

That the sanctuary of Aphrodite was specifically founded by her, at the behest of Hera, no less, according to the scholion, emphasizes the idea of wives who aid their husbands, just as the Corinthian wives are doing during the invasions. By attributing the sanctuary's foundation to Medea (and Hera!), the commentator evokes images of particularly powerful wives chanting prayers (enchantments?) to save their husbands from destruction. Furthermore, if we are to accept that the Corinthian wives reflect Medea, then the Corinthian husbands for whom they pray are themselves reflections of the hero Jason. The myth, in this aspect, ennobles the participants and highlights the good wifely qualities of the women who pray to Kypris.

There is, of course, another side to Medea, one associated with betrayal, infanticide, and banishment. For one reason or another, after returning to Greece, Jason disowned his foreign wife. The most popular version of the tale, as presented in Euripides' *Medea*, is that he opted to marry a Greek wife, thus leading to Medea's banishment from Corinth. In revenge, she kills Jason's new wife and her own children. An older tradition has it, however, that Medea and Jason's children died when Medea left them in Hera's sanctuary at Perachora, and the goddess was negligent on their behalf.[97] Somewhat between these two versions is a third, that Medea killed Jason's bride, and the Corinthians, in revenge, chased her and her children to the sanctuary at Perachora, where they murdered Medea's children (Pausanias 2.3.6). Later, the Corinthians were punished with a plague of infant deaths that was only halted when the citizens established a hero cult in honor of the slain children.[98] In all cases, Medea is forced to flee Corinth. She travels to Athens, where she connives to kill Theseus, is exposed, and flees once again to the east. According to Hesiod (*Theogony* 1001–1002), Herodotos (7.62), and Pausanias (2, 3, 7) she eventually became the eponymous founder of the Medes.[99]

Medea is the foreigner who is consistently driven out of the Greek city. The Corinthians drive her (and her children) from their land; the Athenians do the same. Almost as a form of sympathetic magic in a prayer for deliverance, a reference to Medea summons images of Greeks driving foreign invaders from Greece. Such an ideology of Medea was especially

---

[97] Graf 1997: 35.
[98] Johnston 1997: 50.
[99] Graf 1997: 22, 37; Krevans 1997: 75; Sourvinou-Inwood 1997: 260.

prominent in the mid- to late fifth century, when tales of Medea were "articulated as a mythological representation of the Greek victories over the Persians."[100]

This ideology is then played out in the wording of the epigram – Aphrodite did not give the acropolis to *Median* soldiers. As with Medea, so too with her descendants. Just as Medea was driven from the city (and Greece), so too might the Medes. The use of quasi-homonyms in the epigram and commentary thus creates important mythological links which add a symbolic level of force to the women's prayers.

Finally, reference to Medea ties together the notion of a prayer to Aphrodite with the historical situation of the invading Persians. Once again, Aphrodite was an odd choice for prayers pertaining to military defense (see above). However, if we recall the role played by this goddess in the story of Medea, we see another side to her powers. From the oldest strata of the Medea tale, it is Aphrodite who causes the witch to help the Greek hero against his foreign adversaries.[101] Aphrodite, then, in the context of the Medea narrative, is the goddess who uses feminine powers (such as the magic or prayers of wives) to overwhelm foreigners. Medea, in her persona, ties together those who pray, the divine recipient, and the enemy "prayed away." She is hardly an "irrelevant detail."

It is clear that the originator of Athenaios' version – Khamaileon[102] – had an entirely different set of associations and implications in mind when analyzing the epigram. Prostitutes, not wives, pray for Greece, but not specifically that Aphrodite instill the men with *desire* to fight. There is no reference to the sanctuary's foundation by Medea, and the enemy is called Persian in this version of the epigram, not Median. Thus all the implications of mentioning Medea and her brood are abandoned (powerful wives, husbands as heroes, banishment of eastern enemies, usefulness of Aphrodite in military affairs). Khamaileon's total lack of reference to the dominant themes running through the Theopompan version, I believe, makes it unlikely that he was aware of the historian's take on the epigram, and thus I disagree with Page when he argues that Athenaios meant to suggest that Khamaileon cited both Theopompos and Timaios in his own commentary. Although we cannot speak to Timaios, it is more likely that

---

[100] Sourvinou-Inwood 1997: 265.

[101] Graf 1997: 30; Boedeker 1997: 140.

[102] Page argues that this version actually derives from Timaios. I find this unlikely, based on the following arguments and on Athenaios' own testimony that the narrative comes from Khamaileon.

either Athenaios made an independent reference to the two historians, or, at best, Khamaileon referred to their work on the Persian invasions, but *not* on the epigram itself. As such, Khamaileon's analysis of the epigram is wholly his own, an argument strengthened when we consider his methodology below.

Khamaileon takes a wholly different approach to the Aphrodite-as-recipient-of-war-prayers issue than Theopompos. It would appear that here Aphrodite is approached simply (and reasonably enough) because she is the city goddess. What is of concern is the fact that prostitutes are brought along to intensify the supplication. Thus, what is of interest for Khamaileon is not the prayer recipient, but who prays. Prostitutes are desired, if not necessary, presumably because the goddess invoked is *their* patron.[103]

Other than *who* does the praying, the most notable difference between the Theopompan and Khamaileonic accounts is *when* the praying is done. For Theopompos and his followers, the wives prayed for their husbands (and the Greeks in general) on the arrival of the Medes – thus, a single occurrence. For Khamaileon, the prostitutes routinely (*otan*) prayed on any matter of sufficient importance – thus, an "old custom" (*nomimon . . . arkhaion*). Furthermore, according to Khamaileon, it was traditional that, after the prayers had been offered and the desired aim achieved, the prostitutes were also present at the sacrifices (*kai hysteron epi tois hierois parenai*). In fact, he is quite emphatic about this, repeating this notion later when discussing the example of the Persian invasions – that they made the supplication and were later present (*kai hysteron parousas*) (presumably at the sacrifice, as above).

An old custom then, according to Khamaileon, where Corinthian prostitutes pray to the city goddess, *their* goddess, on matters of importance and later attend sacrifices. The players (prostitutes), nature of the custom (habitual rather than singular), subsequent activities (sacrifice), and subject of the epigram and pinax (prostitutes not wives) are all different in Khamaileon's account from what we see in Theopompos, and if it were not for the common epigram, it would be difficult to believe that both men were discussing the same thing.

---

[103] As Dillon notes: "After all, it would be particularly appropriate for the prostitutes to invoke Aphrodite's aid in consuming the warriors with lust (eros) to annihilate the enemy; that prostitutes had 'heaven-sent power' from Aphrodite, their especial goddess, which they use while praying, also makes sense" (Dillon 2001: 201).

BRINGING IT BACK TO PINDAR

How, then, does this discussion of the Simonides epigram shed light on the issue of sacred prostitution in Pindar? For one thing there is the fact that Khamaileon, author of the meretricious version of the epigram commentary, is also the originator of Athenaios' commentary on Pindar's *skolion*.[104] Furthermore, there are a remarkable number of commonalities in his treatment of the two poems. Both claim to reveal a Corinthian *nomimon* — tradition (*nomimon esti arkhaion; hyparkhontos oun tou toioutou nomimou peri tên theon*), presumably the same one. Both have citizens involving prostitutes in prayers to Aphrodite, either inviting them to join in the supplications (*symparalambanesthai pros tên hiketeian*) or leading them to the goddess once the supplications were fulfilled (*epaxein autêi kai tas hetairas*). Likewise, in both instances the prostitutes who took part in the prayer/dedication were later present at the sacrificial rituals (*hysteron epi tois hierois parenai; kai hysteron parousas; hysteron . . . para tên thysian . . . pros tas hetairas . . . synethusan*).

Khamaileon wrote his commentary on the Simonides epigram in his work *On Pindar* according to Atheniaos. Amusingly, he did not reference Simonides' epigram in his works on Simonides, at least as we have it preserved.[105] Presumably, although it is impossible to know for certain, he wrote his commentary on Pindar's *skolion* in the same work. The most logical explanation for why Khamaileon would deal with these two texts together, especially in a work on Pindar, is that he was invoking a perceived common Corinthian custom to elucidate both poems. Khamaileon clearly believed that there was a tradition (*nomimon*) in Corinth whereby the citizens made a point of including prostitutes' prayers along with their own in matters of importance and including them in religious rituals. He then passed the notion of this "old custom" along to Athenaios, who recorded for posterity that it was customary in Corinth to "bring courtesans to Aphrodite."

But is this nothing more than circular reasoning on the part of Khamaileon? At a loss to explain why Xenophon would bring prostitutes to Aphrodite's sanctuary (assuming Khamaileon took a literal interpretation of *alsos*), did he invent a Corinthian "old custom" that not only explained the Pindaric reference, but also could be invoked to shed light

---

[104] Wehrli 1969, fr. 31.
[105] *Ibid*: 58–59.

on Simonides' epigram as well? And, once this so-called custom was applied to both poems, could they be used to "confirm" each other?

For, as has long been understood, the early Hellenistic biographers, or, such as Khamaileon, biographer–literary critics, had very little material on which to base their biographies and commentaries. To quote an authority on the evolution of Greek biography, A. Momogliano noted that

> Hellenistic *érudits* had little direct evidence for the lives of archaic, or even of classical, poets. The technique of extracting information about the lives of writers from their works was both a legitimate and an extremely dangerous substitute for direct information. It helped Hellenistic erudition out of an impasse, but it also opened the door to the most irresponsible exploitation of literary documents.[106]

One author especially notorious for this kind of "irresponsible" inference was our own Khamaileon, of whom Momigiano wrote,

> Chamaeleon was prone to infer the personal circumstances of his poets from what they wrote. Thus poems by Sappho and Anacreon were used as evidence of their love affairs. Aeschylus was not only the first to introduce drunkards into tragedy, but wrote while under the influence of alcohol: a motto by Sophocles was quoted in confirmation. Corinthian customs were adduced to explain why Pindar mentioned *hetairai* in poems celebrating Corinthian winners.[107]

Khamaileon is brought to task once again by M. Lefkowitz in her study of first-person references in Pindar:

> Chamaeleon, cited in the Ambrosian *vita* as the source of the story about Pindar and the bees[108] . . . , appears consistently to have developed his narratives from the texts, using as documentation inference and probability. We may catch a glimpse of his methodology from a fragment of his commentary . . . on Pindar's encomium for Xenophon of Corinth (fr. 122), who (we are told) had vowed to give prostitutes to Aphrodite if he won at the games. . . . The assertions "it is evident" and "as seems

---

[106] Momigliano 1993: 70. In another particularly delightful quotation on this topic, Momigliano says, "The relation between poetry and life was in itself a problem which exercised ingenuity and encouraged perversity in the handling of literary evidence." *Ibid*: 88.

[107] *Ibid*: 70.

[108] That bees once built a honeycomb in the poet's mouth when he was a child, thus explaining his frequent reference to honey-sweet things in his poetry.

likely" provide reassurance in the absence of confirming data from other sources.[109]

Even van Groningen felt the need to mention about Khamaileon that "Les savants commentateurs, dont nos scolies dérivent, ne l'ont, apparemment, guère pris au sérieux."[110]

All of these quotations have been invoked for two reasons. They show that there is no compelling reason whatsoever to assume that Khamaileon's commentary regarding Pindar is even vaguely accurate, truthful, or credible. Likewise, they show that there is an especially longstanding tradition of disregarding Khamaileon's commentary about the Corinthian matter specifically. Those modern scholars studying Khamaileon from a biographical point of view, as opposed to as a possible source for the history of sacred prostitution, reject his commentary on Pindar generally and on Pindar's Corinthian works specifically. There is likewise no reason to assume that he is any more credible when it comes to Simonides or his Corinthian epigram. Khamaileon being the main source for Athenaios' commentary, Athenaios himself must be used very cautiously as a historiographic source as far as Corinthian prostitution is concerned.

CONCLUSIONS

Although Corinth was famous in antiquity for both its cults to Aphrodite and, even more so, its prostitutes, there is no compelling reason to assume that there was an especially close relationship between the goddess and the city prostitutes, not such that the prostitutes would be invoked as religious intermediaries or intensifiers of prayers. Our exclusive evidence for such a notion comes from Khamaileon, and he is notoriously unreliable.

Neither Pindar's *skolion* nor Khamaileon's commentary on it provides evidence for sacred prostitution. In reality, neither source suggests that there was any kind of *permanent* dedication of prostitutes to Aphrodite in ancient Corinth; both merely refer, in one way or another, to "bringing" prostitutes to Aphrodite. There is no vocabulary in play such as *anatithêmi* (to dedicate) or even a simple *didômi* (to give). As the next chapter will show, it is likely that neither Khamaileon, nor Athenaios, nor even later Strabo thought what Pindar was describing was sacred prostitution, but rather a form of sacral manumission that was just becoming popular in Pindar's day. To this we turn in our study of Strabo's hierodules.

[109] Lefkowitz 1991: 93.
[110] Van Groningen 1956: 21.

CHAPTER SEVEN

STRABO, CONFUSED AND MISUNDERSTOOD

A FULL 25% OF OUR CLASSICAL SOURCES FOR SACRED PROSTITUTION, both implied and inferred, come from Strabo (see Chapter 3). According to the *Geography* written by this first-century polymath from Asia Minor, sacred prostitution was supposedly practiced in Babylon, Corinth, Pontic Comana, Eryx, Egyptian Thebes, and Armenia. In fact, if one were to maintain Oden's hypothesis of sacred prostitution as accusation, Strabo, even more so than Herodotos, would be our primary accusational culprit.

And yet a closer look at Strabo's data reveal that he was no more writing about sacred prostitution than was Pindar. The only place where Strabo appears to be discussing this so-called practice is in his Babylonian *logos*, much of which he takes from Herodotos. Strabo does not function as independent, corroborating evidence for Herodotos in this case; rather, the Roman-age geographer merely repeats second or third hand what had been passed down to him in apparently garbled fashion. Strabo appears to be confused about Babylonian sacred prostitution, and his description, as we shall see, betrays his mistrust of the evidence.

In all other instances, it is the modern audience that is confused. Aspects of Strabo's working vocabulary have become confounded over the millennia so that terms that bear no relation to sacred prostitution have come to be translated as "sacred prostitute." This vocabulary – such as hierodule, *pallakis*, and even *kataporneuô* – will be reconsidered and ultimately redefined below. In the end, it will be clear that Strabo does not discuss sacred prostitution in his work; we, the modern audience, have merely misunderstood him.

16.1.20: BABYLON

It is customary for all Babylonian females, according to some oracle, to "mingle" with a foreigner, arriving before some Aphrodision along with many hand-maids and a retinue; each one is crowned with a cord. And he [the foreigner[1]], having approached places upon her knees as much silver as is seemly, has sex with her going far from the *temenos*. The silver is considered sacred to Aphrodite.

πάσαις δὲ ταῖς Βαβυλωνίαις ἔθος κατά τι λόγιον ξένῳ μίγνυσθαι, πρός τι Ἀφροδίσιον ἀφικομέναις μετὰ πολλῆς θεραπείας καὶ ὄχλου· θώμιγγι δ᾽ ἔστεπται ἑκάστη· ὁ δὲ προσιὼν καταθεὶς ἐπὶ τὰ γόνατα, ὅσον καλῶς ἔχει ἀργύριον, συγγίνεται, ἄπωθεν τοῦ τεμένους ἀπαγαγών· τὸ δ᾽ ἀργύριον ἱερὸν τῆς Ἀφροδίτης νομίζεται.

Such is the evidence Strabo provides for the sacred prostitution practiced in Babylon. The region and the vague description, following along in most details with Herodotos' 1.199 account, have generally been accepted as supporting evidence for Herodotos, and thus that sacred prostitution was indeed practiced in Babylon. However, a number of important issues cloud this apparent supporting evidence. On one hand is the fact that, when examined side by side, it is evident that the majority of Strabo's *ethôn tôn para tois Assyriois* is taken to one extent or another from Herodotos' Babylonian *nomoi*. As such, the Strabonian account need not be taken as independent witness, but as a mere copy or retelling of the Herodotean narrative. This is bolstered by the fact that Strabo never visited Babylon himself, and thus must have been dependent on another author or authors for his accounts of Mesopotamia.[2] On the other hand, differences in the two accounts indicate that the work of at least one other author is present in the Strabonian account.[3] Furthermore, as the following analysis will show, some of the data presented in Herodotos were not supported by this alternate account, leading to subtle yet important differences between the Strabonian and Herodotean versions that ultimately discount this passage (and Herodotos 1.199!) as actual evidence for sacred prostitution in Babylon.

What follows is the full Babylonian *nomoi* as presented in Herodotos followed by the Strabonian Assyrian *ethos*.

---

[1] On why the translation "foreigner" here is preferable to "stranger," see Chapter 4, note 1.
[2] Dueck 2000: Chapter 1.
[3] A fact noted as early as 1811 by Fr. Jacobs.

HERODOTOS 1.194–200

Such are the issues pertaining to their boats, and this is how they dress: in an ankle-length linen khiton. And another, woolen khiton goes about that one and a white mantle is tossed over. They wear rustic sandals much like the slippers worn by the Boiotians. They grow their hair long and [wear] it up in a turban; they anoint the whole body [with oil]. Each one has a seal and a hand-wrought cane. On each cane is some decoration, either an apple or a rose or a lily or an eagle or some other thing, for it is not their custom to have a cane without a design. This is what I have to say concerning their physical habits; these are their customs.

Once a year the following is done in each village. When the maidens are of age to marry, they lead them all together into one place with a crowd of men standing around them. Standing them up one by one, the herald sells them, starting with the most beautiful among them, and whenever she has been sold – fetching a lot of gold – then he puts the next most beautiful up for sale. They are sold for the purpose of cohabitation (= marriage). Many prosperous Babylonians who were of marriageable intent would contend with each other to buy the prettiest girls; but those of the common folk who sought marriage – those who had no need for good looks – they instead would receive money as well as the uglier maidens. For indeed, as the herald finished selling off the prettiest of the *parthenoi*, he would stand up the ugliest, or if some one of them were crippled, and he would put her up for "sale"; whoever wanted the least gold for her got to take her home. The gold came from the pretty maidens, and thus the pretty ones provided a marriage for the ugly and crippled ones. It was not permitted for anyone to give away his own daughter in marriage according to his own designs, nor could one lead away a purchased maiden without providing a guarantee: He had to provide a guarantee that he would marry her so as to take her away. If the couple should not get along, the custom permitted the return of the money. Anyone who wanted could even come from a different village to buy a wife.

Now this was indeed their wisest custom; in truth now it has ceased to exist, and they have hit upon something new. For since being conquered they have been in distress and their households in ruins, and every one of the poorer class prostitutes his female offspring.

Their second wisest custom is this – they carry out their sick to the agora, for they do not use doctors. Going up to the sick people they consult about the illness, if someone he knows, or even he himself ever suffered from a similar ailment. The one approaching consults and advises such things as he did to escape a similar illness, or the person he knows who did. It is not acceptable to go by the sick person in silence before asking what illness he has. They bury their dead in honey, and they use dirges like those in Egypt. Whenever a Babylonian man should have sex with his wife, he sits to fumigate himself upon an incense burner, and opposite him his wife does the same. And the two of them bathe at dawn. They touch no jars before bathing. The Arabs do the same things.

The most shameful of the customs among the Babylonians is this: It is necessary for every local woman to sit in the sanctuary of Aphrodite once in life to "mingle" with a foreign man. But many do not deign to mingle with the others, thinking highly of themselves because of their wealth, and they set themselves before the sanctuary having arrived in covered chariots, with many a maidservant in tow. But the majority act thus: In the *temenos* of Aphrodite many women sit wearing a garland of string about their heads. Some come forward, others remain in the background. They have straight passages in all directions through the women, by which the foreigners passing through might make their selection. Once a woman sits there, she may not return home before someone of the foreigners tossing silver into her lap should mingle with her outside the sanctuary. And in tossing he must say thus: "I summon you by the goddess Mylitta." The Assyrians call Aphrodite Mylitta. The silver is of any amount, for it may not be rejected: This is not their sacred custom, for the money becomes sacred. The woman follows the first man who tossed her silver, nor may she reject anyone. When she should have mingled, having discharged her obligation to the goddess, she leaves for home, and after this time you might not take her, offering gifts no matter how great. Those who are attractive and tall go home quickly, while those homely in these respects wait about a long time, being unable to fulfill the law; some among them wait about for three or four years. And in some areas of Cyprus the custom is similar to this.

Such are the customs of the Babylonians. But there are three tribes who eat no grain, but only fish, which they catch and dry in the sun. Then, they toss it onto a mortar and sieve it through a piece of muslin. And one may wish to eat it kneaded into cakes, another baked like some kind of bread.

STRABO *GEOGRAPHY* 16.1.20

In other respects they are like the Persians, but particular to them is that they establish three wise men as leaders of each tribe who, bringing forth the marriageable girls to the public, auction them off to the bridegrooms, always starting with the more valuable ones [brides]. In this way marriages are accomplished. And as often as they "mingle" with one another they stand apart from each other offering incense; at dawn they bathe before touching any vessel, for just as it is customary to bathe after coming from a corpse, it is nearly the same for sex. It is customary for all the Babylonian females, according to some oracle, to "mingle" with a foreigner, arriving before some Aphrodision along with many hand-maids and a retinue; each one is crowned with a cord. And he [the foreigner] having approached places upon her knees as much silver as is seemly, has sex with her going far from the *temenos*. The silver is considered sacred to Aphrodite. There are three magistracies, that of the former soldiers, that of the most honorable men, and that of the old men, besides the one established by the King. It is for this one to give away the maidens and to try cases of adultery. It is for the second to try cases of theft, and for the first, cases of violence. They place the sick out where three roads meet to question passers-by if anyone should know a cure for the illness, and no one is so vile of the passers-by that he, in such an encounter, does not suggest a cure, if he knows of any. Their clothing is a linen khiton, ankle-length, and a woolen apron, a white cloak, long hair, and sandals like slippers. They carry seals and canes, not plain, but decorated, having on it an apple or rose or lily or some such thing. They anoint themselves with sesame oil. They sing dirges for the dead as the Egyptians and many others; they bury them in honey, having smeared them with wax. There are three tribes without grain. They are marsh-dwellers and fish-eaters, living lives very like those in Gedrosia.

Similarities occur in issues of bride auction, sexual impurity and fumigation, sacred prostitution for Aphrodite, the public display of the sick, dress, burial rites, and the three tribes who live on fish rather then grain. The texts are so similar that it is impossible to believe that Strabo did not derive these things directly or indirectly from Herodotos.

ADDITIONAL SOURCES?

The problem, of course, lies in the issue of "directly or indirectly." There is considerable debate concerning to what extent Strabo made use of Herodotos, and how the geographer knew of the historian's work. D. Dueck has argued that there is no trace of Herodotean influence in Strabo.[4] L. Prandi argues that although there is considerable dependence in Strabo on Herodotos, the geographer only knew of the latter's work

---

[4] Dueck 2000: 46.

indirectly, through intermediary authors such as Ephoros, Eratosthenes, and Kallisthenes.[5] D. Ambaglio is more subtle in his approach. He argues that in many instances, especially with the briefer references, there is no real need to look for intermediary sources between the geographer and the historian; in such cases, the Strabonean material reflects the Herodotean.[6] Problems emerge when Strabo presents a variation on Herodotos, at which point issues of intermediary sources become relevant; "In realità, a misura che il campo di riferimento si allarga, si manifestano nella traditione straboniana di Erodoto approssimazione, fraintendimenti ed errori."[7] In such cases, Ambaglio sees influences from Posidonios, Ephoros, Demetrios of Skepsis, and Kallisthenes. O. Murray is entirely equivocal in his approach to this problem. Initially he claims that "the great majority of the references to Herodotus in Strabo come not from his own reading but through earlier writers, like Eratosthenes." Then, in the footnote to this statement, he adds, "there are a number of passages where Strabo reproduces information in Herodotus without mentioning his name: it is unlikely that all these passages come though an intermediary. The problem needs further investigation."[8] A final hypothesis is that Strabo used Herodotos just as the rest of us do: He read the original work of the historian and then considered his text in light of other historians, geographers, and ethnographers. In some instances he accepted Herodotos' data; in others, he rejected or corrected materials from the *Histories* with the works of the later authors.

Frequent references to Herodotos in Strabo suggest that the geographer was aware of the former's *Histories* (1.2.23, 1.2.29, 1.3.18, 3.2.14, 6.3.6, 7.3.8, 9.4.14, 10.1.10, 10.3.8, 10.3.21, 11.14.16, 12.1.3, 12.3.9, 12.8.5, 13.1.59, 13.2.4, 13.4.5, 13.4.7, 14.4.3), and there are enough condemning remarks to suggest that he had read the actual text (1.2.35, 1.3.22, 11.6.3, 12.3.21). In a very few instances Strabo specifically states that his references to Herodotos come through an intermediary source (e.g., 2.3.4, Herodotos via Posidonios). More often, he does not. In some cases, Strabo is clearly taking information from the *Histories* without citing any source (e.g., 10.3.8, 16.1.20). Such is the case with our tale of Babylonian sacred prostitution, making it quite difficult to determine how reliant Strabo was on Herodotos directly and what other sources

---

[5] Prandi 1988: *passim*, esp. 58.
[6] Ambaglio 1988: 75.
[7] *Ibid*: 75–76.
[8] Murray 1972: 210.

may have influenced his narrative. Nevertheless, there are details in the Assyrian *ethos* that make it evident that Strabo had at least one other work on Babylon at his disposal when writing up his text. Such details are the three wise men in charge of each tribe, the reference to "some oracle" in the section on sacred prostitution, the three tribunals as well as the one "appointed by the king," and finally the fact that the Babylonians use wax as well as honey in their burial rituals.

Clearly there was at least one other source for Strabo's Assyrian customs. Furthermore, I would argue that the second(ary) source had actually visited Babylon and given a narrative from personal autopsy. For the account as it appears in Strabo suggests that the second(ary) author did *not* witness a number of the details mentioned in the Herodotean narrative. The *ethos* as described in Strabo serves at least in part to merge conflicting reports, although whether this dovetailing was done by Strabo himself or the second(ary) author remains debatable.

DIFFERENCES IN DETAILS

Two stylistic details are of considerable importance in comparing the Strabonean account with the Herodotean. To begin, quite simply, Strabo's is shorter, giving far fewer details than his fifth-century predecessor's. Furthermore, Strabo's account is chronologically flat. For the *ethos* section conjugated verbs are in the present tense, as are the majority of infinitives and participles. Aorist participles (e.g., *katatheis*) show aspect, but not tense. There is one perfect tense verb. As such, there is no distinction between the customs as they existed in Herodotos' time, the second(ary) source's time, and Strabo's own day. Furthermore, and perhaps more importantly, there is no sense of temporality to the *ethoi* themselves. This manifests in two ways. On the one hand, there is no sequence of events to the customs or rites recorded – actions happen, but not necessarily in a specific or interdependent order. On the other hand, there is no sense of the customs themselves changing over time, marking perhaps the biggest distinction between Strabo and Herodotos.

The shortening and flattening of the Herodotean *nomoi* in the Strabonean *ethos* is well displayed in Strabo's version of the Babylonian marriage auction. Herodotos is quite specific about this practice. *Once a year* the girls are gathered together; they are auctioned off *starting* with the most beautiful and *proceeding* to the ugly ones. Different pricing accompanied each girl. *Once* a guarantee of marriage was rendered, *then* the couple went home. *If, in the future*, they did not get along, a refund was possible. However, this practice *had since* expired, and *now* all the poor Babylonian families prostitute their daughters. By contrast, Strabo recounts how the three wisest men of each tribe auction off the marriageable girls (later restated as "giving the maidens" *parthenous ekdidonai*), always starting with the more valuable. Later, Strabo informs us that the same elders who auction off the maidens are also responsible for trying issues of adultery. There is no mention either of the beauty scale or of the price scale, nor of the required guarantees, the laws, or the potential refunds. Most especially, there is no mention of the fact that this practice ceased to exist and was replaced at the lower levels of society with prostitution.

Something similar happens when we consider the two accounts of sacred prostitution. Herodotos informs us that all the Babylonian *gynaikes*, *once* in their lives, must undergo this ritual. The rich act one way, the majority in another. Each woman must wait at the sanctuary – with roads running among them – until a foreigner picks her, throwing her money and summoning her with a specific formula. *Then* they go away from the sanctuary to fulfill the ritual, *after* which she goes home and is *henceforth* immune from adulterous seduction. Strabo gives no sense of which females in the Babylonian population undergo this rite, he merely calls them *Babyloniais*. He only copies Herodotos' description of the wealthier women, and while the females go to *some* Aphrodision, there is no mention of waiting around or of roads. In some order a foreigner approaches the female, gives her a respectable amount of silver, "is with" her, and leads her far away from the sanctuary. H. L. Jones opted to translate this latter part as "The man who approaches the woman takes her far away from the sacred precinct, places a fair amount of money upon her lap, and then has intercourse with her."[9] In the absence of chronological indicators, though, and following the order of the verbs given, we are left with an approach, giving of silver, "being with," and leading from the sanctuary. This would seem to suggest that all aspects of the ritual, contrary to Herodotos, occur at the sanctuary itself, and that the foreigner only "leads away" the women once the rite is complete (i.e., she has completed her duty and may now go home). What does appear in Strabo that is missing in Herodotos is the fact that these women engage in this ritual "because of some oracle" (*kata ti logion*).

The differences in the two accounts of Babylonian sacred prostitution presented in Herodotos and Strabo have been interpreted in different

---

[9] Jones 1983 [1930]:227.

ways. F. Jacobs believed that although Herodotos was the originator, Strabo made use of at least one later, additional, intermediary source when composing his own version of the custom.[10] L. Kurke, interpreting the Herodotean accounts of both bride auction and sacred prostitution as symbolic of regulated versus unregulated economies, suggests that Strabo is attempting to soften the harsh realities presented in Herodotos. "These changes combine to make Herodotus's narrative more palatable, for part of its disturbing effect inheres in the painfully inequitable distribution of resources (both money and looks) on the women's side, *and* the lack of correlation between the indiscriminate amount of money and the qualities of the woman it buys."[11] That Strabo argues that the foreigner offers the women "however much [money] as is seemly" suggests to Kurke that there is actually a standard price, not an indiscriminate and arbitrary amount of money offered to the woman and goddess.

By contrast, B. MacLachlan argues that differences between the two accounts derive from the fact that both Herodotos and Strabo took their accounts from an unknown, independent, possibly earlier author. "[Strabo] does not discuss the status of the woman, but adds a couple of minor details in his description which indicated that he did not simply copy Herodotos but took the information from an independent source or from an earlier one upon which Herodotos also drew."[12] Both Herodotos and Strabo then picked and chose which aspects of this initial account to present in their works.

Jacobs's hypothesis is the most likely. As stated above, we know that Strabo must have relied on at least one additional source for his Assyrian *ethos* besides Herodotos; so much is evident in the data that do not come from Herodotos, such as the three tribunals. Furthermore, as stated above, I believe that whoever this second(ary) source was had actually been to Babylon himself and was thus an eyewitness to what he recorded. Many of the differences between the Herodotean and Strabonean accounts, other than simply length, might be attributed to an attempt on the part of either Strabo or his source to mesh Herodotos' account with an autopsy that did not support Herodotos.

For that which concerns sacred prostitution, Strabo's narrative presents the data as given by Herodotos in such a way as to account for the fact that no one actually sees the ritual taking place (an issue often mentioned by

[10] Jacobs 1837 [1811]: 27.
[11] Kurke 1999: 232.
[12] MacLachlan 1992: 149–150.

Assyriologists when confronting this tale – see Chapter 2). What should be conspicuous in the Herodotean account? Scores if not hundreds of women of marriageable age sitting around a temple/sanctuary with roads among them, all waiting for foreign men walking up and down these roads to toss them silver and to take them away for sex. Some of these women have entourages, some sit on the ground, some for years.

These visible aspects are removed in Strabo. The nature of the women themselves is hidden: we are given no nouns such as *gynaikes, parthenoi*, or even *korai*, we are simply given the substantive adjective *Babyloniais* with no clear identification of the females involved. Nor do we know where they are; Strabo places them at *some* (*ti*) Aphrodision. We have no knowledge of which temple or sanctuary, or where it necessarily is. As a result, we should not be overly surprised when we do not see the expected females around a specific temple in the city of Babylon. The eyewitness apparently did see wealthy women with great retinues going about the city, including the various temples, and these women were apparently adorned with "cords." So much conforms to the account of Herodotos and is readily presented. The roads, however, are missing, as is the summoning formula. The order of the exchange ritual is also not clearly presented. In some order a foreign man approaches, leads away, dedicates silver, and "is with" the woman in question. If we are to take the actions in just that order, it would also explain why this ritual, so carefully recorded in Herodotos, is not actually visible in the city of Babylon: the donation of money and the implied sexual activity take place "far away." And "far away" from an unspecified initial sanctuary at that.

A similar process of correction and accommodation might be seen in Strabo's account of the so-called marriage auction. One must recall that, according to Herodotos, the marriage auction no longer took place in his time. Nevertheless, Strabo records the custom as if it were still occurring. Once again, the Strabonian account is much shorter than that of Herodotos, containing no information concerning the ranking according to beauty (Strabo merely says *entimoteras* – "more valuable"), the raising or lowering of price depending on beauty, the need to pay men to take the ugly girls, the guarantees of marriage and the legal prescriptions involved. The additional information provided by Strabo is that the brides are auctioned off by a tribunal of three elders, who are also responsible for trying cases of adultery.

It appears likely that Strabo is here recording some actual legal aspects of Mesopotamian marriages as practiced in the late first millennium and conflating them with, or perhaps interpreting them through the lens of, Herodotos. According to M. T. Roth, it was not uncommon to officialize marriage through contract in Persian through Seleukid Mesopotamia, most especially in instances where money or property was being exchanged as dowry or brideprice. A scribe would be required to draw up this contract, in which it was recorded that the bride's agent (usually a family member of the bride, or possibly even the bride herself) "gave the woman in marriage" (*nadanu ana aššuti*).[13] The Akkadian *nadanu* reflects Strabo's use of the word *ekdidonai* ("to give") later in the *ethos* when referring to the marriage auction. Furthermore, ten of the contracts studied by Roth had clauses pertaining to adultery (although all dating from earlier periods). Thus the scribe drawing up the marriage contract is also involved in issues pertaining to the future wife's possible infidelity. Finally, Roth notes that the most consistent feature of all the marriage contracts is the issue of money: "the transmission of wealth is the most frequent and probably the most important consideration in the documents we call marriage agreements."[14] Although not all of the brides with written contractual marriage agreements were necessarily wealthy, there is a focus on property and exchange in the contracts. This might accord with Strabo's statement that the "auctioneers" always began with the "most valuable" brides.

Contractual marriages were still to be seen in Mesopotamia, a fact no doubt noticed by Strabo's second(ary) source. The wide-scale prostitution of the poor as recounted by Herodotos, by contrast, was not. Thus Strabo resurrects the notion of bride-auction, but not as Herodotos described it. In Strabo, tribal elders "auction off" the brides to the bridegrooms in order to accomplish marriages. Later, Strabo alters his vocabulary, claiming that these men merely "give away" the brides, much as is recorded in the indigenous Mesopotamian marriage documents. There being no ranging of brides by beauty, or need to pay men to take the ugly girls, these details are absent from Strabo. Once again, it appears that Herodotos' accounts are used as some kind of framework upon which to build an account of Mesopotamian moeurs. But these accounts are heavily corrected to conform to what one actually *sees* in Mesopotamia.[15]

---

[13] Roth 1989: 3.

[14] *Ibid*: 28.

[15] One might just as easily imagine sickly beggars on the roads; thus the Herodotean/Strabonian account of the sick placed in public places to receive advice on healing. Likewise, the accounts of three tribes living off of fish rather then grain suggests the southern marsh Arabs and their heavily aquatic lifestyle. See also Reade 1997: *passim* on this aspect of Mesopotamian life.

One final note of possible interest in this account is Strabo's tendency to adjust his vocabulary when discussing his "corrections" to the Herodotean narratives. As noted above, when Strabo first mentions the auctioning off of brides, he uses the verb *apokērussô*. Later, he claims that the tribal elders *ekdidomi* the *parthenoi*. Likewise, in his account of the sacred prostitution ritual, Strabo first claims that all the *Babyloniai mignysthai* with a foreigner, following Herodotos. Later, he claims that the foreigner simply *synginetai* ("is with") with the female. This "toning down" of the vocabulary, starting with Herodotean terminology but then replacing it with more neutral words, may indicate Strabo's concern that the original vocabulary did not actually reflect the reality as perceived by a different tourist to Mesopotamia.

Who was this second(ary) source for the Babylonian *nomoi*? The most likely candidate is Kallisthenes, as suggested by Prandi.[16] Much of Strabo's Mesopotamian material incorporates references to Alexander's excursion there, and thus historiographies and geographies from the days of the Macedonian hegemony appear to have been primary sources for the Roman-age geographer. As stated above, the treatment of specific details in the Assyrian *ethos* suggests that the second(ary) author was an eyewitness of Mesopotamian, or at least Babylonian, customs, and we know that Kallisthenes traveled to Mesopotamia with Alexander's retinue. Of particular importance is the way that Kallisthenes himself seems to have treated Herodotos' materials. As both Ambaglio and especially Prandi note, Kallisthenes was prone to editing and adding on to Herodotos' narratives without specifically mentioning that he was altering any text. So Prandi notes, "Delle tre notizie che gli attribuisce, però due si trovano nelle Storie mentre la terza, oltretutto poco corretta geograficammente, non presenta corrispondenza alcuna e sembra appartenere semmai a Callistene che senza dubbio <<seguiva Erodoto>> ma probabilmente lo <<aggiornava>>."[17] Likewise, Ambaglio admits that when discussing the Araxes River, "appare l'ipotesi che Strabone abbia fatto passare per Erodoteo, in perfetta buona fede, un dato che Callistene aveva aggiunto alla sua citazione di consenso nei confronti dello storico di Alicarnasso."[18] Strabo's account of Babylonian sacred prostitution, then, ultimately derives from Herodotos, but probably with some editing on the part of Kallisthenes, from whom Strabo probably took the account.

---

[16] Prandi 1988: 58.
[17] *Ibid*: 63; see also Prandi 1985: 82–93 for the Herodotos–Kallisthenes–Strabo triad.
[18] Ambaglio 1988: 78.

In the end, Strabo's account of sacred prostitution does not provide good evidence for such a custom in Babylon. It is evident that the geographer's account is based primarily on Herodotos, whose own account of this practice as actual history was debunked in a previous chapter (Chapter 4). The differences present in Strabo's narrative do not indicate that there was an independent source corroborating Herodotos' account. Quite to the contrary, the majority of differences present in 16.1.20 seem apologetic, accounting for the fact that many of the details in Herodotos are not actually visible in Babylon. This is not only so for sacred prostitution, but also for the Herodotean construct of Babylonian bride auction.

8.6.20: CORINTH

The sanctuary of Aphrodite at Corinth was so rich that it had possessed more than a thousand hierodules, courtesans, whom both men and women used to dedicate to the goddess. The city was frequented and enriched by the multitudes who resorted there on account of these women. Masters of ships freely squandered all their money, and thus the proverb,
"Not for every man is the voyage to Corinth."

τό τε τῆς Ἀφροδίτης ἱερὸν οὕτω πλούσιον ὑπῆρξεν, ὥστε πλείους ἢ χιλίας ἱεροδούλους ἐκέκτητο ἑταίρας, ἃς ἀνετίθεσαν τῇ θεῷ καὶ ἄνδρες καὶ γυναῖκες. καὶ διὰ ταύτας οὖν πολυωφελεῖτο ἡ πόλις καὶ ἐπλουτίζετο· οἱ γὰρ ναύκληροι ῥᾳδίως ἐξανηλίσκοντο, καὶ διὰ τοῦτο ἡ παροιμία φησίν·
οὐ παντὸς ἀνδρὸς ἐς Κόρινθον ἔσθ' ὁ πλοῦς.

In many ways, Strabo's account of Corinthian *hetairai*, and his account of Corinth in general, is diametrically opposed to his narrative concerning Babylon. This is especially so in two major points: Strabo very clearly states that he traveled to Corinth himself, and thus was an eyewitness to what he saw there; and the geographer is quite explicit about the chronology of his observations. Nevertheless, as with the Babylonian account, Strabo here also relies on the works of earlier scholars when constructing his description of Corinth. Once again, then, as with Babylon, at least part of Strabo's understanding of Aphrodite's prostitutes in ancient Corinth might be attributed to a misreading of earlier sources. Additional complications emerge when we consider that Strabo added in to his account social and religious customs pertaining to his own time and culture.

Strabo begins his discussion of Corinth by informing the reader, at the end of 8.6.19, that he himself beheld a village from the peak of Acrocorinth: *kai hêmeis apo tou Akrokorinthou katôpteusamen to ktisma*, "And we saw the settlement from Acrocorinth." In 8.6.21 Strabo indicates that he perceived the circuit wall of the city upon the slopes of the hill. Likewise, P. W. Wallace has argued that the geographical organization of Strabo's Corinthian description appears to be based upon a bird's-eye view of the city from the top of the acropolis.[19] Unlike Babylon, then, Strabo offers a first-hand account of Corinth.

However, a first-hand account is really only viable in the present tense, so to speak. Strabo's presence on Acrocorinth in the first century CE allows the geographer no greater authority regarding the city's past, which is when Strabo places the city's practice of dedicating prostitutes to Aphrodite. This is presented in three ways. First there is the grammar of the passage itself. Unlike the Babylonian passage, Strabo is quite explicit about the past tense concerning the wealth of Aphrodite's temple. The temple *was* (*hupêrxen* – aorist) so wealthy that it *had* possessed (*ekektêto* – pluperfect) more than a thousand hierodules, whom men and women *used to* dedicate (*anetithesan* – imperfect). The use of the pluperfect especially emphasizes the past and noncontinuous nature of this practice.

Furthermore, later, in 8.6.21, Strabo makes reference to the contemporary (to him) temple of Aphrodite on Acrocorinth, which he describes as a *naidion*, or smallish temple. There are no references to the temple's current wealth or to any hierodules, *hetairai* or otherwise.

Finally, Strabo commences his description of Corinth with a contrast between the city's illustrious past and its "present." He begins 8.6.20 with the statement that Corinth was called "wealthy" because of its *emporion* or commerce, being well-placed at the isthmus of continental Greece. He then goes on to describe how dealing with this isthmus was far preferable to dealing with the Straits of Sicily and/or the sea beyond Malea, and thus, from ancient times, Corinth became wealthy on trade. Such wealth was then augmented by the Isthmian Games. The Bakkhiadai clan took advantage of this wealth in making themselves tyrants of the city, continuing into the reigns of Kypselos and his descendants. Strabo finishes his description of the city's wealth with his commentary on the temple of Aphrodite and its prostitutes. Section 8.6.21 then transfers to the city's present, narrating what Strabo himself saw (*kai autoi de eidomen*) after

[19] Wallace 1969: *passim*.

the Roman restoration of the city. The past-versus-present transition is presented subtly in an extended *men . . . de . . .* construction introducing both sections. Section 8.6.20 begins "*Ô de Korinthos aphneios* men *legetai dia to emporion.*" The *men* is not complimented by a *de*, and a second *men . . . de . . .* construction begins when Strabo discusses the city's two harbors. Section 8.6.21, however, begins "*tên* de *topothesian tês poleôs,*" with the *de* here picking up the *men* commencing Section 8.6.20. This extended *men . . . de . . .* construction creates a contrast between ancient Corinth and the "modern" city. Although it would seem most logical that the break between ancient and contemporary should be before and after the Roman destruction, Strabo's reference at the beginning of 8.6.21 to the late Classical and Hellenistic scholars Hieronymos and Eudoxos shows that this is not Strabo's reckoning. Nevertheless, the geographer is quite explicit that the prostitutes present on Acrocorinth were a thing of the past, not present at the site's little *naidion* now; thus, once again, Strabo was not an eyewitness of the custom he claims to describe.

Strabo's reference to Hieronymos and Eudoxos at the beginning of section 8.6.21 shows that he consulted alternate sources for his description and study of Corinth, a fact rendered all the more obvious by the geographer's discussion of the city's early history. As was the case with Babylon, who Strabo's sources were remains problematic – for example, Strabo does not credit any earlier authors with the accounts of the Bakkhiadid tyranny or the rise of Kypselos. Furthermore, his account of the latter rather contradicts at least one well-known account of this tyrant – that of Herodotos, who is quite insistent that the Kypselid dynasty only lasted two, not three, generations. (*Histories* 5.92ε: "Yourself and children, but not your children's children." "*autos kai paides, paidôn ge men ouketi paides.*").

HIERODOULEIA

One of the most important elements in this study of Strabo's Corinth and its cult of Aphrodite is the geographer's use of the word "hierodule." Technically, it means "sacred (*hieros/a*) slave (*doulos/doulê*)," and the term was present in the ancient Greek vocabulary in the Mycenaean Age, with references to *te-o-jo do-e-ra* and *te-o-jo do-e-ro* ("slave (f./m.) of the deity") in the Linear B tablets from Pylos.[20] However, the word "hierodoulos" as a technical term disappeared from the Greek cultic vocabulary and

[20] Hooker 1980: §268.

only reappeared in the third century BCE, first in Egypt and then in the eastern Hellenistic territories.[21] To refer to the ancient prostitutes of, for example, Pindar's Acrocorinth as hierodules is a blatant, although common, anachronism, seen not only in Strabo but far too frequently in modern scholarship, where the word is automatically taken to mean "sacred prostitute" (e.g., Wilamowitz, Gulick, van Groningen, Williams, Vanoyeke, Kurke, Dillon).[22]

What did Strabo understand by the word "hierodule"? It is only when he is discussing Corinth specifically, both in 8.6.20 and in 12.3.36, that he juxtaposes the term with the word *hetairai*, and thus, apparently, prostitution was *not* a normal aspect of its meaning. Although the word translates from the Greek directly as "sacred slave," this was not quite the definition of the term. There appears to have been three definitions of the word "*hierodoulos*" (m. and f.) in the ancient Greek lexicon, two deriving from ancient Egyptian and Anatolian traditions; the last referring to issues of manumission.

Egyptian

In ancient Egypt, where the word first appears, a hierodule from the Hellenistic period and beyond was a cult functionary self-dedicated to a specific deity or temple, who was exempt from certain aspects of taxation and corvée labor. So much is spelled out in a third-century BCE letter from Philadelphia (P.Cair.Zen 3.59451):

The hierodules of Boubastis, being keepers of the sacred cats,[23] send greetings to Zenon.

The King, acting fairly, sent forth this group [hierodules] throughout the land free from corvée labor, as did Apollonios [the governor] as well. We are [. . .]. Leontiskos, nevertheless, through compulsion sent us off to the harvest, and so that we might not disturb you, we completed the required service he asked of us.

But *now*, a *second* time, Leontiskos has sent us off to do the summer-reaping and make bricks. There are two of us. He keeps the brickmakers

---

[21] Debord 1972: 139; Börner 1960: 152 and 162.

[22] H. Meenee, in her 2007 article "Sacred Prostitutes and Temple Slaves: The 'Sexual Priestesses' of Aphrodite," typically defined hierodules as "young women dedicated to the Love Goddess in order to serve as her 'sexual priestesses.' They are more commonly known as sacred prostitutes."

[23] This is a really good place to insert your own puns and jokes (e.g., "How do you know that the hierodules of Boubastis were sacred prostitutes?" "Because they worked in the holy cat house.")

in Sôphtheis-Ameroïs and Bêsân; they are obliged to perform corvée labor for him as their "tax." You would be acting well, then, to do just as the king and Apollonios the governor had arranged and follow accordingly. Let us protest this matter in your absence. Farewell.[24]

An even earlier, damaged papyrus from Hibeh (1.35, c. 250 BCE), seems to provide similar evidence:

> Petosiris Pokouto and Onnophris Petêsios, hierodules of great Thuê-rios, and the rest of the hierodules greet Sonnophris.
>
> We, in good order, are finishing up the tribute collection to the sanc-tuary under your care; both now and previously we are under your protection. . . . [25]

Rather than actual slaves, or prostitutes, or second-class citizens of any kind, the hierodules appear to have been a somewhat privileged class, free from the corvée labor demanded of the secular population and protected by the king and local officials (at least ideally).

Hierodules were paid for their work, and in some instances at least this pay could be "taxed" back into the religious economy. Pay for sacred service is evident in a second-century papyrus sales receipt recording the finances of public games at Oxyrhyncus (P.Oxy 3.519):

Received from the exegete	42 drakhmai
from the Director	53 drakhmai, 1/2 obol
of which was spent for the revels of the Nile	20 drakhmai
Revels of the Deities	56 drakhmai
for the grooms	16 drakhmai
for the hierodules	14 drakhmai, 84 obols
for (πλου'. .) hierodules	20 drakhmai
for the herald	8 drakhmai
for the trumpeter	4 drakhmai
for the children of the best	6 obols
of the shakers (?)	6 obols
equaling 124 drakhmai and 96 obols.[26]	

That the hierodules could be "taxed" on their professions, whatever they were, for the sanctuaries seems to be implied in a frustratingly damaged

---

[24] Accessed via the Perseus Project. Emphases mine.
[25] Ibid.
[26] Grenfell and Hunt 1903: 254–255.

decree from Ptolemy VIII Euergetes II dating to 140/139 BCE concerning the revenues for a sanctuary of Aphrodite (P.Tebt. 1.6 = berkeley. apis.448):

> King Ptolemy and Queen Kleopatra his sister and Queen Kleopatra his wife send greetings to the generals, and garrison commanders and superintendents of the guards and garrison leaders and caretakers and household administrators and royal scribes and other royal administrators.
>
> The priests have written to us . . . the Fraternal Deities and the Benefactor Deities and the Ancestor-Loving Deities and the Manifest Deities and the Noble Deities and the Mother-Loving Deities and the Benefactor Deities about the sacred land . . . along with the dedicated land of the *kleroukhoi*, and the [moneys] from honors and prophecies and the scribes and liturgies – the revenues from all these have been declared for the use of the sanctuary, and . . . from the properties and those things according to decree by the . . . of these and of the associations in turns and of the hierodules from their trades and manufactures and paid wages, and the collected taxes from men and women in Alexandria and the country for treasuries and phialês and drinking cups, and from the so-called *aphrodisia* and in general those belonging to. . . . [27]

Hierodules also functioned in the secular world, dealing with economics not pertaining to the sanctuaries. One third-century papyrus from Oxyrhynkhitê is a leasing contract where one Eupolis, a private citizen of Athens, leased both land and its revenues to one Alexander son of Kratetos of Cyrênê and to Horos, hierodule of Thoêris.[28] Centuries later, under the Caesars, Satabous Petesoukhou, hierodule of Soukhos (Egyptian crocodile deity), and his brother Papous Petesoukhou filed a real-estate grievance concerning their millhouse in Soknopaios Nesos.[29]

Finally, that hierodules were considered to be particularly blessed appears at the end of a letter dated to 161 BCE addressed to one Sarapion and his subordinates concerning as-yet-undelivered rations of olive

[27] It is interesting to note that Debord (1982: 410, no. 133) believes that this papyrus refers indubitably to sacred prostitution, based, apparently, on the reference to hierodules and *aphrodisia* in the same text. Considering the extent to which hierodules are linked to other deities, such as Bast (above), and that even here they are placed in a separate category than the *aphrodisia*, such a hypothesis is strained at best.

[28] BGU 6.1263 and 1264, accessed via Perseus.

[29] CPR 15.1, access via Perseus.

oil and *kiki* to the royal household. After politely noting the nondelivered state of the goods, Ptolemy advises Sarapion

> ... to write to Mennides the superintendent to render to me both the issue of this year's olive oil ration and the ration of *kiki*, and may no one resist! May it be for you equal to those piously disposed before the deity, both the hierodules and all of those in the sanctuary, and may you receive in turn aphrodisian grace and form, good things and good luck in other matters. Farewell.[30]

A number of the concepts presented above endured into the Roman period. Hierodule "employment" by a specific deity and self-identification as a hierodule even in secular matters appeared above in the first-century papyrus from Soknopaios Nesos. The idea of a temple or sacred employee protected by secular authorities also appears in Josephus Flavius' *Antiquities of the Jews*. Here, in Chapter 11.5.1, when Xerxes permitted the Jews under the authority of Esdras to return to Jerusalem, he sent out letters to the regional governors commanding, among other things, that "you not lay any treacherous imposition or any tributes upon their priests or Levites or sacred singers or porters or hierodules[31] or scribes of the temple." Clearly, even here, a hierodule was understood to be a cult functionary – but not a priest – attached to the temple or sanctuary who was free from secular taxations and impositions.

Anatolian

A second definition of "hierodule," typical in Anatolia, pertained to individuals who were dedicated to the deities and who often were residents of sacred territories (*hiera khora*) where land, objects, and population legally belonged to one or more deities and were under the authority not of the king or other secular powers, but of a (high) priest.[32] Such sacred lands existed since Bronze Age times in Anatolia, where they formed an aspect of the Hittite religious economy.[33] Such sacred lands with their sacred economies and sacred residents (*hierodouloi*) continued to exist in Anatolia

---

[30] UPZ 1.36, accessed via Perseus.

[31] This is obviously Josephus' Greek translation of an originally Aramaic text. What is important here is that he considers the term hierodule to be the appropriate translation of one of the many cult functionaries mentioned. Probably not prostitutes. . . .

[32] Garlan 1988: 113.

[33] Debord 1982: 83–84.

into Roman times, with a plethora of evidence not only coming from Anatolia, but specifically from Strabo himself.

The best inscriptional evidence for the hierodule as a protected resident of sacred land under the authority of a priest appears in the first-century BCE inscription from Nimrud Dağ, composed by Antiokhos I of Commagne (IGLS 1.1). Here, ll. 171–189:

> It is not permissible for anyone, neither dynast, nor priest, nor magistrate, either to enslave these hierodules whom I consecrated to the deities and to my ancestors according to divine will, nor their children, nor their descendants, who belong to this class forever, nor to alienate them in any way, nor to mistreat them in any way, nor to extort corvée services from them, but may the priests take charge of them and may the kings and magistrates protect them.

Additional evidence comes copiously from Strabo. Concerning Albania he relates that (11.4.7) "The office of priest is held by the man who, after the king, is held in highest honor; he has charge of the sacred lands (*hieras khoras*), which are extensive and well-populated, and also of the hierodules, many of whom are subject to religious frenzy and utter prophecies." In 11.8.4 the geographer notes that a small city (*polisma*) sacred to Anaitis in Armenia "mostly belonged to the hierodules." Also in Armenia, by the town of Sebastê (12.3.31), "Has a sanctuary called of Mên Pharnkos, the county town of Ameria which has many hierodules and sacred land (*khôran hieran*); the ordained priest always reaps its fruit." Referring to Pontic Comana (Strabo's own familial homeland), Strabo narrates (12.3.34),

> when Pompey took over the authority, he appointed Arkhelaos priest and included within his boundaries, in addition to the sacred land, a territory of two *skhoinoi* (i.e., 60 *stadia*) in circuit and ordered the inhabitants to obey his rule. Now he was leader of these, and also master of the hierodules who lived in the city, except that he was not permitted to sell them. And even here the hierodules were no fewer in number than 6,000.

Before the time of Pompey, "Zela was not a city, but a sacred precinct of the Persian gods, and the priest was master of everything. It was inhabited by a multitude of hierodules, and by the priest, who had an abundance of resources; and the sacred territory as well as that of the priest was subject to him and his numerous attendants" (12.3.37). Finally, once upon a time in Phrygia, the town of Antiokheia near Pisidia "was a priesthood of one Mên Arkaios, which had a plethora of hierodules and sacred lands (*khoriôn hierôn*)" (12.8.14).[34]

As the evidence especially from 12.3.34 indicates, the hierodules formed a special, separate class within the sacred lands, and their hierodule status, to judge from the Nimrud Dağ inscription, was attained via dedication or descent. To be a hierodule, then, meant to be a consecrated individual or the descendant thereof under the authority of sacred powers, possibly living on consecrated land and, quite importantly, protected from abuse and enslavement. To be a hierodule was antithetical to secular enslavement.

Manumission

The idea of a hierodule as a free, protected individual seems to have brought about a further meaning for hierodule. Here, an individual, possibly a slave-owner, could dedicate a slave to a deity as a hierodule as a form of manumission, protection, and "donation." The evidence for this is primarily epigraphic.

A typical, although frustratingly undated inscription from Lycia relates that:

> Kloinizoas, son of Hermaios, grandson of Onobaros, son of Mnandrasis, liberated to the Meter Oreia as hierodules Akierous and Apionitheis, his own slaves (*paidiskas*). May Kloiniziriaos likewise belong to the goddess beside Opramis, daughter of Areios, and may it not be permitted for anyone to contest this in any way. If not, may he be accountable before the Meter Oreia and may he pay 500 sacred *drakhmas*.[35]

If the word *paidiskas* does in fact refer to Akierous and Apionitheis as slaves, then this dedication may be a form of sacral manumission whereby the girls are dedicated to the goddess as hierodules and remain under her continued protection to the tune of 500 sacred *drakhmas*. So much is also true for Kloiniziriaos and Opramis, who henceforth "belong to the goddess." A similar case appears in inscription SEG, II, 396, where "Aurelia Philipparin Eurodikês releases (*aphiêmi*) the slave (*paidiskên*) named Ariagnê to the goddess Artemis Gazôria as a hierodule. . . . "[36] The verb *aphiêmi* plus the term *paidiskê* indicates that manumission is at issue.

---

[34] All translations Jones 1917.
[35] Darmezin 1999: 163 #198.
[36] Papazoglou 1981: 177, no. 22.

In other instances, the issue of manumission is not quite as clear. An imperial inscription from Cappadocia (Ortaköy) reads:

> To Good Fortune.
> To the Great Goddess Anaitis
> Barzokhara, Phôtis
> and Theôn and Preima
> also [called] Garsê as hierodules
> inviolate in all ways
> for life, [continually] through their descendants
> Flavia Preima [gave]....[37]

A number of inscriptions indicate that the dedicated hierodule either served or maintained an on-going relationship with the deity or deities to whom s/he was "given." According to one imperial-age inscription from Pisidia (Kaynar Kalesi) (see also Strabo 12.8.14):

> To Ploutos and Korê, receptive deities, Poplius Aelius Minoukianus and Petronia Aemilia, daughter of Marcus, his spouse, graciously give according to a vow (*eukhên*) the girl named Hierodoulida, making her a hierodule, so as to serve the deities. And may no one undo this for her or for her children.[38]

A contemporary inscription from Pisidia reads:

> Claudia, daughter of Manos, daughter of Psekas
> hierodule of Ploutos and
> Korê dedicated a bronze statue
> to Korê from her own [resources] and Ia
> her daughter she made and
> her own children.[39]

The meaning of the final line – *kai ian tên thygatera epoiêse kai ta tekna autês* – has caused some difficulties. Bean suggested that the word "hierodule" is implied, and that Claudia was dedicating her own descendants as hierodules, thus dedicating/initiating them into a continuing, inherited sacral status that implied liberty and protection by the deity.[40] However, as shown in the two previous inscriptions, hierodule status is already understood to be inherited; a child born to a hierodule would presumably already be of that class, as is specified when hierodule status is granted. It

---

[37] Harper 1967: 193.
[38] Bean 1960: 47–49, #96.
[39] *Ibid*: #97.
[40] *Ibid*: 49.

is perhaps more likely that Claudia means that the bronze statue she made is of her daughter Ia and her grandchildren, dedicated to the goddess who protected them.

In later years especially individuals designated as hierodules could, in their own turn, dedicate children/slaves to the deities, in some instances as a form of sacral manumission. This not only reveals an on-going relationship with the receiving deities, but shows how wealthy hierodules could grow in their own right. This is most apparent in an inscription from the sanctuary of the Autochthonous Mother of the Gods in Leukopetra, Macedon. Here, in the year 343/459 CE:

> I, Theodotê, hierodule of the Autochthonous Mother of the Gods, speaking before Symphoros, donate a slave of mine named Zoikhê, aged 40 years, to the Autochthonous Mother of the Gods, and Zoikhê's child Theodas, aged 14 years, on the condition that they remain with me for the duration of my life. If someone should try to lay claim to these two bodies (*toutôn doio sômatôn*), he will give to the most holy treasury 1,000 *denarii* and to the goddess herself 1,000.[41]

The *paramonê* clause "on the condition that they remain with me for the duration of my life" is typical of this type of manumission (see below). Theodotê's manumission reflects that of Kloinizoas above: Terminology (*paramonê* clause, vocabulary such as "liberated") shows that manumission is at issue, this manumission is done under the auspices of a deity who protects the dedicated individual(s), and to whom anyone who would contest the manumission then owes a hefty, sacred sum of money.

The different definitions of "hierodule" have a number of points in common. In spite of the -*doulos* element, hierodules are free, either originally, or because they received hierodule-status as the result of a specific type of manumission, or because they are of hierodule descent. They are associated with deities, either because they work directly for them or their sanctuaries (Egypt), or because they are under religious authority as opposed to secular (Anatolia), and they are all personally protected by their gods. There is no one deity especially associated with *hierodouleia*, nor are hierodules of any specific profession within their status. Hierodules pay taxes and owe obedience to sacral and priestly powers, not secular.

How does all this pertain to the topic of this study? Some important points immediately present themselves. First, in spite of the most

---

[41] Petsas *et al.* 2000 174–175, #117.

commonly found definitions for "hierodule" in the research materials, there is in fact no reason to take this word as meaning "sacred prostitute," or, for that matter, "prostitute," or even necessarily "female."[42] In all our sources, hierodules, both male and female, are associated with a variety of deities, also male and female, with little reference outside of Egypt as to their professions. When professions are noted, they tend to be caretakers of sacred lands (as above in Anatolia), cult functionaries (e.g., cat-herders or tribute collectors), and one inscription from Lefkopetra relates that: "Maria, hierodule of the Mother of the Gods and lighter of lamps (lykhnaptria) dedicated to the goddess a child named Theodotê, whom I bought at birth (lit. ex haimatos) and reared."[43] Maria, a declared hierodule, had a job as a lamp-lighter.

In more focused fashion, there remains the question of how Strabo understood and intended the meaning of "hierodule" in the Corinthian context. Did Strabo understand the Corinthian hetairai to have been cult functionaries, as in Egypt? Were they under priestly authority, as in Anatolia? It is evident that Strabo understood these women to have been possessions of the sanctuary, as he associates them with the literal fortunes of the sanctuary ("the sanctuary was so wealthy that. . . ") and he specifically states that this sanctuary "owned" (ekektêto) the hierodules in question.

In all other instances, though, we must recall that Strabo's references to hierodules refer to consecrated and free individuals. Likewise, the epigraphic evidence in both Anatolia and later Macedon make it clear that the dedication of hierodules to any deity implied a degree of manumission, whereby the dedicated individual was no longer to be a slave but exclusively under divine authority. There is therefore a strong probability that what Strabo had in mind was not sacred prostitution, at least as we the modern audience understand it, but a Corinthian custom whereby men and women freed prostitute slaves into the authority of Aphrodite.

Was Strabo correct in this? This is the crux of the problem. Once again, we must keep in mind that Strabo was not a first-hand observer of the tradition he is recording – the Corinthian hierodules are distinctly a thing of the past. Specifically, they are a thing of the Greek past, and Strabo applies the terminology and concept of hierodules to a period when neither technically yet existed. The idea that the sanctuary of Aphrodite in Corinth "owned" hierodules then is a bit of an anachronism.

---

[42] Even Liddell, Scott, and Jones offer in their definition of ἱεροδοῦλος: "esp. of temple-courtesans at Corinth and elsewhere...."

[43] Petsas et al. 2000: 107–108, #39.

Furthermore, we must account for why Strabo not only thought that the Corinthian hierodules were exclusively female, in contrast to every-place else he finds them, but prostitutes. Two ideas come to mind.

One the one hand, of course, is the influence of Pindar and Khamaileon (see Chapter 6). Strabo was clearly well acquainted with Pindar, as he cites the poet numerous times over the course of his *Geography* (3.3.7, 3.5.6, 5.4.9, 6.2.3, 6.2.4, 7.7.1, 7.7.10, 9.2.12, 9.2.27, 9.3.6, 9.5.5, 10.3.13, 12.3.9, 13.4.6, 14.1.28, 14.2.10, 15.1.57, and a fragment from Book 7). There are no references to Khamaileon, and thus it is impossible to determine if Strabo consulted his particular commentaries on this poet, although copious references to Khamaileon in Athenaios show that his work remained accessible well into the third century CE. That Strabo might not wish to associate himself with a scholar as untrustworthy as Khamaileon is certainly possible, for, as van Groningen reminds us, he was hardly taken seriously even by the ancient commentators.[44]

It is in Khamaileon's misinterpretation of Pindar's Corinthian *skolion* (see Chapter 6), as preserved in Athenaios, that we read about the ancient Corinthian custom of "bringing courtesans to Aphrodite in fulfillment of prayers," much like the dedication of the hierodules to Ploutos and Korê *kata eukhên* above. Whether Khamaileon himself may have thought of the "bringing" of *hetairai* to Aphrodite as a type of manumission in the eastern tradition is impossible to judge: he was writing just when such sacral manumissions were making themselves prominent in the Greek world,[45] and it is possible that he invoked the new custom in the inter-pretation of an old poem. Strabo seems to have accepted this "custom," believing that several men and women, just like Xenophon, "brought" prostitutes to Aphrodite's sanctuary in Corinth (one again taking a less than literal translation of the word *also*). If Xenophon could donate one hundred at one shot (misunderstanding "hundred-limbed" in this case), then donations into the thousands were certainly likely. Of course, such "donations" in Pindar's age would not have been called hierodules – the term did not yet exist in Greece.

The use of Pindar/Khamaileon themselves may have been in answer to what was evidently another concern of Strabo's – the meaning behind the expression "Not for every man is the voyage to Corinth," the maxim with which he ends his narrative. The expression seems to have emerged from Middle Comedy, although the exact context is no longer known.

[44] Van Groningen 1956: 21.
[45] Late 5th–4th centuries BCE. Bömer 1960: 18–21.

In modern times Strabo's reference to the adage here, right next to his Corinthian hierodule-*hetairai*, has caused most people to see in the maxim a reference to the numerous, specifically sacred prostitutes of Corinth. But this was not the case in the ancient sources. As late as the tenth-century *Suda*, three alternatives were offered for the expression (O 924):

1) Because of the *hetairai* promised to Aphrodite by the Greeks during the Persian Wars;
2) or, because of the difficulty of navigation in the voyage to Corinth;
3) or, because there were many *hetairai* and only the wealthy could afford it.

Two of the explanations pertain to the infamous prostitutes of Corinth, and it is evident by the tenth century already that the Khamaileonic account had gone on to influence reception of Simonides' epigram as discussed in Chapter 6 – the author in explanation 1 claims that the Greeks promised Aphrodite *hetairai* during the Persian Invasions, combining Pindar's poem with Simonides'. That, as we have already seen, was a misreading of the evidence, and thus offers no actual evidence for Corinthian sacred prostitution. The third explanation in the *Suda* merely refers to the large number of prostitutes in Corinth. These courtesans were, as far as all the other data go, purely secular, and, more to the point, quite expensive. According to Sotion's third-century "The Horn of Amaltheia" as preserved in Aulus Gellius 1.8.4, the maxim applied quite specifically to the secular *hetaira* Lais, who charged an exorbitant amount for her company.

Other authors, such as Horace in his "Letter to Scaeva" (1.17) seemed to take the second interpretation of the maxim, seeing it as merely a reference to things which are difficult to accomplish:

> To perform great deeds and to show fellow citizens their enemies in chains reaches to Jupiter's throne and brings celestial honors. To have been acceptable to the great is not the least praise. But it is not for every man fated to go to Corinth. A wise fellow sits still for fear of failure; so be it then.

There is nothing in the expression "Not for every man is the voyage to Corinth" that pertains to sacred prostitution. In fact, with the exception of Strabo, no other ancient (or even Byzantine) author took this meaning. It was merely Strabo, in somewhat Khamaileonic fashion, who combined the data from Pindar with that of an old, Athenian adage, threw in some Anatolian religious praxis, and thus created an illusion of sacred prostitution.

12.3.36: PONTIC COMANA

The inhabitants [of Comana] are voluptuous in their mode of life. All their property is planted with vines, and there is a multitude of women who work with their bodies, most of whom are sacred (*hierai*). In a way the city is almost a little Corinth, for because of the plentitude of the courtesans, who were sacred (*hierai*) to Aphrodite, there were many who resided there and kept holiday in that place.

καὶ εἰσιν ἁβροδίαιτοι οἱ ἐνοικοῦντες, καὶ οἰνόφυτα τὰ κτήματα αὐτῶν ἐστι πάντα, καὶ πλῆθος γυναικῶν τῶν ἐργαζομένων ἀπὸ τοῦ σώματος, ὧν αἱ πλείους εἰσὶν ἱεραί. τρόπον γὰρ δή τινα μικρὰ Κόρινθος ἐστιν ἡ πόλις· καὶ γὰρ ἐκεῖ διὰ τὸ πλῆθος τῶν ἑταιρῶν, αἱ τῆς Ἀφροδίτης ἦσαν ἱεραί, πολύς ἦν ὁ ἐπιδημῶν καὶ ἐνεορτάζων τῷ τόπῳ.

This text should be the most convincing concerning sacred prostitution in antiquity, for here more than anyplace else we have what appears to be a first-hand account of the practice. Not only was Strabo himself from this region, his relatives were the high priests of Comana.[46] Unlike Corinth, the narrative is presented in the present tense. Notions of accusation, such as hypothesized by Oden, would not seem to apply here (see Chapter 1). The comparison with Corinth would, at first, seem to strengthen not only the argument for sacred prostitution in Comana, but for the same practice in Corinth as well. If there were sacred prostitution practiced in the ancient world, it would have been here.

Of course, this is assuming that Strabo is even discussing sacred prostitution, something which, as we recently discussed, he was not actually doing in his earlier discussion of Corinth. Once again, Strabo's meaning gets lost in translation. Whereas in Corinth untangling the geographer's meaning regarding the "sacred courtesans" of Aphrodite came down to understanding what he meant by "hierodule," so too now we must engage ourselves in what Strabo meant when he claimed that many of the women in Comana – those who worked "with their bodies" – were "sacred."

---

[46] Dueck 2000: 5.

Hiera

The word *hieros/hiera* (m. & f.) in Greek has as its simplest meaning "sacred" or "holy." When referring to humans, however, the word has a very particular set of implications starting in the late Classical period and continuing well into the Christian era. Specifically, the term *hiera* (or *hieros*) refers to a former slave freed via sacral manumission, or to a descendant of such a person.[47] In this way it duplicates to some extent the final meaning of hierodule discussed above – a slave dedicated to a deity and thus freed.

It is generally accepted that the type of sacral manumission that led to *hieros* status was a fictitious "sale" to a deity. The slave, who had acquired the necessary funds by his or her own labor but who was not legally able to use them to purchase freedom, gave the money to a sanctuary, which then gave this money to the slave owner to buy the slave on behalf of the deity.[48] Such is the understanding of numerous manumission records present in the epigraphy, especially numerous at the sanctuary of Pythian Apollo at Delphi. To give an example from the second century BCE,

> Krato, son of Mesateos...has sold to Pythian Apollo a female slave named Irenê, Armenian by race, for three minas of silver; and he has received the price in full. Guarantor: Nikarkhos, son of Erato, according as Irenê has entrusted the purchase to the god, to the end that she is free and not subject to seizure by anybody, doing whatever she may wish, and running off to whomever she may wish.[49]

The text indicates that Irenê "entrusted the purchase to the god," thus having the sanctuary buy her freedom on her behalf. Manumission is clearly at issue, as it is stated that "she is free and not subject to seizure." This makes it evident that we are not dealing with the sale of a slave to become temple property, but a legitimate manumission.

Slaves liberated in such a manner, or possibly simply through the good graces of an owner by way of a sanctuary, were given the appellation *hiera/hieros*. So much is evident on a first-century inscription from Hyampolis, which reads (in part),

> If someone should seize Eukrateia and lead her into slavery...in any way or under any pretext, may he pay 30 minas of silver to Artemis and Apollo, and may it be permitted to whoever wishes to come forward

---

[47] Debord 1972: 141; Sokolowski 1954: 174.
[48] Debord 1972: 136; Westermann 1945: 215.
[49] Westermann 1945: 216, with adaptions.

and seize up to a half of this (sum from him). And may Eukrateia be free (*eleuthera*) using the appellation sacred (*hiera*) to Artemis and Apollo, no longer belonging (*pothêkousa*) to anyone in any way.[50]

The subject of the inscription is to be free (*eleuthera*) and to be designated as sacred (*hiera*) to Artemis and Apollo. Furthermore, much as we saw with the hierodules, in the previous section, Eukrateia's freedom was under the protection of the deities. Anyone who would infringe upon her rights owed money to these gods.

Similar dedications appear throughout the Greco-Roman world in association with a number of different deities. To give but one example, a late third-century BCE dedication to Herakles-Kharops in Koronea reads,

> Gods, Good Fortune. In the arkhonship of Potamonos, the 25th of Thiouios, Asklapion the son of Stroton consecrated his own servant Soteiridas to be sacred (*hiaron*) and free (*eleutheron*) from this day going untouched.[51]

In some instances, the word *hieros/hiera* is replaced with a reference to the deity to whom the slave is being freed, the former slave thus being *tês theou* or *tou theou* or even *kurion einai tên theon*.[52] A dedication from 195 CE claims that Elpidia, the eventually liberated slave, "stays the remaining time with me and Dionysios for the time we live, and after our death no one will wield more power over her than the goddess."[53] A. F. Papazoglou concluded from such examples, "J'incline donc à penser que dans les actes que nous venons d'examiner l'expression τῆς θεου εἶναι serait équivalente à ἐλεύθερον εἶναι et que l'expression κύριον εἶναι τὴν θεόν signifieraient que la personne affranchie était placée sous la protection de la divinité."[54]

The extent to which the sacrally liberated slave remains bound to the sanctuary or the deity who liberated her/him varies. As we saw above, Irenê was free to do whatever and to go wherever she wished. Of course, she also does not bear the title "*hiera*." Several slaves were under a *paranomê* clause, whereby they continued serving their masters until the masters' death, at which point they were freed and divinely protected but no longer bound. A number of considerably later manumission inscriptions make reference to *tas ethimous hêmeras*, functionally the "fixed number

---

50 Darmezin 1999: 117–118, #153.
51 *Ibid*: 93–94, #128. See also *ibid*: 95–96, # 130. See also Debord 1982: 118–124.
52 Papazoglou 1981: 177; Sokolowski 1954: 174.
53 Petas et al. 2000: 111, #43; Papazoglou 1981: 175.
54 Papazoglou 1981: 177.

of days" when discussing the future obligations of sacrally manumitted slaves, sometimes with reference to the law of Tertullianus Aquila.[55] A dedicatory inscription from Leukopetra dating to the Roman period records that

> Petronia Lyka had inscribed (the gift of) my servant Zosimê without reserve to the Mother of the Gods. May no one have authority over her except the goddess. May she serve her all the fixed number of days. . . . [56]

Likewise:

> Aurelianê Kosmia, having the right of three offspring, gives gracefully to the Autochthonous Mother of the Gods a slave named Menoitas, the child of my slave Euphrosynê, whom I, since he was a baby, promised to the goddess, and for this I did not sell him nor give him away nor pledge him. May no one else have authority over this aforementioned slave except the goddess. He will serve the goddess the fixed number of days. . . . [57]

In some instances a slave was liberated to a deity for the purpose of serving as that deity's on-going cult functionary. A second-century BCE inscription from Kos, for example, relates that (SEG XIV, 529):

> Pythion dedicated the temenos [and] this sanctuary of Artemis . . . and Zeus Hikesios and the ancestral deities. Pythion son of Praxilas and the priestess dedicated . . . a young slave (*paidion*) named Makarinos free (*eleutheron*) [and] sacred to the goddess (*hieron tês theou*), so that he might care for the sanctuary and all the sacrificers, ministers, and servants, as many as are in the sanctuary may Makarinos care for them and for all the other matters both sacred and profane just as is written in the sacred register, and the other matters as given by Pythion and the priestess. . . .

To be *hiera*, then, especially in the age of Strabo, identified one as a manumitted slave under the protection of a deity to whom, possibly, some manner of service was required. The designation does not indicate temple ownership of the individual, or that the individual henceforth will earn money for the sanctuary or deity. Quite to the contrary, even those dedicated to the temples, such as Makarinos above, are designated "*eleutheros*."

What about the phrase "to work with the body" (*ergazomenôn apo tou sômatos*)? In some instances, of course, such a construction can refer to

---

[55] Petas et al. 2000: *passim*; Papazoglou 1981: *passim*.
[56] Petas et al. 2000: 97–98, #23.
[57] *Ibid*: 119–120, # 52. See *ibid*: 232 for a full listing of examples.

182

prostitution. Such seems to be the case in Apollodoros' *Against Neaira*, where the orator three times refers to Neaira as having "worked with her body," (59:20, 22, and 108). However, as J. Miner has noted, Apollodoros himself is careful to distinguish such terminology from direct references to prostitution *per se*, where he specifically employs words as *hetaira* or *pornê*. Furthermore, the first two references to Neaira "working with her body" pertain to a period in her life when she was considered to be too young to be a *hetaira*, when Apollodoros himself claims that she acted (59:24) "as though she were a *hetaira*" (*hôs an hetaira ousa*), but not actually one (yet).[58] If anything, Apollodoros seems to use this rather open-ended expression to suggest that Neaira was a "working girl" of some sort without directly defining her as a prostitute.

In other instances where there is no preconceived notion of prostitution, sacred or otherwise, involved, a similar construction is taken simply to mean "self-employed." So much is apparent in a third century BCE papyrus from Magdola, Egypt (P.Enteux 26):

Ktesikles greets King Ptolemy,

I am being wronged by Dionysios and my daughter Nikê. For having raised and reared and educated my daughter myself into young adulthood, and now that I am growing weak in body and eyesight, she is not doing any of the things for me which she should. I wanted to seek justice from her in Alexandria, entreating her, and in the 18th year she signed the King's oath to me in the sanctuary of Arsinoë Aktia to give me 20 drakhmai every month, working with her own body (*ergazomenê autêi tôi idiôi sômati*). And if she should go lax in this, she would either pay me 500 drakhmai or be held to the oath. . . .[59]

LSJ takes the expression *ergazomenê autêi tôi idiôi sômati* here simply to mean "earning her own living." Prostitution is not at issue.

To be a woman who "works with her body" and who is "sacred," then, does not imply a sacred prostitute, nor even a cult functionary. Rather, we might understand that these women lived in the sacred land of Comana, which in itself grants hierodule status, as self-employed individuals.[60]

It is, of course, entirely possible that the *hierai* of Comana were prostitutes, although we must note that Strabo, even in the midst of comparing

[58] Miner 2003: 21–22.
[59] Accessed via the Perseus Project.
[60] Several such dedications are recorded in the epigraphy of this goddess's sanctuary in Edessa, Macedonia. See Papageorgios 1900: *passim*.

them to the hierodules of Corinth, does not call them *hetairai*. Nevertheless, there is no direct relationship between the occupation of the women involved and their status as *hierai*. They are sacred. They may be prostitutes. But they are not specifically "sacred prostitutes," either as a class of workers in Strabo's time or according to the modern definitions.

6.2.6: ERYX

Also inhabited is Eryx, a lofty hill. It has an especially revered sanctuary of Aphrodite; in past times it was filled with women hierodules whom many of Sicily and elsewhere dedicated according to a vow. But now, just like the settlement itself, the sanctuary is depopulated and the plethora of sacred bodies has left.

Οἰκεῖται δὲ καὶ ὁ Ἔρυξ λόφος ὑψηλός, ἱερὸν ἔχων Ἀφροδίτης τιμώμενον διαφερόντως, ἱεροδούλων γυναικῶν πλῆρες τὸ παλαιόν, ἃς ἀνέθεσαν κατ᾽ εὐχὴν οἵ τ᾽ ἐκ τῆς Σικελίας καὶ ἔξωθεν πολλοί· νυνὶ δ᾽ ὥσπερ αὐτὴ ἡ κατοικία λειπανφρεῖ τὸ ἱερόν, καὶ τῶν ἱερῶν σωμάτων ἐκλέλοιπε τὸ πλῆθος.

Chronology and terminology are very much at issue here. Strabo is discussing two different times – the *to palaion* and *nuni* – and, potentially, two different categories of sacred persons – the hierodules and the *hiera sômata*.

The various definitions of "hierodule" continued to function in the Roman period. As shown above, the Anatolian model remained in place even under Pompey. The Egyptian variant, whereby a hierodule is a self-dedicated temple worker, shows up in the Roman epigraphy pertaining to the imported cults of Egyptian deities, especially Isis and Serapis. *IG* 14.1024, for example, dating to the Imperial period and discovered in the city of Rome itself, records

> For the salvation of the autocrat M. Aurelius Antonius of Sebastos Major, to the great god Helios-Sarapis, G. Abidios Trophimianos, a hierodule of the entire assembly of hierodules, in prayer dedicated this.

A longer dedication from Ostia (*IG* 14.914) is similar, and refers to a contingent of hierodules in conjunction with other cult functionaries, such as the sacred singers (*hierophônois*).

The "women hierodules" discussed by Strabo in regards to Eryx seem to have a lot in common with their Corinthian counterparts – both are groups of exclusively women dedicated by men and women/Sicilians and others. Nevertheless, the expression "according to a vow" calls to mind the dedication formulae mentioned above in regards to Anatolia, such as the dedication at Pisidia to Kore and Ploutos.

Hiera Sômata

What about Strabo's second term, the *hiera sômata*? Who and what were these individuals populating the sanctuary of Eryx? From Strabo's perspective, the term "sacred body" or "*tou theou sômata*" (and as well the *hieroi paides*) could function as a synonym for "hierodule" especially in the more occidental regions of Anatolia.[61] The epigraphic evidence from that region indicates that the *hiera sômata* worked for and came under the protection of the temples/deities. That "sacred bodies" worked for the temples is evident in a late third–early second-century BCE building inscription from Didyma, where the temple architect and general manager give a list of expenditures, including an *apologismos tôn gegenêmenôn dia tôn tou theou sômatôn*, "an account of the works done by the bodies of the god."[62] A contemporary inscription from Amyzon honors one Hermias Pankratou for, first among many things:

> ... having performed great services for the demos, and having taken charge of the sacred bodies (*tôn hierôn sômatôn*) carried off in the battle against King Antiokhos and bringing them back again at his own expense, and in other matters which the demos had services of him which he performed enthusiastically and in a timely manner, it seemed good to the demos to praise Hermias Pankratou.... [63]

Evidently the sacred bodies were a group desirable to steal and most honorable to return.

Strabo's Erycine *hiera sômata* might then simply be seen as a synonym for his previously mentioned hierodules. The only odd aspect of this reference is the exclusive sex of the hierodules; in other instances both males and females were dedicated to the various deities, both as hierodules and as *hierai/hieroi*. That male *hiera sômata* existed is evident in the Didyma passage quoted above. Furthermore, there remains the question of whether or not Strabo's Anatolian-based vocabulary (he was from Comana) adequately captures the realities of the Roman institution of so-called *hierodouleia*.

[61] Debord 1982: 87.
[62] Günther 1970: 238 and 240.
[63] Amyzon Inscription 5 (=Robert Amyzon Inscription no. 18), accessed via http://erga.packhum.org/inscriptions/

Fortunately, in the case of Eryx we have additional, first-hand evidence that paints a fuller picture of these individuals sacred to Erycine Aphrodite in the Roman period from an earlier author – Cicero. In his *Div. against Q. Caecilius*, his *Against Verres*, and his *Pro Aulus Cluentius* Cicero sheds considerable light on the status and functions of the Venerii – the "slaves" of Erycine Venus. The passage in Caecilius is at once the most familiar and confusing, ultimately revealing the differences in sacred slavery as it pertained to the Roman west.[64] According to Cicero (17.55–56),

> There is a certain woman, Agonis of Lilybaeum, a *liberta* of Venus Erycina, who was quite well-to-do and wealthy before this man was quaestor. An admiral of Antonius abducted some musician-slaves from her in a violent, insulting manner, whom he said he wanted to use in the navy. Then, as is the custom of those of Venus (*Venerorum*) and those who have liberated themselves from Venus, she invoked religion upon the commander in the name of Venus; she said that both she and hers belonged to Venus. When this was reported to quaestor Caecilius – that best and most just of men! – he commanded that Agonis be called to him. Immediately he appointed a commission [to see] "If it appeared that she had said that she and hers belonged to Venus." The justices judged that it was surely so, nor was there indeed any doubt that she had said this. Then the cad [Caecilius] took possession of the woman's goods, sentenced her into servitude to Venus, then sold her goods and pocketed the money. And so because Agonis wanted to retain a little property by the name of Venus and religiosity, she lost all her fortunes and liberty by the outrage of this cad! Verres later came to Lilybaeum, heard the matter, annulled the judgment, and bade the quaestor to count up and pay back all the money he got for selling Agonis's goods.

The notion of divine protection is strongly reminiscent of what we have seen in the Hellenized east. Agonis, a former slave of Erycine Venus (*liberta Veneris Erycinae*) still claims that both she and her household are under the goddess's protection. And well she might, for this protected status is also recognized and respected by the Sicilian government (for the most part), Cicero, and presumably his audience.

---

[64] I distinguish here between an Anatolian/Greek tradition and a Roman one, contrary to Eppers and Heinen, who see a difference between a Greco-Roman *hierodouleia* and the Erycine/Oriental type complete with nuances of sacred prostitution. "Daß wir auf dem Eryx die orientalische und nicht die rein griechische Form der Hierodulie vor uns haben, wird durch den zugrundeliegended Astarte-Kult und durch die dort wahrscheinlich betriebene Tempelprostitution nahegelegt." (Eppers and Heinen 1984: 228)

It must be noted, though, that the evidence from Eryx actually presents two separate categories of what might be termed in Greek hierodules: those who are free (as with the manumissions seen above) and those who still belonged to the goddess – "*omnium Veneriorum et eorum qui a Venere se liberaverunt*," "all those of Venus and of those who have liberated themselves from Venus." In contrast to the eastern tradition, in the Roman tradition it would appear that sacred slaves were the equivalent of state-owned slaves, with the temple as opposed to the government having ultimate authority over them. This is made clear in two additional passages from Cicero. In his *Against Verres* II, 38.86 Cicero, complaining about Verres's abuses of power and nonstandard use of resources, mentions that when Verres was fleecing the people of Tissa:

> The collector you sent to deal with them was Diognetus – a man of Venus (*Venerium*). A new style of tax-farming – why are the public slaves (*servi publicani*) here in Rome not taking up tax-farming as well through this fellow?

Cicero equates the man of Venus – Diognetus – to a *servus publicanus*, a public slave. That those belonging to deities were not considered to be free as were their eastern cognates is also evident in the cult of another deity – Mars of Larinum. In his *Defense of Cluentius* Cicero discusses a political power-play in this town pertaining to the Martiales – "those of Mars" (15.43):

> In Larinum there are certain men called Martiales, public ministers (*ministri publici*) of Mars and consecrated to this god by the ancient institutions and religious ordinances of Larinum. There was quite a large number of them, and as well, just as the case in Sicily with the many Venerii, so too these men of Larinum were reckoned to be in the *familia* of Mars. But quickly Oppianicus began to demand that these men be free and Roman citizens.

The Martiales, who are likened to the Sicilian Venerii, are neither free nor citizens. Furthermore, they are reckoned to be in the *familia* of Mars. To be in a Roman-style *familia* is not to be a member of the blood clan, a concept better expressed by the word *gens*, but to be a member of a household, including the status of household slave.[65] The Venerii, like

---

[65] Lewis [1891] 1993: 315. "*The slaves in a household, a household establishment, family servants, domestics.*"

the Martiales, then, were slaves belonging to a deity, and thus the temple, but otherwise likened to the state *servi publicani*.

It is easy to understand how the sacred *servi* would be under the protection of their patron deities. However, as stated in Cicero's anecdote about Agonis, she was a *former* Veneria, a *liberta* of Venus Erycina. Nevertheless, she claimed that both she and her own household still fell under the goddess's protection. Thus two classes of sacred slaves, one actual slaves, one freedpersons, but equally under divine protection.

This apparent paradox might be resolved if we consider that manumission from a deity (rather than through a deity as we saw in the east) in Rome functioned similarly to manumission from a human owner. In the words of W. L. Westermann:

> When a slave was manumitted, as a freedman he moved into a position similar to that of a client in the family organization. His former *dominus* became his *patronus*. The *pater familias* had controlled the work services and the movements of his slaves. Also the clients of his household were indirectly affected in their freedom to move by the custom of salutation of the *patronus* at his place of residence at fixed intervals. Since the freedman now rose out of the level of his former servile domination into the range of the patronal domination of the clients it was an easy shift of the control over his right of movement from the old *dominica potestas* to the patronal authority which the head of the household maintained over his clientage. . . . Both the reverent obedience and the labor services were to endure throughout the life expectancy of the freedman.[66]

In this way, even though the former Veneria (or Martialis) was technically now a *liberta*, she remained to some extent within the *famila* of Venus, acquiring the goddess's protection not only for herself, but also for her own household *familia* who might be called upon to help in the service of the deity.[67]

If we might accept that Cicero's Venerii were the Latin "translation" of Strabo's hierodules and *hiera sômata*, we must question Strabo's understanding of the Sicilian practice. For, once again, Strabo claimed that the hierodules (and presumably the *hiera sômata*?) were female. It is

---

[66] Westermann 1945: 220–221.

[67] Reference to continued bonds between a freed slave and a former owner appear in Valerius Maximus 2.6.7, where he notes that a freed slave who cheats his master three times might be reenslaved to that master.

very clear from the Roman evidence, however, that the Venerii of Eryx were not exclusively female. To give a quick summary of the various uses and abuses of these Venerii as enacted by Verres and condemned by Cicero in *Verres II*,

> They acted as provincial police either directly under the governor or indirectly under his agents (3, 61; 74; 89; 105; 143; 200; 228). They made arrests and executed not only the sentences of the governor's court (2, 92–93) but also, it would seem, the decisions of the tithe contractors (ibid., 3, 50); ran errands for the governor and carried out his commands that were not of a judicial nature (3, 55; 4, 32); took charge of the moneys and goods he ordered sequestered (3, 183; 4, 104); acted as bodyguard to his satellites (3, 65); were the beneficiaries of donations forced upon the cities by the governor (3, 143; 5, 141); collected the offerings, dues and emoluments accruing to the temple of their goddess (2, 92–93).[68]

It may be my own deeply rooted sexism showing, but I have a terrible time imagining that these functionaries were female, especially the bodyguards (although I suppose having sacred prostitutes as police, tax collectors, and bodyguards might have contributed significantly to local feelings of good-will toward the Romans...). While some of the Venerii, and thus the *hiera sômata*, were certainly female, as is evidenced by Agonis, many were also male.[69]

How might we understand Strabo's "mistake"? First, we must remember that by the time of Strabo's writing the "plethora of sacred bodies had left." Strabo never actually saw any of these *hiera sômata*, and thus he was writing based on tradition. Furthermore, it is possible that Strabo allowed his knowledge of the Corinthian custom to color his understanding of the Erycinian. In both instances, both set definitively in the past, Strabo understood that the general populace dedicated hierodules to Aphrodite. In both instances, the sanctuary itself was famous for its wealth in times of old (see below). It is possible, then, that Strabo's "knowledge" of Corinth colored his view of Eryx, claiming that only female hierodules (but **not** *hetairai*!) were originally associated with the sanctuary.

As Strabo seems to have understood it, the temple of Aphrodite at Eryx was once populated by a number of female hierodules. Unlike Cicero, he

---

[68] Scramuzza 1936: 326–327, adapted.
[69] For additional inscriptional evidence for servi Veneris outside of Eryx, see Schindler 1998: 194.

was not entirely specific about whether the temple directly owned the hierodules; he merely related that in olden times the temple was "filled with" hierodules, and later, when the going got tough, the sacred bodies left. This stands in contrast with Cicero, who relates that the temple did in fact own Venerii, both female *and* male.

In neither the Strabonic nor the Ciceronian accounts is there any evidence that would suggest that the normal service activity of the hierodules for the temple was sacred prostitution, either for the males or for the females, just as there is no suggestion in the literature that the Martiales, who are compared to the Venerii, are prostitutes for Mars. Nevertheless, the "sacred bodies" are often taken to be sacred prostitutes, the descendants of the female hierodules of earlier times who are also, of course, understood to have been sacred prostitutes.[70] Furthermore, their sacred meretricious profession is generally traced back to the early Phoenician/Punic habitation of the site. The sacred prostitutes of Erycine Aphrodite are a holdover from the sacred prostitutes of Erycine Aštart.[71] As with Corinth, then, sacred prostitution is understood to emerge from an initially Semitic influence.

This, of course, is hogwash. As discussed previously, there is no "Semitic" sacred prostitution (see Chapter 2). The word "hierodule" does not mean sacred prostitute and does not come into use in the Greek (much less Roman) vocabulary until the mid-3rd century BCE. Thucydides fails to mention the temple slaves when discussing the apparent wealth of that sanctuary of Aphrodite of Eryx in 6.46.7–11 of his *Peloponnesian War.*

> And leading them to the sanctuary of Aphrodite in Eryx they showed them the dedications, phiales and wine jugs and incense burners and not an insignificant amount of other paraphernalia which, being silver, presented an appearance of much greater worth by far.

Although it is never safe to argue from negative evidence, the evidence from Thucydides strongly suggests that there were no "sacred slaves" of Erycine Aphrodite in the fifth century BCE, a point *after* the

---

[70] Strong 1997: 181–187; Bonnet 1996: 116–117; MacLachlan 1992: 157; Vanoyeke 1990: 29; Eppers and Heinen 1984: 228; Bömer 1960: 82 only claims that the earlier hierodules were "Tempelhetären," but that the later *hiera somata* belonged in a different category, no doubt due to the evidence of Cicero.

[71] Zucca 1988: 773 and 776; Eppers and Heinen 1984: 228. For more on the cult of Aštart at Eryx, see Bonnet 1996: 115–117.

Greeks had assumed political and cultural control of the island from the Carthaginians, as well as the cult of the Erycinian.[72] There can be no continuity, then, between the supposed sacred prostitutes of the cult of Erycine Aštart and those of Erycine Aphrodite or Venus.

Strabo's section 6.2.6 is not evidence for sacred prostitution in Sicily; it is a commentary on the women dedicated to a temple of Venus and how, in "modern" (for Strabo) times, the temple and town, having fallen on hard times, has fewer temple attendants – hierodules, *hiera sômata*, Venerii – than previously. Nothing indicates that the hierodules had prostitution as an aspect of their temple service, either for the males or the females.

17.1.46: THEBES, EGYPT

But for Zeus, whom they [the Theban Egyptians] honor most, a most beautiful maiden of most illustrious family serves as priestess, [girls] whom the Greeks call *pallades*; and she prostitutes herself, and has sex with whomever she wishes until the natural cleansing of her body; and after her cleansing she is given to a man; but before she is given, a rite of mourning is celebrated for her after the time of her prostitution.[73]

τῷ δὲ Διί, ὃν μάλιστα τιμῶσιν, εὐειδεστάτη καὶ γένους λαμπροτάτου παρθένος ἱερᾶται, ἃς καλοῦσιν οἱ Ἕλληνες παλλάδας– αὕτη δὲ καὶ παλλακεύει καὶ σύνεστιν οἷς βούλεται, μέχρις ἂν ἡ φυσικὴ γένηται κάθαρσις τοῦ σώματος– μετὰ δὲ τὴν κάθαρσιν δίδοται πρὸς ἄνδρα– πρὶν δὲ δοθῆναι, πένθος αὐτῆς ἄγεται μετὰ τὸν τῆς παλλακείας καιρόν.

As ever, what is of critical importance in understanding what is going on in this passage is vocabulary. Three words are of relevance regarding how this passage pertains to sacred prostitution – *pallados*, *pallakeuô* (and its related *pallakeias*), and *synestin*.

PALLAS AND PALLAKEUÔ

The word "*pallados*" is quickly followed by two variations on the word *pallakê* – *pallakeuei* and *pallakeias*. The overall effect, as it has been taken in

---

[72] Serrati 2000: 12; Bonnet 1996: 116.
[73] Translation by Jones 1982 [1932]: 125. My own translation below.

the scholarship, is that the *pallades* are some type of *pallakai*.[74] The word *pallakê/pallakis* being understood to mean "concubine," it has come to be accepted that these *pallades/pallakai/*concubines who "have sex with whomever they wish" served as priestesses to Zeus and were some manner of sacred prostitutes.[75]

However, it is more linguistically correct to read *palladas* as an accusative plural form of the Greek word *pallas, pallados*. When a proper noun, of course, this is an epithet of Athena. Otherwise, the word is defined as "maiden-priestess," possibly originally "virgin, maiden" or even just "girl" in *LSJ*, based partially on this passage in Strabo, the commentaries of Eustathius, and the fact that the word is simply the feminine form of the masculine *pallax* – "a youth."[76] There is no reason based on vocabulary *per se* to suggest that the *pallades* are concubines, much less priestess-concubines, much less sacred prostitutes. The definition "girl" in this instance seems a bit too vague considering the semiunique status these girls enjoyed according to Strabo, and thus it is perhaps better to use the more specific translation of "maiden priestess."

If these priestesses are not concubine-prostitutes, how must one understand Strabo's repeated use of variations of the word *pallakê/pallakeuô* in the passage? Perhaps Strabo himself felt that the term "*pallas*" was too vague, and he made repeated reference to the notion of *pallakeia* as a means to specifying the identity or function of this young priestess. How, then, did Strabo understand the title *pallakê*?

Liddell, Scott, and Jones clearly favored a sacro-sexual interpretation, giving the main definition as "concubine," putting "concubine for ritual purposes" as the first possible definition of παλλακίς/παλλακή in the *Greek–English Lexicon* (citing specifically this passage from Strabo), and "of ritual prostitution" at the end, referring to an inscription from Tralles discussed below.[77]

By contrast, in the middle of the last century it was suggested that in certain instances a *pallakê* might be some kind of prophetess. In the 1940s Karl Latte, in his articles "The Coming of the Pythia" and "Orakel," argued that the word *pallakê* referred to a woman who performed divination incorporating perceived sexual relations with a deity, such as

---

[74] See especially Jones 1982 [1932] : 124–125, who suggests that *palladas* is actually a defectively written *pallakidas*.

[75] See especially Ramsay 1883: 276–277; Robert 1970 [1937], 406; MacLachlan 1992, 151; and Strong 1997: 170–171 and 187–189.

[76] *LSJ* 1968 [1843]: 1293.

[77] *Ibid*.

presented in Herodotos 1.181–182.[78] While discussing the general topography and history of Babylon, the historian mentions,

> On the farthest tower is a large temple, within which lies a large couch, well decked-out, and a golden table beside it. There is no statue erected therein, nor does anyone of mankind pass the night there save one woman alone from the region, whomever the god chooses from all others, as say the Chaldeans, being priests of this god. These ones also say, although I do not think they speak credibly, that the god himself goes regularly to the temple and rests upon the couch, just as in Egyptian Thebes, where they have the same custom, so say the Egyptians (for indeed a woman lies there in the temple of Theban Zeus, and they say that it is not permitted for either of these women to have sex with men), and likewise in Lycian Patara for the prophetess of the god, when there is one – for there is not always an oracle present – when she is there, then she is shut up at night in the temple.

The understanding of the *pallakê* as a prophetess with possible sexual links to a deity was then adopted by A. Laumonier in his study of Carian religion, F. R. Walton in his entry "Prostitution" in the second edition of the *Oxford Classical Dictionary*, and F. B. Poljakov in his study of the inscriptions from Tralles and Nysa.[79]

There is, however, little reason to link the prophetesses mentioned by Herodotos with the cult title *pallakê* – the historian never calls them such himself. Latte's identification of this cult title with prophetesses had more to do with the perceived sexual component of the prophetesses' duties than any semantic connections between prophecy and *pallakeia*. More specifically for our purposes, Strabo, unlike Herodotos, does not liken his Theban *pallades* to oracular women in Babylon and Lycia. Furthermore, Strabo is quite clear about the youth and maidenhood of the girls in question; there is no reference to their being consorts for Zeus. It is unlikely that Strabo had a definition of theoretically sexual prophetesses in mind regarding the Egyptian *pallades*.

The Tralles Inscriptions

It is more likely that Strabo understood these girls to be simple cult functionaries, priestesses in the cult of Zeus. This is supported by two

---

[78] Latte 1940, 14–15; Latte 1968, 164.
[79] Laumonier 1958, 633; Walton 1970: 890; Poljakov 1989, 12.

data from Strabo's next-door neighbor Caria. These are a pair of second-century CE inscriptions from Tralles, Turkey.[80] The first reads

Ἀγαθῆι Τύχηι	Good Fortune
Λ.Αὐρελία Αἰ–	L. Aurelia Aimilia
μιλία, ἐκ προ–	from an ancestry of
γόνων παλλα–	*pallakides* and those
κίδων καὶ ἀνι–	with unwashed feet,
πτοπόδων, θυ–	daughter of L. Aur.
γάτηρ Λ.Αὐρ. Σε–	Secundus Se[i]us[81]
κούνδου Ση[–?]	having been a
ου, παλλακεύσα–	*pallakê* and
σα καὶ[82] κατὰ χρη–	according to an oracle
σμὸν	
Διί.	to Zeus.[83]

The second, quite similar, has

Μελτίνε Μοσχᾶ,	Meltine Moskha,
παλλακή, μητρὸς	*pallakê*, of the mother
δὲ Παυλείνης τῆς	Paulina, of
Οὐαλεριανοῦ Φιλ–	Valerianus Philtate,
τάτης, παλλακευ–	who was a *pallakê*
σάσης ἐπὶ τὸ ἑξῆς	consecutively during two
πενταετηρίσι β',	five-year periods,
ἀπὸ γένους τῶν	from an ancestry of
παλλακίδων, Διί.	*pallakides*. To Zeus.

That the word *pallakê* refers to a cult functionary is apparent in two aspects of the inscriptions: the use of the aorist participle form of the verb *pallakeuô* in both inscriptions, and the reference to the time Meltine's mother spent as a *pallakê* in the second inscription – "two consecutive five-year periods." In both inscriptions the verb *pallakeuô* appears in the aorist participle, either nominative in the case of Aurelia, or genitive

---

[80] Most recently see Poljakov 1989: nos. 6 and 7. Concerning the meaning of the word "*pallakê*" in these inscriptions, see Budin 2003 as *passim*.

[81] Robert 1970 [1937], 406 has [ι] (?)-. The family name Seius is attested in the Roman prosopography, possibly of Etruscan origin. See Schulze 1904, 93.

[82] Poljakov forgets to include the word καὶ here, but it is clearly visible on the inscription and is present in the publications of Ramsay and Robert.

[83] Zeus Larasios, to whom the city of Tralles was sacred. See Laumonier 1958, 505.

in the case of Paulina (being the mother of Meltine). In the Meltine inscription, Meltine refers to herself with the nominative *pallakê*, which might be understood as the equivalent of the present participle.

Use of the aorist participle refering to a sacred function is common in Greek-language inscriptions dating at least as far back as the late Classical period, and according to William H. D. Rouse, "Later, the number of these dedications increases so enormously, that it appears to become the regular thing that an official should make an offering on taking or leaving office."[84] In this instance, the use of the aorist participle implies that the functionary is leaving office.[85]

Parallels come from all over the Greek world well into Roman times. Rouse alone records the following references: ἀρχιεροθύτας (IGS I, 788); δαμιουργήσας (IGS I, 704); ἱεραρχήσας (Thebes IGS I, 2480); ἱερατεύσασα (Athens CIA iii, 94); ἐρητεύσας (Boiotia IGS I, 3097); ἱεροθυτήσας (Rhodes IGS I, 836); θευκολήσασαι (Aetolia IGS iii, 1.421); μολπαρχήσας (Amorgos, BCH xv, 597); ἀγγεῖον ὃ ὑδροφορήσασα ὑπόμνημα ἀνέθηκε (CIG 2855); and Ἀπόλλωνι Πυτίωι ἱαρατεύσας . . . (Itanos, *Mus. Ital.* iii, 588).[86]

The expression ἐπὶ τὸ ἑξῆς πενταετηρίσι β' denotes a 10-year period of activity, broken up into two units of five years each. This would be an awkward way to recount that Meltine's mother was a concubine for 10 years. If, however, a cultic function were held for four- or five-year intervals or annual events, such an expression would indicate how long or how many times Paulina held the cultic position. Because several cultic functions are temporary (one thinks immediately of the Arrhephoroi in Athens), a reference to "terms in office" suports the argument that the *pallakai* were cult functionaries.

These Carian *pallakai* were probably not celibate, at least not permanently, as the priesthood seems to have been passed down in the family (*ek progonon* or *apo genous*). It is possible, however, that a temporary state of celibacy may have been required during ritual periods, as with many Greek priesthoods.[87] This would argue against there being a sexual component to the priestess's ritual duties. Furthermore, if there were some sexual component to the priestess's role, this, according to the

---

[84] Rouse 1975: 260.
[85] *Ibid*: 265. Also "It is fair to assume that where the aorist participle is used, the offering has a direct reference to the office." *Ibid*.
[86] *Ibid*: 264–265, 272.
[87] Connelly 2007: 18.

comparanda offered by Herodotos above and the Egyptians materials below, was directed to the god exclusively, not to mortal, physical men. Finally, the fact that L. Aurelia Aimelia identifies her father by name argues against any prostitutional form of reproduction.

The reference to a defined period of service and the parallels to postofficial dedications suggest that the *pallakai* of the Tralles inscriptions were cult functionaries, although cult functionaries *not* to be defined as sacred prostitutes, as argued above. The fact that both Aurelia and Meltine make a point of noting their descendence from *pallakidôn* makes it clear that the position was honorable and, possibly, maintained within individual families, as were many Greek priest(ess)hoods.

There is evidence that in Anatolia there was a priestesshood dedicated to Zeus whose functionaries were entitled "*Pallakê.*" The word *pallakeuô* shows up in at least two different inscription referring to such a cult functionary's religious service. For Strabo, then, it is possible that the words *pallakeuei* and *pallakeia* mentioned in passage 17.1.46 refer not to prostitution, and not even to diviniation, but simply to a special kind of religious service offered to Zeus by females.

Egyptian Parallels

A final consideration in interpreting Strabo's choice of vocabulary is understanding how certain Egyptian cult titles translated linguistically and conceptually into a Greco-Roman understanding. Strabo was not the first to associate the vocabulary of *pallakeia* with the priestesshoods of Egypt. In his first-century BCE description of Egyptian Thebes, Diodorus Siculus mentioned the tombs wherein were buried the "concubines of Zeus" (*tas pallakidas tou Dios*; 1.47.1). The same terminology – *pallakidas*, the same city – Thebes, and the same deity – Amun–Zeus, appear here as in Strabo. Although none of the priestesshoods discussed below appear to be quite the direct cognates of Strabo's *pallades*, they all display elements that a Classical author could associate with *pallakeia*, and a few do appear to share significant details with Strabo's description.

It is most likely that Diodoros at least was writing about priestesses known as the "God's Wife of Amun," an office held by royal women at least as far back as the seventeenth Dynasty.[88] That such significant women as Queen Hatshepsut could hold this title would certainly also

---

[88] Robins 1993: 149–156; Robins 1985: 71.

justify Strabo's designation of "most illustrious family." The title "God's Wife of Amun" could easily be translated into the Greek language and cultural understanding as "Concubine of Zeus," as Zeus' actual wife was, of course, Hera. The title "God's Wife" may have implied some theoretical aspect of divine sexuality on the part of these women, although certainly not as sacred prostitutes. According to G. Robins,

> A second title 'god's hand,' which sometimes follows that of 'god's wife,' refers to the hand with which the creator god masturbated to produce the first divine pair, Shu and Tefnut. . . . Clearly, then, the titles 'god's wife' and 'god's hand' have sexual reference, but how this translated into temple cult is unknown. Nevertheless, we can conjecture that the holder was probably responsible for rituals meant to stimulate the god sexually, so that he would continually re-enact the original creation of the universe and thereby prevent the world from falling back into chaos.[89]

These extremely high-ranking priestesses certainly did not "prostitute themselves and have sex with whomever they wished," but were reserved for god and husband, and they had children within the familial context.[90] In later dynasties, it is possible that even this aspect of their lives changed, as political considerations caused later Pharaohs to impose celibacy upon some of these priestesses, who acquired their successors via adoption.[91]

The title conforms well to Diodorus' reference to *pallakidas tou Dios*, although the fact that these priestesses served well into adulthood and marriage strongly argues against seeing them in Strabo's description, where the girls in question only serve until the onset of adolescence. A second possibility is the Divine Votaress, another priestesshood held by the highest-ranking female members of ancient Egyptian royalty. Although in the Bronze Age holders of this office might be married (as was the wife of Ramses III), by the Libyan period the title was given to the adopted successor of the previously named Wife of Amun.[92] As such, it is possible that the title was associated with younger women, even girls.

A third, although far less probable, Egyptian cognate for the "concubines of Zeus" may be found in the *heneret* – the female musicians of the

---

[89] Robins 1993: 153.
[90] Teeter 1999: 25; Robins 1993: 152.
[91] Robins 1993: 153–155.
[92] Lesko 2002: "Royalty's Role" and "New Cultic Roles for Women in the First Millennium."

Egyptian temples. The confusion of the *heneret* with concubines is not rare. According to B. Lesko, even modern Egyptologists have identified these women, mistakenly, as "concubines of the god," probably in reference to their service to Amun in his role as ithyphallic fertility deity. As the role of these women was to please this god with their music and dancing, the assumption was that their service increased the god's fertility by way of divine sexual stimulation. Thus, the "stimulators" of the fertility god were, in a sense, his "concubines."

However, as Lesko also notes, the term *heneret* is consistent in its orthography and usage whether in the context of a god's cult, a goddess's, or even a funeral. Thus, these functionaries are not specifically associated with Amun's sexual life, and the translation "(divine) concubine" is not accurate.[93] Furthermore, Robins points out that the élite female cultic musicians served in the cults of both male and female deities, once again emphasizing the fact that the role of these women in relation to their deities was not specifically sexual.[94] And, once again, this cultic function was often held by older, married women and thus is not a good parallel for Strabo's *pallades*.

There are a number of reasons that Strabo would have referred to a class of Egyptian female cult functionaries as performing *pallakeia*, none of which necessarily entail a sexual component, much less a reference to prostitution. On the one hand there are the Carian women who functioned as *pallakai* to Zeus Larasios for series of 5-year service intervals. Strabo being a native of Anatolia, there is a good possibility that he was familiar with this term as a cultic title. On the other hand, there is the Greek translation of at least one Egyptian cult title as "concubine of Zeus," which Strabo may have combined with his knowledge of the Carian office title. In neither case is there any suggestion that any of these cultic *pallakai* were actively sexual in their duties. Quite to the contrary, all evidence concerning the Egyptian "God's Wife of Amun" or "Divine Votaress" suggests that she was either secularly married or officially celibate.

SYNEIMI

What, then, about the word *syneimi*? It is here typically taken as meaning "to have sexual relations with," although more generally the word simply

---

[93] *Ibid*: "New Kingdom."
[94] Robins 1993: 145.

means "to be with" (*syn* = with; *eimi* = to be), also taken as "to be engaged in." In fact, there are several variations of meaning for this term as presented in LSJ, only one of which, and a small entry at that, refers to sexual intercourse.[95] There is no good reason to assume that Strabo implied a sexual meaning for the word here, especially as he explicitly refers to the *pallades* in question as *parthenoi*. It is only if we are specifically looking for sacred prostitutes that we would assume the erotic connotations.

It is possible to offer a new, nonsexualized translation of passage 17.1.46:

> But for Zeus, whom they [the Thebans] honor most, a most beautiful maiden of most illustrious family serves as priestess, [girls] whom the Greeks call *pallades*; and she serves as a functionary and accompanies whomever/attends whatever [rites?] she wishes until the natural cleansing of her body; and after her cleansing she is given to a man/husband; but before she is given, a rite of mourning is celebrated for her after the time of her religious service.

Whatever cult functionaries Strabo intended, there is no reason to associate the Egyptian *pallades* with sacred prostitutes. None of the possible Egyptian referents were concubines or prostitutes, and there are Classical cult functionaries called *pallakai* who also cannot be shown to have been cultically sexual: It is only later commentators who mistakenly ascribe a sexual role to their functions.

11.14.16: ARMENIA

All the sacred things of the Persians both the Medes and the Armenians hold in reverence, but the Armenians especially revere those of Anaitis; and in various regions [temples?] are established, and especially in Akilisenê. And they dedicate there male and female slaves; and this is not remarkable. But even the most illustrious men of the nation dedicate [their] maiden daughters, for whom it is the custom to be prostituted a long time in the goddess's temple/before the goddess, after these things being given in marriage, no one disdaining to live with her. Something similar Herodotos also says about the Lydian females, that they all prostitute themselves. In such a kindly way they treat their lovers that they both furnish hospitality and give in return gifts, often much more than they receive, being well supplied from their affluent households. They

---

[95] *LSJ* [1843] 1968: 1705.

do not receive just anyone of the guests, but mostly those of equal rank to themselves.

Ἅπαντα μὲν οὖν τὰ τῶν Περσῶν ἱερὰ καὶ Μῆδοι καὶ Ἀρμένιοι τετιμήκασι, τὰ δὲ τῆς Ἀναίτιδος διαφερόντως Ἀρμένιοι, ἔν τε ἄλλοις ἱδρυσάμενοι τόποις, καὶ δὴ καὶ ἐν τῇ Ἀκιλισηνῇ. ἀνατιθέασι δὲ ἐνταῦθα δούλους καὶ δούλας. καὶ τοῦτο μὲν οὐ θαυμαστόν, ἀλλὰ καὶ θυγατέρας οἱ ἐπιφανέστατοι τοῦ ἔθνους ἀνιεροῦσι παρθένους, αἷς νόμος ἐστὶ καταπορνευθείσαις πολὺν χρόνον παρὰ τῇ θεῷ μετὰ ταῦτα δίδοσθαι πρὸς γάμον, οὐκ ἀπαξιοῦντος τῇ τοιαύτῃ συνοικεῖν οὐδενός. τοιοῦτον δέ τι καὶ Ἡρόδοτος λέγει τὸ περὶ τὰς Λυδάς· πορνεύειν γὰρ ἁπάσας. οὕτω δὲ φιλοφρόνως χρῶνται τοῖς ἐρασταῖς, ὥστε καὶ ξενίαν παρέχουσι καὶ δῶρα ἀντιδιδόασι πλείω πολλάκις ἢ λαμβίνουσι, ἅτ᾽ ἐξ εὐπόρων οἴκων ἐπιχορηγούμεναι· δέχονται δὲ οὐ τοὺς τυχόντας τῶν ξένων, ἀλλὰ μάλιστα τοὺς ἀπὸ ἴσου ἀξιώματος.

As with Babylon, so too for Armenia: Strabo never visited nor saw first-hand the region he described. According to his own testimony (2.5.11), the easternmost reach of the geographer's travels was the western border of Armenia; he did not go into the interior. Thus, as with Babylon, Strabo was dependent on an alternate source for the topographic and ethnographic information in Book 11.14, including our current point of concern: 11.14.16 – the Armenian cult of Anaitis/Anahita. Unfortunately, Strabo is not forthcoming about his sources for this passage, citing only Herodotos in a side reference to Lydia. F. Lasserre claims that Strabo's source for this passage was an obscure, first-century BCE geographer/ethnographer named Apollodoros of Artemita[96] who authored a work entitled "Parthian Matters" (*Parthika*).[97] However, Lasserre provides no argument for this assessment. It is true that Strabo does cite this author on numerous occasions in Book 11 specifically (11.7.3; 11.9.1; 11.11.1; 11.11.7; 11.13.6).[98] However, he is not cited once in Section 14, which actually pertains to Armenia. One idea may support Lasserre's claim. Although Strabo discusses the sacred land of Akilisenê, he does not mention the central holy city of Erez, where was located Anahita's temple. This temple, as Pliny the Elder informs us in his *Natural History* (33.4.24), was sacked by the troops of Marc Antony. The absence of this datum may suggest that we are at least dealing with a first-century BCE source.

---

[96] *FGrHist* 779.

[97] Lasserre 1975: 13–15.

[98] See Nicoli 2001, Appendix II for a full survey of authors cited in Strabo Book 11.

As with Babylon so too with Armenia: there are several accurate data in the description, followed by a reference to some form of sacred prostitution, which the language of the text makes clear Strabo found strange. The initial information in Strabo's text pertaining to Anahita's cult in Armenia might all be confirmed in alternate sources. The importance of Akilisenê as a cult region sacred to Anahita is attested in writings both Classical and Armenian. Dio Cassius (36.48.1 and 36.53.5) refers to the entire region of Akilisenê as *tên Anaitin khôran*, while Pliny, in his *Natural History* (5.34 and 33.4.24, as above) refers to the district as Anaetica – the "land of Anaitis."[99] Likewise, the Christian-era, Armenian author Agathangelos, in his *History of the Armenians* (3.48), relates that "In the first year of the reign of Trdat in Greater Armenia, they went to the province of Ekeleats to the village of Erez, to the temple of Anahit in order to sacrifice there."[100] Likewise, later in the narrative, St. Gregory "came to the neighboring province of Ekeleats. Here the demons appeared in the places of worship of the most important shrines of the Armenian kings, in the temple of Anahit in the town of Erez."[101]

That *douloi* and *doulai* were dedicated to the goddess in Akilisenê, a matter which Strabo claims was "nothing remarkable," has parallels in other Anatolian cults of Anahita. Strabo himself notes that the small Pontic city of Zela had a temple primarily dedicated to Anaitis, and that the town (*polisma*) for the most part belonged to the hierodules (11.8.4). In this respect the district mirrored other sacred lands in Anatolia, such as the Comanas (see above), where the residents, like the land, were considered to be sacred to the deity, thus termed hierodules. Furthermore, the sacral manumission aspect of *hierodouleia* was also associated with the cult of Anahita, as is evidenced in the imperial-age inscription given above from Cappadocia (Ortaköy), where three girls are given to Anaitis as hierodules (see above).[102] As such, the data given by Strabo have parallels in alternate sources.

And then there is the reference to the apparent sacred prostitution of upper-class Armenian girls. This datum has no confirmation in any alternate sources, not even the Christian sources that would be most inclined to malign their pagan predecessors. As M. L. Chaumont notes,

---

[99] Chaumont 1965: 173 and 180.
[100] Thomson 1976: 61. Translation by Thomson. Ekeleats is the Armenian form of Akilisenê.
[101] *Ibid*: 325.
[102] Harper 1967: *passim*.

"Au reste, le fait qu'Agathange, qui n'avait aucune raison d'épargner la divinité la plus représentative de la dernière période du paganisme, ne fait pas la moindre allusion à un semblable usage. . . . "[103] Furthermore, Strabo makes use of an inverted litotes to express his own mild incredulity about the practice: whereas the fact that people dedicated male and female slaves was *ou thaumaston*, the fact that the most illustrious citizens dedicated even (*kai*) their daughters, by natural extension of the sentence's syntax, was. Thus we begin our consideration of Strabo's attestation of Armenian sacred prostitution on very shaky ground. We do not know the source of the information; the datum is not confirmed in any other sources; and Strabo himself seems to find this practice he only knows through alternate sources to be odd.

How odd? To begin, Anahita is an odd goddess to be associated with prostitution of any kind. It would appear that although the goddess emerged as a Zororastrian adaptation of the Mesopotamian goddess Ištar (who could more logically have been associated with prostitution), she also absorbed the attributes of a water goddess, and came ultimately to known as *anahita*, the "Immaculate One."[104] The Greco-Roman deity to whom she was most often compared was Artemis/Diana in the function of a "pure" fertility goddess. So much is attested in Plutarch's *Lucullus* (§24), the *Annals* of Tacitus (3.63),[105] and the Anatolian epithets of Artemis as Artemis Anaitis and possibly Artemis Persike.[106] Her role as fertility goddess in Armenia specifically is attested in Agathangelos (*History of the Armenians* 68) who calls her "the great Anahit, who gives life and fertility to our land of Armenia."[107]

Like Ištar, Anahita also had her militaristic side, and as such she could also be syncretized with Athena. According to Chaumont, the goddess received at her temple in Staxr the severed heads of enemies killed in battle,[108] whereas Agathangelos (127) records a blessing offered by the pagan king Trdat, offering fertility from Aramazd, protection from Anahit, and valor from Vahagn.[109]

Only one ancient source, Berossos, syncretized the goddess with Aphrodite. It appears that this was because of Anahita's epithet "Golden,"

---

[103] Chaumont 1965: 175.
[104] Boyce 1987 [1979]: 61.
[105] Garsoïan 1989: 347.
[106] Brosius 1998: *passim*.
[107] Thomson 1976: 77 (translation by Thomson).
[108] Chaumont 1965: 172.
[109] Thomson 1976: 139.

in reference to her famous golden statues in both Erez (Pliny *Natural History* 33.4.24) and Ashtishat (Agathangelos 809). The Armenians themselves associated the Greek Aphrodite with their goddess Astlik, the wife of Vahagn (Agathangelos 809).[110] That Berossos came to associate Anahita with Aphrodite through similar statue iconography seems apparent in his Fragment 12, where he discusses the origins of Persian cult statues, claiming that Artaxerxes "first set up the statue of Aphrodite Anaitis and showed respect to it at Babylon, Susa, and Ekbatana, in Persia and Bactria, and at Damascus and Sardis."[111] In other respects, though, such a syncretism was quite unusual – Anahita being more commonly associated with Artemis, whereas Aphrodite was syncretized with Astlik – and Verbrugghe and Wickersham claim that the syncretism with Aphrodite is "understandable" mainly because sacred prostitution functioned in the cults of both goddesses.[112] This is not a good argument.

Anahita, then, is not a goddess whom we would expect to command a cult of sacred prostitution, a fact that is intensified when we consider the total lack of corroborating evidence for this so-called Armenian custom anywhere else. Additional problems emerge when we consider Strabo's actual description of the "prostitution." At first it should not seem that there is any ambiguity with the concept Strabo is describing. He uses the word *kataporneuô*, "to prostitute." The geographer uses this word one other time, in passage 6.1.8, when describing the punishment meted out to the daughters of Dionysios II of Syracuse – they were prostituted out before being strangled (see Chapter 8). He also compares them to some of the most famous "prostitutes" in ancient history – the Lydians, "all"[113] of whom "prostitute themselves."

But then Strabo goes on to describe the prostitution as practiced by the Armenian noble girls. According to Strabo, the girls are permitted to choose which men they give themselves to, men who are inevitably of an equal rank with the girls themselves. Likewise, there is no reference to payment for "services rendered" *per se*, but Strabo does mention that the girls "give in return" (*antididoasi*) even more gifts (*dôra*) than they receive. As Beard and Henderson describe it, it is "nothing like *any* form of prostitution – truly (as Strabo announces) a 'wonder.'"[114]

---

[110] *Ibid*: 347–349.
[111] Verbrugghe and Wickersham 2000 [1996]: 62.
[112] *Ibid*: 62, note 51.
[113] On the universal, as opposed to limited, prostitution of Lydian women, see Chapter 8: Klearkhos.
[114] Beard and Henderson 1998: 70. Emphasis in original.

Strabo then attempts to rationalize such a custom by finding a previously attested equivalent for it, and what he comes up with is the
Herodotean reference (1.93) to the self-prostitution of Lydian women.
This brings up a number of cogent points. First of all, Strabo does not
choose to compare the Armenian "sacred prostitution" with the Babylonian, even though he was clearly familiar with it. It is possible that Strabo
did allude to the Mesopotamian reference through his use of the word
xenôn when describing the girls' lovers (*erastais*), thus paralleling the *xeinoi*
who made use of the Babylonian women's services. However, the word
xenôn in passage 11.14.16 seems to reflect the word *xenian* in the previous
line. As such, rather than a case of "foreign lovers" as we saw in Herodotos
(see Chapter 4, note 1), I believe here we have upper-class Armenian
young ladies treating proper guests with appropriate hospitality. There
is no need to see a connection to Herodotos, and it appears that the
understanding of Armenian-style sacred prostitution was distinct from
the Babylonian model, especially in the volition and "return payments"
exhibited by the Armenian noble girls.

Secondarily, the Lydian model offered by Herodotos is not a form
of "sacred" prostitution. Although the Lydian women may prostitute
themselves before marriage (to earn their dowries, as Herodotos tells us),
there is no sacral component to their actions.[115] This would not appear to
be the case in the Armenian model, where Strabo expressly states that
the girls are prostituted (*kataporneutheisas*) *para têi theôi*. The *para* in this
instances is usually taken to mean "at the house of," in this instance of the
goddess, and thus at the temple, presumably at Erez. Of course, Strabo
never actually mentions this temple, even when discussing the cult of
Anaitis in Akilisenê. We do know, however, that the land of Akilisenê
was regarded generally as belonging to the goddess (see above), and it
is thus possible to offer an alternate reading of this line, where the girls
are prostituted "in the presence" of the goddess. In either event, there
should be a sacral element to the prostitution that is not attested in the
Lydian comparandum.

An additional similarity between the Lydian model and the Armenian,
and definitely not the case in the Babylonian, is that this prostitution
takes place before the marriage of the *parthenoi*. In the Lydian model, the
prostitution might almost be seen as a necessary step in the preparation

---

[115] Although see Chapter 8: Klearkhos, for the early confusion of the Lydian and "sacral"
versions of premarital prostitution.

for marriage (the acquisition of the dowry), whereas in Armenia the girls are "prostituted" for a long time before being given in marriage.

So, in his understanding of Armenian sacred prostitution, Strabo likens the practice not to a clearly sacral model as seen in Babylon, but to a secular, prenuptial model as seen in Lydia (at least according to Herodotos). Furthermore, this (sacred) prostitution does not really fit a definition of what would be called prostitution *per se*, insofar as the girls pick their lovers (*erastais*) and do not generate an income on the perceived sale of sex. If anything, they pay their lovers.

The apparent contrast between the word *kataporneuô* (and perhaps even *porneuô* as pertaining to the Lydian women) and the description given of this practice might be resolved if we consider the ancient Greek categories of sexual exchange and the linguistic terminology that accompanied them. Prostitution itself, in its most basic form, is simply "the exchange of sex for something else of value."[116] However, there were, and still are, circumstances when such a definition is not entirely accurate. In ancient Greece this is most evident in homoerotic, and especially pederastic, relationships.[117]

Ephoros (F149), for example, records the Cretan custom of "ritualized homosexual rape."[118] Here, the lover (*erastes*), after notifying the (*eromenos*) beloved's family of his intentions, set up a mock kidnapping which resulted in the lover and beloved spending about two months alone together. At the end of this period, the *erastes* returned the *eromenos* to his family along with many expensive gifts, including clothing.[119] Here we see an exchange of gifts (*dôra*) for sexual access, but the ritualized nature of the act seems to preclude a categorization as prostitution.

Likewise, vase paintings from Attica reveal scenes of older males offering gifts (hares or roosters) to younger men while pointing at the younger men's genitalia (see Fig. 7.1).[120] The "courtship" of youths was entirely acceptable in Athenian culture, and although the official policy was that such relationships remained chaste (Aiskhines 1. 135–136), the vase paintings also reveal older/younger lover pairs wrapped in amorous embrace

---

[116] Miner 2003: 30.

[117] The following examples come from fifth- and fourth-century Greece, making them contemporary with Strabo's comparandum of Herodotos' Lydia and accounting for his choice of Greek terminology.

[118] The term is Dover's (1978: 189).

[119] Dover 1978: 189–190.

[120] Insert your own "rooster" pun here.

Figure 7.1.

(see Figure 7.2). The exchange of the "gift" for sexual access could, technically, be defined as prostitution, although it generally is not.

Generally, that is. For in some instances it could be difficult to distinguish between the exchange of gifts and sex – what we in modern times call "dating" – and prostitution. This is most obvious in Aiskhines' *Against Timarkhos*. Here the orator accuses the citizen Timarkhos of having sold his body as a prostitute, thus disqualifying himself for a number of civic prerogatives. Aiskhines, though, has a terrible time arguing that what Timarkhos did qualified as actual prostitution, rather than merely sharing the sexuality and resources of other men ("dating"). This first becomes apparent in §52, when Aiskhines must convince the jury that the number of Timarkhos' lovers precludes identifying Timarkhos as

206

Figure 7.2.

simply a *hetairêkôs*, or "little companion," but makes him a full-fledged prostitute (*peporneumenos*). Later, in §75, Aiskhines argues further,

> What shall we say when a young man leaves his father's house and spends his nights in other people's houses, a conspicuously handsome young man? When he enjoys costly suppers without paying for them, and keeps the most expensive flute-girls and hetairas? When he gambles and pays nothing himself, but another man always pays for him? . . . Is it not perfectly plain that the man who makes such demands must himself necessarily be furnishing in return certain pleasures to the men who are spending their money on him?[121]

[121] Translation Adams 1917, adapted.

In §160 Aiskhines reminds the jury that no written contract is required to define or to prove a case of prostitution. In §159, having distinguished on *ethical grounds* the difference between a true beloved (*eromenos*) and a whore, Aiskhines asks the jury into which category Timarkhos belonged. In short, there was no clear-cut means of distinguishing between an exchange of gifts and sexuality in some kind of pseudo-courting or dating ritual and prostitution.

There are no comparanda for heterosexual relationships. Normal courtship for marriage would be arranged between a bride's family and either the groom himself or his family. Gifts, of course, were offered, but to the bride's family, and physical/sexual access to the bride was not permitted until after a wedding ceremony.[122] To have sexual access to a female outside of marriage was either rape (*bia*) if by force, fornication (*moikheia*) in the absence of force or payment, or prostitution in the presence of payment. A premarital exchange of gifts with a potential bride directly does not appear to have been an option.

This, however, is what seems to be described in Strabo's Armenian *logos*: a premarital exchange of gifts between noble girls and potential suitors (members of the same socioeconomic status), where the exchange is direct between the females and males, possibly, if not probably, indicating some manner of direct physical access between the two ("dating"). Or, in ancient Greek, with no concept, and thus no word for such a scenario: prostitution.[123] Going further, one might see in this Armenian practice a sacral component whereby the courtship of the noble girls took place under the supervision of either the goddess herself (*para têi theôi*) or her priests. This confusion between prostitution and what might be termed direct courtship explains how Lydian women could have been prostitutes while preparing for marriage. And remember, Herodotos tells us that the Lydian women, much like the Armenian girls, chose their own husbands, a direct result of "dating."

In the end, Strabo 11.14.16 does not provide good evidence for sacred prostitution. We know that Strabo himself was not a witness to the practice he describes, nor do we know his source (Apollodoros of Artemita?), or how his source came by this information, or even if, as was the case

---

[122] The outlier case of Sparta is left out of this more general description.

[123] I realize that the example of Penelopê does conform to this model of direct contact and exchange in courtship. However, her example is understood to be tragic and abnormal; she is an older woman (not a virgin), and her son does try to run interference between her and her suitors. Her atypical scenario can at best be seen as midway between standard Greek practice and the Armenian (and Lydian) "aberration."

with Babylon, the description was fictional to begin with. Strabo seems to have misgivings about it. Everything that we do know about the identity and cult of Anahita herself suggests that she was not a goddess normally associated with prostitution of any kind. Furthermore, the description of the so-called prostitution does not sound like prostitution at all, but rather courtship, where the girls involved picked their "lovers" (*erastais*) and returned gifts more valuable than those they received. Add to this the absence of any other data for the practice of sacred prostitution in the ancient world, and in Armenia specifically, and this hypothesis falls apart entirely.

CONCLUSIONS

Strabo is our single most important source for sacred prostitution in the ancient world. As stated at the beginning of this chapter, about a quarter of our data come from him alone. And yet, Strabo did not create the myth of sacred prostitution, nor do I think he actually believed in the practice himself. None of Strabo's references to *hierai* or hierodules pertain to sacred prostitution as we understand it. Even his few passages that do seem to speak directly about the topic, such as with Babylon or Armenia, are riddled with doubt, not to mention serious historiographic methodological errors. What this does confirm, though, is that Oden's hypothesis of sacred prostitution as an accusational literary motif is not, in the end, accurate. Strabo, our main source for sacred prostitution, did not accuse anyone, really. He merely reported the facts as he understood them, more or less accurately as we have come to see. Sometimes, certainly, he was confused. Other times, especially by us, misunderstood.

CHAPTER EIGHT

KLEARKHOS, JUSTINUS, AND VALERIUS MAXIMUS

T HREE AUTHORS WHO HAVE BECOME MIRED IN THE SACRED PROSTI-
tution debate are Klearkhos of Soli, Pompeius Trogus as epito-
mized by Justinus, and Valerius Maximus. Klearkhos was a fourth-century
BCE Peripatetic philosopher whose works are now mostly preserved in
Athenaios' third-century CE *Deipnosophistai*. A fragment coming from the
fourth book of Klearkhos' *Lives* (FGH 6 = Wehrli 43a) has been used
to argue for the existence of sacred prostitution in Lydia, Cyprus, and
Epizephyrian Lokris in southern Italy. As the evidence will show, this
reference has consistently been read out of context, so that Klearkhos'
actual subject matter – the wages of decadence – has been eschewed in
favor of the sacred prostitution meaning.

Valerius Maximus wrote during the reign of Tiberius in the first century CE and authored the work *Memorable Deeds and Sayings*, a handbook
for Romans studying the art of declamation. In the second book of this
work (2.6.15), Valerius castigates the Punic women of Sicca in northern Africa for... something. He actually is not very explicit. Because
the passage implicates a Semitic population, involves a temple of Venus,
and makes reference to dowries, memories of Herodotos have influenced
scholars to see in this passage a reference to sacred prostitution.

Between these two authors comes Pompeius Trogus, who wrote a universal history in the first century BCE. This extensive work unfortunately
no longer survives except in fragments in the works of Valerius Maximus,
Velleius Paterculus, Frontius, and Q. Curtius Rufus,[1] and in an epitome
written by Justinus – *Epitoma Historiarum Philippicarum Pompei Trogi* – in
what was probably the late second to early third century CE.[2] There are

---

[1] Yardley and Heckel 1997: 7 and 19–20.
[2] *Ibid*: 8–11.

numerous problems with trying to derive Trogus' original data out of the *Epitome*, not the least of which is trying to determine how many data were interjected by Justinus himself in his process of summation. J. C. Yardley's recent work on the language of Pompeius Trogus and Justinus has been especially helpful in this regard. For the purposes of this book, it appears that both passages under consideration – 21.3 pertaining to Lokris and 18.5 pertaining to Cyprus – derive from Justinus per the chronology of the vocabulary.[3] It is entirely possible, then, that elements from later than the reign of Augustus might become implicated in the analysis of Justinus' *Epitome*, in spite of the earlier date of Pompeius Trogus.

As a final note, it must be recognized that Valerius Maximus and Justinus created their respective works as tools for the practice of rhetoric and declamation.[4] As Peter Brown, citing H.-I. Marrou, once artistically expressed the concept:

> ... performances of the master rhetoricians of the late classical age [were like] the virtuoso techniques of a Hot Jazz trumpeter; they could bring out themes deeply embedded in their own memory and held at readiness for themselves and their hearers by centuries of tradition and could weave such themes into new combinations. These new combinations often had a topical relevance all the more cogent for being expressed in ancient, easily intelligible terms.[5]

For both authors, this means that historical accuracy was not as important as usable exempla. The data become jumbled; dates, people, and places

---

[3] Concerning the Lokrian material Yardley notes (Yardley 2003: 155) that

21.3.1 *callido commento...*
PHI does not parallel before Papin. Dig. 3.2.20 *praef. callido commento*, Ulpian Dig. 27.9.9 *praef. callidum commentum*. *TLL.*3.1867.57–58.
21.3.4 *adtaminet*
Late verb, not paralleled before Porphyrio on Hor. Ep. 1.3.9; cf also HA Gord. 27.2, Servius on Georg. 1.268, Aen. 4.507, etc. *TLL* 2.115.82–116.32 ...
For that which concerns the Cypriot material (Yardley 2003: 216):

18.5.4 *dotalem pecuniam* ('dowry')
Paralleled only in the Digest: 23.3.54 *praef.* (Gaius) *ex dotali pecunia*, 23.3.56.3 (Paul.) *dotalis pecunia*, 24.3.53 *praef.* (Tryphoninus) *dotalem pecuniam*, etc.: TLL 5.1.2054.33ff. In the Speech of Mithridates, Trogus uses *dotem* (38.5.3 *in dotem dedisset...*, cf. also 3.3.8 *sine dote nubere*), making it more likely that *dotalem pecuniam* is a usage of Justin.

[4] Yardley and Heckel 1997: 17–18; Bloomer 1992: 19 and 49.
[5] Brown 1996 [1978]: 8.

are swapped around to create better examples or tighter analogies, thus tampering with the historical information we can actually derive from these sources. This will have profound implications for the study of sacred prostitution.

This chapter will proceed by site – Epizephyrian Lokris, Cyprus, Sicca – rather than by author, as it is in the combinations of textual data from these authors that the mirage of sacred prostitution emerged in both the ancient and modern scholarship.

EPIZEPHYRIAN LOKRIS: JUSTINUS AND KLEARKHOS

Two texts are commonly cited as showing that sacred prostitution was practiced in ancient Epizephyrian Lokris (henceforth: Lokris).[6] These are passage 21.3 from Justinus' *Epitome* of Pompeius Trogus, and a passage from Klearkhos of Soloi as preserved in Athenaios' *Deipnosophistai* (FGH 6 = Wehrli 43a). The translation from Justinus is as follows:

Justinus 21.3:[7]

When the Lokrians were being pressed by the war with Leophron, tyrant of the Rhegians, they had vowed – if they were victorious – that on the feast-day of Venus they would prostitute their virgins. As the vow was *intermisso* (paused, interrupted, neglected, omitted, ignored, left unfulfilled), when they were waging a losing war with the Lucanians, Dionysios summoned them into an assembly; he urged them to send their wives and daughters into the temple of Venus as ornately decked-out as possible, from whom 100 chosen by lot would enact the public vow and would – for the sake of religion – stand for one month in a brothel (before this all the men would swear that no one would touch any of them). So that the matter would not harm the virgins who were releasing the state by the vow, they made a decree that no virgin would marry until those girls were given to husbands. Approving of

---

[6] There are also archaeological data brought to bear on the Lokrian sacred prostitution debate, whereby the "Stoa ad U," the tablets from the temple archives of Zeus, and even the Lokrian *pinakes* are offered as evidence for sacred prostitution in the city. However, because these data rely almost exclusively on the literary evidence for their links to sacred prostitution, I am leaving them out of this study. On these topics see especially Schindler 1998: 130–136; also Amantini 1984: 43–46 and Graf 1981: 177–179.

[7] Latin text below.

this plan, which accommodated both superstition and the modesty of the virgins, all the women in full earnest and decked out to the nines convened in the temple of Venus. Dionysios, having stationed soldiers there, despoiled them all and turned over the matrons' jewellery into his own treasure chest. He killed the husbands of the wealthier women; he tortured some to make them hand over their husbands' wealth. He ruled six years by these means. He returned to Sicily after being turned out of the state by a conspiracy of Lokrians.

The passage from Klearkhos as typically cited in the modern literature is actually only a fragment of the fragment, the one considered in Chapter 3 as pertaining to issues of translation in sacred prostitution studies. This reads as follows:

Klearkhos:

Not only the women of the Lydians are free to those present, but also those of the Epizephyrian Lokrians, and those about Cyprus, and simply of all those expiating their own girls by "companionship."[8]

οὐ μόνον δὲ Λυδῶν γυναῖκες ἄφετοι οὖσαι τοῖς ἐντυχοῦσιν, ἀλλὰ καὶ Λοκρῶν τῶν Ἐπιζεφυρίων, ἔτι δὲ τῶν περὶ Κύπρον καὶ πάντων ἁπλῶς τῶν ἑταιρισμῷ τὰς ἑαυτῶν κόρας ἀφοσιούντων.

Let us consider Klearkhos first before delving into the matter of the Lokrian *votum*. The Klearkhos fragment fragment is used as evidence for sacred prostitution in Lokris as well as in Cyprus, Lydia, and any-place else one would choose to find the practice under the rubric of "all those."[9] As early as 1952, C. Turano noted that "Che il rito della sacra prostituzione fosse praticato a Locri Epizefiri risulta da quanto ci è riferito da Clearco di Soli, nel passo riportato da Ateneo..., sec-ondo il quale non soltano le donne dei Lidi erano solite prostituirsi con chiunque si imbattesse loro, ma anche quelle dei Locresi Epize-firii e dei Ciprioti; tutti costoro votavano alla prostituzione le loro figli-uole...."[10] According to S. Pembroke, writing on this topic in the 1970s, "Cléarchos, péripatéticien peu scrupuleux, parle de la prostitution des femmes à Locres Epizéphyriennes comme d'un traite permanent de leur

---

[8] The linguistic analysis of this fragment appears in Chapter 3.

[9] A minority opinion, espoused by Musti and Graf, is that this passage of Klearkhos refers not to sacred prostitution, but to the Lokrian origin tale wherein the women of eastern Lokris had sex with their slaves when the Lokrian men were away at war. Graf 1981: 176.

[10] Turano 1952: 248.

société, et la met en parallèle avec celle des Lydiens."[11] C. Sourvinou-Inwood, when attempting to understand the Lokrian votum described by Trogus, claimed that "This problem is usually considered and interpreted in terms of 'sacred prostitution,' a practice which Klearchos believed to take place regularly at Locri."[12] L. S. Amantini, in his study of sacred prostitution in Lokris, begins with "La testimonianza richiama alla mente un accenno alla prostituzione a Locri Epizefirii da parte di Clearco di Soli."[13] R. A. Oden, citing Athenaios directly, claimed that "A piece of symposium literature by the late second-century author Athenaeus repeats the charge that the Lydians and the Cyprians both give up their daughters to prostitution as part of a sacred rite."[14] This concept of parents handing over their daughters to sacred prostitution is echoed by B. MacLachlan, who wrote, "In addition, the Cyprian historian Clearchus, preserved in Athenaeus, says that the women of Lydia, like those of Cyprus and western Locri, are dedicated by their parents to strangers, as prostitutes."[15] R. A. Strong concludes, "In summary, Clearchus seems to suggest here that some kind of religious prostitution involving free women was an ongoing practice of the inhabitants of Epizephyrian Locris."[16] B. Goff wrote, "Klearchos in Athenaeus 12.516a claims that the families of Italian Locri vowed to prostitute their daughters if they were victorious in war,"[17] obviously confusing Klearchos with Justinus 21.3. Most recently, J. Karageorghis was so certain that Klearchos was here discussing sacred prostitution that she specifically translated the term *hetairismos* as "sacred prostitution," thus giving the impression that sacred prostitution was so well ingrained in Greek culture that there was a technical term for it.[18]

As ever in the debate about the existence of sacred prostitution, the value of Klearchos' evidence is set in the arena of whether or not Klearchos himself was a reliable source. J. Redfield calls Klearchos "a notably sensationalistic writer."[19] Both Pembroke and R. Schindler suggest that Klearchos was about as reliable as, say, Khamaileon, and that his

[11] Pembroke 1970: 1269.
[12] Sourvinou-Inwood 1974: 186.
[13] Amantini 1984: 39.
[14] Oden 1987: 142.
[15] MacLachlan 1992: 151.
[16] Strong 1997: 112.
[17] Goff 2004: 156.
[18] Karageorghis 2005: 52.
[19] Redfield 2003: 412.

testimony concerning Lokrian sacred prostitution should thus be handled with extreme care, if not jettisoned outright.[20]

What makes this all somewhat humorous is that if one were to read the *entire* fragment as presented in Athenaios, one would realize that Klearkhos was not writing about sacred prostitution at all. The full text is as follows.

Klearkhos frag. 6 apud Athenaios 12.515 (Wehrli F 43a):

The Lydians through wanton luxury decked out parks and, making them into gardens, lounged in their shade, believing it more luxurious that the rays of the sun never fell on them. And proceeding further in their hybris, they led together the wives and maiden [daughters] of others to the place celebrated as "Chastity Place" because of the act, and there molested them. And in the end they, having become totally effeminate at heart, switched over to the life of women, wherefore this life-style even found for them a female tyrant, one of the molested women – Omphalê. She first began to wreak a fitting vengeance on the Lydians. For to be ruled by a woman and suffering outrage is a sign of violence (*or:* a sign of their lifestyle). She herself, being both licentious and taking revenge for the outrageous things that had happened to her, handed over to the slaves the maiden daughters of the masters in that very place in the city where she had been molested by them. Having here gathered them together she forced the mistresses to lie with the slaves. And so, the Lydians, euphemizing the harshness of the deed call the place "Sweet Embrace." Not only the women of the Lydians are free to those present, but also those of the Epizephyrian Lokrians, and those about Cyprus, and simply all of those expiating their own girls by "companionship." In truth, it appears to be a reminder of and revenge for some ancient outrage.

The commonly cited fragment fragment appears in a longer passage about the wantonness of the Lydians, which itself, to judge from the other passages that Athenaios claims come from Klearchos' *Lives*, Book 4, is Klearkhos' topic of discussion. That is, what is at issue here is not prostitution, sacred or otherwise, but the evils of a wanton lifestyle.[21] The Lydians, as Klearkhos tells us, were so decadent that they routinely molested/raped

---

[20] Schindler 1998: 130; Pembroke 1970: 1269–1270.
[21] According to Athenaios 12.522d, another account in Book 4 of Klearkhos' *Lives* relates the excessive luxury and effeminacy of the people of Tarentum. This is just one more example to complement those to follow.

free wives and maiden daughters. Eventually they paid the price for these actions. Becoming so debauched, according to our Peripatetic moralist, they allowed a queen to come to power – Omphalê. She, having been molested herself, sought revenge on the Lydians by having the wives and daughters of the free citizens sexually partnered with their slaves. Thus, violent, inappropriate sexuality found its retribution in further inappropriate sexuality (possibly violent).[22] Certainly, as Klearkhos' fragment tells it, it is a revenge for an earlier outrage.

As stated above, this fragment comes from Book 4 of Klearkhos' *Lives*. So too does another passage preserved in Athenaios, this one referring specifically to our comparandum Epizephyrian Lokris. Once again, according to Klearkhos,

Klearkhos apud Athenaios 12.541c–e (Wehrli F 47):

Dionysios son of Dionysios, scourge of all Sicily, came to the city of the Lokrians as a mother-city (for Doris, his mother, was Lokrian). Strewing the largest house of those in the city with creeping thyme and roses he sent for the maidens of the Lokrians in turn, and he being naked himself left off no disgrace rolling about the spread with their naked (bodies). And indeed after a short time the outraged men seizing in hand his wife and children set them on the street and were utterly licentious with them. And when they were sated with their violence, stabbing needles under their finger nails they killed them. They ground up the bones of the dead ones in a mortar and the remaining bits they divided up as meat portions, cursing those who did not taste them. The reason why they ground up the flesh in spite of its impiety was so that the meal might be eaten entirely as they ate bread. The remaining bits they threw into the sea. And Dionysios himself ended his life pitifully as a tambourine-bearing mendicant priest of Kybele. One must thus beware of so-called wantonness, it being the overthrower of lives, and regard hybris as the destroyer of all.

The situation in Lokris is similar to what we saw in Lydia and it is *this* anecdote, not Justinus' later narrative, that Klearkhos is referencing in fragment 6. In Lokris, it was one man – Dionysios II – who committed hybris by sexually molesting the maidens of Lokris. Once again, the afflicted parties sought a comparable revenge: The citizens of Lokris raped and tortured Dionysios' daughters to death. Neither prostitution nor religion features

---

22 See also Athenaios 12.540f, where Klearkhos is quoted as comparing the wanton lifestyle of Polykrates of Samos to the "effeminate practices of the Lydians."

in either account. Rather, the two texts coming from the same work deal with issues of sexual impropriety, violence, and violently sexual revenge.

If we let go of preconceived notions of sacred prostitution and consider the texts as we have them, it becomes far more likely that what Lydia, Lokris, Cyprus, and whatever other regions Klearkhos had in mind had in common was a story of violent sexual impropriety (rape or otherwise) that found vengeance in the violent rape or enforced sexual impropriety of women/girls. Either the initial indulgence in wanton hybris, or the vengeance thereof – the purging of the citizens' anger – may be the *aphosioô* referred to by Klearkhos, while the reference to inappropriate sexuality (in whatever form) is subsumed in the extremely rare word *hetairismos*. The women of Lydia, Lokris, etc. are not "free to those present" in the sense that they have free, open access to whomever *they* choose. Rather, any stranger has access *to them*, because they, as the stories about them reveal, were not protected from sexual violence.

Klearkhos' use of the vague and uncommon term *hetairismos* did cause confusion, and not just in the modern scholarship. Two later historians who apparently made use of Klearkhos in their own histories also read prostitution into their readings. When recounting the history of Dionysios II in Lokris, Strabo has this to say:

Strabo, Geography, 6.1.8:

They [the Lokrians] are believed to be the first to use written laws, and having been under good laws for a very long time, Dionysios – having been kicked out of Syracuse – made most lawless use of all. He, going to the chamber, lay before marriage with those dressed for marriage. And gathering together the ripe maidens he released clipped doves in the *symposia*, and he ordered them [the maidens] to run about naked to catch the doves, shod in unmatched sandals – one high, one low – for the joy of the disgrace. But he paid the price when he went back to Sicily to take back his domain. For the Lokrians, having destroyed his garrison, freed themselves and made themselves masters of his wife and children. There were two daughters and the youngest of his sons, being still a child, for his other son Apollokrates was fighting with his father on the campaign. And Dionysios pleaded greatly that the Lokrians hand over the persons for whatever they wanted – both Dionysios himself and the Tarantines on his behalf – but they did not give them up; they endured a siege and the ravishing of the countryside, pouring out their hearts especially on the daughters. For *having prostituted them* they strangled them, then, having burnt the bodies they ground up the bones and cast them into the sea.

We get a similar account from Aelian in his *Varia Historia* 9.8:

> When the younger Dionysios arrived in the city of the Lokrians (as his mother Doris was Lokrian), seizing the houses of the greatest people in the city and having them strewn with roses and creeping thyme and other flowers he sent for the daughters of the Lokrians and was with them in a most licentious manner. He paid the price for this. For when his tyranny was overthrown by Dion, then the Lokrians *prostituted his wife and daughters*, and without restraint they all raped them, especially those whose daughters were ruined by Dionysios. When the rapists became glutted, they killed the women, stabbing them under their fingernails with needles. They ground up their bones in a mortar, and ripping the meat off of the bones they cursed anyone who did not taste it. Anything that remained they threw into the sea.

The theme in both later accounts is similar to what we see in Klearkhos: Dionysios treated the virgins of Lokris with sexual violence, and in return his own daughters (and wife) were raped, tortured, and killed (and ground up and cast into the sea). Once again, we are dealing with the expiation of anger through sexual violence. What is interesting is the use of words pertaining to prostitution in both Strabo and Aelian. Strabo, unlike Klearkhos, claims that the Lokrians prostituted the daughters of Dionysios (*kataporneutheisas*) before killing them, while Aelian mentions that the Lokrian men somehow prostituted them (*kateporneusan*) by raping them. It is likely that both historians were attempting to rationalize Klearkhos' use of the word *hetairismos* in his own history of the events at Lokris, implying, somehow, prostitution in the story of hybris, debauchery, rape, and revenge.

Klearkhos is not a source of evidence for sacred prostitution, and he cannot be used to argue that the Lokrians practiced this so-called rite. Far more pertinent in this regard is Pompeius Trogus/Justinus, who is the sole author to record for us that, in the early fifth century BCE, the Lokrians once vowed to prostitute their daughters to Venus. Let us consider this passage now.

Justinus 21.3:[23]

Dein cum rapinae occasio deesset, universam civitatem callido commento circumvenit. Cum Reginorum tyranni Leophronis bello Locrenses premerentur, voverant, si victores forent, ut die festo Veneris virgines suas prostituerent. Quo voto intermisso cum adversa bella cum Lucanis gererent, in contionem eos

---

[23] English translation above.

Dionysius vocat; hortatur ut uxores filiasque suas in templum Veneris quam possint ornatissimas mittant, ex quibus sorte ductae centum voto publico fungantur religionisque gratia uno stent in lupanari mense omnibus ante iuratis viris, ne quis ullam adtaminet. Quae res ne virginibus voto civitatem soluentibus fraudi esset, decretum facerent ne qua virgo nuberet priusquam illae maritis traderentur. Probato consilio, quo et superstitioni et pudicitiae virginum consulebatur, certatim omnes feminae inpensius exornatae in templum Veneris conveniunt, quas omnes Dionysius inmissis militibus spoliat ornamentaque matronarum in praedam suam vertit. Quarundam viros ditiores interficit, quasdam ad prodendas virorum pecunias torquet. Cum his artibus per annos sex regnasset, conspiratione Locrorum civitate pulsus in Siciliam redit.

One of the first points to consider regarding Justinus' narrative is that it does not hold together well. The passage begins with the reference to a *votum* sworn a century before when Lokris was at war with Rhegion. The use of the word *intermisso* makes it extremely difficult to determine if the *votum* was in abeyance or even ever carried out. At any rate, by the time of Dionysios II it was not being fulfilled, so the tyrant reminded the Lokrians of their discarded vow. However, the remedy Dionysios comes up with differs considerably from the original *votum*. Originally, the city's virgins were to be prostituted on one day – the feast of Venus. In the new version, 100 virgins and matrons were to be chosen from the full lot of Lokrians, and they were to be set up in a brothel for a month. However, when the new *votum* was being enacted, reference is made specifically to the ornately decked-out matrons, with special reference to their husbands. The virgins who figured so prominently in the first two sections of the text now disappear, as the story moves from an original vow pertaining to the city's virgins to a story about the despoiling of the city's matrons. This is not a coherent narrative. In fact, it would appear that passage 21.3 consists of four separate elements. (1) There is the brief introductory sentence claiming that Dionysios needed an excuse to despoil the Lokrians (he was not yet well established and comfortable in the city, as he apparently grew in subsequent narratives). (2) There is a reference to the supposed old *votum* of the fifth century. (3) There is a transitional passage in which Dionysios proposes a new execution of the old *votum*. (4) Finally, there is the account of how Dionysios despoiled the matrons of Lokris and murdered their husbands.

There are other unnerving aspects of this passage from Justinus. Once the supposed sacred prostitution "parallel" in Klearkhos is discarded, Justinus' *votum*-account is wholly unique in the extant corpus for Lokrian history. This casts grave suspicion upon Justinus' account of Lokrian sacred prostitution. It is the sole reference to a rather unusual *votum* recorded some four centuries after the supposed *votum* was enacted, and three centuries after Dionysios rather awkwardly pretended to resurrect it. Furthermore, this uniqueness stands in contrast with the immediately preceding passage (21.2.9–10), which shows strong similarities to the data derived from Klearkhos, Strabo, and Aelian:

> [Dionysios] was accepted as a refugee by his allies, the Locrians, and then, as if he were their legitimate leader, he seized the acropolis and subjected them to his characteristic ruthlessness. He ordered the arrest of the wives of leading citizens so he could ravish them; he abducted virgins before their marriage and gave them back deflowered to their betrothed; he either banished from the state or had executed all the richest citizens, confiscating their property.[24]

As James Redfield argued in his treatment of this passage in his masterful work on ancient Epizephyrian Lokris, much of this narrative consists of stereotypes pertaining to notions of Greek tyranny.[25] I would argue that in the latter two portions of the text (Sections 3 and 4 as enumerated above), Justinus is indeed likening Dionysios II to prototypical tyrants of both Greece and, as I argue it, Rome.

Once again, a quick statement as to authorship and chronology. Although the *Epitome* is based upon a much longer work written by Pompeius Trogus in the first century BCE, Yardley has shown that certain portions of the text, due to their language and chronological implications, might be attributed to Justinus rather than to Trogus. For example, in passage 41.5.8, Justinus claims that the Parthians entitled their kings Arsaces just as "the Romans use the names Caesar and Augustus."[26] As Yardley and Heckel have argued, this Roman practice was not conventional in Rome until the reign of Antoninus Pius, thus too late for Trogus but well in keeping with the chronology for Justinus.[27] Likewise, in passage 2.10.2 Justinus claims that primogeniture is the natural type of succession for all peoples, an idea more typical of Rome under the emperors than under Augustus.[28] Furthermore, historiographic influences later than Trogus

---

[24] Trans. Yardley and Develin 1994: 169.
[25] Redfield 2003: 288.
[26] Yardley and Develin 1994: 257.
[27] Yardley and Heckel 1997: 5.
[28] *Ibid*: 12.

appear in the *Epitome*, including Aulus Gellius, Pseudo-Quintillian, and, most importantly here, Suetonius.[29]

According to Yardley's study of the language, passage 21.3 would appear to owe more to Justinus than to Trogus.[30] As such, we should not be surprised to find influences here extending into the second or even third century CE. Likewise, because Justinus may have been an orator, his interests tended toward the moralizing more than toward the accurate. Thus, to quote Yardley and Heckel on Justinus' accuracy as an historian, " . . . he confuses historical characters bearing the same name, he conflates historical events and is often not scrupulous about chronology . . . he is not a good historian . . . concerned not with accuracy or chronology or sources, but with historical exempla."[31] Therefore, we should not necessarily expect total historical accuracy from Justinus, nor should we be surprised to find (stereotypical) attributes casually transferred from one character to another.

Such a mélange is evident in passage 21.3. The references to Dionysios II are combinations of apparently accurate historical data (as offered by several other historians; see above) and stereotypes of tyranny. The stereotypes used are Herodotos' depiction of Corinthian Periandros in Book 5.92 of the *Histories*,[32] and developing narratives pertaining to Demetrius Poliorcetes in Plutarch, and to Caligula in Suetonius and Dio Cassius.[33]

In the final section of passage 21.3, Justinus narrates that Dionysios, "having stationed soldiers [in the sanctuary of Venus], despoiled all the women and turned over the matrons' jewellery into his own treasure chest. He killed the husbands of the wealthier women; he tortured some to make them hand over their husbands' wealth." On the one hand, this conforms well to passage 21.2 in which, following other attested historical narratives, Dionysios "ordered the arrest of the wives of leading citizens" and "either banished from the state or had executed all the richest citizens, confiscating their property." The specifics of the violation, however, are heavily predicated upon the prototype established in Herodotos. In his *Histories*, 5.92, Herodotos records that in an attempt to soothe his wife Melissa's ghost, Corinthian Periandros enacted the following scheme:

> Periandros sent all the Corinthian women to the temple of Hera, and they went to the "festival" decked out in their finest apparels. But

[29] *Ibid*: 13.
[30] Yardley 2003: 155–156.
[31] Yardley and Heckel 1997:17–18.
[32] Berve 1967: 663; Graf 1981: 177.
[33] My thanks to Kimberly Huth for drawing my attention to the Caligula parallel!

Periandros, having placed spearmen in ambush, stripped them all at once, both free woman and servant, and bore the clothing to a hole and burnt it, calling upon Melissa.[34]

There are several parallels: The setting in a temple (Hera for Herodotos, Venus for Justinus), the city's women wearing their finest clothes and adornments, the tyrant having placed guards/spearmen in the temple in advance, the despoiling of the women. The final portion of Justinus' 21.3, then, rather than a historical account of Dionysios' sojourn in Lokris[35] (once again, there are no parallels), appears to be a literary construct used with the intent of highlighting Dionysios' tyrannical persona.[36]

The previous portion of the narrative (my Section 3 above) is a bit more complex. Here, Dionysios suggests that the Lokrians, in an attempt to conciliate Venus for a vow either abandoned or left unfulfilled,

send their wives and daughters into the temple of Venus as ornately decked-out as possible, from whom 100 chosen by lot would enact the public vow and would – for the sake of religion – stand for one month in a brothel (before this all the men would swear that no one would touch any of them). So that the matter would not harm the virgins who were releasing the state by the vow, they made a decree that no virgin would marry until those girls were given to husbands.

The differences between this set up and the specifics of the original *votum* could be rationalized easily enough: The women have to remain a month to make up for the lost time; they wait in a brothel because of the extended temporal commitment; matrons as well as virgins go because those matrons did not fulfill the *votum* when *they* were virgins, etc. But this is to make excuses for a narrative that hardly holds up to scrutiny to begin with. The presence of both virgins and matrons in this section partially derives from the passage's function as a bridge between the original *votum*, which included only virgins, and the Periandran conclusion, which involved the despoiling (and then some) of the city's matrons. Including matrons in the revised *votum*, so to speak, legitimized their required presence at the end of the narrative. The detail that the virgins so prostituted would be the first to be married off (or,

---

[34] A variation on this story is in Diogenes Laertios' *Lives and Opinions of the Eminent Philosophers* 1.96.

[35] Contra Muccioli 1999: 351–352, although he does admit that this account is "particolari fantasioni e romanzati."

[36] Graf 1981: 177, "la storia narrata de Giustino non può essere che una finzione, modellata dopo Erodoto."

specifically, that no other virgins could marry before them) also seems to derive from details in passage 21.2. Here, Justinus (once again with support from other historians) claims that Dionysios "abducted virgins before their marriage and gave them back deflowered to their betrothed." Thus, the virgins in question would be the first to be married off because the virginal victims of Dionysios were already on the verge of marriage.[37]

As with the end of passage 21.3, here it appears that there is a secondary source that provides some of the specific details of Justinus' account. In this instance, it is another tyrannical leitmotif that evolved over the course of the first through fourth centuries CE – the tyrant's establishment of a brothel in a temple or palace, and his despoiling or pimping of free boys and women therein. The earliest such reference is Plutarch's account of Demetrius Poliorcetes' depredations in the Athenian acropolis; a contemporary tradition records Caligula's establishment of a palatial brothel; the final evolution implicates Messalina.

According to Plutarch (*Demetrius* 24), "Demetrius wrought such hybris in the acropolis upon free boys and women of the city that the place seemed far more pure when he merely debauched with Khrysis, Lamia, Demo, and Antikleia, those whores!" Here we see the combination of prostitution (at least as far as Plutarch was concerned) with the ravaging of free boys and women in the temple of Athena.[38]

This leitmotif intensifies when applied to the Roman emperor Caligula. As Suetonius wrote in the late first century CE, Caligula, "setting aside a suite of Palace rooms, decorated them worthily, opened a brothel, stocked it with married women and free-born boys, and then sent his pages around the squares and public halls, inviting all men, of whatever age, to come and enjoy themselves."[39] Caligula, then, put up for sale in a brothel married women. When Dio Cassius refers to this same occurrence in Book 59.28.9 of his early third-century *Roman History*, he writes about "the rooms established in the palace itself, both the wives of the foremost [citizens] and the children of the most revered, these ones he sat in the rooms to outrage, fleecing everyone by means of them." By the time Sextus Aurelius Victor was writing in the fourth

---

[37] This seems more likely to me than Graf's suggestion that this passage reflects back to notions of premarital ritual defloration as supervised by the city matrons. See Graf 1981: 177.

[38] Many thanks to Daniel Ogden for bringing this reference to my attention.

[39] Graves 1979: 174.

century, this pimping motif had transferred from Caligula to Messalina (*Epitome de Caesaribus* 4.5):

> His wife Messalina was at first almost everywhere making use of the "right" of adultery, and because of this many men, refraining out of fear, were killed. Then, even more harshly incensed, she displayed like whores along with herself the wives and virgins of the noble families, and the men were compelled to attend.

The relationship between temple/palace/brothel in both Justinus and the Demetrius and Caligula narratives is further intensified by the archaeology of Lokris. According to Redfield, when Dionysios arrived,

> It was at this time that the U-shaped stoa passed out of use; the Temple of Aphrodite was actually demolished and replaced by a secular building – the so-called House of the Lions, a luxurious house which looks remarkably like a residence fit for a tyrant. Possibly Dionysius demonstrated his hybristic power and wealth by actually moving into the precinct of the goddess.[40]

According to Klearkhos (above), Dionysios took hold of the biggest house in the city, decked it out with roses and herbs, and molested the city's women there. If, as the archaeology suggests, Dionysios set himself up at the site of the temple of Aphrodite, then there is a correspondence between the temple and his "palace." The city's matrons and virgins, then, going to the temple for the lottery would, as seen in later years, have headed to the palace, the parallel of Caligula's brothel, to begin their rite of prostitution.

The motif of prostituting the city's wives and children/maidens functions as a reference to the tyrannies of Demetrius and Caligula in much the same way the despoiling of matrons in a temple calls to mind the tyranny of Periandros. Furthermore, this tyrannical pimping motif was clearly evolving as Justinus was writing in the late second–early third century CE. As such, the motif of setting up for sale the city's matrons and virgins not only serves as a narrative bridge, but links Dionysios II to Demetrius and Caligula as epitomes of tyrannical decadence. These narratives pertaining to Dionysios in Lokris ought not to be seen as historically accurate, but as tyrannical leitmotifs.

What, then, of the original *votum*, supposedly vowed a full century before the arrival of Dionysios II and thus, apparently, free of tyranical

---

[40] Redfield 2003: 222. For more archaeological data, see Schindler 1998: 153–159.

reimaging? In many respects the *votum* falls within the normal parameters of ancient Greek "human dedications." As summarized by Redfield, using the dedication of the East Lokrian maidens to Trojan Athena as an example,

> The ritual... has the familiar shape of an initiation: There is an elaborate phase of separation (adornment, transport, and threat of violence) followed by a phase of liminality (degradation and service)... The ritual, further, involves seclusion and service, which are characteristic of women's ritual roles.[41]

The Epizephyrian Lokrian *votum* partakes of a number of these elements. The prostitution of the maidens suggests both adornment and a threat of violence (both concepts are picked up by Justinus in the latter part of the passage). The fact that they are prostituting themselves makes them, at least temporarily, liminal in their own society. The fact that they are free girls so acting qualifies both as degrading and, being in the interest of the greater community, also as service. The notion of seclusion must remain questionable, as there are no details as to where this prostitution would take place. If in a brothel per Justin's later reconstruction, then this could constitute a form of seclusion. In many ways, except for the rather odd use of prostitution, the *votum* is well in line with Greek religious practice.

However, it cannot be denied that our provenance, so to speak, for this tale is somewhat suspect. The only extant reference to it is in Justinus, recording the facts some four centuries or more since the event supposedly transpired. The wording of the narration is ambiguous as to whether or not the prostitution of the virgins ever even took place, since *intermisso* potentially means either "lapsed" or "ignored."

Nevertheless, it also seems unlikely that Justinus would have made up this *votum* at this point in the Dionysios narrative, if only because it fits so poorly with the following text. As discussed above, passage 21.3 does not hold together well. It begins with a reference to prostituting virgins at a festival and changes over the prostitution of virgins and matrons at a brothel for a month, before switching over to the Periandros motif. The wording of the original *votum* causes undue contortions in the remaining narrative, suggesting that the idea and structure of the *votum* were already present before Justinus' reworking.

Ironically, I believe, Justinus (possibly Trogus) invented the Lokrian *votum* out of the very same texts that we now use as supporting evidence

---

[41] Redfield 2003: 89.

for this matter: Klearkhos frag. 6 and Pindar's *Pythian* 2. As discussed in Chapter 3, the vocabulary used in the Klearkhos fragment is both rare and ambiguous. The word *hetairismos* only appears twice in our extant corpus, in this passage from Klearkhos and a first-century CE inscription from Egypt. The Egyptian inscription *seems* to refer to prostitution, or at least to female wage-earners whose job is described as "companionship." The word *aphosioô* pertains to sanctification or expiation, neither of which definitions seems to make much sense in the Klearkhos passage, so that later editors, at least, tweaked the definition to include "to dedicate."[42] Thus, a passage that, as discussed above, refers to the purging of wrath through rape becomes understood as a religious dedication of girls to prostitution. Justinus/Trogus, then, may have gotten at least part of his *votum* of prostitution from such a misreading of Klearkhos. That the inference of prostitution was already present in Roman-period writings is evident in the works of Strabo and Aelian, who included prostitution in their accounts of the vengeance on the daughters of Dionysios II in Lokris.

Concerning the Lokris–Cyprus connection, Klearkhos was not the only author to link Cyprus and the daughters of Lokrians. Pindar, in his *Second Pythian Ode* dedicated to Hieron of Syracuse, also juxtaposes these two concepts. Lines 15–18 of the *Ode* pertain to the priest-king of Paphos Kinyras, beloved of both Apollo and Aphrodite. This is immediately followed in lines 18–20 by a reference to Lokrian maidens standing by their houses to sing the praises of Hieron:

> The voices of the men of Cyprus often shout the name of Cinyras, whom golden-haired Apollo gladly loved, Cinyras, the obedient priest of Aphrodite. Reverent gratitude is a recompense for friendly deeds. And you, son of Deinomenes, the West Lokrian girl invokes you, standing before the houses: out of the helpless troubles of war, through your power she looks at the world in security.[43]

The reference here to Lokris, as discussed in the scholia, pertains to Hieron's rescue of that city from Rhegion.[44] As Woodbury suggests, based on a study of the chronologies involved, this conflict between Rhegion and Lokris is the same as that described by Justinus in passage

---

[42] The Herodotean sense of "to conciliate" as seen in 1.199 hardly seems appropriate here.

[43] Translation from the Perseus Project.

[44] Amantini 1984: 42 with Greek text of scholia; Woodbury 1978: 286–288.

21.3.[45] According to Pindar, it would seem that the Lokrian maidens are especially grateful to Hieron for saving their city. The question is, "why them?"

The answer could simply be that girls are the most vulnerable members of any society, and thus the least citizens, so to speak, of Lokris come out to thank Hieron for saving the city from destruction, the *parthenoi* speaking for the city as a whole. In addition, the fact that they are praising from their homes (*pro domôn*) intensifies the idea that they have not been dragged off into servitude through military defeat. Furthermore, Lokris was known for the high status of the females in their society. If Pindar were aware of this, and he certainly could have been, the reference to the Lokrian maidens may have functioned as a very culturally aware reference to that city.

But if we combine the "evidence" from Pindar with the "evidence" from Klearkhos, almost in Khamaileonic fashion, we might come up with something different. The Lokrian maidens, like the Cypriot, were at some time "religiously dedicated to 'companionship'/prostitution" (Klearkhos). Kinyras, to judge from both Apollodoros' *Bibliothekê* (3.14.3) and Ovid, was known in Roman times for having fifty daughters who, through the wrath of Aphrodite, "cohabited with strangers" before ending their lives in Egypt.[46] Justinus may have read the link Kinyras–Cyprus–Aphrodite–daughters–prostitution into his interpretation of Pindar, so that, just as with the Cypriot allusion, the Lokrian daughters were also threatened with some kind of prostitution in relation to Aphrodite, a threat somehow resolved when Hieron saved them from Rhegion (Pindar).[47]

And thus the notion of the Lokrian *votum* emerged. Once, when Lokris was threatened in a war with Rhegion (Pindar), the Lokrians vowed to prostitute their daughters in relation to Venus (Klearkhos). Hieron came in and saved the day, very much to the relief, apparently, of the Lokrian maidens (Pindar). This, of course, left it rather ambiguous as to whether the vow was then fulfilled (Klearkhos *versus* Pindar); were the Lokrians *victores*, thus having to prostitute their daughters (going against the perceived reading of Pindar)? Or were they instead passively saved, thus nullifying the *votum*? Justinus merely recorded that the *votum* was *intermisso*, leaving that entire question open-ended.

---

[45] Woodbury 1978: 288. See also Redfield 2003: 205 for archaeological evidence of synchronicity.

[46] Karageorghis 2005: 52.

[47] By contrast, Graf suggests that Kinyras' role in the poem was merely as a well-known emblem of piety and prosperity. Graf 1981: 177.

Passage 21.3 is not evidence for sacred prostitution in Lokris or any-where else. The original *votum* appears to be a historiographic construction combining certain stock motifs of "human dedication" in the Greek tradition with evidence from Klearkhos and Pindar. We can hardly fault Justinus for coming up with the same interpretation of the Greek evidence that most modern scholars have. This *votum* is then used to introduce a narrative about Dionysios II, the "scourge of Sicily." Unlike Justinus' previous description of Dionysios in passage 21.2, this Lokrian account has no parallels in other authors, such as those of Klearkhos (as preserved), Strabo, or Aelian. By contrast, the narratives presented do have strong parallels with other "tyrant motifs," notably Periandros of Corinth, as has long been recognized, and Caligula. As Redfield put it:

> In fact, Justin need not have been reliant on sources of any kind; his account in large part consists of commonplaces about the tyrant: "he changes inherited lawful ways and forces women and executes without trial" (Herodotus 3.80.5) . . . I suggest that these stories record through the transformations of folk narrative the Locrian experience of Dionysius the Younger.[48]

CYPRUS: JUSTINUS 18.5.4

When discussing the abduction of eighty Cypriot girls by Phoenician colonists on their way to Carthage, Justinus relates that:

> It was a custom in Cyprus to send young girls down to the sea-shore on specific days before their marriage to earn money for their dowry by prostitution, and to offer Venus libations for the preservation of their virtue in the future.[49]

Such is passage 18.5.4 of Justinus' *Epitome* of Pompeius Trogus as translated by J. C. Yardley and R. Develin (1994), currently the only full translation available in English. The references to prostitution, libations to Venus, and most especially the island of Cyprus all call to mind Herodotos' chapter 1.199, where, after a description of the Babylonian custom of sacred prostitution to Mylitta/Aphrodite (Venus), Herodotos mentions that a similar custom existed on parts of the island of Cyprus. It is no wonder, then, that this passage has become mired in the sacred prostitution controversy.

---

[48] Redfield 2003: 288.
[49] My translation is at the end of this section.

However, the Latin text of the passage reads,

Mos erat Cypriis virgines ante nuptias statutis diebus dotalem pecuniam quaesturas in quaestum ad litus maris mittere, pro reliqua pudicitia libamenta Veneri soluturas.

There is no unambiguous reference to prostitution in the text; the virgins do not "*se prostituerent,*" as with Justinus' Lokrian *votum,* or earn their dowries "*meretricio.*" The only word in the text that Justinus gives us regarding the girls' employment, the only word that would lead one to the conclusion that the girls are hooking, is *quaestus.*

As any word for profit, acquisition, or gain, this word can of course be related to prostitution. In such cases, though, the word is usually accompanied by other vocabulary that fleshes out the sexual source of the *quaestus.* One of the most common means of referring to meretricious employment is by the expression "*quaestum corpore facere,*" literally "to make a profit from the body." Thus the Tabula Heracleensis, dating to c. 45 BCE, includes in those excluded from magistracies and council memberships "*queive corpore quaestum / fecit fecerit.*"[50] Ulpian, citing an Augustan statute on prostitution, identifies such a practitioner as one who "*palamve corpore quaestum faciet feceritve.*"[51] Likewise Livy, *Ab Urbe Conditum* (28.33): *Duas mulieres compertum est Vestiam Oppiam Atellanam Capuae habitantem et Paculam Cluviam quae quondam* quaestum corpore fecisset, *illam cottidie sacrificasse pro salute et victoria populi Romani. . . .* In the *Annals* of Tacitus we find (2.85) *Eodem anno gravibus senatus decretis libido feminarum coercita cautumque ne* quaestum corpore faceret *cui avus aut pater aut maritus eques Romanus fuisset.* In a slight variation of this terminology, Plautus, in his *Cistellaria* (5.563), claimed that all Etruscan girls "dotem quaeras corpore."

Even more explicit terminology could be used, not merely referring to use of the body, but deliberately to prostitution – *meretricio.* Thus Cicero in his *Philippics,* referring in rather insulting fashion to Antony, says (18): *sed cito Curio intervenit qui te a* meretricio quaestu *abduxit.*

However, as with any word for profit, acquisition, or gain, *quaestus* can have nonmeretricious connotations as well, and in fact this is the more common usage.[52] Cicero, in his *Pro P. Quinctio* refers to a young man whose father left him no inheritance, so he (3) *vocem in quaestum contulit,*

---

[50] McGinn 1998: 32–33.

[51] *Ibid*: 62.

[52] In his lexicon of Justinus' *Epitome,* Eichert defines *quaestus* as Erewerb, Gewinn 5,4,4; *divitiarum* 9,8,6; plur. *quaestus militiae* 14,3,10. Only the final definition has insb. Gewinn durch Buhlschaft 18,5,4. No reason is offered for the "durch Buhlschaft" in the final analysis. Eichert 1967: 151.

made a living from his voice. The same author, in his *Pro Flacco*, tells of a man for whom (19.56) *haec pecunia tota ab honoribus translata est in quaestum et faenerationem*, all his money was earned in honorable fashion through employment and interest-bearing loans. Tacitus, in his treatment of the Germans and their sports, claims that their young men, competing in the nude, do so for honor, *non in quaestum tamen aut mercedem*, receiving neither profit nor pay. No references to prostitution are implied or inferred in these latter examples, partially, probably, because males are involved, but also because there is no vocabulary that would specify sex as the source of profit, nor does the context imply such.

It is a matter of debate, then, whether prostitution should be read into (or out of) this passage. Then there is the secondary question – is this potential prostitution related to the virgins' other seaside activity, the pouring of libations to Venus? If a "yes" can be offered to both questions, then the passage appears to be about sacred prostitution.

HERODOTEAN PROTOTYPE...

How one chooses to answer these questions depends very much on the extent to which one sees the influence of Herodotos in Chapter 18.5.4. The question is to what extent Justinus himself relied on Herodotos for the details of this Cypriot prenuptial practice, or to what extent modern interpreters read the passage through a lens of Herodotos.

As far as Trogus' own sources are concerned, there is no doubt that he had access to Herodotos, although it is clear that he also made use of other sources for the early histories, such as Thucydides, Ktesias, Ephoros, and Theopompos, among others.[53] Trogus made especial use of Herodotos in his sections on Persian and Lydian history, which makes it evident that the author was well acquainted especially with book 1 of the *Histories*. Thus, in the *Epitome* 1.4–10, Trogus recounts Herodotos' life of Cyrus, from the tale concerning Astyages' dream of the grandson who would replace him through to Zopyrus' ruse to help Cyrus conquer Babylon. Section 1.7 is a brief excursus relating, in backward order, the Herodotean story of the Lydian Dynasty, starting with the defeat of Croesus and ending with the ascension of Gyges. The details in Book 1 of the *Epitome* follow Herodotos quite closely, suggesting a deep familiarity with the Carian historiographer for those sections most relevant to the sections of the *Histories* that furnished the comparanda for Justinus' supposed Cypriot practice.

---

[53] Yardley and Heckel 1997: 30.

There are three passages in the first book of Herodotos that could be thought to have contributed to the genesis of passage 18.5.4: 1.1–4, 1.93, and, of course, 1.199. The first, the opening of the *Histories* generally, is a description of Phoenician and Greek girls who were abducted and carried off by boats at either the seashore or a port. Passage 1.93 is a reference to the prenuptial practice of Lydian working-class girls of prostituting themselves to acquire dowries. The last is Herodotos' discussion of Babylonian sacred prostitution.

What are the similarities between Herodotos' references to prostitution and abduction and Justinus' Cypriot account? In Chapter 1.199 of the *Histories*, Herodotos claims that the women (*gynaikes*) of Babylon wait in the sanctuary of Mylitta/Aphrodite to prostitute themselves with a foreigner, once, for a token payment sacred to the goddess. Afterward, they cannot be tempted into adultery. For Justinus, Cypriot virgins work (somehow, possibly prostitution) and pour libations to Venus at the seashore for the preservation of their future chastity.

Unlike passage 1.199, though, the Cypriot females are virgins and are collecting dowries. The latter part of this statement at least may refer to Herodotos 1.93. Here, Herodotos related that "Working-class girls in Lydia prostitute themselves without exception to gather money for their dowries, and they continue this practice until marriage. They choose their own husbands." This passage refers to a purely secular kind of prostitution, possibly even a kind of dating (see Chapter 7). Nevertheless, over the years and centuries (and millennia), it appears that authors both ancient and modern have somewhat mixed-and-matched this Herodotean account of Lydian secular prostitution with that discussed in Section 1.199 – Babylonian sacred prostitution – so that elements of one have come to influence the understanding of the other.[54] The idea

---

[54] There are numerous examples of such "cross-fertilization" and mistaken details among the various sources for sacred prostitution, both in the ancient authors and the modern. Oden, in a discussion of Lucian's *Syrian Goddess*, records that, "In the *Syrian Goddess*, a second-century A.D. text attributed to the satirist Lucian of Samosata and descriptive of the religious rites at the city of Hierapolis near the Euphrates River, we read that the women of the city 'shave their heads, as do the Egyptians when Apis dies . . . '" (Oden 1987: 142.) A slip of the keyboard (not adding in the words "of Byblos" after the second "city") makes it sound as though the religious rite in question is taking place in Hierapolis, not in Byblos. Beard and Henderson, in their refutation of sacred prostitution in the Classical repertoire, conflate Lucian's account of Byblian sacred prostitution with Justinus' account of the Cypriot prenuptial rite, referring to "the Adonis festival at Byblos, that requires women to crop their hair, or else, as a forfeit, go down to the sea-shore. There they 'become prostitutes for one day . . . '"

of prostituting oneself under the auspices of a deity for the sake of acquiring a dowry appears in Valerius Maximus's *Memorable Deeds and Sayings*, 2.6.15, where he claims that matrons possibly prostitute themselves for dowries going forth from the temple of Venus (see below); in Plautus' *Cistellaria* (5.562–3, mentioned above), where "*ex Tusco modo, tute tibi indigne dotem quaeras corpore*"; and in Strabo 11.14.16, where the geographer claims that noble girls in Armenia prostitute themselves at the temple of Anaitis before marriage, although here they pointedly do not need to acquire dowries, as they already come from the wealthiest families. On the flip side, as we have seen, Trogus' Lokrian *votum* has been taken as both sacred prostitution and prenuptial ritual simultaneously.[55] According to Aelian's *Varia Historia*, written in the third century CE, "The Lydians had a custom whereby the women had relations with men before they married. But after they were married they were chaste."[56] The chastity after promiscuity/marriage is not a detail presented in Herodotos 1.93, but rather in 1.199.[57]

If Justinus, like other ancient authors, conflated the two accounts of prostitution in Book 1 of the *Histories*, this might explain how Cypriot virgins would prostitute themselves for dowry money (*dotalem pecuniam*). Finally, influence from the beginning of the *Histories* could help to explain the girls' presence at (and, as will be discussed, abduction from) the seashore instead of a sanctuary. Chapters 1.1–4 relate how, in Argos, Phoenicians abduct women who came down to the shore to shop. Later,

(Beard and Henderson 1998: 70). There is no reference to a "sea-shore" in Lucian's Byblian account, although there is such a reference in Justinus. Lightfoot calls Beard and Henderson to task for this slip-up and then goes on to make one of her own, claiming that "for Herodotus, as for other ethnographers, it [sacred prostitution] is usually a prenuptial rite" (Lightfoot 2003: 325). As we saw in Chapter 4, there is nothing in Herodotos that suggests that Babylonian sacred prostitution was prenuptial; if anything, use of the word *gynaikes* and the placement of the passage after references to bride-auction and marital intercourse rather argue that the Babylonian ritual happens *after* marriage. Goff, in her study of prostitution and religion in ancient Greece, claims that Klearkhos recorded that the residents of Epizephyrian Lokris consecrated their daughters to prostitution for Venus (Goff 2004: 156). This notion is wholly unique to Justinus.

[55] Graf 1981: 177.
[56] Johnson 1997: 86.
[57] Worthy of note: The passage about the Lydian women comes just a few lines down from the declaration that "The Assyrians gather their nubile maidens all together into one city. They put them up for public auction, and each man leads home as his bride whichever girl he purchases" (*Ibid*). There can be little doubt as to where Aelian got his references.

almost in revenge, some Greeks, probably Cretans, abducted Europa from the port at Tyre. The abduction of women by boat is a well-known Herodotean motif, and it explains how young, vulnerable women would be so easily accessible to travelers by sea.

A combination of details from Herodotos 1.1–4, 1.93, and 1.199 could be seen to have generated the creation of Justinus' 18.5.4. The practice takes place on Cyprus, just as Herodotos, at the end of 1.199, claims that a practice similar to that of the Babylonians occurs in certain parts of Cyprus. That it takes place on the coast, sacred to Aphrodite, may pertain to both Herodotos 1.1–4 and 1.199. The idea that this occurs before marriage to earn money for a dowry derives from Herodotos 1.93. There is no reference to the money acquired being sacred, as was the case in 1.199 (possibly because the money is already earmarked for dowries); however, the ritual does involve at least a libation to Venus, our Romanized equivalent of Mylitta/Aphrodite. This libation is associated with the girls' chastity, much as Herodotos says of the Babylonian women that, after their period of prostitution, "you cannot have them, offering no matter how much money."

Although we saw in Chapters 2 and 4 that Herodotos' account of Babylonian (and for that matter Cypriot) sacred prostitution was not historical but metaphorical, we also saw in Chapter 7 that by the first century BCE there was at least some ambiguity on the part of Augustan historiographers concerning this fact, such that Strabo would include a watered-down version of the Babylonian narrative in his *Geography*. Thus, although Trogus cannot be providing supporting evidence for Herodotos' chapter 1.199 in a historical sense, he certainly could have used Herodotos as a source, and thus offered simple repetition of the Babylonian *logos*. If Justinus used Herodotos as his source for this passage, then the word *quaestus* could be understood to refer to prostitution, and its acquisition could be understood to be related to the pouring of libations to Venus in the following clause. The passage, although not providing evidence for historical sacred prostitution, at least links one more such text to Herodotos.

... Or Independent, Roman Account?

If, however, we consider the fact that Justinus was responsible for the final formation of Chapter 18.5.4 (see above), additional ideas come into play. For we are dealing not only with issues of historiography, but also with literary/poetic/rhetorical embellishment. As Yardley has argued, Justinus made use of poetic language in his *Epitome*, reflecting back on

Augustan-age authors such as Vergil and Ovid.[58] Furthermore, it has been argued that Justinus was a teacher of rhetoric,[59] and thus one should not be surprised to find an emphasis on parallels, exempla, or other attributes that would improve the declamatory quality of his narratives. Chapter 18.5.4, then, might be analyzed as a combination of historiography and literary motif. Furthermore, those literary motifs are more Roman than Greek/Herodotean. Let us, then, consider passage 18.5.4 from a literary/rhetorical perspective.

Justinus' reference to the Cypriot custom occurs in a brief excursus in Book 18 of the *Epitome*, when Justinus pauses briefly in his recitation of the exploits of Pyrrus of Epiros to recount the foundation legend of Carthage. According to legend, Carthage was founded by the Tyrian princess Dido/Elissa, who fled from Phoenicia after her brother Pygmalion murdered her husband, known as Acherbas or Sychaeus. This tale is known from three extant, pre-Christian sources: a fragment of Timaios of Tauromenion dating to the third century BCE, this passage from Justinus, and, most famously, Book 1 of Vergil's *Aeneid*.[60]

According to Timaios, preserved in an anonymous *De mulieribus* (*FGH* 82(23)),

> Timaios says this concerning the one called Elissa in the Phoenician language. She was the sister of Pygmalion, King of Tyre, and he says that Carthage was founded by her. For when her husband was killed by Pygmalion, she, placing all her possessions into small ships, fled along with some citizens, and having suffered many hardships she went to Libya, and after her long wanderings Dido was welcomed in local fashion by the Libyans. Having founded the above-mentioned city, when the King of the Libyans wanted to marry her, she refused. But, being compelled by her citizens, she, alleging some rite by which to release herself from her oath, prepared and kindled a huge fire by her home, and she threw herself into the fire from her house.

Justinus' narrative is longer and more elaborate. According to him, Tyre passed to the kingship of Pygmalion after the death of his and Elissa's father Mutto. Pygmalion was named king, and Elissa was married off to her uncle Acherbas, a very wealthy priest of Herakles (Melqart). Lusting after Acherbas's wealth, Pygmalion murdered him, although he had no

---

[58] Yardley 2003: 188–189.
[59] *Ibid*: 5; Yardley and Heckel 1997: 17–18.
[60] Josephus Flavius, in his *Against Apion* 1.18, refers to the foundation of Carthage by King Pygmalion's sister, but he does not name her or tell her story.

idea where the priest had actually hidden his goods. At first, Elissa seethed passively, but later, she tricked her brother into believing she was moving back in with him. Under this pretext, she stowed all of her possessions on board some ships, and then made it look as though she were tossing Acherbas's goods overboard. Pointing out to her helpers that Pygmalion was going to be furious, she persuaded them to join her in exile, along with some of Acherbas's noble colleagues.

They first made a stop in Cyprus, where the priest of Jupiter offered to join them, asking only that the priesthood remain within his family. Then comes the passage quoted above. Elissa had eighty of these girls seized and taken on board so that the men might have wives and the future city descendants. Then, turning back to Tyre, Justinus relates how Pygmalion was thwarted in his designs to pursue Elissa *et al.* both by his own mother and by prophesies from the deities.

Elissa and her company arrived finally in northern Africa, where the story proceeds much as narrated by Timaios, ending in Elissa's death when pressured to marry a Libyan king. Justinus ends by noting that, as long as Carthage remained unconquered, Elissa was worshipped as a goddess.

Vergil's story is somewhat different, most notably in including Aeneas in the narrative. This is actually strange. The chronology of events, even as held by the ancients, shows that Troy fell some three centuries before the founding of Carthage. Chronologically speaking, then, Aeneas lived some 300 years before Dido/Elissa, making any dating on their part somewhat tricky.[61] However, Dido, the exotic, oriental queen who tries to seduce Aeneas away from his destiny and the glory of Rome (or, at least, Italy), serves as a perfect mirror of Cleopatra, who did pretty much the same thing to Julius Caesar and Marc Antony. Vergil, patronized by Julius Caesar's heir Octavian, has good reason to reflect contemporary events in an epic glorifying the earliest history of Rome while simultaneously sowing the seeds for Rome's "future" wars with its "ex" Carthage. The affair of Dido and Aeneas is a literary construction, only partially based on the "historical" Dido. Nevertheless, a number of the same legendary elements appear even in Vergil. In Book 1.484–522, Venus tells her son Aeneas how Dido left Tyre after her brother Pygmalion had treacherously killed her husband, the priest Sychaeus. Gathering her dead husband's treasure, Dido left Tyre with a group of people all feeling disgruntled with the king. They came to the site of Carthage, which Dido acquired by paying for as much space as she could surround with a bull hide.

[61] Desmond 1994: 26.

Although still courted by a Libyan king, Vergil's Dido kills herself when abandoned by Aeneas.

In all these versions, Justinus is unique in making reference to a stop in Cyprus, and especially so in referring to the abduction of the eighty girls who were in the process of acquiring dowries (somehow) and pouring libations to Venus as a prenuptial rite. Why did Justinus include this narrative in his history of the foundation of Carthage? The Cypriot interlude does not appear in Timaios, nor in Vergil, where we would almost expect it seeing as the story is being narrated by Venus, Goddess of Cyprus, herself. A number of factors seem to have contributed, above and beyond any "prototype" possibly created by Herodotos.

First, there is the simple historical factor: In the ninth century BCE, when Carthage was founded, the Phoenicians were also colonizing the island of Cyprus, especially at the site of Kition.[62] Either Trogus or Justinus may have here preserved a memory of Cyprus' role as stepping stone in the foundation of other, western Phoenician/Punic settlements. Aubet offers an interesting analysis:

> Moreover, it can apparently be inferred from [Justinus'] story that there was a significant Cypriot embassy among the contingent of Tyrian people who accompanied Elissa . . . It will be remembered that Elissa's name has a direct connection with the ancient name for the island of Cyprus (Alashiya) and that the name of the king of Tyre contains the Cypriot form of the god Pmy.[63]

As Trogus/Justinus is the main Roman source for the role of Cyprus in the colonization of Carthage, it is difficult to determine how well this part of the history was known to Roman historians generally. However, his details fit so well with the archaeological evidence, as well as with the evidence of the epigraphy (such as the Nora Stele) and the onomastics (see above), that it is unlikely that Trogus/Justinus fabricated the historiography. Furthermore, the early history of both Phoenicia and Carthage was preserved (minus the references to Cyprus) in other contemporary historians, most notably Josephus Flavius. Combined, these data suggest that to one extent or another the role of Cyprus in the early colonization efforts of Phoenicia was still known in the Augustan Age and later.

[62] Aubet 2001: 214–218; V. Karageorghis 1988: *passim*; Michaelidou-Nicolaou 1987: *passim*.

[63] Aubet 2001: 217. The Phoenician form of Pygmalion's name is attested as Pumayy-aton, possibly a combination of the Phoencian deity Pumay as attested on the Nora Inscription (see Aubet 206–209) and the Canaanite/Israelite Elyon (*Ibid* 208).

Just as important, though, are the literary qualities inherent in the Cypriot prenuptial ritual. At first glance, one (especially if one is a Hellenist) might be inclined to think that the abduction of girls from a religious ritual must foreshadow a future disaster on the part of the abductors. In such a way, Justinus' Cypriot maidens might reflect the Spartan maidens who were attacked during a religious ritual to Artemis in the countryside by the Messenians, thus eventuating the conquest of Messenia by the Spartans (Pausanias 4.4.2). The abduction of the Cypriot girls, then, might serve to foreshadow the eventual conquest of Carthage at the hands of the Romans (an important theme for Vergil, as discussed above, and a very good explanation for why Timaios, writing in the early third century BCE, might not have thought a symbolic reference to the Punic Wars overly important in his own texts).

And yet the abduction of the Cypriot girls is not presented in a negative light in Justinus. Concerning placement, this narrative comes between two passages highlighting the apparent sanctity of Elissa's actions. Just before, the crew from Tyre is joined by a priest of Jupiter in Cyprus, recognized as a sign of good omen. Immediately following, Pygmalion is warned not to chase after his sister by numerous divine seers who claim that he would be punished if he hindered the foundation of the city. Furthermore, Justinus specifically states that Carthage's demise came about due to events that happened after the death of Elissa, when the Carthaginians, to avert a plague, began to practice ritual infanticide. The abduction, therefore, has nothing to do with the eventual conquest of the city. There is nothing inauspicious about the Cypriot interlude or the abduction.

In fact, as J. A. Arieti has argued, rape narratives often initiate auspicious developments in Roman historiography.[64] For example, in his early *History of Rome*, Livy initiates several great political developments with a rape (or attempted rape) narrative. To quote Arieti:

The rape of the vestal virgin Rhea Silvia, supposedly by Mars, results in the birth of Romulus... The rape of the Sabine maidens results in the assurance of a continuing population for the new city and later an alliance with the Sabines. The rape of Lucretia brings about the fall of the monarchy and the establishment of the Republic. The rape of Roman prostitutes by Sabine hooligans leads directly to the establishment of the dictatorship. Finally, the attempted rape of Verginia leads

[64] Arieti 2002 [1997]: *passim.*

to the dissolution of the Second Decemvirate and the re-establishment of the Republic.[65]

In the Roman historiographic tradition, rapes or abductions might herald in positive changes or developments. This is especially so for the Roman rape narrative that most closely parallels the Cypriot narrative in Justinus – the rape of the Sabine women.[66] The similarities between the Sabine and Cypriot stories are striking.[67] In both instances, the abductors are groups of primarily male refugees, either just in the process of founding (Romans) or looking for (Tyrians) a new home. In both instances, the young women are abducted during a religious ritual, the Consualia in the case of the Romans, libation-pouring for the Cypriots. In both cases, the purpose of the abduction is the same. For Elissa, it was "so that her young men might have wives and her city a posterity." For the Romans, as Livy put it, their concern was that "a shortage of women meant that Rome's greatness was fated to last for a single generation, since there was no prospect of offspring at home nor any prospect of marriage with their neighbours." (*History of Rome* 1.9)[68] Even the final fates of both chief "abductors" – Elissa and Romulus – are the same, as both end up being revered as deities by their own populations, Romulus as Quirinus, Elissa as herself.[69]

A combination of historical accuracy and Roman literary precedent offer a more likely origin tale for Justinus' Cypriot prenuptial rite. While details from Herodotos may have (subconsciously) influenced either Trogus' or Justinus' construction of the imagery, the girls' age, placement, activities, and religious context can be explained as a parallel to the story of the Sabine women – marriageable girls engaged in a religious ritual in a vulnerable location abducted for the purpose of wedlock and procreation.

Without a clear and definite Herodotean precedent, the argument for prostitution as a definition for *quaestus* is weakened. It is not necessary for the plot, so to speak, to have the girls hooking, nor is there anything in the

---

[65] *Ibid*: 209.

[66] Desmond 1994: 26.

[67] A thousand pardons for the horrible and unintentional alliteration of this sentence.

[68] Translation from Lefkowitz and Fant 1992: 177, adapted.

[69] A similar tendency to equate the founding of Rome with the founding of Carthage is also present in the *Aeneid*: Both cities are founded by widowed refugees fleeing west at the behest of the deities and who establish their cities on territories containing animal or human heads. My thanks to Aislinn Melchior for help with Rome/Carthage literary parallels.

historiographic tradition that would implicate the Cypriots in premarital, much less sacred, prostitution. As such, a more neutral translation of Trogus' chapter 18.5.4 is possible:

> It was a custom among the Cypriots to send virgins before their weddings to the sea-shore on certain days to acquire dowry money by employment, and to pour libations to Venus for their remaining chastity.

SICCA VENERIA: VALERIUS MAXIMUS 2.6.15

I shall tie to this glory [that of the Indian women who commit suttee] the infamy of the Punic women, so that it might appear baser by comparison. For at Sicca is a temple of Venus in which the matrons used to gather and going forth from there for profit they used to acquire dowries by illicit use of the body, undoubtedly to join with such a dishonest bond honest marriages.

> *Cui gloriae Punicarum feminarum, ut ex conparatione turpius appareat, dedecus subnectam: Siccae enim fanum est Veneris, in quod se matronae conferebant atque inde procedentes ad quaestum, dotis corporis iniuria contrahebant, honesta nimirum tam inhonesto vinculo coniugia iuncturae.*

As ever, the acquisition of money for dowries, with a temple of Venus nearby, has led to interpretations based on sacred prostitution. H. J. Walker, whose translation is one of the very few available in English, annotates this passage with the explanation, "Temple prostitutes were found in sanctuaries of the Phoenician goddess Astarte (Venus)."[70] An interesting analysis has been offered by S. Montero, who, after noting that "las mujeres cartaginesas . . . se entregan a la prostitución sagrada,"[71] added:

> Valerio parece seguir . . . al historiador Trogo Pompeyo según el cual era costumbre de los chipriotas enviar a las muchachas a la playa antes de la boda para ejercer la prostitución y obtener así dinero para la dote y para libaciones en honor de Venus a la que pedían la honestidad que deberían mantener en el futuro. La reina Elissa ordenó raptar al menos a ochenta de esas muchachas, y embarcándolas consigo, las llevó a África . . . Aunque Valerio atribuye la práctica de la prostitución sagrada a las matronas cartaginesas éstas serían, en realidad, descendientes se las muchachas chipriotas.[72]

[70] Walker 2004: 61, no. 97.
[71] Montero 2004: 53.
[72] *Ibid.*

Put simply, Montero related this passage to the one discussed in the previous section of this chapter. The sacred prostitution of the Cypriot girls abducted by Elissa was transferred along with the girls to northern Africa. The fact that Valerius Maximus was known to use Pompeius Trogus as a source, especially for his foreign materials,[73] would support this interpretation. The fact that Pompeius Trogus may not have been discussing prostitution at all, of course, creates certain problems with this analysis.

Should we even understand prostitution (of any sort) to be at issue in this passage? The matter hangs on what Valerius meant by *corporis iniuria*, the means by which the *matronae* earned dowry monies. Technically speaking, there is no reference to sex implied in the word *iniuria*. According to the *Harpers Dictionary of Classical Antiquities*, *iniuria* is understood as follows:

> In general, iniuria is whatever is not ius; hence a violation of law. In a special sense, it denotes a wrong against one's person as distinguished from a wrong against one's property. It involves an insult (ὕβρις, contumelia) and must include an intent to act unlawfully (dolus). Instances of iniuria are assault, noisy abuse (convicium), libellous writings, insulting gestures, spitting at a man (*Ad Q. Fratr.* ii. 3, 2), dunning him for a debt in such a way as to injure his credit, etc.[74]

Or, perhaps more simply: "*iniuriae sunt, quae aut pulsatione corpus, aut convicio aures, aut aliqua turpitudine vitam cuiuspiam violant*" (Auct. Her. *4*, 25, 35.)

This, of course, brings up the possibility that the Punic women were acquiring dowry money by mugging people, literally an *iniuria* (assault) against the body (*corporis*). Maybe they threatened to spit at people who didn't pay up.

This seems unlikely, though, especially if Valerius Maximus was not, as I suspect, a Monty Python fanatic. Nevertheless, the lack of specificity of the word *iniuria* has led to considerable problems of both translation and interpretation. Either the sins of the Punic women were so well known that detail was superfluous, or the details of the surrounding text were meant to supply what Valerius refused to state openly. Let us consider these details.

---

[73] Bloomer 1992: 99–108.
[74] Written by H. T. Peck. Accessed via the Perseus Project, Chicago.

To begin, Valerius introduces this passage in reference to his preceding exemplum, his exceedingly high praise of the Indian practice of suttee. In §6.14 Valerius notes that polygyny was an ancient custom among the Indians. When the husband died, the wives competed to see who loved him the most; she who won got the very high honor of being allowed to burn herself with the husband's body on his funeral pyre. This passage is then "tied" (*subnectam*) to the disgraceful account of the Punic wives (*matronae*). So Valerius has set up a scenario where extremely loyal wives of one husband competing to make the ultimate sacrifice for him are contrasted to the shameful behavior of the African women.

I would argue that what we have here is a focus not merely on women, but on the relationships between wives and husbands. The quality of these relationships is enacted physically. The Indian women physically sacrifice themselves. The Siccan women, by contrast (*ex conparatione*), commit *corporis iniurias* for *quaestum*. What physical thing can a married woman do according to Valerius' Roman ideology that would count as an *iniuria*, especially if the underlying notion is that it is a disgrace, rather than an honor, toward her husband? Most likely, Valerius is here accusing the Siccan women not so much of prostitution *per se*, but of profitable, meretricious adultery. In this way, the polygyny of the Indians might be contrasted with a sort of polyandry on the part of the Punic people.

In referencing adultery Valerius would be highlighting one of the significant legal developments under Augustus, predecessor of Valerius' own emperor Tiberius and someone Valerius was generally anxious to praise.[75] These are the *Leges Iulia et Papia*, a series of new legislations regulating the marriages, reproduction, and overall sexual morals of the Romans.[76] According to the dictates of the *Leges*, adultery on the part of married women became an official criminal offence,[77] and, of especial interest, convicted adulteresses were equated with prostitutes.[78] As such, the meretricious air of the passage stems not so much from the women's being prostitutes, but being adulteresses, the functional equivalent.

Part of this equation stemmed from notions of sexual impurity, of course.[79] But even more significant was the notion that wives acquired

---

[75] Bloomer 1992: 204–207.

[76] *Lex Iulia de maritandis ordinibus* (18 BCE), *lex Iulia de adulteriis coercendis* (17 BCE), and the *lex Papia Poppaea* (9 CE). Knust 2006: 39.

[77] Gardner 1986: 127.

[78] *Ibid*: 129; McGinn 1998: 156–171, 222.

[79] McGinn 1998: 170: "Social convention unambiguously identified sexual promiscuity with prostitution."

material advantages, one might even call it *quaestus*, from their illicit affairs.[80] This was of such concern that the *lex Iulia de adulteriis coercendis* did not merely condemn adulterous, meretricious wives, but also potentially complacent husbands who willingly accepted the profits of their wives' extramarital relationships. One passage from this statute reveals much about the relationship between adultery, *quaestum facere*, and notions of prostitution:

> He is regarded as having made a profit out of the adultery of his wife who has received something in return for her committing adultery, and, whether he has accepted something rather often or just once, he is not to be let off, since a man is rightly to be regarded as having made a profit from the adultery of his own wife if he has received something in return for allowing his wife to commit adultery in the manner of a prostitute.[81]

> *Quaestum autem ex adulterio uxoris facere videtur, qui quid accepit, ut adulteretur uxor: sive enim saepius sive semel accepit, non est eximendus: quaestum enim de adulterio uxoris facere proprie ille existimandus est, qui aliquid accepit, ut uxorem pateretur adulterari meretricio quodam genere.*[82]

Similar to the notions of *quaestum corpore facere* that we saw in the previous section, here we have issues of *quaestum ex adulterio facere*, as the wife herself *adulterari meretricio quodam genere*. The new laws made a strong connection between adultery and prostitution, even in situations where the cuckolded husband was completely oblivious of the affair. Thus McGinn: "the identification of the adulteress as a prostitute is fundamental to the adultery law and operates independently of the presence of a *lenocinium* [husband/pimp]."[83]

One extremely important difference between the adulterous wife and the prostitute, however, was that prostitution was not illegal for the prostitute.[84] A later legal clause, possibly reflecting back to the early imperial period, states,

> If a woman who has been found guilty of having committed illicit sexual intercourse with you on showing the facts has everywhere openly offered her body for sale and as a prostitute has made herself available

---

[80] *Ibid*: 185.
[81] McGinn 1998: 221. McGinn's translation.
[82] Ulpian (4 *de adult.*).
[83] *Ibid*: 222.
[84] Gardner 1986: 130–134.

indiscriminately in the manner of a prostitute, the charge of adultery against her ceases.[85]

Si ea quae tibi stupro cognita est passim venalem formam exhibuit ac prostituta meretricio more vulgo se praebuit, adulterii crimen in ea cessat.

According to Valerius, the Punic matrons were acquiring money by illicit means. As the infamy of their actions was, based on comparison with the Indian wives, somehow related to their husbands, it is probable that the *corporis iniuria* Valerius refers to is some type of profitable, and thus meretricious, adultery.[86] However, the *matronae* were specifically not prostitutes, since their *quaestum* was acquired via *iniuria*. Profit for sex would not have been *iniustus* for actual prostitutes.

Between the clearly stated identification of the women as *matronae* and the identification of their "sin" as "*corporis iniuria*" for "*quaestum*," adultery, and not (sacred) prostitution, seems to be the thrust of Valerius' passage 2.6.15, although the adultery itself is understood to be profitable, and thus meretricious in its own right. Two other details of this passage then cry out for explanation, especially once the rubric of sacred prostitution is removed. Why do the women gather at a temple of Venus, and why on earth are married women collecting dowries? A few possibilities come to mind.

It is possible that Valerius was adding a hint of historical or ethnic accuracy by mentioning, by Roman name, the chief goddess of the Punic peoples – Tanit-Aštart. Furthermore, a reference to the temple of Venus may have served to make the actions of the matrons more scandalous. Although references to Venus usually summon notions of sexuality and, of course, prostitution, we are here considering Venus under the auspices of the Julio-Claudian regime. As such, Venus is not so much a wanton, adulterous sex-goddess but mother of Aeneas, *genetrix* of the Julian clan, and in many respects national mother. That the city matrons would convene by the temple of a goddess who oversees the ultimate marriage bond to proceed forth to disgrace that marriage adds a note of impiety to the Punic women's actions.

Finally, a reference to the city temple and the Punic women's going forth from it indicates that what the women are doing is in public. Rather than carefully hiding their adulterous behavior, the matrons of Sicca virtually advertise their actions, thus showing a lack of shame as well as

---

[85] Dioclet., Maxim. C 9.9.22 (a. 290). McGinn 1998: 219. McGinn's translation, adapted.
[86] McGinn 1998: 142, no. 19.

a lack of continence. This in itself brings up yet another parallel with prostitution as defined under the Augustan laws. Not only do prostitutes make a profit with their bodies (*corpore*), they do so publicly (*palam*).[87]

As for dowries, it is certainly possible that the women were acquiring dowries for someone other than themselves. Perhaps here Valerius is castigating the women for selling themselves to acquire dowries for their daughters, thus valuing descendants above spouses. Since Siccan dowries are made via meretricious adultery, Siccan marriages are somehow tainted.

HERODOTEAN PROTOTYPE...

Another possibility is that, once again, to some extent Valerius modeled this passage on a Herodotean prototype, the same muddled references to Herodotos 1.199 and 1.93 mentioned in the previous section. Although Valerius certainly knew about Herodotos (he mentions the historian by name in Book 8.13.5), it is more likely that Valerius "got his Herodotos" not from a direct reading of the Carian historian himself[88] but through the filter of Pompeius Trogus, who, as discussed above, was well acquainted with the first book of the *Histories* at least. Pompeius Trogus was one of Valerius Maximus' most important sources, and so it is possible to hypothesize a now unknown reference to the prostitution of the Babylonian and Lydian women in Trogus not preserved in the remaining epitomes.

If a Herodotean prototype exists in this passage, the presence of the temple of Venus might be understood as a reference back to the temple of Mylitta in Herodotos 1.199, whereas the fact that the Siccan matrons "proceed forth from it" may reflect back to Herodotos' claim that the women of Babylon leave the sanctuary to "mingle" with their foreign men. That the Siccan women acquire dowries may once again be a sign of the conflation of Lydian and Babylonian types of prostitution – the women gather at the temple of Venus (1.199) to collect dowry money (1.193) by *corporis iniuria* (1.193 and 1.199).

That Valerius chose to transplant this anecdote from Babylon/Lydia to northern Africa is well in keeping with his overall tendency to dehistoricize and departicularize his exempla to make them more universal. To quote M. Bloomer:

---

[87] *Ibid*: 124–131.
[88] Bloomer 1992: 145.

[Valerius Maximus] excised anecdotes from their historical surroundings, from the patterns and details that give a particular event its individuality. Great men doing great things and the despicable doing the reverse swiftly become moral categories, not historical events. . . . One Scipio can easily be granted the feats of another (7.5.2), just as a Roman replacement must be found for a Marathonian hero (3.2.22).[89]

To transfer scandalous behavior to Punic women, to that society most villainized by the Romans, conforms to Valerius' methodology overall.[90]

. . . AND TYPICALLY ROMAN

All of this is likewise in keeping with standard Roman techniques of accusation against a "rival" city or community. As J. W. Knust has argued, accusations of adultery, especially on the part of a city's women, were a particularly damning kind of condemnatory rhetoric, not only vilifying the individual participants, but suggesting that the entire community is corrupt and on the verge of collapse due to the inability of the men to control their women. Thus,

> Individual men could be evaluated according to their success at controlling women; cities could be evaluated in similar terms. . . . Following the rise of Augustus, Horace claimed, chastity was restored; Rome had finally mastered "her" women. Juvenal made the opposite claim; he satirized the corruption of Rome by describing the fornications of Rome's "good women" in exquisite detail, including those of the Empress Messalina. Lucian, in his characterization of Rome as an ideal place for hedonists, remarked that the city was awash in its adulteries (*Nigr.* 15–16). . . . According to the logic of this discourse, "good" cities are populated by "proper" women who preserve their chastity and defer to their husbands, but "bad" cities are overrun with adultery and fornication (e.g. Plut. *Cat.Mai.* 8.2–3).[91]

In the end, it is not necessary to see a reference to Herodotos in this passage of Valerius. As discussed above, all elements of the exemplum do make sense without any reference to the *Histories*. The matrons of Sicca are condemned because they publicly commit adultery and make a profit from it. That profit is then used to fund dowries, possibly for the women's own offspring. However, as with the *Letter of Jeremiah* in

---

[89]   *Ibid*: 19.
[90]   *Ibid*: 49.
[91]   Knust 2006: 43.

Chapter 5, a number of the details in the account make more sense if they somehow reflect back onto Herodotos, especially in this instance with Punic matrons collecting dowries. Most assuredly, modern commentators would not have perceived a reference to sacred prostitution in this passage if they did not read it through the lens of Herodotos.

CONCLUSIONS

As with Strabo, so too here: sacred prostitution is more a mirage than a historical fact. In the four texts considered here – Klearkhos frag. 6, Justinus 18.5 and 21.3, and Valerius Maximus 2.6.15 – only one actually pertains to sacred prostitution in any way: Justinus' reference to the *votum* of Lokris, which itself is probably not historical. In the other three instances, there is no reference to sacred prostitution. Klearkhos was writing about the violence and retribution that attend extremely decadent behavior; Justinus' Cypriot reference is a reflection of Livy's rape of the Sabine women; and Valerius Maximus was not writing about prostitution *per se*, but lucrative adultery. Once again, it is only by reading sacred prostitution *into* the texts that we have found it there.

CHAPTER NINE

ARCHAEOLOGICAL "EVIDENCE" FROM ITALY

THIS SHORT CHAPTER IS FURNISHED IN THE INTEREST OF THOROU-
ghness and to correct some popular misconceptions about sacred
prostitution in central Italy. The two regions in Italy once implicated
in the sacred prostitution debate on the basis of physical remains –
Etruscan Pyrgi and Italic Rapino – have since been reconsidered, so
that few scholars still consider these regions to be associated with sacred
prostitution.[1] Nevertheless, it is worthwhile to look at the history of the
sacred prostitution debate at Pyrgi and Rapino for two reasons. On the
one hand, there are still a number of publications available that discuss
sacred prostitution as having been practiced at these sites, and thus there
is still the need to banish that specter in the literature (especially with
Pyrgi). On the other hand, the ways in which sacred prostitution came
to be associated with these two areas offer a fascinating insight into how
this vicious cycle functions. For, in the absence of literary testimonia,
the sacred prostitution idea only emerged in association with Pyrgi and
Rapino through some rather gratuitous circular reasoning and apparent
wish-fulfillment.

PYRGI

The suggestion that sacred prostitution occurred at ancient Pyrgi brings
the sacred prostitution debate into a whole new community: the
Etruscans of Italy. The idea that sacred prostitution might have existed
here has at its base, no doubt, the fact that the Etruscans, like the Greeks,
were heavily influenced by the Phoenicians during the early evolution

---

[1] There is not a peep about prostitution of any sort in Nancy Thomson de Grummond
and Erika Simon's 2006 publication *The Religion of the Etruscans*.

of their society. Thus, as in the case of Greece, sacred prostitution can be blamed on early, eastern, Semitic influence (see Chapter 2). Furthermore, as a link between Phoenicia and Rome, the Etruscans might then be signaled out as the means by which sacred prostitution came into the Roman orbit. The theoretical connections between Rome, the Etruscans, and Pyrgi are spelled out by G. Colonna:

> Gli esempi di prostituzione sacra nel mondo antico sono numerosi, specie alla periferia della grecità, ma per i Romani dell'età di Plauto la pratica evocava, a quanto sembra, in primo luogo gli Etruschi, e forse in particolare il vicino santuario di Pyrgi, ormai romanizzato e impoverito, ma ricco ancora di un passato che non era facile dimenticare.[2]

One of the more recent and commonly accessible books on ancient Etruria reveals much about notions of sacred prostitution at Pyrgi. In N. Spivey and S. Stoddart's 1990 publication *Etruscan Italy* the authors recount this concerning the Pyrgi sanctuary with its "holy brothel":

> [A]longside Temple B [...dedicated to Aštart] there is a structure divided into multiple small cells. A charitable interpretation of these would be that they are shops, or perhaps hostel accommodations for those seeking a medical cure; but ports are never very salubrious places, and given that there is a Roman reference to the *scorta Pyrgensia* ('the Pyrgi harlots'), and given the presence of the Astarte-Aphrodite cult, it seems likely that the structure was a brothel of some official nature within the scope of the sanctuary. Figure 75 gives the excavator's idea of how these little love-nests may have looked.[3]

There is a drawing, figure 75, labeled "Brothels at Pyrgi," showing little rooms with a bed clearly visible in one. Upon the bed lies a woman visible and naked from the waist down. Her pubic hairs are clearly visible, giving, apparently, no doubt as to what she must be doing there.

The above quotation casts into high relief the three categories of "evidence" used to argue for sacred prostitution at Pyrgi: The presence of an Aštart cult, the literary reference to the *scorta Pyrgensia*, and the sanctuary architecture itself.[4] Let us consider each of these in turn.

The cult of Aštart at Pyrgi, syncretized with the Etruscan regnal goddess Uni, is attested on three gold lamellae dating to circa 500 BCE and

---

[2] Colonna 1984–1985: 65.
[3] Spivey and Stoddart 1990: 125. "Love-nests"????
[4] Glinister 2000: 28.

discovered in 1964 at the sanctuary.[5] These three plaques, one in Phoenician, one an Etruscan paraphrase of the former, and one separate text
composed by the same man, are dedications to Uni-Aštart by the Etruscan "king" Tiberius Velianas.[6] Concerning the introduction of the
goddess's cult at Pyrgi,

> It is likely that the sanctuary was primarily dedicated to the Etruscan
> Uni. However, when pressure from Greeks and Romans encouraged
> the forging of closer alliances between Etruscans and Carthaginians,
> Tiberius Velianas opened the door to a multi-ethnic interpretation of
> the sanctuary. Or, more simply put, he recognized an *interpretatio* syn-
> cretism between the queen goddess of the Etruscan pantheon – Uni –
> and the queen deity of the Phoenicio-Carthaginians – Ashtart.[7]

The idea that a cult of Aštart would encompass ritual prostitution is
based on several flawed and circular arguments. The first is evident in a
pair of references presented by G. Barker and T. Rasmussen in their 1998
publication *The Etruscans*. According to these authors, "At Pyrgi it has
been suggested that there were temple courtesans in the service of the
love goddess Astarte."[8] Concerning the sanctuary itself they write that the
architectural feature mentioned above "has been tentatively interpreted
as a series of rooms for sacred prostitution in devotion to the Phoenician
love goddess Astarte."[9] The idea seems to be that Aštart is a love goddess,
and thus ritual sex would be appropriate to her. Certainly, as some have
argued, it was the influence of her cult in the west that brought sacred
prostitution to the Greeks.

But Aštart is not a love goddess. Although her iconography does have
erotic elements, what we know of the goddess based on the epigraphic
evidence of her cult in the Levant, Cyprus, and abroad all suggests that
Aštart, like Uni, is a queenly goddess, a protector of the royal family (at
least in Tyre), and a warrior goddess.[10] The only reason this Levantine
deity is associated with love (as well as sex and fertility) is because of the
syncretism that exists between Phoenician Aštart and Greek Aphrodite.
However, as I have discussed elsewhere, the relationship between Aštart
and Aphrodite is hardly the direct, one-to-one *interpretatio* syncretism

---

[5] Bonfante 2006: 13.
[6] Bonnet 1996: 121; Serra Ridgeway 1990: 519.
[7] Budin 2004: 136.
[8] Barker and Rasmussen 1998: 111.
[9] *Ibid*: 224.
[10] Budin 2004: 107–8; Budin 2003b: 225–228; Bonnet 1996: *passim*.

usually imagined. Although these goddesses are closely identified on Cyprus, both being, ultimately, the "Goddess of Cyprus" to that island's different ethnic populations, the links between them beyond the island are no stronger than those they both have with other goddesses. Aphrodite is not only seen as a Greek Aštart, but a Greek Atargatis, Isis, Argimpasa, and even Kybele. Aštart is likewise identified with Isis, the Balat Gubal, and Egyptian Hathor.[11] Neither Isis nor Kybele is identified as a "sex" or "love goddess" because of her relationship to Aphrodite; there is no reason to assume the same for Aštart. Aštart is not a love goddess.

Furthermore, because the presence of an actual goddess of sex – Aphrodite – does not lead to the establishment of sacred prostitution (see Chapters 4 through 8), there is no reason to suppose that the cult of a Levantine warrior goddess would. Finally, as we have seen in Chapter 2, there is no evidence for any sacred prostitution in the Near East itself (or, for that matter, Carthage), Phoenician Aštart's home turf. A cult of sacred prostitution could most certainly not have followed Aštart to Italy if it did not exist in the place from which it supposedly emigrated. All in all, the fact that Aštart was worshipped at Pyrgi does not offer any evidence, no matter how slight or indirect, that sacred prostitution would somehow be a part of her cult here.

The second bit of evidence used to support the notion of sacred prostitution at Pyrgi is what Spivey and Stoddart called "a Roman reference to the *scorta Pyrgensia* ('the Pyrgi harlots')." The reference in question is a fragment from Lucilius (Luc. fr. 1271 Marx), a satirist of the first century CE, as preserved in a *scholion* to the *Aeneid* (10.184 = 10.258) as written by Servius, a commentator of the fourth century CE.

The fragment by Lucilius reads "*scorta Pyrgensia.*" That's it; there isn't much to go on. The text from Servius is not much more helpful:

Old Pyrgi: this was a most noble fortress at that time when the Tuscans practiced piracy; for their metropolis was there: thus later, it is said, it was captured by Dionysios, Tyrant of Sicily, about which/whom Lucilius '*scorta Pyrgensia.*'

Pyrgi Veteres hoc castellum nobilissimum fuit eo tempore quo Tusci piraticam exercuerunt; nam illic metropolis fuit: quod postea expugnatum a Dionysio Tyranno Siciliae dicitur, de quo Lucilius 'scorta Pyrgensia.'

Quite simply, the surrounding commentary by Servius offers little more information than Lucilius alone.

[11] For an extensive treatment of this topic see Budin 2004: *passim.*

Nevertheless, the usual interpretation, based on the fact that a cult of Aštart existed at Pyrgi, is that these *scorta* are sacred prostitutes. Thus Colonna, "Oggi che sappiamo del culto di Astarte nel santuario è inevitabile postulare un collegamento tra esso e le prostitute ricordate da Lucilio: dove potevano trovarsi le < <prostitute di Pyrgi> >, a quanto pare passate in proverbio, se non nel santuario di Astarte?"[12] F. R. Serra Ridgeway repeats these sentiments when considering the series of rooms by Temple B at the sanctuary (see below): "it might represent the quarters where the priestesses practiced sacred prostitution, as is well known in other sanctuaries of Astarte, particularly the one at Erice in Sicily, and as the proverbial mention of the *scorta pyrgensia* in the literary tradition seems to confirm."[13] Far more reticent, admirably so, on this matter is J.-R. Jannot in his work on Etruscan religion. Although considering the possibility of sacred prostitution at Pyrgi, Jannot nevertheless says quite simply of this interpretation of the Lucilius fragment, "Lucilius writes of the *scorta pyrgensia* ('the debauchery of Pyrgi'), and Servius... alludes to the same tradition: but is this sufficient evidence and a correct interpretation?"[14]

Probably not. The textual evidence leaves us with two important points of ambiguity – the meaning of *scorta* and how Lucilius' phrase is meant to relate to the rest of Servius' text. The original meaning of *scortum* (singular) is quite simply "leather, hide."[15] Only later does it take on the meaning of "a harlot, prostitute."[16] The prostitute in question can be either male or female.[17] The reference to *scorta* Pyrgensia in Lucilius, then, can be referring to either male or female prostitutes, or, quite possibly, to hides or leather. Our context gives us no way to determine.

Likewise, we do not know for certain the antecedent to the relative pronoun (*de*) *quo* in Servius. As a singular masculine or neuter, the *quo* may refer to the *castellum* in the first phrase of the text, or to Dionysios toward the end. As Dionysios is closer, and the primary actor in the secondary clause of the text, the syntax works out better if Dionysios is the antecedent, rather than the fortress itself.

What, then, does Dionysios have to do with the *scorta* of Pyrgi? One possibility, as suggested by F. Glinister, is that this emphasized Dionysios'

[12] Colonna 1984–1985: 65. See likewise Colonna 1985: 128.
[13] Serra Ridgway 1990: 522. On Eryx/Erice, see Chapter 7.
[14] Jannot 2005: 194, no. 48.
[15] Adams 1983: 322.
[16] The definition as given in C. T. Lewis's Latin lexicon.
[17] Adams 1983: 322.

reputation for sexual misconduct[18] (although not, as we have seen, to the extent as did his son Dionysios the younger; see Chapter 8). Dionysios, then, may have been infamous for his relations with the city's prostitutes.

This, however, seems somewhat unlikely in light of what we know of this episode from Diodoros Siculus. According to this historian, in the ninety–ninth Olympiad (385 BCE), Dionysios I attacked the sanctuary of Pyrgi under the pretext of combating piracy (*Bibliothekê* 15.14):

> Dionysios, in need of money, set out to make war against Tyrrhenia with sixty triremes. The excuse he offered was the suppression of the pirates, but in fact he was going to pillage a holy temple, richly provided with dedications, which was located in the seaport of the Tyrrhenian city of Agylle, the name of the port being Pyrgi. Putting in by night, he disembarked his men, attacked at daybreak, and achieved his design; for he overpowered the small number of guards in the place, plundered the temple, and amassed no less than a thousand talents. When the men of Agylle came out to bring help, he overpowered them in battle, took many prisoners, laid waste their territory, and then returned to Syracuse. From the booty which he sold he took in no less than five hundred talents.[19]

There is no reference to prostitutes or the rape of the local populace, or even of Dionysios lingering to enjoy his victory. What we do have is a description of military conquest with an emphasis on the loot stolen from the temple and the acquisition of prisoners. If *scortum* in this instance retained its original meaning, Servius may have had in mind the carting off of the city's wealth in leather bags. Or, possibly, the sale of the prisoners, which, as Diodoros relates, contributed to the additional 500 talents acquired through the attack on Agylle. As stated above, *scorta* can refer to male prostitutes as well as female.

The paucity of information makes it impossible to know what either Lucilius or Servius had in mind when referring to the *scorta Pyrgensia*. One thing is rather clear, though, and this is that there is no good reason to associate the *scorta*, whatever they were, directly with the sanctuary at Pyrgi. Although Diodoros does make it clear that Dionysios intended to attack the sanctuary, he makes no reference to prostitutes. Servius, although mentioning Lucilius' *scorta*, makes no reference to the sanctuary, referring rather to the pirates' *castellum* and *metropolis*. As Dionysios was famed for having destroyed the town sanctuary, the later reference to

---

[18] Glinister 2000: 30.
[19] Translation from the Perseus Project.

scorta Pyrgensia in relation to Dionysios could also simply refer to prostitutes becoming common in the city *after* its conquest, and thus after
the despoiling of the temple. In such a case, the *scorta* are whores, but of
the common, secular, economically depressed variety.[20] In the absence
of any clarity in this issue, it is best not to overburden the text with a
sacred prostitution interpretation.

Finally, there is the sanctuary architecture itself. The structure specifically linked to the sacred prostitution question is a series of about 17
small (2×3 m) rooms running along the temenos wall on the south side
of Temple B, contemporary with the temple, and thus dating to the very
end of the sixth century.[21] Based on the gold lamellae mentioned above,
the temple was dedicated to Etruscan Uni–Phoenician/Punic Aštart, and
thus the series of rooms was understood to belong to this cult as well.

It was the excavator G. Colonna who first suggested that these rooms
were the "cribs" of "hierodules" of Aštart, "l'edificio in cui veniva prat-
icata la prostituzione sacra, da parte di sacerdotesse che, così facendo, si
identificavano e si sostituivano alla dea, secondo l'antico rito orientale,
che a Cipro ha dato origine al culto della Afrodite.... "[22] He based this
identification on three pieces of evidence, two literary, one historical.
The first is a passage from Plautus' *Cistellaria* (5, 562–563), in which a
slave woman mentions how, "in the Tuscan fashion, all their girls shame-
fully earn a dowry by their body" (*ex Tusco modo, tute tibi indigne dotem
quaeras corpore*).[23] This, however, is a fictional, and even comedic, reference to a secular type of prostitution, which even Colonna compares to
Herodotos 1.93, in which purely secular Lydian girls are saddled with the
same accusation.

Colonna's second literary reference is to Lucilius' *scorta Pyrgensia* mentioned above. As already discussed, this cannot serve as evidence for sacred
prostitution in Pyrgi. Finally, coming full circle, Colonna presents the
argument that sacred prostitution took place in association with Temple
B at Pyrgi because the temple was dedicated to Aštart, and the cult of
Aštart, as he claimed, was linked to the practice of sacred prostitution
throughout the Mediterranean:

> Ora è noto che il culto di Erice aveva come connotato più appariscente
> la prostituzione sacra, che lo accompagnò in quella sua riconosciuta

---

[20] Glinister 2000: 30–31.
[21] Colonna 1984–5: 59.
[22] *Ibid*: 64.
[23] On the expression *quaero corpore*, see Chapter 8.

filiale che fu Sicca Veneria. Quindi pienamente plausibile che sia stato introdotto anche a Pyrgi, come un sontuoso dono regale, conseguenza di un voto personale di Thefarie, novello Cinera, ad Astarte.[24]

As we have already seen in Chapter 7, there was no sacred prostitution in Eryx, in spite of cults of both Aštart and Aphrodite. As discussed in Chapter 8, there was, likewise, no sacred prostitution at Sicca Veneria. The false comparanda betray the historical argument, rendering it null and void.

In contrast to these faulty arguments for sacred prostitution at Pyrgi, and thus the presence of a sacred brothel of sorts, a far simpler explanation has been offered for the series of rooms by Temple B. Quite simply, they may have served as a *katagôgion*, a hostel or "motel" for those visiting the sanctuary. Colonna himself suggests as much in his initial publication of the structure, claiming that, "L'aspetto complessivo della costruzione, che comprendeva almeno 17 celle, forse 20, ricorda quello di un καταγώγον, di un ostello."[25] M. Cristofani, writing a decade later, came to the same conclusion, not only in noting the similarity of the structure to other known hostels in the Greco-Roman world, but in arguing that all aspects of the architecture and iconography of Temple B at Pyrgi pertain to the Roman (or, if possible to know, Romano-Etruscan) world. To see a sacred brothel by Temple B would be to impose a level of Phoenician/Punic influence that does not otherwise appear at the site.[26]

The supposed presence of sacred prostitution at Pyrgi is based on a series of circular arguments. The fact that Aštart, syncretized with Uni, was worshipped at Pyrgi opened the door to the possibility that any reference to prostitution in any way applicable to Pyrgi must refer to specifically sacred prostitution. Thus, Lucilius' *scorta Pyrgensia* were interpreted as sacred prostitutes, even in the absence of a reference to the sanctuary (or anything else, for that matter . . .). Plautus' mention of "Tuscan" prenuptial prostitution became affixed to the sanctuary at Pyrgi. A series of small rooms comparable to hostels throughout the Greco-Roman world came to be seen as a holy brothel because Aštart was worshipped there, and the literary "evidence" "argued" for the presence of sacred prostitutes at Pyrgi. But once we recognize the fact that Aštart herself had nothing to do with sacred prostitution, the entire body of evidence breaks down.

---

[24] Colonna 1984–1985: 67.

[25] *Ibid*: 59, with full citations of comparanda.

[26] Cristofani 1996: 79. Likewise, J. MacIntosh Turfa has noted that there is no Punic material among the hundreds of votives excavated at Pyrgi (personal communication).

RAPINO

The Rapino Bronze, a third-century BCE Marrucinian–Oscan dialect inscription composed in the Latin alphabet, was discovered in the early nineteenth century in a cemetery about a mile southeast of Rapino.[27] After initial publications in the later nineteenth century, especially by Mommsen and Vetter, the piece was lost after the Second World War and only recently reemerged at the Pushkin Museum in Russia.

The text pertains to the economic arrangements of an apparent joint cult of Jove and Ceres in the Marrucinian community. It is the source of the revenue in this cult that brings the bronze into the sacred prostitution debate. According to the most common translations and interpretations of the text, revenues might be derived from the sale of unconsumed sacrificial meat. However, in the 1990s A. La Regina proposed an alternate interpretation of the text, whereby what was for sale was not meat, but the slave girls of Jove, whom he identified as sacred prostitutes.[28]

The inscription as transliterated by Vetter and preserved in Martínez-Pinna and Glinister reads,

> aisos pacris totai
> maroucai lixs
> asignas ferenter
> auiatas toutai
> maroucai ioues
> patres ocres tarin
> cris iouias.agine
> iafc esuc agine asum
> babu poleenis feret
> regen[ai] peai cerie iouia
> pacrsi eituam am<.>aten
> s uenalinam ni ta[g]a nipis ped
> i suam.[29]

The translation, as devised by Vetter, Wallace, Martínez-Pinna, and Glinister might be put together as follows:

> May the gods (be) propitious. (A) regulation(s) for the Marrucinian community. The sacrificial flesh, judged propitious for the Marrucinian community by the oracle of Jove the father and of the Tarincrine mount,

---

[27] Glinister 2000: 21; Wallace 1984: 101.

[28] La Regina 1997a: *passim.*

[29] Glinister 2000: 21; Martínez-Pinna 1998: 203.

is brought forth. Let the Jovian priestess place them on sale, at the appropriate price, to enhance the treasury of Ceres. May it be propitious. They have collected (?) the money received from the sale. Let no one touch any but his own.

By contrast, La Regina offers the following emendations to the text and thus a different translation:

> aisos pacris totai
> maroucai lixs
> asignas ferenter.
> auiatas toutai.
> maroucai ioues.
> patres ocres tarin
> cris iouias. agine
> iafc esuc agine asum
> ba[-]u [-]poleenis feret
> regen[-] di[-]i cerie. iouia.
> pacrsi. eituam am. aten
> s uenalinam. ni ta[-]a. nipis. ped
> i. suam

> (presi gli auspici:) gli dei (sono) favorevoli;
> legge per il popolo marrucino:
> le (ancelle) giovie di Giove padre dell'arce Tarincra assegnate
>   in servitù, dopo che il popolo marrucino avrà preso gli
>   auspici su di esse, siano poste in vendita;
> le ponga in vendita, al giusto prezzo (?), la sacerdotessa
>   giovia per accrescere il tesoro do Cerere;
> (presi gli auspici: gli dei) sono favorevoli;
> (i Marrucini) hanno stabilito che nessuno tocchi il denaro
>   ricavato dalla vendita se non quando ne abbia il diritto.[30]

In this instance, what is being sold to augment the treasury of Ceres is the slave girls (*ancille*) of Jove "*(ancillae) Ioviae adsignatae (in servitutem)*".[31]

The main problem with this interpretation (among many, according to Glinister) is that the word for slave-girls/sacred prostitutes – *ancillae* – does not actually appear in the text of the Rapino Bronze; La Regina interjected the word himself. The only reason to place this word in the text is to force the law to be about sacred prostitution in the absence of

---

[30] La Regina 1997a, 1997b.
[31] La Regina 1997a.

any other supporting data. Sacred prostitution in inferred, not implied (much less stated).

This, of course, brings up the question of why La Regina would see sacred prostitution in a random Marrucinian text that not only does not pertain to prostitution, but even to Venus/Aphrodite. Once again, it is a matter of circular reasoning and, to a certain extent, wish fulfillment. At the end of his article on the Rapino Bronze and its sacred prostitutes, La Regina notes several references to the practice of sacred prostitution in ancient Italy:

> Il nome di Marte legato ad una notizia sulla practica dell "hierodouleia" in ambiente sabino (Dion. Hal. II, 48, 1–4) e così la connessione . . . con Venere, suggeriscono che anche nel santuario lucano fosse praticata la prostituzione sacra. . . . una dedica (Vetter 107) a Venus Erycina, Herentatei Herukinai, il cui culto era sicuramente praticato, come del resto anche a Roma, dalle meretrici. Un decreto istitutivo della prostituzione sacra emanato con riluttanza a Locri Epizephyrii nel IV secolo a.C. è ricordato da Giustino (XXI, 3, 2–7).[32]

The nonexistence of sacred prostitution in relation to such things as *hierodouleia*, the cult of Erycine Venus, and Epizephyrian Lokris has been discussed in previous chapters. What is important to note here is that these faulty references then opened the door to the creation of new references in a text which, on the surface, does not seem to be about sex in any way.

However, once the door is opened, different types of rationalization are free to enter. For La Regina, this consists of pulling references to Venus into the cults mentioned in the text and of finding a vocabulary for sacred prostitution in the ancient Italic dialects. Concerning Venus, La Regina notes a prominent joint cult of Ceres and Venus throughout the Marrucinian and neighboring communities. The reference to the treasury of Ceres in the Rapino Bronze, then, might also be linked to a theorized joint treasury with Venus. Likewise, Venus, like Herakles, was frequently linked in cult with Jove, even acquiring the epithet "Jovian," as in the title of the priest "*sacerdos Iovia Veneria*" (CIL X, 1207). The Rapino Bronze, then, which does not actually mention Venus, does mention two of her typical cojoiners – Ceres and Jove – and thus a link to Venus herself might be postulated. This is a stretch at best.

Then there is the desire to create a vocabulary for sacred prostitution, much as we saw in Chapter 2 for Near Eastern cult functionaries and

[32] *Ibid.*

in Chapters 3 and 8 for the Greek word *hetairismos*. In this instance, La Regina refers to the first-century BCE Herentas Inscription from Corfinium, a funerary dedication for a priestess (*sacaracirix*) of what La Regina claims was a joint cult of Venus and Ceres, wherein Venus is dubbed Urania (a link to Venus' "Oriental" manifestation?). The translation of the priestess's cult title *pristafalacirix* is given as *praestabulatrix*, "ossia un'incaricata delle prostitute."[33] The text and translation as given by Wallace read as follows:

> . . . pracom. . . .
> usur.pristafalacirix.prism.petieu.ip.uiad
> uibu.omnitu.uranias.ecuc.empratois
> clisuist.cerfum sacaracirix.semunu.sua[.]
> aetatu.firata.fertlid praicime.perseponas
> afed.eite.uus.pritrome pacris puu.ecic
> lexe.lifar.dida.uus.deti.hanustu.herentas

. . . tomb. . . . Prima Petiedia, *praestabulatrix*, wife of . . . , *ip.uiDad/ uibDu.omnitu*. She was laid to rest at the bidding of Urania. The priestess of the Cerfes departed for the abode of Persephone, her own life having been? copiously. May you go forward propitiously, you whom it is permitted to read this. May hanustu? Herentas give you wealth.[34]

Although it is true that the text names Urania as the individual who laid Prima Petiedia to rest, there is no indication here that this is the name of a divinity, much less one to whom Prima was a priestess. *If* we might see a reference to Aphrodite Ourania in this passage, the goddess here would appear to have more to do with mortality than sex. Furthermore, Prima is not named as a priestess of Urania, but of the Cerfes (which La Regina takes as Ceres, thus creating a further "link" between Ceres and Venus that then supports his argument for bringing Venus into the interpretation of the Rapino Bronze). However, without the link to Venus (Urania), there is little reason to suggest that the cult title *pristafalacirix/praestabulatrix* should be read as "sacred prostitute," especially considering that the text states quite clearly that Prima Petiedia was married (*usur*).

There is, in the end, no reason to support La Regina's suggestion that the Rapino Bronze pertains to sacred prostitution. The "word" for sacred prostitute – *ancillae* – is not even in the text, but is inserted by La Regina on the speculation that this was just one more reference to an institution

---

[33] *Ibid.*
[34] Wallace 1984: 92.

that his (mis-)readings of other documents, such as Justinus 21, 3, created. What is fascinating in this instance, though, is to see how the process of logic works in the creation of new sources of "evidence" for sacred prostitution in the ancient world. Because authors believe that sacred prostitution existed, evidence is tweaked and manipulated to place references to that institution into texts, inscriptions, and even, as we saw with Pyrgi, architectural structures. This then creates new "evidence" that will then be used to support further hypotheses concerning the relevance of sacred prostitution to various texts, inscriptions, and architectural structures, until it seems that there is a whole world of evidence supporting the existence of sacred prostitution in the ancient world. And so the myth survives and grows.

CHAPTER TEN

THE EARLY CHRISTIAN RHETORIC

E VEN MORE NUMEROUS THAN PASSAGES FROM STRABO IN THE HIS-
toriography of ancient sacred prostitution are the references that
appear in the early Christian literature. Although different scholars cite
different passages as referring to sacred prostitution, a "complete" list
includes no fewer than 10 authors: Paul of Tarsus, Clement of Alexandria, Arnobius of Sicca, Lactantius, Eusebius of Caesaria, Athanasius of
Alexandria, Firmicus Maternus, Augustine of Hippo, Sokrates Scholasticus, and Sozomen. Each one of these has been used to support the notion
of sacred prostitution existing in one of the regions mentioned previously
in this work – St. Paul for Corinth, Clement and Lactantius for Cyprus,
Athanasius and Augustine for Phoenicia.

Nevertheless, the evidence derived from the early Christian sources is
not entirely credible. Although St. Paul does discuss the problems of *pornoi*
and *porneia* in the congregation at Corinth, he himself never refers to any
links with the local cult of Venus. Furthermore, as recent scholars such
as R. Kirchhoff and K. Gaca have discussed, Paul's definition(s) of the
terms *pornos* and *porneia* are quite distinct from the traditional pagan (and
modern) meanings, and thus must be categorized and studied differently.[1]

Then there is the biased nature of the writings. With the (slight) exception of Eusebius and his "followers" Sokrates and Sozomen, who were
composing church histories, each of the remaining texts supposedly referring to sacred prostitution is accusational, ranging in genre from apologetic, as with Lactantius, to polemic, as with Firmicus Maternus. It is the
purpose of these pieces to show that (proto-orthodox[2]) Christianity is

---

[1] Gaca 2003: 172; Kirchhoff 1994: 196.
[2] As Ehrman 2003: 7 has discussed, there was no such thing as Christian "Ortho-
doxy" in the first three centuries CE. As such, I am here using his terminology of

not merely a legitimate religion, but infinitely superior to the pagan religions and so-called Christian heresies with which it was competing. It is to the benefit of the authors' arguments to present both paganism and alternate forms of Christianity in the worst possible light. Often this was accomplished via a condemnation of sexual moeurs, whereby the Christian authors accused their opponents of egregiously lustful behaviors.[3] References to sacred prostitution in such a context cannot so much be taken for historical evidence as for a type of condemnatory rhetoric.

Finally, as was the case with Strabo, the "references" to sacred prostitution in the early Christian writings are far more imagined than real. Of all the authors mentioned above, only two actually refer to sacred prostitution *per se* in their works: Athanasius and Augustine, both of whom offer an extremely general, undetailed description of sacred prostitution in "Phoenicia." There is no reference to sacred prostitution – defined as the sale of a person's body for sex where some or all of the money is dedicated to a deity – in any of the other sources. Instead, the passages typically interpreted as pertaining to sacred prostitution fall into three categories: attempts to redefine and regulate newly emergent Christian sexual moeurs, descriptions of Aphrodite/Venus herself being a whore, and simple Christian lust-rhetoric. Let us consider these before moving on to the data that actually refer to the topic of this book.

PAUL AND THE PROSTITUTES

There are two epistles written by Paul of Tarsus that are brought into the debate on sacred prostitution – 1 Corinthians 5–6:15–19[4] and 1 Timothy 2:9–15. The passage in 1 Timothy, pertaining to the city of Ephesos in Asia Minor, will be dealt with in the following chapter for reasons that will become obvious. That 1 Corinthians has become muddled in the matter of sacred prostitution rests on two factors: various references to *porneia* in the text and, far more importantly, a preconceived notion of sacred prostitution occurring in Corinth.

This latter datum cannot be overemphasized, for at no other time when Paul makes references to *porneia* (or *pornoi*, etc.) does specifically

---

"proto-orthodoxy" to refer to the Christian apologetic literature that would come to be viewed, for the most part, as "Orthodox" in later eras.

[3] Knust 2006: *passim*; Ehrman 2003: 197–202.

[4] I have never actually seen these passages used as evidence for sacred prostitution, but rather it has been common to interpret the passages in question in light of such a supposed practice in Corinth.

sacred prostitution become implicated. Thus in his first letter to the Thessalonians (4:3), Paul tells his addressees that it is "the desire of God, the one revered among you, to hold yourselves off from *porneia*." But no one considers this *porneia* to be of a sacred variety. Likewise Ephesians 5:3, Galatians 5:19, and Colossians 3:5. It is exclusively in Corinth that New Testament scholars have seen the shadow of sacred prostitution lurking behind Paul's prohibitions. This is most clearly evident in J. Héring's work *The First Epistle of Saint Paul to the Corinthians*, where the author states, "Perhaps we should remember that '*pornoi*' were in general sacred prostitutes, slaves attached to the service of a pagan temple (notably to a temple of Venus–Aphrodite), who were supposed to put those who worshipped there in communion with the deity they served – a further reason for looking upon union with such as having a strongly negative religious value."[5]

This notion has been seriously challenged in more recent literature, usually on the grounds that sacred prostitution never existed in Corinth to begin with (although this has not stopped scholars from recognizing the institution as existing farther east).[6] Additional arguments have been raised on the grounds that Paul's entire concept of *porneia* is different from the traditional, pagan meanings. The passages in question are as follows (1 Corinthians 5–6):

> Generally it is heard that there is *porneia* among you, and that it is of a kind not existing among the Gentiles, insofar as some man is keeping a wife of his father's. And you have become quite full of yourselves! Would you not be better off lamenting, so that one who acts thus is taken from the midst of you? For I, being distant in body, am near in spirit, and as one near in spirit I have judged in the name of the Lord Jesus the one who has done this. When you have gathered together and my spirit is with the power of our Lord Jesus, hand over this man to Satan for the destruction of his flesh, so that his spirit might be saved on this day of the Lord. . . .
>
> I have written to you in my letter not to associate with whores, not at all meaning the whores of this world or the arrogant and rapacious or idolaters, since you would then need to leave this world. But now I have written to you not to associate even if someone called a brother should be a whore or braggart or idolater or smart-mouth or drunkard or rapacious; do not eat with such a one! For what is it for me to judge

---

[5] Héring 1962: 45.
[6] *Inter alia* Baugh 1999: 445–447; Kirchhoff 1994: 46–47; Murphy-O'Connor 1987: 56–58; Saffrey 1985: 373–374; Conzelmann 1975: 12.

those without? Is it not for you to judge those within? Those without
God judges. Drive out the wicked one from among you!

. . .

Don't you know that your bodies are limbs of Christ? Would you then
make the limbs of Christ the limbs of a whore? It must not be so! Or
do you not know that the one clinging to the whore is one body (with
her)? For they will be, they say, the two as one flesh. The one clinging
to the Lord is one (with him) in spirit. Flee *porneia!* All sin, if a person
commits it, is outside of the body; but to commit *porneia* is to sin against
the body itself.

Ὅλως ἀκούεται ἐν ὑμῖν πορνεία, καὶ τοιαύτη πορνεία ἥτις οὐδὲ ἐν τοῖς
ἔθνεσιν, ὥστε γυναῖκά τινα τοῦ πατρὸς ἔχειν. καὶ ὑμεῖς πεφυσιωμένοι
ἐστέ, καὶ οὐχὶ μᾶλλον ἐπενθήσατε ἵνα ἀρθῇ ἐκ μέσου ὑμῶν ὁ τὸ
ἔργον τοῦτο πράξας; ἐγὼ μὲν γάρ, ἀπὼν τῷ σώματι, παρὼν δὲ τῷ
πνεύματι, ἤδη κέκρικα ὡς παρὼν τὸν οὕτως τοῦτο κατεργασάμενον
ἐν τῷ ὀνόματι τοῦ κυρίου Ἰησοῦ συναχθέντων ὑμῶν καὶ τοῦ ἐμοῦ
πνεύματος σὺν τῇ δυνάμει τοῦ κυρίου ἡμῶν Ἰησοῦ παραδοῦναι τὸν
τοιοῦτον τῷ σατανᾷ εἰς ὄλεθρον τῆς σαρκός, ἵνα τὸ πνεῦμα σωθῇ
ἐν τῇ ἡμέρᾳ τοῦ κυρίου.

. . .

Ἔγραψα ὑμῖν ἐν τῇ ἐπιστολῇ μὴ συναναμίγνυσθαι πόρνοις, οὐ πάν-
τως τοῖς πόρνοις τοῦ κόσμου τούτου ἢ τοῖς πλεονέκταις καὶ ἅρπαξιν
ἢ εἰδωλολάτραις, ἐπεὶ ὠφείλετε ἄρα ἐκ τοῦ κόσμου ἐξελθεῖν. νῦν δὲ
ἔγραψα ὑμῖν μὴ συναναμίγνυσθαι ἐάν τις ἀδελφὸς ὀνομαζόμενος ἢ
πόρνος ἢ πλεονέκτης ἢ εἰδωλολάτρης ἢ λοίδορος ἢ μέθυσος ἢ ἅρπαξ,
τῷ τοιούτῳ μηδὲ συνεσθίειν. τί γάρ μοι τοὺς ἔξω κρίνειν; οὐχὶ τοὺς
ἔσω ὑμεῖς κρίνετε; τοὺς δὲ ἔξω ὁ θεὸς κρινεῖ. ἐξάρατε τὸν πονηρὸν ἐξ
ὑμῶν αὐτῶν.

. . .

οὐχ οἴδατε ὅτι τὰ σώματα ὑμῶν μέλη Χριστοῦ ἐστιν; ἄρας οὖν τὰ
μέλη τοῦ Χριστοῦ ποιήσω πόρνης μέλη; μὴ γένοιτο. ἢ οὐχ οἴδατε
ὅτι ὁ κολλώμενος τῇ πόρνῃ ἓν σῶμά ἐστιν; ἔσονται γάρ, φησίν,
οἱ δύο εἰς σάρκα μίαν. ὁ δὲ κολλώμενος τῷ κυρίῳ ἓν πνεῦμά ἐστιν.
φεύγετε τὴν πορνείαν. πᾶν ἁμάρτημα ὃ ἐὰν ποιήσῃ ἄνθρωπος ἐκτὸς
τοῦ σώματός ἐστιν· ὁ δὲ πορνεύων εἰς τὸ ἴδιον σῶμα ἁμαρτάνει.

What, then, is *porneia?* Rather than "prostitution" *per se,* it is here better
understood as "fornication." For Paul, this is any expression of sexuality
by Christians other than sex in Christian wedlock (which should only
occur as a means of avoiding *porneia* anyway, chastity being preferable –
1 Corinthians 7:1–2). *Porneia* is a lack of physical temperance expressed

in specifically sexual terms.[7] Thus, in 1 Thessalonians 4:3–5, when Paul urges his "brothers" to be pleasing to God, he commands them: "to hold off from *porneia*/fornication, to know, each one of you, how to preserve your body in sanctity and honor, not to suffer desire like those Gentiles who do not know God."

By extension, a *pornos* (masculine) is a Christian man who engages in a form of sexuality other than that deemed appropriate by Paul – a fornicator. In 1 Corinthians 5, this is the man who "keeps" (*ekhein*) his father's woman/wife (*gynaika*).[8] Paul is remarkably taciturn about what, exactly, that man is doing with his father's *gynaika*, or the circumstances of the father, or the status of the *gynaika*,[9] but he is quite emphatic that the *pornos'* relationship to her is an abomination for which he should have his flesh handed over to Satan. A tad extreme, perhaps, but it certainly gives no indication whatsoever that the *pornos* in question is a prostitute (one who sells sex), much less one in any way connected with a cult of Venus.

Finally we come to the most critical character in the study of Paul's supposed relationship with Corinthian sacred prostitution – the whore (*pornê*) whose limbs are contrasted with those of Christ, whose embrace must be avoided lest one become one with her. This is the character whom Héring identified as the sacred prostitute who brought worshippers into communion with Venus. But, once again, the term *pornê* here has a different meaning than in the standard Greek. As with the masculine form seen above, a feminine *pornê* is a woman who engages in illicit sex; who, in the somewhat sexist model provided by Paul, causes men to commit fornication and thus turn away from God (or, even worse, causes God to turn away from them). Thus R. Kirchhoff, "Πόρνη nennt Paulus nicht speziell eine Prostituierte, sondern jede Frau, mit der ein christlicher Mann nach Paulus' Meinung nach nicht sexuell verkehren darf, d.h. eine, die nicht die einzige Sexualpartnerin und also die Ehefrau ist."[10] Perhaps most importantly for Paul, she is a non-Christian woman in a committed relationship with a Christian man. To quote K. Gaca:

> The so-called whore ... is any woman who is religiously alien to, or alienated from, Paul's missionary communities. She is not only a prostitute plying her trade in Corinth, let alone a more specialized cult

---

[7] As Gaca notes, Paul seemed far less concerned about physical "sins" such as eating food sacrificed to pagan deities.

[8] On the ambiguity of the Greek word *gynê*, see Chapter 4.

[9] Knust 2006: 76.

[10] Kirchhoff 1994: 196.

prostitute of Aphrodite. The harlot could just as easily be a daughter under the watchful eye of her conservative Greek parents, a real girl-next-door type whose mother is a priestess of a goddess or god, for Paul is referring to the danger of a Christian man joining in a marital or other committed sexual partnership with any woman dedicated to gods other than or in addition to the Lord.[11]

The *porneia* that St. Paul urges the Corinthians to flee is not sacred prostitution, or even prostitution, but fornication.[12] It is any sexual relationship that might come between the good Christian and God, be this for the usual, "sinful" reasons such as adultery, or for the newer reason – that such a relationship will turn the participant to deities other than Christ.

VENUS THE WHORE: CLEMENT OF ALEXANDRIA, ARNOBIUS OF SICCA, LACTANTIUS, AND FIRMICUS MATERNUS

A significant aspect of early Christian apologetic was the denigration of pagan deities. This was typically achieved in two ways. On the one hand, pagan "deities" were claimed to be nothing more than mere mortals, a practice called euhemerism after its originator, the Hellenistic author Euhemeros of Messenê. He suggested that the deities of old were not really deities, but great (or possibly infamous) men and women who came to be deified only in later generations. His writings were translated into Latin by Quintus Ennius in the third century BCE, and through him went on to influence pagan and Christian philosophers alike, most notably Cicero (*De Natura Deorum*, Book 1).

On the other hand, divine or not, those pagan deities were simply scandalous, and worship should be denied to anyone who behaves thus. Not only were their antics immoral and disgusting, but they taught by example such behaviors to their followers, who thus became themselves immoral and disgusting. As Athanasius put it in his fourth-century *Contra Gentes* (26):

For from Zeus they [the Greeks] have learned pederasty and adultery, from Aphrodite fornication; and from Rhea licentiousness, from Ares

---

[11] Gaca 2003: 172.

[12] Gaca makes the additional argument that Paul adopted the Biblical metaphor that "to whore" = apostasy, as discussed in Chapter 2 for the Hebrew Bible. Thus, *porneuein* is an especially damning sin as it is not merely physical incontinence, but a direct violation of the first commandment. See Gaca 2003: Chapter 6.

murder; and from the others other such things which the laws punish and every temperate man avoids. So is it right, then, to believe these to be deities, who do such things, and is it not better to consider them to be less rational than dumb animals because of the licentiousness of their ways? Is it right to think them humans who worship them, and is it not better to pity them, as less rational than dumb animals and less spiritual than the soulless? For if they spoke with their souls' mind, none of them would have fallen headlong among these, nor denied the true God, the father of Christ.

In this spirit, Clement of Alexandria, Arnobius of Sicca, Lactantius, and Firmicus Maternus all relate that Cypriot Venus was a prostitute. For Clement, Venus was a goddess whose mysteries on Cyprus had the initiates pay the deity as if she were a whore. For Arnobius, Lactantius, and Firmacus Maternus, Venus was a human, a euhemerized "goddess" famous for her lustful nature and obscene rites. In all cases, it is the goddess herself who is the prostitute; there is no reference to prostitution being a part of her cult.

There are two main sources for the "Cypriot Venus the Whore" motif: Ovid and Clement of Alexandria himself. It was Ovid who wrote that Cypriot Venus first created the "profession" of prostitution in Amathus. Thus in his *Metamorphoses* 10.238–242:

> The foul Propoitides [in Amathus] would not acknowledge
> Venus and her divinity, and her anger
> made whores of them, the first such women ever
> to sell their bodies, and in shamelessness
> they hardened, even their blood was hard, they could not
> blush anymore; it was no transition, really,
> from what they were to actual rock and stone.[13]

And so Venus, logically enough, invents prostitution on the island of Cyprus.

Clement of Alexandria, writing in the late second century CE after his conversion to Christianity, was emphatic about exposing the stupid and perverse nature of Greco-Roman religion, and especially the so-called mysteries.[14] These he desecrated (literally) in his work *Hortatory Address to the Greeks*, wherein he revealed the mysteries of such cults as Dionysos (accusing the Bacchantes of cannibalism), Demeter and Korê (multiple

---

[13] Humphries 1983: 241.
[14] Meyer 1987: 243.

generations of incest), and, of course, Cypriot Aphrodite/Venus. Thus, in his *Hortatory Address to the Greeks*, 2.12–13, Clement wrote:

> Now then, and high time too, I shall reveal those orgies of yours, full of deceit and monstrosity. And if you have been initiated, you will laugh all the more at those hallowed stories of yours. And I shall speak openly about the hidden things, not abashed to say what you are not ashamed to revere. So then this "Foam-born" and "Cyprus-born," the one beloved of Kinyras[15] (I speak of Aphrodite, the "genital-lover because she was born from genitals," from those genitals cut off of Ouranos, the lustful members which, after being cut off, violated the waves). Thus she becomes for you the worthy fruit of wanton members. In these rites of maritime pleasure a token of her birth – a lump of salt and a phallus – is given to the initiates of the art of adultery. The initiates bring a coin to her, as a lover to a *hetaira*.

Ἤδη δέ, καὶ γὰρ καιρός, αὐτὰ ὑμῶν τὰ ὄργια ἐξελέγξω ἀπάτης καὶ τερατείας ἔμπλεα. καὶ εἰ μεμύησθε, ἐπιγελάσεσθε μᾶλλον τοῖς μύθοις ὑμῶν τούτοις τοῖς τιμωμένοις. ἀγορεύσω δὲ ἀναφανδὸν τὰ κεκρυμμένα, οὐκ αἰδούμενος λέγειν ἃ προσκυνεῖν οὐκ αἰσχύνεσθε. ἡ μὲν οὖν "ἀφρογενής" τε καὶ "κυπρογενής," ἡ Κινύρᾳ φίλη (τὴν Ἀφροδίτην λέγω, τὴν "φιλομεδέα, ὅτι μηδέων ἐξεφάνθη," μηδέων ἐκείνων τῶν ἀποκεκομμένων Οὐρανοῦ, τῶν λάγνων, τῶν μετὰ τὴν τομὴν τὸ κῦμα βεβιασμένων), ὡς ἀσελγῶν ὑμῖν μορίων ἄξιος [Ἀφροδίτη] γίνεται καρπός, ἐν ταῖς τελεταῖς ταύτης τῆς πελαγίας ἡδονῆς τεκμήριον τῆς γονῆς ἁλῶν χόνδρος καὶ φαλλὸς τοῖς μυουμένοις τὴν τέχνην τὴν μοιχικὴν ἐπιδίδοται· νόμισμα δὲ εἰσφέρουσιν αὐτῇ οἱ μυούμενοι, ὡς ἑταίρᾳ ἐρασταί.

Here Aphrodite/Venus' whorelike nature is expressed in the way that her initiates pay for their initiation: They pay the goddess as if she were a *hetaira*.

The ideas of Venus the founder of prostitution and Aphrodite who received the wages of a whore were then combined with notions of euhemerism. Thus, Venus came to be regarded as a mortal woman who lived in Cyprus and was a friend of King Kinyras of Paphos, whom Kinyras deified and honored.

Such is the character whom we come across in the writings of our next three early Christian authors. Arnobius of Sicca,[16] like Clement,

---

[15] On Kinyras as priest/founder of Cypriot Aphrodite's Paphian temple see Pindar *Pyth.* 2:15–17 and Tacitus *Historiae* 2:3.

[16] This is the same city of Sicca in northern Africa as mentioned by Valerius Maximus in the passage discussed in Chapter 8. The fact that Arnobius felt no need to mention

was anxious to denigrate the pagan religions from which he was a recent convert. Writing his *Adversus Nationes* in the first years of the fourth century CE,[17] he was obviously heavily influenced both by the theories of Euhemeros and by the works of Clement of Alexandria. In Book 4.24 of his work he asks, "What about the Cypriot king Kinyras, by whom, we've declared, the prostitute (*meretriculam*) Venus was consecrated into the number of the divinities?" In Book 5.19 he goes on to narrate,

> Nor shall we pass by those hidden rites of Cypriot Venus, of which the founder, it is said, was King Kinyras, in which the participants render a fixed payment as if to a prostitute and receive back phalloi given as a sign of her divine beneficence.

> *Nec non et Cypriae Veneris abstrusta illa initia praeterimus, quorum conditor indicatur Cinyras rex fuisse, in quibus sumentes ea certas inferunt ut meretrici et referunt phallos propitii numinis signa donatos.*

The presentation of Venus as a whore was an important aspect of Arnobius' rhetoric overall. For Arnobius, a physical existence, and certainly one that implicated passionate emotions such as lust or hate, was incompatible with immortality, and thus divinity. In Book 4.28 he states that "Where there are weddings, marriages, childbirth, nurses, arts, debilities; where there is liberty and slavery; where there are wounds, slaughter, bloodshed; where loves, desires, passions; where there is every frame of mind coming from restless emotions – there you have nothing divine."[18] Likewise in Book 7.3 implicating the notion of libido and sexuality specifically, Arnobius claims:

> For what is overcome by pleasure, must be subject to its opposite, sadness, nor is that which trembles with joy and is exalted by trivial gladness capable of existing free from the anxiety of grief. The gods, however, ought to be free from either emotion, if we want them to be eternal and without the frailty of mortals.[19]

Arnobius' student in rhetoric was Lactantius, who wrote his *Divine Institutes* during the last great persecution of Christians under the Tetrarchs in the early years of the fourth century CE.[20] The *Divine Institutes* and

the "matrons of Sicca" and the "Temple of Venus" in his polemic against the pagans may be additional evidence that the accusations of Valerius were groundless.

[17] Simmons 1995: 93.
[18] Translation by Simmons 1995: 249.
[19] *Ibid*: 250.
[20] Bowen and Garnsey 2003: 3.

Arnobius' *Adversus Gentes* appear to have been written simultaneously, and neither betrays knowledge of the other in spite of the close relationship between the authors. Lactantius was extremely well-versed in his Latin classics, and he is notable among early Christian apologists as relying primarily on the pagan literature rather than Christian scripture in his defense of his new religion.[21] The influence of Ovid, Ennius/Euhemeros, and probably Cicero[22] (although not Clement) is evident in his take on the Cypriot cult of Venus. In Book 1.17 of his *Divine Institutes* he writes,

> She first, as it is contained in the *Sacred History*, instituted the art of prostitution and was the instigator among women in Cyprus to prostitute themselves publicly. She ordered this so as not to appear alone among other women as immodest and desirous of men.

> *Quae prima, ut in Historia Sacra continentur, artem meretriciam instituit auctorque mulieribus in Cypro fuit uti vulgo corpore quaestum facerent[23]: quod idcirco imperavit ne sola praeter alias mulieres impudica et virorum appetens videretur.*

While in Book 5.10.15 he asks, "How will [pagan worshippers] maintain their modesty when they worship a goddess [Venus] who is naked and adulterous, the prostitute of Olympus?"[24]

These themes come together again in the writings of Firmicus Maternus, who, in the mid-fourth century CE[25] wrote his *The Error of the Pagan Religions*, wherein, following in the footsteps of Clement of Alexandria, he attempted to desecrate the pagan mysteries by revealing and mocking them. In Book 4.10 of this work Firmicus Maternus fulminates,

> I hear that Cypriot Kinyras gave a temple to his prostitute friend – her name was Venus – and that he also initiated to Cypriot Venus very many people and offered many useless consecrations. He even established that whoever wanted to be initiated into Venus' secret should give to her in exchange one penny of payment in the name of the goddess. What kind of secret it is we should all understand in silence; we cannot openly discuss such things because of their shamefulness. Well did the

---

[21] *Ibid*: 15–21.
[22] *Ibid*: 5 and 13; Edwards 1999: 217.
[23] On the expression *corpore quaestum facere* as meaning "to practice prostitution," see Chapter 8.
[24] Bowen and Garnsey 2003: 302, adapted.
[25] Meyer 1987: 207.

lover Kinyras establish the laws of prostitution – he ordered the fee from his priests to be given to divinized Venus as to a whore.

Audio Cinyram Cyprium templum amicae meretrici donasse – ei erat Venus nomen – , initiasse etiam Cypriae Veneri plurimos et vanis consecrationibus deputasse, statuisse etiam ut quicumque initiari vellet secreto Veneris sibi tradito assem unum mercedis nomine deae daret. Quod secretum quale sit omnes taciti intellegere debemus, quia hoc ipsum propter turpitudinem manifestius explicare non possumus. Bene amator Cinyras meretriciis legibus servit: consecratae Veneri a sacerdotibus suis stipem dari iussit ut scorto.

For all of their vehemence and animosity, none of the above apologists and polemicists actually makes reference to sacred prostitution. The closest we might come is the statement by Lactantius that Venus taught the women of Cyprus to prostitute themselves, even demanding it (*imperavit*) of them. However, it is also quite clear that Lactantius did not regard Venus as a goddess, merely a wanton if euhemerized woman who was concerned with how she appeared among other (presumably mortal) women (*praeter alias mulieres*). Furthermore, his concern was not that a goddess *per se* demanded prostitution of her followers (which could qualify as sacred prostitution as established in this work), but that erroneously identifying the whore Venus as a goddess worthy of reverence would induce her worshippers to follow her example. Thus he asks: How will her followers maintain modesty when they worship the prostitute of Olympos?

In all other respects, Clement, Arnobius, Lactantius, and Firmicus Maternus complain about the impropriety and shamefulness of revering and calling by divine titles a female of such bad repute. As could only be expected, the rites associated with such a "goddess" are themselves shameful (certainly none of our authors will openly say what they are! Best to leave that to prurient imaginations). They involve salt and model phalloi – which are logical considering the myths pertaining to Venus – and a denigrating payment as if to a prostitute/whore (*meretrici/scorto*). But the "whore" is the goddess herself, not her initiates nor her cult personnel.

RHETORIC OF LUSTFULNESS: EUSEBIUS AND THE PAGANS OF PHOENICIA

As J. W. Knust discussed in her 2006 work *Abandoned to Lust*, the ancient Christians and pagans spent a lot of time calling each other perverts. Within Christianity itself there was also quite a bit of name-calling and sexual-accusation-making among the various sects. It is in the milieu of this sexual flame war that Eusebius of Caesaria must be understood.

There are two passages from Eusebius, both from his *Life of Constantine* (*VC*), that are frequently held up as evidence for sacred prostitution: the descriptions of the cults of Aphrodite at Aphaka in Lebanon (§3.55) and Heliopolis/Baalbek in Syria (§3.58). According to the usual modern understanding, both of these regional cults practiced sacred prostitution.[26] To these two passages really should be added two others: Eusebius' description of the cult of Aphaka in his *Laus Constantini* (§8) written several years before his *Life of Constantine*, and in many places a source for this latter work;[27] and Book 2.14 of his *Theophany*.

Concerning the sanctuary of Aphaka, Eusebius relates (*VC* 3: 55 and *LC* 8[28]),

> This was a grove and *temenos*, not among the cities nor among meeting-places or city-centers, such as the many that grace the cities with ornament; this one was off the beaten path and away from the junctions and highways, built for the shameful demon Aphrodite in the highlands of Lebanon in Aphaka. It was a school of wrongdoing for all lacking self-control, and they ruined the body with great indolence. Some men were not men but effeminates, utterly denying the dignity of their nature, revering the demon with womanish sickness. And furthermore there was illicit intercourse among women,[29] and ruinous sexual liaisons, unspeakable and infamous practices enacted in this temple as in a lawless and ungoverned land. No one was witness to these deeds, as no one of righteous men dared to go anywhere near there.[30]

> ἄλσος δὲ τοῦτ᾽ ἦν καὶ τέμενος, οὐκ ἐν μέσαις πόλεσιν, οὐδ᾽ ἐν ἀγοραῖς καὶ πλατείας, ὁποῖα τὰ πολλὰ κόσμου χάριν ταῖς πόλεσι φιλοτιμεῖ-ται· τὸ δ᾽ ἦν ἔξω πάτου, τριόδων τε καὶ λεωφόρων ἐκτός, αἰσχρῷ

---

[26] Lightfoot 2003: 329; Cameron and Hall 1999: 303; Millar 1993: 217 and 284; Hajjar 1985: 232; Thomson 1971: 69, n. 26.[1].

[27] Cameron and Hall 1999: 34.

[28] The descriptions are identical.

[29] There is some ambiguity concerning the translation of the phrase γυναικῶν τᾶυ παράνομοι ὁμιλίαι. Cameron and Hall (1999: 144) take the more traditional approach, translating it as "unlawful intercourse *with* women." Drake (1975: 98 and 168) translates it as "illegal intercourse *between* women . . ." (emphasis mine in both cases). The first translation suggests illicit heterosexual intercourse, while the latter presents homosexual union. As the previous statement referred to homosexual relations between men, it is possible that this latter clause may parallel it by referring to similar "unlawful" acts between women. A similar idea and construction are presented in Romans 1:26 (see below). The final clause referring to "ruinous sexual liaisons" would perhaps then encompass all the illicit heterosexual unions.

[30] Eusebius offers no explanation of how he knows what's going on at the grove in spite of the fact that no "good" people go there. . . .

δαίμονι Ἀφροδίτης, ἐν ἀκρωρείας μέρει τοῦ Λιβάνου ἐν Ἀφάκοις ἱδρυμένον· σχολή τις ἦν αὕτη κακοεργίας πᾶσιν ἀκολάστοις, πολλῇ τε ῥαστώνη διεφθορόσι τὸ σῶμα. γύνιδες γοῦν τινες ἄνδρες οὐκ ἄνδρες, τὸ σεμνὸν τῆς φύσεως ἀπαρνησάμενοι, θελείᾳ νόσῳ τὴν δαίμονα ἱλεοῦντο· γυναικῶν τ' αὖ παράνομοι ὁμιλίαι, κλεψίγαμοί τε φθοραί, ἄρρητοί τε καὶ ἐπίρρητοι πράξεις, ὡς ἐν ἀνόμῳ καὶ ἀπροστάτῃ χώρῳ κατὰ τόνδε τὸν νεὼν ἐπεχειροῦντο· ἔφορός τε οὐδεὶς ἦν τῶν πραττομένων, τῷ μηδένα σεμνῶν ἀνδρῶν αὐτόθι τολμᾶν παριέναι.

His comments regarding Heliopolis/Baalbek in his *Vita Constantini* are rather general:

> Such was the case in Phoenician Heliopolis, where those honoring unbridled Pleasure[31] by name gathered together to commit shameless fornication with spouses and daughters.

> οἷον ἐπὶ τῆς Φοινίκων Ἡλιουπόλεως· ἐφ' ἧς οἱ μὲν τὴν ἀκόλαστον ἡδονὴν τιμῶντες προσρήματι, γαμεταῖς καὶ θυγατράσιν ἀναίδην ἐκπορνεύειν[32] συνεχώρουν.

He offers a slightly more explicit view in his *Theophany*:

> What manner of things they did in imitating their deities we can contemplate in our Phoenician neighbors, as we see what even now is seen in Baalbek, how the old, demonic vice and vestiges of the grievous evils are still there, so that the women there cannot bind themselves in lawful wedlock until they have been violated in illegal union and have taken part in the unlawful mystery cult of Aphrodite.[33]

The first point which the attentive reader will notice is that none of these passages refers to prostitution. The atrocities committed at the shrine of Aphrodite at Aphaka include homosexuality and "ruinous sexual liaisons," but not prostitution. In his *VC*, "shameless fornication" took

---

[31] The usual translation here is "pleasure by the name of Aphrodite." However, there is no mention of the name Aphrodite in the Greek text; her name is supplied in the Latin translation: "*qui obscoenam libidinem Deae Veneris vocabulo afficiunt.*" In this instance, Eusebius may have intended to deify the concept of pleasure generally (Thomson 1971: 25, n. 4).

[32] The word *ekporneuein* is only attested in Christian sources and has as its most common meaning "to commit fornication" (LSJ). To refer to prostitution, the verb must govern the accusative. Here, the verb governs the dative. Rather than taking this phrase as referring to prostitution *per se*, then, I have translated it in accordance with the most common meaning for the verb.

[33] This text is only preserved in the Syriac (Gressmann 1992: V). I give here my translation from the German text in Gressman and Laminski 1992: 85.

place at Heliopolis, but not necessarily prostitution, and not in the context of the temple – Eusebius merely related that the Heliopolitans did such things in that city. Thus, once again, sacred prostitution is not at issue. According to the *Theophany* some type of illegal sex, violation even, takes place in conjunction with (?) the mystery cult of Aphrodite at Heliopolis/Baalbek. The description given, however, speaks more to prenuptial defloration, possibly by rape, than to prostitution, associating Baalbek more with Sodom than Babylon.

What is present in these passages is the leitmotif of sexual accusation. The accusations Eusebius chose to cast are typical of the rhetoric of sexual misconduct from Classical antiquity through the early centuries of Christian polemic. On the one hand, in the *Theophany* we once again see condemnation of the immorality of the ancient deities and especially of how their followers, in imitation of divine precedent, act immorally. Thus the passage quoted above begins, "And not only this, but from the stories they made about their deities they received every accommodation to lead base and lawless lives, destroying their souls and bodies through every sort of lust."[34] In this he is reminiscent of Athanasius' *Contra Gentes* quoted above, where he complains that humans learned fornication from Aphrodite.

On the other hand, we see a number of motifs supposedly pertaining to the sex lives of the pagans specifically – lack of restraint, homosexuality (both lesbianism and especially the passive participation of "effeminate" males), and fornication/incest. These motifs show up continually throughout the condemnatory literature. Thus a common vibe might be felt in the Hellenistic forgery *The Letter of Aristeas*, wherein "Eleazer" praised the Jews in claiming that (§152–153)

> [M]ost other men defile themselves by promiscuous intercourse, thereby working great iniquity, and whole countries and cities pride themselves upon such vices. For they not only have intercourse with men but they defile their own mothers and even their daughters. But we have been kept separate from such sins.[35]

In the first century CE St. Paul wrote to the Romans about those who had denied God's will (Romans 1:26–27):

> On account of this God hands them over to dishonorable passions. For their women exchanged natural intimacy for unnatural,[36] and likewise

---

[34] Gressman and Laminski 1992: 85; my translation from the German.

[35] Translation from http://www.ccel.org/c/charles/otpseudepig/aristeas.htm.

[36] Once again, this may be evidence that women were exchanging heterosexual intercourse for homosexual.

the males, fleeing the natural intimacy of women, burned in their hunger for each other – men performing the shameful act with men.

In the late second century CE,[37] the Christian apologist Minucius Felix defended his faith against accusations leveled by one M. Cornelius Fronto, who claimed that Christians (*Octavius* 9:6–7)

> [G]ather at a banquet with all of their children, sisters, mothers, people of either sex and every age. There, after full feasting, when the blood is heated and drink has inflamed the passions of incestuous lust, . . . the tale-telling light is upset and extinguished, and in the shameless dark lustful embraces are indiscriminately exchanged; and all alike, if not in act, yet by complicity, are involved in incest, as anything that occurs by the act of individuals results from the common intention.[38]

Certainly the most amusing account of sexual debauchery in the early Christian rhetoric comes from the fourth-century *Panarion* of Epiphanius of Salamis. In Book 26 of this work Epiphanius describes the rites of the Phibionites/Borborites, who have "enslaved their bodies and souls to fornication and promiscuity."[39] What follows is a précis of their so-called practices based on the translation of F. Williams (1987).

First off, as Epiphanius tells us (26.4.1), "they hold their wives in common."[40] When they get together for their sacred feasts they consume a great deal of food and wine, the latter filling their veins and causing them to go mad for each other. The married couples split up as husbands tell their wives to go perform the *agapé* with another man (4.3–4). They have sex, but avoid impregnation via *coitus interruptus*, gathering the semen in their hands, which they then consecrate to God and eat (4.5–7). They also eat menstrual blood, calling it the blood of Christ (4.8).[41] If a woman does become pregnant (we all know how well *coitus interruptus* works as birth control), they abort the fetus and eat it, calling it the "perfect Passover" (5.4–6). Some men masturbate and eat their own semen (11.1). Furthermore, "these persons who debauch themselves with their own hands – and not just they, but the ones who consort with women too – finally get their fill of promiscuous relations with women and grow ardent

---

[37] Price 1999: 112.
[38] Translation by Knust 2006: 4.
[39] Williams 1987: 84.
[40] *Ibid*: 85.
[41] Epiphanius seems to have a fixation on semen and menses, for he makes almost identical accusations against the Simonians in 21.4.1 and the Nicolaitans in 25.3.2.

for each other, men for men" (11.8).[42] "For they never have their fill of copulation . . . They are always having intercourse and committing fornication" (11.9–10).[43]

We have no idea where Epiphanius came up with this. According to Williams, "The literary sources of Sect. 26 are unknown; there may be some points of contact with Irenaeus. Epiphanius claims personal experience as his source of information, but also indicated that what he says is in part based on reading."[44] B. Ehrman offers a robust analysis of the problem of Epiphanius' "sources":

> I don't think anyone doubts that as a young man Epiphanius had personal contacts with members of the group. He explicitly recounts the advances of his two "seductresses,"[45] and there seems to be little reason to think that he made up the story . . . On the other hand, this surely cannot be taken as some kind of warrant for the accuracy of his report concerning the group's private sex rituals. Epiphanius never says that he actually participated in or even witnessed any of the group's activities . . . Quite to the contrary, he explicitly states that he spurned these women *before* they had enticed him into joining the sect. Nor can we think that the women had actually divulged to him what the group was doing behind closed doors. Epiphanius does say that they told him about their group. But he is remarkably vague concerning *what* they told him, and he does *not* indicate that they revealed to him their secret rituals. He clearly had read a good deal of their literature . . . But he never claims that he found the group's orgiastic and cannibalistic practices described in them. And it stretches all credulity to think that they could have been: These books could hardly have been "how-to manuals."[46]

A number of the issues brought up with the preceding narratives are reflected in the accounts of Eusebius. He is a Christian condemning pagans, as with St. Paul. He accuses the devotees of Aphrodite of incontinence – "lacking self-control and ruining the body with great indolence" – just as the Phibionites "enslaved their bodies and souls to fornication and promiscuity." Homosexuality is at issue, just as in Paul's

---

[42] Williams 1987: 92.
[43] *Ibid.* Most major atrocities are accounted for here – adultery, gluttony, masturbation, spilling (and eating!) of seed, homosexuality, and, of course, baby-eating.
[44] Williams 1987: 82, n. 1.
[45] Recounted in passage 26.17.4.
[46] Ehrman 2003: 200–201, excerpted. Emphases in original.

letter to the Romans[47] and Epiphanius' *Panarion*. So too, at Heliopolis specifically, was incest – an indiscriminate fornication in the presence of spouses, mothers, and daughters – just as in the *Letter of Aristeas* and Minucius Felix's *Octavius*.

And, perhaps most importantly of all, there is no clear source for the information. Just as Epiphanius could not (or at least did not) offer a coherent account of how he came by his knowledge, so too did Eusebius muddle himself in regards to his account of Aphaka. He insisted that no one was witness to the events that occurred at the rural sanctuary, since "no one of righteous men dared to go anywhere near there." Where, then, did Eusebius get his information?[48] Likewise, the accounts of Heliopolis are not consistent. According to the *VC* fornication occurs with wives and daughters; according to the *Theophany*, prenuptial rape is mandatory. Furthermore, as Y. Hajjar noted in his study of the cults of Heliopolis/Baalbek, all references to the *porneia* of this city (which Hajjar accepts as sacred prostitution in the cult of Venus) appear *exclusively* in Christian authors, Christian authors writing about a city where paganism remained well-entrenched through late antiquity, thus giving the Christian authors a cause for grudge.[49] The declared lack of sources combined with the strongly rhetorical nature of the narratives, and especially their similarities to other such rhetorical accounts in terms of sexual aberrations, suggests quite emphatically that Eusebius' accounts of the goings-on at Aphaka and Heliopolis should not be taken as historical facts, but as accusational literary constructions.

> The claims made by Eusebius in III.54–8 should be treated with caution. He gives few specific examples, twists his material to give it an apologetic meaning, and embeds his statements within a context of highly coloured and tendentious rhetoric.[50]

Not only are these texts *not* evidence for sacred prostitution at either of these sites, they are not even evidence for the cults of Aphrodite generally in Late Antiquity.

---

[47] As the evidence from Athanasias below will indicate, Eusebius may have been specifically thinking of St. Paul's letter to the Romans when making his accusations against the cult at Aphaka.

[48] This is known as the Captain Jack Sparrow Conundrum: "No survivors? Then where do the stories come from, I wonder?"

[49] Hajjar 1985: 232, "L'existence de la prostitution sacrée à Héliopolis nous est révélée par Eusèbe de Césarée et d'autres écrivains chrétiens qui constituent notre unique source dans ce domaine."

[50] Cameron and Hall 1999: 305.

COMING FULL CIRCLE: ATHANASIUS, SOKRATES, SOZOMEN (AND HERODOTOS!)

The following three texts have a familiar air about them. Athanasius, in his *Contra Gentes*, offers a description of Phoenician sacred prostitution reminiscent of Herodotos or Lucian before he delves into the "problem" of Phoenician homosexuality. If that latter issue calls to mind Eusebius, then so too do the works of Sokrates Scholasticus and Sozomen, both of whom refer in Eusebeian fashion to the debauchery and fornication that took place at Heliopolis/Baalbek before Constantine had the good grace to end Aphrodite's reign of perversion. But there are details present in the works of these two authors that derive from sources independent of Eusebius. Sokrates, for his part, mentions that maidens were specifically prostituted to foreigners (*xenois*), and Sozomen tells us that the maidens of Hieropolis were prostituted to any first-comer (*prostukhontos*) before being married off. Foreigners, prenuptial rituals, random strangers – once again, details from Herodotos come to mind. And well they should. As the evidence shows, all three of the following writers were influenced to one extent or another by the "Father of Historiography," and it appears that references to sacred prostitution (as with Athanasius) or foreigners (as with Sokrates) might be attributed to Herodotean influence.

Athanasius: Christian Invective and Herodotean Ethnography

Immediately preceding the passage quoted above about the scandalous behavior of the Greek deities, Athanasius, in his *Contra Gentes*, had this to say about the pagans (26):

> Women in times past used to sit themselves among idols of Phoenicia, offering to these very deities there the earnings of their own bodies, believing that by prostitution they supplicated this goddess of theirs and that they brought out her good-will by these things. And men, rejecting their nature and no longer wishing to be men, morph to the nature of women, doing these things to please and honor the mother of the so-called deities among them.

> Γυναῖκες γοῦν ἐν εἰδώλοις τῆς Φοινίκης πάλαι προεκαθέζοντο, ἀπαρχόμεναι τοῖς ἐκεῖ θεοῖς ἑαυτῶν τὴν τοῦ σώματος ἑαυτῶν μισθαρνίαν, νομίζουσαι τῇ πορνείᾳ τὴν θεὸν ἑαυτῶν ἱλάσκεσθαι, καὶ εἰς εὐμένειαν ἄγειν αὐτὴν διὰ τούτων. ἄνδρες δὲ, τὴν φύσιν ἀρνούμενοι καὶ μηκέτι εἶναι θέλοντες ἄρρενες, τὴν γυναικῶν πλάττονται φύσιν, ὡς

ἐκ τούτων καταθύμια καὶ τιμὴν τῇ μητρὶ τῶν παρ' αὐτοῖς λεγομένων θεῶν ποιοῦντες.

Accusing them of lewdness, Athanasius then quotes from Paul's letter to the Romans, passage 1.26–27 (quoted above), where the saint accuses the unbelievers of homosexuality.

A number of the ideas presented in this passage have precedents in earlier Biblical and Christian writings. The reference to idols no doubt emerges from Athanasius' overall theme in the *Contra Gentes*, which is the vanity of worshipping idols as if they were deities. In this respect the work is similar to the "Letter of Jeremiah" discussed in Chapter 5. References to the illicit sexualities of both women (prostitution) and men (homosexuality) derive from a combination of Eusebius and ultimately St. Paul, whom both authors followed on this topic. The women's location in Phoenicia probably derives from Athanasius' following of Eusebius' *Theophany* (2.14–15), where Eusebius writes about the mandatory prenuptial rape of the women of Baalbek and the homosexuality of its men, ending with a quotation from Paul's Letter to the Romans 1.26–27.[51]

However, there are extremely important differences between Eusebius' (and Paul's) account and that of Athanasius. Athanasius is explicit in his reference to and description of what must be defined as sacred prostitution. The women of old (*palai*[52]) sat before (*proekathezonto*) idols, offering wages (*mistharian*) earned through the sale of their bodies either to deities (*theois*), or specifically to a goddess (*tên theon*). In prostituting themselves they believed that they were acting in a religious fashion (*nomizousai têi porneiai tên theon heautôn hilaskesthai*).

These are the details that come from Herodotos. Athanasius used not only scriptural sources in his work, but also Classical data. Beyond such Christian authors as the Evangelists, Paul, Clement, and Eusebius, the *Contra Gentes* also takes examples and ideology from, *inter alia*, Plato (§6 – spiritual charioteer, §9 – snails, §10 – trip to Peiraios); Euhemeros (§§9 and 10); Homer (§11 – death of Sarpedon, §12 – adultery of Aphrodite and Ares); and Herodotos. Athanasius uses data from the first four books of the *Histories* in the mockery he makes of pagan beliefs in §§23–26. All in all, there are no fewer than eight Herodotean references in these four sections of the *Contra Gentes*.

---

[51] Thomson 1971: 69, n. 26, '.

[52] Contrary to Eusebius' account, which was quite insistent that the debauchery at Baalbek still took place.

Athanasius	Herodotos
23.23–27: For concerning the abominations in Egypt it is not possible to speak, anyone can see that the cities have rites opposite and conflicting to each other, and those in one town are always rushing to revere the opposite thing of that of their neighbors. Indeed the crocodile is worshipped as a deity among some of them, while it is thought to be utterly disgusting to those next-door.	2.42.2: For all the Egyptians do not revere the same deities alike, except for Isis and Osiris, whom they call Dionysos. 2.69.1: Crocodiles are sacred to some of the Egyptians, but for others not, and they speak of them as if they were enemies.
23.32–35: And quite amazing, as the historians relate, the Pelasgians learned the names of the deities from the Egyptians, even though they do not believe in the deities of the Egyptians but worship others.	2.52: Previously the Pelasgians prayed to the deities and made all types of sacrifices to them, as I know from hearing it in Dodona; but they called none of them by name, for they had heard none yet . . . But then much later they learned the names of the other deities (other than Dionysos, which they learned later), names that had come from Egypt.
24.6–7: The Egyptians revere the ox and the Apis calf, and others sacrifice these to Zeus.	3:27–29: *General discussion of the Apis calf as worshipped by the Egyptians and killed by Cambyses.*
24.9–11. The Libyans have a sheep god called Ammon, while among others [the sheep] is slaughtered in sacrifice to many deities.	2.42: The Egyptians render the statues of Zeus as ram-faced, and from the Egyptians the Ammonites . . . It seems to me the Ammonites derived this name for themselves from this, for the Egyptians call Zeus Amon. And the Thebans do not sacrifice rams, but they are sacred to them because of this. But on one day of the year, during the festival of Zeus, they kill and flay one ram and clothe the statue of Zeus in its skin.

25.9–11: For the Skythians called Taurians carry off to sacrifice to the one among them called Virgin those from shipwrecks and as many Greeks as they capture.

4.103.1: Of these the Taurians practice the following custom: They sacrifice to the virgin the shipwrecked and those of the Greeks who put out to sea whom they capture.

25.15–19: And others [Skythians], whenever they return from wars and are victorious, then they sort out into hundreds the captured, and taking one from each of these groups they sacrifice them to Ares, as many as are picked out for one hecatomb.

4.62: As many as they [Skythians] capture alive in wars they sacrifice to Ares one man out of a hundred men, not as they do the cattle, but in a different manner.

26.1–4: *The sacred prostitution of Phoenician women.*

1.199: *The sacred prostitution of Babylonian women (see Chapter 4).*

According to Herodotos' account of the ritual in Babylon, every Babylonian woman must sit in the sanctuary of Aphrodite until a man pays her for sex. The money, as Herodotos tells us, becomes sacred (*ginetai gar hieron touto to argyrion*). The women do this to "discharge their obligation to the goddess" (*aposiôsamenê têi theôi*). Such details reflect the non-Eusebeian elements in Athanasius' account: The women sit among idols, offering a goddess pay through prostitution, thus supplicating and cheering her.

Athanasius' reference to the prostitution of women before Phoenician idols comes at the end of a series of ethnographic references derived at least in part from Herodotos, forming a bridge between the pagan "ethnography" and the Christian authors by linking female prostitution with male homosexuality and the quotation from Paul. If Athanasius' account, contrary to those of Clement, Lactantius, and Eusebius above, actually refers to sacred prostitution in the Near East, this has far less to do with an actual account of Near Eastern religion or even necessarily Christian rhetoric than it does with Athanasius' sources. Once again, it is merely Herodotos lurking in the background.

INTO THE FIFTH CENTURY – SOKRATES AND SOZOMEN

Both Sokrates and Sozomen followed in the footsteps of Eusebius in writing church histories, both rather unimaginatively called *Ecclesiastical History*. Both works contain information about the fornication of maidens at Heliopolis before Constantine arrived, built a church in the city, and outlawed the traditional pagan practices. Because of similarities in the narratives – Constantine, Heliopolis, prostitution – it has been assumed that, like their predecessor Eusebius, both Sokrates and Sozomen were also writing about sacred prostitution. However, a look at their respective texts will show that, once again, sacred prostitution has only been read *into* their stories.

Sokrates, *Ecclesiastical History* 1.18.7:

> [Constantine] commanded that another church be built in Phoenician Heliopolis on account of the following. What kind of law-maker the Heliopolitans had at the start I cannot say, but his character as such was revealed by the custom of the city. For the local law commanded that the women/wives be held in common among them, and because of this the parentage of those born to them was indeterminate (for no one could determine the parents of the offspring), and they allowed the maidens to be prostituted to the foreigners present.

> Ἑτέραν δὲ ἐκκλησίαν ἐν Ἡλιουπόλει τῆς Φοινίκης κτισθῆναι ἐκέλευσε δι᾿ αἰτίαν τοιάνδε· Ἡλιουπολῖται τινὰ μὲν ἔσχον ἐξ ἀρχῆς νομοθέτην, οὐκ ἔχω εἰπεῖν, ὁποῖος δὲ ἦν τὸ ἦθος, ἐκ τοῦ ἤθους τῆς πόλεως δείκνυται· κοινὰς γὰρ εἶναι παρ᾿ αὐτοῖς τὰς γυναῖκας ἐγχώπιος νόμος ἐκέλευσεν, καὶ διὰ τοῦτο ἀμφίβολα μὲν ἦν τὰ τικτόμενα παρ᾿ αὐτοῖς (γονέων γὰρ καὶ τέκνων οὐδεμία διάκρισις ἦν), τὰς δὲ παρθένους τοῖς παριοῦσι ξένοις παρεῖχον πορνεύεσθαι.

Sozomen, *Ecclesiastical History* 5.10.7:

> And so I add my own opinion, that what led the Heliopolitans to such utter savagery against the holy maidens [feeding them to pigs] was the prohibition, contrary to what was their ancestral custom previously, of prostituting there their maidens to any first-comer before they joined their fiancés in marriage. For Constantine, destroying the temple of Aphrodite in Heliopolis, first then built a church among them, and he utterly forbade them by law to enact their customary *porneias*.

> Ὡς δὲ συμβάλλω, εἰς τοσαύτην ὠμότητα κατὰ τῶν ἱερῶν παρθένων προήγαγε τοὺς Ἡλιουπολίτας τὸ κωλυθῆναι, καθὸ πάτριον ἦν αὐτοῖς πρότερον, ἐκπορνεύεσθαι παρὰ τοῦ προστυχόντος τὰς ἐνθάδε παρθένους, πρὶν τοῖς μνηστῆρσι συνελθεῖν εἰς γάμον. Ὁ γὰρ Κωνσταντῖνος καθελὼν τὸν ἐν Ἡλιουπόλει τῆς Ἀφροδίτης νεών, τότε πρῶτον παρ᾿ αὐτοῖς ἐκκλησίαν ἐδείματο, καὶ νόμῳ διεκώλυσε τὰς συνήθεις ἐπιτελεῖν πορνείας.

For Sokrates, the polyamorous residents of Heliopolis prostituted (or possibly, permitted fornication with) their maidens to foreigners. There is no indication that this prostitution/fornication occurred under the auspices of a deity or temple. As such, specifically sacred prostitution is not at issue, although the familiar rhetoric of sexual accusation most certainly is (on holding spouses in common, see above: Phibionites). For Sozomen, the city's residents prostituted their daughters to any random man before marriage. Although this practice was stopped by law in conjunction with the destruction of the temple of Aphrodite,[53] there is once again no direct link between the prenuptial prostitution of maidens and the goddess' cult. Once again, no sacred prostitution.

Nevertheless, the details in these accounts do, as with Athanasius, show a joint dependence on both Eusebius and Herodotos. That both Sokrates and Sozomen were familiar with, and even influenced by, Herodotos has been made well manifest in P. van Nuffelen's 2004 study of their *Histories*. Sokrates was at least well versed in his Classical Greek historians, including Herodotos, Thucydides, and Xenophon.[54] Although he was less stylistically influenced than Sozomen, elements of Herodotean narrative do come across in his work. To give one (rather amusing) example: in Book I, chapter 12 of his *Ecclesiastical History*, Sokrates relates the story one Spyridon and his virgin daughter Irene. A neighbor had once entrusted a certain treasure to the maiden, which she hid via burial, and then died. When Spyridon was called upon to find the treasure, he summoned his daughter's ghost at her tomb. She emerged and revealed the location of the neighbor's property. This must be the world's most cleaned-up version of Herodotos' account of Periandros of Corinth consulting the ghost of his wife Melissa (recounted briefly here in Chapter 8) in the *Histories*, 5.92.

Sozomen not only was familiar with the work of Herodotos, but, according to van Nuffelen, based much of his historiographic style on the *Histories*:[55]

> Chez Sozomène, l'imitation d'Hérodote semble aussi jouer un rôle. Nous avons déjà attiré l'attention sur l'usage répétitif de λέγουσι et ses formes apparentées, le renvoi aux indigènes, la présentation régulière de plusieurs versions. On pourrait ajouter la formule ὧν ἴσμεν et un passage à charactère ethnographique comme des renvois au <<père de l'historiographie>>.[56]

---

53 Although it is commonly assumed that Eusebius referred to the destruction of Aphrodite's temple in Heliopolis at the behest of Constantine (Cameron and Hall 1999: 146 and 304–305), Eusebius actually made no such claim. Direct reference to the temple's destruction comes only with Sozomen.

54 Van Nuffelen 2004: 4.

55 *Ibid*: 247 and 259.

56 *Ibid*: 261.

For Sokrates, the fact that the Heliopolitans held their wives in common could be attributed to Christian invective as easily as it could to references to, say, the Nasamones in Herodotos (4.171, see Chapter 4). However, the fact that the maidens were specifically prostituted to foreigners is a detail present *only* in Herodotos and his imitator Lucian. Although it is possible that Sokrates may have been familiar with Lucian's *De Dea Syria*, thus rationalizing the easy transference of ideas from Babylon to Phoenicia/Syria, it is certain that the historian was sufficiently familiar with Herodotos to have acquired details about "oriental" prostitution from him.

Likewise with Sozomen. What is distinctive in his account, other than the pigs and the actual destruction of the temple, is his insistence upon the randomness of the "Johns." They are not foreigners, as with Sokrates, but firstcomers. But this is also highly reminiscent of Herodotos, who claimed that the Babylonian women "follow the first man who tossed her silver, nor may she reject anyone." Rather than focusing on the detail of foreignness, Sozomen focused on the notion of "first man." Furthermore, as discussed in Chapter 8, Sozomen made the fairly typical link between Herodotos 1.199 and 1.93, where Herodotos claimed that working-class Lydian girls prostituted themselves for dowries. As such, Sozomen turned his prostitution into some manner of prenuptial ritual, a common motif as we have seen.

The fact that none of the descriptions of the fornication/prostitution at Heliopolis agree with each other, in spite of the clear reliance of multiple authors on Eusebius (who, for that matter, was also inconsistent in his accusations against that city), argues rather strongly that the early Christian writers really had no idea what, if anything, actually went on there. The close relationship between the details presented especially in Athanasius, Sokrates, and Sozomen and those of Herodotos 1.199 indicate that the influences on the accounts pertaining to Heliopolis were far more literary than historic, with Eusebius and Herodotos contributing far more than any actual reality.

PULLING IT ALL TOGETHER: AUGUSTINE'S *CITY OF GOD* 4.10

But then are there two Venuses, one a virgin, the other a women? Or perhaps three: one of virgins, a sort of Vesta; one of spouses; the other of prostitutes? To this one even the Phoenicians used to give a gift from their daughters' prostitution, before they united them to husbands.

An Veneres duae sunt, una virgo, altera mulier? An potius tres, una virginum, quaze etiam Vesta est, alia coniugatarum, alia meretricum? Cui etiam Phoenicis donum dabant de prostitutione filioaru, antequam eas iungerent viris.

By this point the attentive reader should be able to pick this passage apart without further commentary.

RECONSIDERING THE EVIDENCE

Chapters 2 and 3 presented the texts most commonly used as evidence for sacred prostitution in the ancient world. As it turned out, none of the ancient Near Eastern materials indicated the presence of such a practice. Perhaps more interesting, not only did the Classical texts not prove the existence of sacred prostitution, but also the majority of them made no reference to sacred prostitution whatsoever. If we were to gather a list of actual sources for this so-called religious practice, we would only come up with seven. Herodotos 1.199 certainly counts, as does Lucian's imitative *DDS.6*. Strabo 16.1.20 and 11.14.16 mention variations (and rather extreme variations at that concerning Armenia) on the theme, even if the geographer barely expresses credence himself. Justinus' description of the *votum* of Epizephyrian Lokris counts, as do Athanasius' and Augustine's comments on the rites of the Phoenicians. Six authors, seven references, spanning 1,000 years. Herodotos is directly or indirectly responsible for four (himself, Lucian, Strabo 16.1.20, and Athanasius); the others are independent of him.

As we have seen, the other so-called sources do not pertain to sacred prostitution. Pindar's *skolion* celebrated the "bringing" of prostitutes to a bunch of drunken Corinthians, misinterpreted by Khamaileon as a Corinthian custom (and so implicating Simonides), misread by Athenaios probably as sacral manumission. The *Letter of Jeremiah* does not mention prostitution, merely promiscuity, and not even a promiscuity associated with religion. Klearkhos wrote about rape and retribution; Justinus about the Sabine-like kidnapping of Cypriot maidens; Valerius Maximus about the adulterous matrons of Sicca. Strabo had much to say about the different types of hierodules throughout the Roman Empire, many from his own home town. But hierodules are not sacred prostitutes, and these texts do not apply to them. Likewise for Egyptian priestesses, as well as those from Tralles – the handmaidens to Zeus. Several early Christian authors complained about the immorality of the pagans and their deities, especially Venus the whore, but only two actually make reference to those pagans prostituting their daughters in her honor.

Six authors, seven references, 1,000 years. This was not a popular topic. Perhaps it is telling that even authors such as Sokrates Scholasticus and Sozomen, who were well acquainted with Herodotos and had every reason to denigrate their pagan neighbors, felt no need to make the sacred prostitution accusation, explicitly or otherwise. Strabo certainly thought it was strange. When read appropriately, not even Athenaios mentions it in his remarkable compendium of things meretricious. If the ancients thought about the idea of sacred prostitution at all, it was a quaint literary novelty, or perhaps some bizarre and utterly local religious custom, or even a vow made under unbearably adverse circumstances, and we cannot tell if they ever actually did it anyway. . . . Whatever it was, it was neither common nor well known.

It is difficult to determine if or when the ancient authors came to believe in the myth of sacred prostitution. Strabo gives us our first inklings that, maybe, perhaps, sacred prostitution might have existed. He is willing to repeat Herodotos' claims about the women of Babylon, even though he seems to express extreme skepticism on the topic. Likewise, his ethnography of the Armenians contains a "wonder" – the sacred prostitution of noble girls to Anaitis. As with Babylon, Strabo only finds this reference to sacred prostitution in a land which he himself had never personally visited, which may be why he was willing to include the information "on spec." It is nevertheless not entirely clear if he believed the accounts he reported, just as Herodotos made clear the fact that he reported what he heard, even if he did not believe it. It is also rather difficult to determine what exactly Strabo understood the Armenian ritual to be. He did not have our background in sacred prostitution studies, and, as discussed previously, he may have had an odd, semi-"barbaric" notion of courtship ritual in mind, rather than what we would now call sacred prostitution.

I would suggest that Justinus believed at least in the vow of the Epizephyrian Lokrians. Nevertheless, perhaps like Strabo, his belief stemmed primarily from a lack of data, a lack highlighted by the ambiguous details he offers. Justinus (presumably Pompeius Trogus before him) cannot tell (or at least cannot tell us) if the prostitution ever took place. It was *intermisso* – maybe never done, maybe done for a while and stopped. Who knows? Whatever it was, it served as a jumping off point for a series of tyrannical leitmotifs to characterize Dionysios II, which themselves were more literary than real. If the sacred prostitution of Lokrian girls took place, this does not seem to have been particularly important to Justinus.

Did the Christians *believe* the accusation? Once again, this can be terribly difficult to determine. The continued use of the rhetoric of lust must have been meaningful to some extent, as they continued using it. Furthermore, every new accusation helped to foster belief in the accusation that went before. Nevertheless, as we saw with both Eusebius and Epiphanius, the authors themselves denied having any ability to know about their topics while writing about them. At least in their own minds they must have had some sense of fabrication. However, their rhetoric was probably quite convincing to their audiences. Whatever Eusebius might have known or thought about the rites of Aphaka, his readers may have been more than willing to accept his narratives as Gospel truth (we certainly do today as far as sacred prostitution is concerned). Likewise for Athanasius, Augustine, and so forth.

Did Athanasius believe the evidence and anecdotes he took from Herodotos? Once again, I think that this is rather difficult to determine. What is important, though, is that he was willing to use this "evidence" in his rhetoric because he thought that it would be effective, and believable, and it certainly seems that his readers were willing to accept his accusations as true.

In the end, I doubt that many of the authors who contributed to the sacred prostitution myth entirely believed what they wrote. Herodotos certainly knew what he was doing, as did Lucian. Strabo was skeptical but inclusive, as was Justinus. Athanasius and Augustine had a different template for "true." But in the end, what is more important for the rise of the myth is that their *readers* believed what they wrote, either through misunderstanding of nuance or naïvité or, just the opposite, basing assessments on what appeared to be a long line of evidence stretching back beyond the author in question (e.g., Lucian is confirmed by Strabo and Herodotos). The myth of sacred prostitution probably dates back to the fifth century BCE, when some fellow went home to tell his family what he heard from Herodotos today ("You won't *believe* what they do in Babylon . . . !").

CHAPTER ELEVEN

LAST MYTHS

COROLLARY

THERE IS AN IMPORTANT COROLLARY TO THE SACRED PROSTITUTION myth. According to this corollary, sacred prostitution never existed, but was primarily an invention of the Victorians, especially Sir James G. Frazer in his work *The Golden Bough*, based on biased Classical sources, notably Herodotos. Thus for G. Leick, "[T]he 'sacred prostitute,' who engages in sex as a magical rite in the context of some fertility cult or officiates in the rites of Inanna/Ištar, belongs to the 'Golden Bough' school of historical anthropology."[1] The fullest discussion of this corollary is presented by J. Assante:

> Prostitutes fornicated with strangers in and around the temple precincts, in the city streets, squares and taverns, while highly specialized hierodules copulated with kings in beds elaborately prepared for sacred marriage rituals. This vision was largely derived from the 19th century view of ancient Mesopotamia as a forum of naive and primitive sexual freedom allowable before the Old Testament prophets imposed their more austere mores. The notion of Mesopotamia's sexual freedom . . . was anachronistically based in the 19th century version of it as an exclusively male preserve. Philologists and art historians read the unmarried women attested in cuneiform as prostitutes, sacred or secular. . . . Aside from the avant-garde, which was fast legitimizing erotica as a worthwhile academic pursuit, a number of historical "authorities," unduly influenced scholars of the ancient Near East. Chief among them was Herodotus. . . . The deviancy of Mesopotamian sexual activity seemed

[1] Leick 1994: 150–151. Leick does accept the existence of some kind of sacred prostitution, but not necessarily the "fertility cult" model devised, according to her, by Frazer.

287

confirmed by the Old Testament writers who accused idolaters of harlotry and adultery.[2]

Most recently, C. Stark, in her work on Old Testament *Kultprostitution*, wrote

> Die moderne Interpretation und Wahrnehmung anderer, grösstenteils vergangerner religiöser Vorstellung wurde und wird wesentlich von dem monumentalen Werk des schottischen Gelehrten Sir J. G. Frazer (1854–1941) beeinflusst.
>
> . . .
>
> Das Werk James Frazers hat nicht nur der Religionsethnologie und Anthropologie wichtige Impulse verliehen, sondern wurde auch von der historische-kritischen Bibelwissenschaft rezipiert und weiter bearbeitet. So ist er neben Herodot der zweite bedeutende Gewährsmann für Erwähnungen von Kultprostitution.[3]

COROLLARY COROLLARY

Ironically, there is a corollary to the "Victorian Corollary." According to this mode of thought, sacred prostitution did exist, and the desire to deny this stems from a "Victorian mentality" (i.e., extreme psychosexual repression). The inability to believe that some ancient societies revered their deities through sexuality goes hand in hand with the inability to see piano legs (excuse me: limbs) without fainting. Whether one believes in sacred prostitution or not, the thinking goes, is a matter not of evidence or methodology but of the extent to which one is repressed. Thus W. Johansson, when writing about the possible acceptance of homosexuality in ancient Israel, wrote

> I suspect that the effort to deny the sexual role of the kedeshim and *kedeshoth* represents the last gasp of the Victorian striving to blot out the merest suggestion that homosexual activity had ever been approved or tolerated by any society.[4]

---

[2] Assante 1998: 6.
[3] Stark 2006: 29 and 35.
[4] W. Johansson, Associate Editor of the *Encyclopedia of Homosexuality*, in response to Greenberg's review thereof, as published in the SOLGA Newsletter 13(1), Feb. 1991. My thanks to D. Greenberg for this reference!

Likewise, B. MacLachlan, in her full study of sacred prostitution in the ancient world, prefaced her study with the comment that

> It is not surprising perhaps to find Victorian divines and classical scholars simply unable to contemplate the idea [of sacred prostitution]; it is more surprising to find scholars of our own time continuing this resistance.[5]

Speaking more generally but typically of the "modern" desire to deny the relationship between prostitution and the sacred, H. Meenee claimed that

> For the modern mind, to define any kind of prostitution as "sacred" seems like a contradiction in terms. Hence some scholars deny that such customs [sacred prostitution] existed, trying hard to persuade their readers that all ancient texts referring to them are either inaccurate or misunderstood.[6]

Neither of these corollaries is accurate. As the evidence will show, the myth of sacred prostitution existed in modern scholarship well before the Victorians, in many of the same forms and with many of the same theories that we still hold about it today. Frazer no more invented sacred prostitution than Herodotos accused oriental barbarians. Likewise, the Victorians were themselves quite enthralled with the "exotic, erotic Orient," and sacred prostitution provided them with the opportunity to discuss sex under the rubric of academia. The Victorians were more likely to accept the notion of sacred prostitution, not less.

A MODERN HISTORIOGRAPHY OF SACRED PROSTITUTION

As discussed briefly at the end of the last chapter, the myth of sacred prostitution probably goes back to the fifth century BCE, when someone who listened to Herodotos first believed in the Babylonian *logos*. As details from Strabo and Lucian, among others, seemed to confirm this belief, no doubt the myth grew stronger over time. The Septuagint was created in the Hellenistic Age, and the Vulgate in the fourth century CE, and, as we have already seen, problems of translation gave a vague sense of sacred prostitution there as well, especially in terms of the *qedešîm* and *qedešôt*, the "sacred ones" who were both initiates and whores, *meretrices* and *effeminati*.

---

[5] MacLachlan 1992: 145–146.

[6] Meenee 2007. I suppose that I am the quintessential example of such a "scholar."

The rise of Christianity and the coming of the Dark Ages did not completely deter people from reading Herodotos, Strabo, and certainly Augustine and the Bible *inter alia*, and so there is no reason to suppose that the notion of sacred prostitution disappeared, only to be resuscitated by the Victorians some 1300 years later. As long as these works were read, the myth continued to exist. Occasionally, the idea even reemerged in new texts. For example, in 'Imad ad-Din's (1125–1201) history of the Third Crusade, the author wrote about the contingent of Frankish whores who had come to join the Crusaders in "companionship":

> They arrived after consecrating their persons as if to works of piety, and offered and prostituted the most chaste and precious among them. They said that they set out with the intention of consecrating their charms, that they did not intend to refuse themselves to bachelors, and they maintained that they could make themselves acceptable to God by no better sacrifice than this. . . . They dedicated as a holy offering what they kept between their thighs.[7]

Rather than a literary motif, though, the notion of sacred prostitution as a historical reality, one that must be considered when examining alternate aspects of ancient life and religion, already appeared in the German scholarship two centuries ago, before the Victorian Age. Different authors, naturally enough, had different understandings of this "odd" institution. Some wrote about the universal worship of the Mother Goddess and her fertility cult, including the annual death and resurrection of the Vegetation God, of which sacred prostitution was a part. Or, possibly, sacred prostitution was really a manifestation of ritual defloration, perhaps a sacrifice of virginity to the Goddess. Maybe it was a lifestyle choice. Maybe it was a career path. Whatever it was, it could be understood and documented. What is especially notable is the fact that the various scholars who studied this problem made use of the same data sets; the core sacred prostitution corpus has been in place for a long time. As will become strikingly apparent, Frazer's *Golden Bough* comes at the *end* of a long line of inquiry into the sacred prostitution myth.

THE NINETEENTH CENTURY CONFRONTS SACRED PROSTITUTION[8]

There are two reasons that an examination of "modern" sacred prostitution studies should begin at the dawn of the nineteenth century. The first

---

[7] Gabrieli 1989: 205. A million thanks to my husband, Paul Butler, for this citation!

[8] A slight play on the title of F. Manuel's masterpiece *The Eighteenth Century Confronts the Gods*.

is a change in the way post-Enlightenment scholars approached the idea of myth and religion. Before the eighteenth century, because of a combination of alternate theories about the historical process and a somewhat belligerent religiosity, pagan religions and their myths were approached either as allegories or through the ideology of euhemerism.[9] For pre-Enlightenment scholars, then, pagan deities were to be understood either as philosophical symbols or as great heroes and monarchs who were deified (presumably *post mortem*) by a grateful populace. These approaches left two possible interpretations of ancient myth and religion. On the one hand, in a more charitable mode, the allegories of the ancients contained within them high philosophy and moralizing teachings, cast in the guise of gods and heroines to make their messages more comprehensible to the unwashed, illiterate masses. On the other hand, if the ancient deities used to be humans, they were a horrid lot, castrating parents, raping girls and boys, marrying siblings. Furthermore, as F. Manuel has noted, such condemnation, or at least ridicule, of the pagan religions was inevitably bound up in the continued debates pertaining to the on-going Reformation movement in Europe. "The late seventeenth-century exposures of paganism and its survivals in contemporary European society were invariably presented as pious works of God, excising from Christianity the remnants of false patristic traditions about idolatry so that the fabric of the true religion might be strengthened."[10] Such an approach inevitably did away with the profound distinctions between different world views as manifested in religion, making it difficult to appreciate the alternate ideologies that would, for example, demand from women the sacrifice of virginity as a manifestation of religious piety.

This began to change during the eighteenth century as a new mode of thinking started to emerge. Once again, to quote Manuel,

> By the eighteenth [century] . . . the tide had turned completely. One of the striking expressions of the new scientific and material civilization of western Europe was an overwhelming tendency to become matter-of-fact, to eschew wonder, to reduce the fantastic to a commonsense narrative. There was a general movement to de-allegorize, to perceive the ordinary where previous generations had sought occult connotations. The world was obvious, the cloud of past obfuscations had lifted, things were to be described as they were and as they should appear to reasonable people not possessed by romances or religious enthusiasm.[11]

[9] Ackerman 2002: 2.
[10] Manuel 1959: 22.
[11] *Ibid*: 26.

The second reason for beginning a search for modern notions of sacred prostitution at the beginning of the nineteenth century is the larger world to which the post-Enlightenment scholars had access. As we shall see, most of the authors who wrote about sacred prostitution, to one extent or another, believed in notions of social evolution and thought that expressions of earlier stages in such evolution could be studied in the societies of "primitive," "savage" peoples. European contacts with the New World, India, and central Africa contributed to a new understanding of human social developments and thus shed new light on the "evolution" of religions. J. Rosenbaum, then, understood the ritual defloration aspect of sacred prostitution in parallel with Indian lingam-worship, whereas Frazer understood the role of the Biblical *qedešôt* through parallels with West Africa. By confronting "savage" peoples, the Europeans became willing to confront "savage" customs.

A combination of these factors – a new matter-of-fact ideology and growing contacts with the exotic – prepared the Europeans to deal with issues of sexuality, especially as it pertained to religion:

> By the latter half of the eighteenth century the idea that sexual orgies and the display of phallic symbols played a prominent role in pagan worship was widely diffused in the learned literature on antiquities . . . By the 1780's these practices, which in the Renaissance had either been merely alluded to and passed over quickly as aberrations or spiritualized, began to loom in the darkness of heathen religion. Perhaps the reproduction of the wall paintings and statuary excavated at Herculaneum which graphically depicted Priapic ceremonials and licentious myths contributed significantly to the spread of a new appreciation of ancient religion. . . . Travelers in the East who described the prevalent temple prostitution, the dancing girls and the dancing boys, focused attention upon identical practices of ancient paganism which, though mentioned in the Bible, in Lucian, and in patristic literature, had previously been squeamishly avoided as too abominable to discuss.[12]

The studies of sacred prostitution here considered emerged out of these developments. Authors such as Heyne and Jacobs were educated and developed their own ideologies in the latter half of the eighteenth century and were themselves influential on Rosenbaum. The following survey of studies is not exhaustive. It attempts merely to provide the more important treatments of ancient sacred prostitution in European scholarship. Some authors, such as Ramsay and Sandys, are limited in scope, focusing only

---

[12]   *Ibid*: 259–260.

on one or two sources for the sacred prostitution myth. Others, such as Rosenbaum, Bachofen, and Frazer, provide more universal treatments. I have provided extensive quotations from these various works, the longer passages in translation from the Latin or German. I warn the reader that what follows will be very repetitive. This is deliberate. I hope to show by this to what extent sacred prostitution studies have not really changed in the past 200 years.

In 1804 C.G. Heyne wrote an article attempting to explain Herodotos' Babylonian rite of Mylitta in the context of several similar rites practiced throughout the ancient Near East. His "De Babyloniorum Instituto religioso, ut Mulieres ad Veneris Templum Prostarent" begins with a standard description of Herodotos 1.199:

> Templum apud Babylonios fuit Veneris, quo nomine ab Herodoto appellatur, hoc est, numinis, quod com Venere comparari solebat, Mylittae. *In eo templo, seu in eius septo . . . sederunt mulieres, complures numero, coronam in funiculi modum tortam circa caput habentes*: ornamenti genus, quo religatae feminae in monumentis quoque Graecis et Etruscis visuntur, pro fascia seu diademate. Inter mulieres ex ordine sedentes, *sune utrinque praetendo*, media erat via, qua externi viri Babylonem commeantes incederent, et, quam vellent, sibi quisque eligerent, numo, mox in sacrum inferendo, in eius gremium iniecto, cum verbis, quibus is se Mylittam deam eius caussa invocare significat; tum illa furgit, virum sequitur, cumque eo congressa domum redit, iam se religione exsoluisse, et debita deae rite persoluisse arbitrata; et ab eo inde tempore pudorem illa feruat.[13]

After considering two related Herodotean passages – the auction of brides in Babylon and the prostitution of Lydian girls for dowries – Heyne comes back to the passage of interest:

> We have seen two customs of the Babylonians, one born from the other. Just as previously the girls were farmed out at public auction, so later the girls themselves earned a dowry by the base use of their bodies, offering them for sale. There remains a third, which we see after these other two, which was infamous in Babylon: They surrendered their daughters' modesty to foreign men at the temple of Mylitta. . . . This was an annual custom of the people, when sacred festivals were held at the temple, and the various peoples congregated there. And since it was necessary for the girls to get dowries by prostituting their bodies, it

---

[13] Heyne 1804: 31–32. Italics indicate where he is quoting directly from a Latin translation of the original Greek.

became advantageous, I believe, to make a profit by a greater amount of licentiousness and a more sumptuous price. And so they set them up at the temple, hardly worthy of reverence! It was so easy to combine this with the religious affairs of the temple that, being turned into a religious institution, the girls were seen to have consecrated their bodies to Venus, handing over part of their price to the temple, using the remainder as dowry money so that they might find a man to marry. And there were men who led away home a number of these girls as wives from the temple. And it possibly followed that marriage with a girl so consecrated to Mylitta was particularly attractive from a religious perspective; and so finally it became the norm among the Babylonians that no one wanted to enter into marriage with any girl except those who had prostituted themselves, having consecrated their bodies to Mylitta at the temple. And so the religious custom was maintained to dedicate the flower of one's virginity to the goddess, and the girls offered themselves to passers-by before the temple in sacred space.

. . .

Now from these diverse ritual institutions by one means or another others were propagated and led forth to other peoples, especially in Asia, by the Assyrians and Babylonians. All bore this mark . . . , that girls about to be married consecrated to the goddess the fees earned through the defloration of their bodies. This act and many others have been passed down diligently by authors. So in Phoenicia women are said to sit before the temples consecrating the fee for using their bodies to the goddess, and in this way they provide themselves with her good-will. Augustine related a similar custom concerning marriages. *Venus*, he says, *cui etiam Phoenices donum dabunt de prostitutione filiarum, antequam iungerent eas viris.* Noble was the temple of Atargatis in Hierapolis, also known as Bambyca, not far from the Euphrates. Here they maintained the same religious custom, and this endured until the time of Constantine. It was forbidden to marry a girl of Hierapolis until she prostituted herself to others. The Phoenicians established a similar custom in their colony on Cyprus. Justinus remembers this about the Cypriots in the passage where Dido sets out – "Elissa," he said, "set out heading for Carthage and came by ship to Cyprus. She had her companions seize the girls so that they might marry and the new colony have progeny." *Mos*, he said, *erat Cypriis, virgines ante nuptias flatutis diebus dotalem pecuniam quaesituras in quaestum ad litus maris mittere, pro reliqua pudicitia libamenta Veneri soluturas.* There is another example from a Phoenician colony in Africa, Sicca of New Numidia, a city named for Venus. The author is Valerius Maximus. If there were not comparable stories, the matter would hardly be believable. *Siccae*, he says, *fanum est*

Veneris, in quod se matronae conferebant, atque inde procedentes ad quaestum, dotes, corporis inuria, contrahebant; honestua nimirum tam inhonesto vinculo coniugia iuncturae. The word *matronarum* is not well used here, referring to older brides.

. . .

Doubtlessly this absurd religious custom spread mainly in the Orient; it did not integrate as easily among the Greeks, save for the passage in Justinus: *Locrenses bello pressi vouerant, si victores forent, ut die festo Veneris virgines suas prostituerent.* However, they were later remembered as not entirely fulfilling the vow and were obliged to make harsh amends. Other peoples had a different belief, that the girls went to the temple for the sake of consecrating their virginal bodies. Thence, the goddess being propitiated by this divine rite, the girls entered into sweet matrimony. Connected to this were other flourishing rites among other peoples.... And furthermore, we note that these rites were profitable to the priesthood, as we have seen above regarding the Phoenicians, Assyrians, and Babylonians. I shall add another example from Phoenician Byblos. While a religious rite demanded the shaving of the head, *quotquot mulieres tonderi nolebant, multam soluebant huius modi, ut per unum diem venasles starent, forma quaestum facturae, solis tamen peregrinis copia sui facta, utque ex mercede sacrificium pararetur.* Among other peoples and especially the Assyrians, the stupidity of superstition was so advanced that they consecrated daughters to the temples so that here, their flower of youth plucked, they might be summoned by husbands and taken away. One example is in Strabo, in the famous temple of Anaitis in Armenia. They so honored religious tradition that they did not provide slaves to fortify the temple, but truly *ut illustrissimi eius nationis filias suas virgines ei dedicarent, ac lex esset, ut longo tempore apud deam constuprate, deinde nuptum darentur; nemine talis mulieris coniungium dedignante.* In this region the cult of the goddess was extensive, whom some called Luna, others Bellona, the proper name of the goddess in Comana, whose priests enjoyed a mark of authority, both in Pontic Comana and Cappadocian. Assigned to the temples were fields and slaves — hierodules; *multae quoque habebantur mulieres quaestum corpore facientes, pleraeque sacrea* [Strabo XII]. And the temples had woman servants, as we remember of the shrine of Astarte....[14]

Seven years later Fr. Jacobs took Heyne to task for this assessment. Jacobs' 1811 article "Ueber eine Stelle beim Herodot," begins with a description of two passages in Herodotos – the Marriage Auction in 1.196 and the

[14] Heyne 1804: 36–41, excerpted.

Rite of Mylitta in 1.199 – and their parallel passages in Strabo (16.1.19–20). The author then presents Heyne's analysis of Herodotos 1.199 (see above). Finally, Jacobs presents his own views of the rite explained by Herodotos and Strabo, taking a very different approach than did his predecessor:

> The two customs – the auction occurring in Herodotos' own time and the one concerning the worship of Mylitta – have nothing to do with one another. The first one has nothing to do with religion. Its use was purely economic, such that as far as possible no girl remained unmarried and the attractive young women provided means for the ugly. The second custom was clearly religious from its inception.
>
> In our opinion it is quite unlikely that, if the girls in the temple precinct sell themselves to men for a base profit, this sort of prostitution could *become* religious just because of the holy place where it took place. This goes against the nature of religion. What is profane in the eyes of the people can never be religious or holy. Surely it can happen that the conception of a deity and the belief in his/her innate power, deeds, and customs give rise to the dominant conceptions of his/her morality, and that these can run contrary to the usual laws of village life. The resulting practices thus stand alone and are independent of daily life. Thus it is no wonder when one hears that the Babylonian women – in spite of sleeping with a random foreign man – remain loyal, true, and honorable at home. This act of copulation was a sacrifice – as Herodotos clearly stated – a duty to appease the goddess, not an act of lust.
>
> . . .
>
> But why foreigners? And why was every Babylonian woman so bound once in her life? This is not explained in Heyne's hypothesis. This explanation completely fails to address the fact that the law pertains not to brides, but to family women. πᾶσαι γυναῖκες says Herodotos, not κόραι, not παρθένοι. In the report about the auction of the daughters he uses these latter words.
>
> We should now present a straightforward analysis on the sense and origin of this odd custom, and so we must express at the outset that we shall not achieve any holistic, all-encompassing answer. We shall be pleased if, in our search, we find the relevant spirit of the old religious belief, and if nothing else, we might illuminate a bit of the darkness of this Herodotean narrative.
>
> We must first here remember the intensity with which the deities enjoyed protecting their privileges (τιμάς, *munia*), so that they had no reservations about severely punishing any affronts or negligence to their

dignity. The race of deities, as Euripides had Aphrodite say (Hippol. 8), enjoys their honors, which humans must provide for them. . . .

These honors, as demanded by the deities, were twofold. On the one hand were adoration and sacrifice. But no less important were actions seen to be particularly appropriate to the conception of the deity and provided by those under a divinity's special care. And so singers and poets served the Muses and Phoebos, insofar as they used their noble art. And so warriors worshipped Ares and brought him bloody offerings on the battlefield. And whoever used the works of Artistic Pallas (Ἐργάνη) honored her thusly. The Babylonian Mylitta was, like Pontic Anaitis, the goddess of procreation, and *Venus genetrix*; her honor (τιμῆ) was the enhancement of every endeavor. And as in the temple of Phoenician Astarte, or Armenian Anaitis, or Corinthian Urania, where a certain number of hierodules served with their bodies, so too in Babylon through a similar ideology the high honor of Mylitta expanded to become an obligation of temple service for the full population of Babylonian women. But now the fulfillment of this duty in its real sense and scope was no longer feasible, and so through another twist the custom arose by which every woman, aristocratic or low-born, rich or poor, was obliged once in life to subject her body to a compulsory embrace in the service of the goddess. That this self-sacrifice – as such an action must have appeared to any honorable woman – had the greatest publicity was appropriate to the honor of the goddess. And so we ought not to wonder if the well-born women sought to redeem themselves from the worship of the highly celebrated goddess by giving the greatest solemnity to their actions. In this sense we understand, and the evolution becomes comprehensible, that the self-resignation should be to a foreigner. Were it a local man – one who had already submitted to the dominion of the great goddess and who was bound to her worship – who touched a woman who presented herself as the bound worshipper of the goddess, this would be a criminal offense in her domain, as a sacrilegious injury to her due honors.[15] Such considerations do not impede the foreigner. Being foreign both to the worship of the goddess and to the land, he acquired the woman through a legal slave-sale; and she, having given herself over and fulfilled her duty to the goddess, is now released from her obligation.

. . .

In later times this practice continued in several southern lands in Asia, as well as the majority of the east Indian islands. . . . Such a custom probably also reigned in Antiquity amongst the Chaldeans, and it may have

---

[15] Jacobs never does explain his rationale for this.

endured a long time until the people, having achieved a better under-standing of religion, stopped the practice. Then perhaps some catastro-phe occurred and the consulted oracle (noted by Strabo) demanded that they appease the goddess, and thus they readopted the custom narrated by Herodotos.[16]

In 1838 J. Rosenbaum published his first edition of *Geschichte der Lust-seuche im Altertume,* rendered in English as *The Plague of Lust.* Theoretically, it is on the history of venereal disease in antiquity, although the work is definitely more historiographic than scientific. Rosenbaum's description, decades before the advent of the Victorians and at least a generation before the rise of the Myth and Ritual School, sounds hauntingly familiar:

It was at Babylon then that the cult of Venus originated as *Mylitta* worship, spread over the inland parts to Mesopotamia as the Sabaean religion, and was passed on by the Phoenicians to the seaboard peoples as Astarté-worship. For at the spot where this cult first arose, it lasted longest in its original purity, and *Herodotus* could report how at Babylon the daughters of the country were compelled once in their life-time to give themselves for money to a strange man to win the favour of the goddess, then to return to their dwelling all the more virtuous for the sin, and neither promises nor gifts, however great these might be, availed ever again to draw them into the arms of a stranger.... This custom we find again carried still further amongst the Armenians, who *Strabo* says consecrate their daughters for some considerable length of time to Anaitis, and only after this suffer them to marry. Herodotus relates the same custom of the Lydians, degenerated in the same way as had been the case in later times at Babylon, for here too the lower classes used to abandon their daughters to prostitution for a livelihood. Still in its original purity the usage reached the Phoenicians, but with them also would seem to have early degenerated, although in particular towns of Phoenicia the practice appears to have been followed only under certain circumstances. *Lucian* relates that the women, of Byblus, where was a Temple of Ἀφροδίτη Βυβλίη (Venus of Byblos), *if* they would not allow their hair to be cut off at the Funeral-feast of Adonis, were bound in honour of Venus for one whole day to abandon their bodies to strangers. Among the Carthaginians also, as in Cyprus, maidens had to earn their dowry, and the Tyrant Dionysius introduced the same custom, no doubt, with a secondary design of profit for himself, amongst the people of Locri.

[16] Jacobs 1837 [1811]: 29–34, excerpted.

As to the *reason* for this custom, one might be found in the opinion that prevailed almost universally in Antiquity amongst the Asiatic peoples, that the first-fruits of everything were consecrate to the Deity, and accordingly the virgin's hymen must be offered up to Venus. But this will not in any way explain why the self-surrender must nearly always take place with a *Stranger* . . . of all people in the world . . . [I]n Antiquity, as to this day amongst many savage peoples, not only was the menstrual blood . . . held to be impure, but also the blood that flowed when a virgin was deflowered, from the rupture of the hymen, and consequently the act of defloration as well . . . must necessarily cause injury to the man. This also explains why Herodotus (loco citato) says γυναῖκες (women) and not simply κόραι or παρθένοι (girls, virgins). . . .

The dwellers on the sea-coast, who enjoyed more active intercourse with the rest of the world, left to strangers the polluting act of defloration, whilst among inland peoples this office was undertaken for those of the higher classes by the priests, else an idol, specially appropriated for the purpose, a Priapus or Lingam was employed. Subsequently several mistaken reasons may well have been alleged for the custom. . . .

We must then take into consideration *several* causal factors to help us to an explanation for the custom in question. The original motive may very well have been in every case the consecration of the maiden's virginity to the goddess, – Hieroduli (Temple hand-maids) in the earlier meaning. . . . Little by little the custom lost its purer character. After a time it ceased to be any longer one of universal obligation, and became binding only for the poorer classes, who found in it an opportunity of earning a dowry for their daughters. Meantime the rich adopted the habit of presenting female slaves to the temple of the goddess, thereby giving occasion for the establishment of the regular Hieroduli, – who subsequently grew into *filles de joie* in the proper sense, and laying the foundation of the brothel system.[17]

. . .

As regards the cult of Aphrodité itself and the manner in which it was celebrated in Greece . . . we will limit ourselves here to mentioning the female Hieroduli who as bondswomen of Aphrodité dwelt within the precinct of her Temple, and performed the necessary observances of honour. These were, as already pointed out, of Asiatic origin, and to be found in greater numbers particularly at Ameria and Comana in the Pontus, where they united with the temple-service the traffic of their bodies . . . , just as in later times male Hieroduli gave up their persons for Paederastia.

---

[17] Rosenbaum 1901 [1838]: 17–25, excerpted.

When the cult of Venus came into Greece, the Hieroduli were introduced along with it. But they stripped off in Greece their Asiatic character, which they assumed again only in particular sea-port towns at
the period of the decline or the moral greatness of the Nation, in places
where the temple of Aphrodité Πόρνη (Harlot) was found. Specially
was this so at Corinth, in which city were more than a thousand female
Hieroduli, who were presented as slaves to the Temple.[18]

. . .

The offerings made at [Venus'] shrines were no longer to win an assurance of posterity; they became bribes paid to buy a free opportunity for
the indulgence of sensuality. They degenerated into fornication-fees,
as her temples did into brothels. The priestesses of Astarté or Mylitta
stood at the beck and call alike of strangers and natives, and the opportunity was ever open for sexual enjoyment. Hence too it is that a special
designation for the brothel will be looked for in vain in Asia. The thing
existed there without the name being required; and the State found
no need to establish an institution, which had long ago, without any
intervention on its part, taken form under the cloak of religion.[19]

In 1861, just two years after the appearance of Darwin's *Origin of Species*,
and thus when notions of evolution were all the rage, J.J. Bachofen
published his *Mutterrecht* ("Mother Right"). According to his hypothesis, all societies go through three distinct stages of development from
"low" or "primitive" culture to "high" or "spiritual" culture. First is the
tellurian ("earthy") in which there is no marriage, recognized paternity,
agriculture, or social organization other than the relationship between
mother and children. Second is the lunar stage, in which there is agriculture and marriage within settled communities. Finally, there is the solar
stage, marked by recognized paternity (leading naturally to patriarchy),
a division of labor, and individual ownership.[20] All peoples, then, had at
their beginning a period when, paternity not being recognized, mother
right, or even what we would call matriarchy, held sway. Consequently, all
societies maintain at their core a memory, preserved in myth and ritual, of

---

[18] *Ibid*: 30–31. Concerning the imported slave women at Corinth, Rosenbaum adds,
   "These were purchased by the Greeks, and handed over as offerings to the temple
   of Aphrodité under the title of Temple-servants or 'Hieroduli'; and acquainted as
   they were with the needs of their fellow-countrymen, sought in every way to supply
   them, – as was in particular the case at Corinth" (p. 69).

[19] *Ibid*: 65.

[20] Campbell in Bachofen 1967: *xix*.

the days of matriarchy and, by logical extension, the worship of a Mother Goddess rather than a transcendent Father God.

In the section on Lycia, the quintessential matriarchy according to Herodotos, Bachofen uses several Classical sources, notably Herodotos and Strabo, to display various ancient societies along the evolutionary line and how these communities regulated (or not) reproduction. It is here that we see some of Bachofen's earliest references to what would be understood as sacred prostitution in the modern literature. Discussing dowries, Bachofen relates:

> Aus Sextus bemerkungen über die Entstehung der Dos, womit das bekannte Plautinische *tute tibi dotem quaeris corpore* von dem etruskischen Weibe übereinstimmt, erhält das Geschenk, das jeder Augiler der Braut bringt, seine Erklärung. Es ist das Hetärengeld, das die Ausstattung bildet, wie auch in dem Mysterien der Eingeweihte Aphroditen ein solches *aes meretricium*, die *stipes*, in den Schoß legt, dagegen von ihr den Phallus erhält. Die nachfolgende pudicitia insignis zeigt uns die Augiler im Stande der Ehe und den anfänglichen Hetärismus nicht nur durch sie nicht ausgeschlossen, sondern selbst also Sicherstellung ihrer späteren Strenge und Keusschheit. Wir finden alle diese Züge bei Babyloniern, Lokrern, Etruskern wieder.[21]

There is much that is familiar here. Once again we see the relationship between dowry and prostitution. The mysteries revealed by Clement of Alexandria and Arnobius of Sicca appear again, Aphrodite herself exchanging a phallus for the wages of a whore (*aes meretricium*) as the girls do for their dowries. The "John" is a foreigner, a chance-comer. The act itself is an *obsequens* to the Goddess. As to why this meretricious dowry seeking was necessary and, most important for this study, religious, Bachofen explained as follows:

> Der Ehe Ausschließlichkeit beeinträchtigt das Recht der Mutter Erde...Darum muß das Weib, das in die Ehe tritt, durch eine Period freien Hetärismus die verletzte Naturmutter versöhnen und die Keusschheit des Matrimonium durch vorgängige Unkeusschheit erkaufen....Er ist ein Opfer an die stoffliche Naturmutter, um diese mit der späteren ehelichen Keusschheit zu versöhnen.[22]

---

[21] Bachofen 1975 [1861]: 80.
[22] *Ibid*: 83.

More important for Bachofen's study of sacred prostitution, though, is his later work *Die Saga von Tanaquil*, published in 1870. Looking at the oriental origin of certain aspects of Classical culture, Bachofen dedicated one and a half subchapters to the study of ancient *kultische Prostitution*:

§8 It is very important and meaningful for the study of the myth of Tanaquil to develop a core understanding of this hetaeric conception. An important prototype is the Babylonian Mylitta, whose unrestrained Nature-principle rose to dominance throughout the Near East, changing the original spirit of the cult to her own conception. Mylitta followed the principle which underlay the natural world in its entirety – the creative principle hampered by no human law. The confining shackles of marriage are contrary to this principle. A proponent of this creative *ius naturale*, Mylitta demands full submission of everyone; she raises all barriers off the lower spheres from men, recognized in the *ultronea creatio* of the swamp.

In the accounts which Herodotos 1.199 and Strabo 16 give us concerning the worship of Mylitta, we find all the themes of her presence. From every girl of this population the goddess demands free devotion to the man who calls her to sexual intercourse. The summons takes place in the name of Mylitta and in the sacred space of her temple. The man's payment is a payment to Mylitta and belongs to the temple treasury. The cord about the girl's head is a symbol of the sacrifice of her chastity. Prostitution is thus cultic, an act demanded by religion. When taken further, the goddess is content with a single act of devotion from the woman and henceforth confers the most absolute chastity upon the ensuing marriage. Thus comes to the fore with all clarity the motif of expiation vis-à-vis *matrimonium* as regards the Mylitta principle.

From Babylon the hetaeric Mylitta principle spreads out over all lands subject to the Assyrian culture. We find it in Lydia, where the names γλυκὺς ἀγκών or ἀγνέων denote the sacrifice of chastity particularly in the realm of the sacred. Likewise in the Elian Βάδυ, which is clearly tied to Lydia via Herakles; and endlessly in the service of Aphrodite Pornê at Abydos, which in the surviving mythus surely displays the essence of the Sacaea...

Another route of the expansion of cultic prostitution leads towards Syria, Phoenicia, and Cyprus. Under various names and in a plethora of cult forms the same Law of the *Hetaira* rises to dominance in all these lands. A salient example appears in Syrian Askalon. This place is connected to Babylon via Semiramis and to Sardis and its Heraklid royal house through a myth of Xanthus. The city is the residence of a goddess whom the ancients called Aphrodite Urania, and furthermore they claimed that this city was the origin of the Cypriot Venus sanctuary at Paphos, and thence the island of Kythera, Corinth, and Athens. That this Askalonian Urania was worshipped with prostitution is proven not so much by the θήλεια νοῦσος she gave to the Skythians as by the myth of Semiramis, who coincides with Aphrodite Urania and who imposes her hetaeric principle even on Derketo, especially in the mandatory Cypriot worship which is particularly important for the understanding of cultic *hetairismos*. Herodotos equated the Cypriot example explicitly with the Babylonian, equating Aphrodite Urania with Mylitta. The descriptions which Arnobius, Firmicus Maternus, and Clement of Alexandria provide concerning the *initia Cypriae Veneris* testifies to a very close relationship with the Babylonian conception and custom. The practice of prostitution on the sea-shore is understood by Justinus to be like the Babylonian practice in the midst of the sanctuary – both being an expiation for marriage; while Athenaios equates it with the custom of the Lydians, and this is confirmed in several other reports. The founder of the Cypriot worship of Mylitta and its licentious mysteries is Kinyras. The temple at Paphos as well as the one at Amathus can be traced back to him, and the foundation of the entire cult can be seen to go back to his love for a harlot, whom the king deified. In Metharmê [Myrrha], the daughter of Pygmalion, with whom Kinyras begat the licentious Adonis (called Κύρις on Cyprus) existed the epithet "consecrated lust-whore" ["*Buhldirne*"].

The same phenomenon appears in two Syrian sanctuaries: at Byblos, the domain of Kinyras-Adonis, and at Aphaka in Lebanon. The first appears in the *Syrian Goddess*, chapter 6, where the Byblian Baaltis-Venus demands of every woman the sacrifice of her chastity or the equivalent in hair-cutting. The "love price" becomes the property of the goddess's treasury. The temple at Aphaka was also bequeathed by Kinyras. At that place was a grove in which all sorts of licentiousness were practiced as a gift of the goddess.

The same custom of Mylitta also found entry into Phoenicia thanks to Dido-Elissa, who might be placed in very close relationship with the worship of Cypriote Aphrodite and in whose encounter with Aeneas might be understood as a manifestation of Omphale-Semiramis. Elissa carried off from Cyprus 80 "lust-whores," assuring the long life of the custom through the future assimilation of these Venus-worshippers. . . . In Sicca Venera a temple was equated with the Erycinian temple and associated with the cultic prostitution of women, just as in the case of Babylonian Mylitta.

The same *hetairismos* appeared at Corinth in a different guise. This was the setting for lustier Aphrodite servants than among the other peoples. However, it was not the underlying principle that changed, merely the style of its portrayal and practice. The delight of the goddess in prostitution was especially revealed in that the intercession of the hierodules was required in the direst of situations.

Finally, the Babylonian Mylitta principle reached as far as Italy and the isle of Samos. We have elsewhere explained at length (*Mutterrecht* § 138–139) how the idea of cultic *hetairismos* was interwoven with the entire epic history of the Epizephyrian Lokrians, and here we make only a reference to the general testimony of Athenaios, especially as it highlights Justinus' narrative about the Lokrian matrons' sacrifice of chastity during the war against Leophron and the Rhegians. For in the vow the old Aphrodisian law comes forth with all clarity....

For Samos we possess the testimony of Eustathius. The duty to sacrifice one's chastity in honor of Hera here reveals a new lowering of standards. The physical union occurred before the festive wedding ritual. The myth takes this custom back from Hera's licentiousness. That it derives from the law of Mylitta is known not only from Eustathius, who compared the unchaste cult of Anaitis with that of Hera, ... but also from the frequent equation of Hera and Aphrodite, and finally by the festivals of Nonae Caprotinae, a Sacaean cult to honor the hetaeric Juno, already discussed. The nature of Urania most assuredly cannot be missed in the worship and attributes of Samian Juno.

§9 Since we have followed the spread of the Babylonian Mylitta principle over Syria, Phoenicia and the neighboring coasts and islands to Italy, and we have highlighted the origin point of the hetaeric cult, let us turn to inner Asia to examine the dominion of the same issue among the Armenians and to clarify the same remarkable expression.... In Akilisene, the land between the Euphrates and the Taurus Mountains, is the sanctuary of Anaitis, where the noblest daughters of the population sell themselves as consecrated "lust-whores" in service to the goddess. They enjoy high regard, and no one disdains them as they choose spouses of their own rank. This prostitution differs from the Babylonian only in that the consecration to Anaitis does not involve every woman, as in the Mylitta rite, but those enjoying rank and status. On the large trade route to Armenia lies Comana, whose goddess received a similar cult, although not bearing the name Anaitis. Strabo 12 likens the place of pilgrimage to Corinth, as neither the *hetairai* nor the foreigners who seek them are few.[23]

In 1883 W. M. Ramsay, while working on his compendium on the geography and history of Phrygia, published a number of unedited inscriptions from Asia Minor. Number 19 from this set was the Tralles inscription discussed here in Chapter 7, wherein a woman named L. Aurelia Aimilia

---

[23] Bachofen 1951 [1870]: 93–98.

dedicated an *anathema* to Zeus after her period of *pallakê*-ship. According to Ramsay:

> Aurelia Aemilia belonged to a family in which the ancient custom was retained that the women should in their youth be *hetairai* in the service of the temple. The custom was common in the native religions of Asia Minor, . . . [Aurelia] acted as a hierodoule like her ancestors in obedience to an order from the oracle.[24]

Other than a reference to Strabo, however, Ramsay gives no indication as to his methodology in defining the Tralles *pallakai* as sacred prostitutes ("*hetairai* in the service of the temple"). His reasoning is better expressed in his masterwork *The Cities and Bishoprics of Phrygia*, published between 1895 and 1897. Here, in the section entitled "Matriarchal System," after discussing the Mother Goddess worship prevalent in this region, Ramsay reveals:

> The religion originated among a people whose social system was not founded on marriage, and among whom the mother was head of the family, and relationship was counted only through her. Long after a higher type of society had come into existence in Phrygia, the religion preserved the facts of the primitive society. . . . The inscriptions reveal to us cases in which women of good position felt themselves called upon to live the divine life, under the influence of divine inspiration. The typical case is recorded in an inscription of Tralleis.
>
> The commentary on this inscription is contained in Strabo's account . . . of the social customs which existed in Akilisene in his own time, and which, as he says, formerly existed in Lydia [Strabo 11.14.16, quoted here by Ramsay]. The inscription shows that the custom survived in Lydia as late as the second century: the person here concerned is of good rank, as is proved by the Latin name of her family. She comes of ancestors who have served before the god with asceticism (unwashed feet) and prostitution; she has served in the same way in accordance with the express orders of the god.[25]

Ramsay, then, takes the word *pallakê*/*pallakis* as "sacred prostitute" because he believes that Aurelia Aimilia was engaged in whatever activity Strabo claimed that Armenian girls did, which Strabo himself compared to what Lydian girls did. Of course, as we saw in Chapters Four, Seven, and Eight, Strabo's understanding of Lydian prostitution was derived

---

[24] Ramsay 1883: 276–277. See Budin 2003a on this inscription and later interpretations.
[25] Ramsay 1975 [1895–1897]: 94–95.

from Herodotos, who claimed that Lydian girls practiced a purely secular kind of prenuptial sacred prostitution. But the conflation of sacred with prenuptial prostitution was so common in the literature, both ancient and modern, we can hardly hold Ramsay accountable for this methodological *faux pas*.

More important for his analysis, though, was Ramsay's apparent reliance on the theories of Bachofen. Ramsay believed that the Tralles inscription pertaining to L. Aurelia Aimilia could be understood in light of that region's continued use of aspects of its primitive religion. That primitive religion, understood through Bachofen, consisted of Mother Goddess worship, a certain indiscriminate sexuality, and, above all, the need for girls to prostitute themselves in honor of the Goddess before settling in to a nice, honorable, patriarchal marriage. The Tralles inscription proved Bachofen to be correct, and Bachofen provided the key to interpret the Tralles inscription. Both then "confirmed" Strabo's accounts, and the vicious cycle continued.

Most nineteenth-century scholars writing on ancient sacred prostitution focused on its role as prenuptial ritual, either as an initial sacrifice of chastity in honor of a nature goddess, or as a ritual defloration that protected the groom from the danger of virginal blood. In 1893 W. Hertz, when considering notions of prenuptial rite and dowry in his essay "Die Sage vom Giftmädchen," wrote about

> die bekannte babylonische Sitte, zu Ehren der Mylitta die Jungfrau an Fremde preiszugenben, auf jenen Abergluaben zurückführen. Dieselbe religiöse Prostitution herrschte auf Kypros bei Phönikern und Puniern, Syrern und Juden, bei den Ägyptern, den Armeniern, den Hellenen, den Indern und Hinterindiern.
>
> Doch wenn auch änliche Beweggründe damit ursprünglich im Spiele gewesen sein können – was wohl vermutet, aber nicht bewiesen werden kann – , so wie uns diese Bräuche geschichtlich bezeugt sind, unterscheiden sie sich wesentlich von den bisher besprochenen. Denn weit entfernt, alsber abgelohnt zu werden, hatte der Liebhaber den für die Gottheit ihre Keuschheit opfernden Jungfrauen ein Geldgeschenk zu geben, das dem Templeschatz anheimfiel.[26]

Likewise, in 1887 H. H. Ploss wrote in his study of *Das Weib in der Natur- und Völkerkunde* that the "sacred" prostitution found amongst the Phoenicians and Babylonians was a form of prophylactic defloration (thus

---

[26] Hertz 1905: 215–217.

following directly in the theories of Rosenbaum that virginal blood was dangerous).[27]

The last author to write about sacred prostitution as a prenuptial safety measure was M. P. Nilsson, in his 1906 publication *Griechische Feste von Religiöser Bedeutung*. Of especial interest is the fact that Nilsson did *not* believe that the practices narrated by Herodotos, Justinus, and the like were sacred in nature. Rather, they were practical acts that only over time came to be misunderstood as ritual.

The other matter pertaining to the Paphian festival concerns the sacrifice of virginity. This custom came to Cyprus from several places and was not native to Paphos. So Justinus relates, as he claims that the sacrifice took place at a festival (*statutis diebus*). Herodotos related the same but places it in Babylon, where the women once in life go to the temple of Mylitta and must sell themselves to the first foreigner. The custom was not bound to a single, specific day – neither there, nor in Armenia, nor in Lydia, and thus not in Cyprus either. Justinus offers few details. One links his account with the reference in Herodotos to the Lydians: *dotalem quaesituras pecuniam*. That a festival took place is evidenced by the common, old motif of the abduction of maidens: Dido sought to acquire wives for her companions and in so doing wound up adopting and preserving this rite with its Semitic flavor.

Justinus was right in one thing: The maidens were selling themselves before marriage. We find the same thing in Lydia (according to Herodotos 1.93, the maidens acquired their trousseaux just as today the girls in the wilds of Biskra do; there is no naughtiness after marriage), Syria, North Africa, and Akilisene in Armenia, where prostitution was associated with the cult of Anaitis. Likewise the Epizephyrian Lokrians vowed to prostitute their maidens. This is not attested in Babylon, although it is highly likely. The woman must once in life submit to this sacrifice, after which she maintains perfect chastity. These two details and the routine nature of the entire affair reveal that that these isolated practices do not belong to a licentious cult as people tend to assume, accusing the Semitic religion of unrighteousness in many respects. It is here clear that it is the maidens who sell themselves, never married women. Furthermore, she must always do so with a foreigner. The explanation lies in the widely held belief that first intercourse with a maiden is dangerous, and to counteract this a less delicate age permitted the perilous abduction of its maidens by foreigners. The Babylonians

---

[27] Ploss 1887: 302–303.

must have believed that every act of intercourse between a man and women exposed them to dangerous power, as Herodotos explains the fumigation and bathing rituals in 1.198. . . .

Originally these practices had nothing to do with religion, and so it remained with the Lydians. When they took on cultic aspects, they seemed similar to the rites of sexuality, and so they were quickly accepted as belonging to that realm. The fee earned by the maidens was seen as a sacrifice to the goddess and left in her temple. Like other acts so undertaken for divinity, the maiden resided in the temple, and thus it became temple prostitution. Naturally, the maidens also served as temple-slaves, and if the superstitious fear of youth diminished, what remained is what we see in Comana, this then proceeding to Corinth. The same thing appears today in India within certain castes.[28]

EXCURSUS – CORINTH: A DIFFERENT THING ENTIRELY

The historians, ethnographers, and nascent anthropologists of the nineteenth century who studied sacred prostitution mostly stuck to historiographic texts, primarily Herodotos, Strabo, and Justinus. By contrast, the literary scholars who considered this issue did so in the context of poetry. The works of Pindar, Simonides, Athenaios, and Khamaileon discussed in Chapter 6 were already the subject of considerable debate in the early nineteenth century. In his 1821 analysis of Pindar's thirteenth Olympian Ode and its accompanying *skolion* (frag. 122), A. Boeckhius claimed that

> Many things are known about the *meretriculis* of Corinthian Venus – ἱεροδούλοις, who as slaves of the goddess employ their services and offices to earn a profit of sorts for their Lady, and for this reason the poet said σὺν δ' ἀνάγκα πᾶν καλόν. At this point Venus herself, the ματέρ' Ἐρώτων οὐρανίαν was understood to be listening in. . . . She is said to be the Lady of Cyprus. Clearly Paphian Venus is Οὐρανία, about whom see Herodotos I, 105; Pausanias 1.14.6 (this Venus whom the Corinthians worship is Οὐρανία). . . . You will note that Uranian Venus is by nature a *genetrix* and Mistress who gathers together all things and promotes generation, and thus she even presides over physical love, contrary to what Plato supposed of her in his *Symposium*. Nor was this base union with religious matters astonishing, being propagated in Cyprus and Greece by the unchaste and lascivious Syrian Mother.[29]

[28] Nilsson 1906: 365–367.
[29] Boeckhius 1821: 611.

By the 1850s it was becoming increasingly obvious that the women extolled by both Pindar and Simonides were not wives, but prostitutes. In 1856, E. Köpke criticized Plutarch for shoddy scholarship in so identifying the Corinthian *matronas*, "Vehementissime falsus est Plutarchus, quum perversa scriptura perductus de statuis cogitaverit, quae matronis Corinthiacis essent positae."[30] In 1889 in his "Commentariolum grammaticum IV" U. von Wilamowitz-Moellendorff combined the bodies of evidence provided by Pindar and Simonides by way of Khamaileon and Athenaios and determined that the subjects of both the *skolion* and the epigram (see Chapter 6) were "clearly" prostitutes. Furthermore, they were not merely Corinthian "girls" plying a meretricious trade; they were specifically sacred prostitutes:

> Theopompos understood that it was the wives who were honored [in the epigram] and so he rendered his sweet tale. Khamaileon cross-referenced the epigram with the song from Pindar and perhaps some other documents pertaining to the customs of the Corinthians, and he concluded that in both the vow made by Xenophon in the song and the one fulfilled by the Corinthians in the epigram, it was prostitutes who were honored. ὅταν ἡ πόλις εὔχεται περὶ μεγάλων τῇ Ἀφροδίτῃ, συμπαραλαμβάνεσθαι πρὸς ἱκετείαν τὰς ἑταίρας ὡς πλείστας, καὶ ταύτας προσεύχεσθαι τῇ θεῷ καὶ ὕστερον ἐπὶ τοῖς ἱεροῖς παρεῖναι. This occurred in the Persian War, and they were painted ἰδίᾳ (i.e., alone amongst the population). τὰς τότε ποιησαμένας τὴν ἱκετείαν καὶ ὕστερον παρούσας. Khamaileon veritably saw the truth, it cannot be doubted, whatever might be corrected in his explanation. For he incorrectly understood from an older custom that some of the girls of Corinth practiced the art of prostitution; and therefore he affirmed that a great many of them were invited to the public sacrifices, stood before the populace, and were painted together, all as referring to a single thing. In truth, they were *servae Venereae*, who in the temple earned a profit by their bodies (*corpore faciunt*) and in sacred matters appeared hardly different than even the Deliades of Delos. So much Pindar explains in his oft-cited text [fr. 122]; the girls whom he seriously and graciously calls πολύξεναι νεάνιδες ἀμφίπολοι, Πειθοῦς ἐν ἀφνειῷ Κορίνθῳ, αἵ τε τὰς χλωρᾶς λιβάνου ξανθὰ δάκρη θυμιᾶτε, πολλάκι ματέρ' Ἐρώτων οὐρανίαν πτάμεναι νόημα ποττὰν Ἀφροδίταν. He continues his commemoration of the girls' sacred functions ὑμῖν ἄνευθεν ἐπαγορίας ἔπορεν, ὦ παῖδες, ἐρατειναῖς ἐν

---

[30] Köpke 1856: 25.

εὐναῖς μαλθακᾶς ὥρας ἀπὸ καρπὸν δρέπεσθαι. σὺν δ' ἀνάγκᾳ πᾶν καλόν. These were public slaves, not *libertinas* or even free women. Xenophon vowed that if he won at the Olympics he would dedicate 50 slaves to Venus. When he fulfilled the vow, Pindar sang ὦ Κύπρου δέσποινα, τεὸν δεῦτ' ἐς ἄλσος φορβάδων κορᾶν ἀγέλαν ἑκατόγγυιον Ξενοφῶν τελέαις ἐπήγαγ' εὐχωλαῖς ἰανθείς, which Khamaileon can be seen to have correctly interpreted in the form we have preserved in Athenaios.[31]

In 1902, M. Boas followed up on Wilamowitz' theories with great fervor in his *De Epigrammatis Simonideis*. Here he extolled:

And so a great man of keen intellect understood Khamaileon when he explained Corinthian Xenophon and the prostitutes celebrated by Pindar, whom Xenophon promised to Venus if he should return to his homeland an Olympic victor as requested. He understood that what was recorded was a Corinthian sacrifice of an earlier age, at which women were present, and he saw that they were not *matronas*, but *meretrices*. . . . As we saw above, it was Ephoros who was the literary source for both this Corinthian epigram [that of Simonides] and others; *he* made the mistake, by which those women came to be understood as the wives of the Corinthians. This error was passed on from Ephoros to Theopompos, to Plutarch's source, and to Plutarch himself.[32]

Finally, in his 1915 publication of the Odes of Pindar for Harvard University's Loeb series, J. Sandys could offer the following commentary on Pindar's fragment 122:

Xenophon of Corinth, before competing for the Olympic crown in 464 B.C., vowed that, in the event of his success, he would devote a hundred courtesans to the service of the temple of Aphroditê in that city. On the occasion of the fulfillment of his vow, the following ode was sung in the temple of the goddess, while the hundred women danced to the words of the song. The same Olympic victory was celebrated in the thirteenth Olympian ode.[33]

THE TWENTIETH CENTURY: FROM PRENUPTIAL RITE TO FERTILITY

At the dawn of the twentieth century, a change occurred among the Germans in the study of ancient sacred prostitution. The scholars found

---

[31] Wilamowitz-Moellendorff 1889: 4–5.
[32] Boas 1905: 58.
[33] Sandys 1915: 580–581.

a new interest – fertility – and this is where most modern students of ancient sacred prostitution pick up the thread of scholarship. In his 1905[34] publication *Wald- und Feldkulte*, W. Mannhardt provides once more a highly familiar description of ancient sacred prostitution, although focusing primarily on Byblos, Cyprus and Babylon. Here, though, Mannhardt presents the ancient custom so-called as related to fertility ritual, downplaying the previously popular notion of prenuptial rite. Sacred prostitution represents the union of Aphrodite (played by the female prostitutes) and Adonis, the man from the "foreign" land of death. This Adonis is in turn presented as the genius of the Korngeist, a manifestation of the dying and rising Vegetation God.

In Byblos the women cut their hair during the mourning festival, as did the Egyptians when Apis died. Those, however, who did not wish to submit to this sacrifice were obliged to assemble for a day at the market-place to show themselves to foreigners and to sell their beauty to one of them. The proceeds were consecrated to the goddess. This must have occurred in the latter part of the festival. In Paphos and Cyprus existed the same custom, as the etiological narrative reveals: The lovely sisters of Adonis – daughters of Kinyras, the founder and hero of Paphos, and the Cypriot Metharme – the maidens Orsedike, Laogara, and Braisia had sold themselves to foreign men in accordance with the will of an angered Aphrodite. Perhaps this portrays a variation on the Byblian practice, as Justinus XVIII.5 reports that this practice occurred on Cyprus when the young girls, about to be married, set out for the shore on certain days to earn a dowry by selling themselves to foreign men. The Babylonian practice described by Herodotos I.199 – that every woman once in life, in the sanctuary of Mylitta, had to give herself to the first foreign man who tossed a piece of money into her lap – must as well originally derive from an orgy[35] or something similar, from which it had since become disassociated. Or, more likely, did such a festival actually take place – misunderstood by Herodotos – where the woman . . . had to remain throughout the entire festival until such time as she found a lover, and where the ugly ones often had to do this over the course of three or four years before someone finally chose them? With these festival customs, the same, constrained moralizing sentiments appear: Total and strict chastity is undoubtedly endured and demanded outside of the festival and in marriage. Deriving from a view of life which is quite different from our own, they were not

---

[34] Second edition.
[35] The original German has here "Duzifeste," literally an "intimacy festival."

immoral in regards to common lust. They were symbolic and mystic expressions of a religious belief, and their divine and sanctified origins, at least originally, were far from the beastial sensuality and wild eroticism which they and other field processions later degenerated into in the worship of Aphrodite Pandemos.... The women sacrificing their chastity imitated the example of Aphrodite herself, who remarried the returning Adonis. They acted as images, path-followers, and copies of the goddess. The Cypriot cult reveals this thusly: Those who were initiated into the cult of Aphrodite in the temple built by Kinyras received a small phallus and gave a piece of money "*mercedis nomine*" into the hand of the goddess herself. Every woman represented the goddess, and so the foreigner, who appeared to her and enjoyed her love, represented the returning Adonis, logically a stranger from a foreign place – the land of death. I must suggest the possibility, even probability, that the foreigner here is even understood in terms of the Phrygian Litys custom, in which he was taken for the Corn-Spirit during the harvest, bound in a sheaf, and beheaded, either in reality or symbolically.

At so, finally, we come to our most famous pariah, Sir James George Frazer. By now it should be reasonably clear that Frazer is hardly to blame for the development of the sacred prostitution myth. Several eminent and at the time well-respected scholars had already done much to fashion the contours of the myth in the previous century, including (as we shall see below) Frazer's own mentor W. Robertson Smith. Interestingly, *in spite of* this, Frazer originally gave little thought to sacred prostitution in the original formulation of his masterpiece *The Golden Bough*. When this was first published in 1890, Frazer did not include a word about sacred prostitution, in spite of an extensive treatment of Adonis in this first edition. It was only later, in a revised and expanded edition of 1907, that Frazer turned his attention to this apparent institution. This chronology is confirmed by Frazer's own letters. In a letter written to E. Sidney Hartland on 18 October 1907, Frazer wrote:

In the new edition of "Adonis," I have considered the question of sacred prostitution in Western Asia much more fully than before ... You are wrong to set aside so cavalierly the testimony of Eusebius as to the prostitution of married women. He was a contemporary of the practices, he lived in the country, he was bishop of the diocese, and he was taken to task by Constantine (who abolished the sacred prostitution) for remissness in dealing with the heathen practices of his people. He is therefore a witness of the highest authority, and is not to be put out of court in favour of the later historian Socrates, who lived in Constantinople and was born long after the custom was abolished.[36]

It is immediately apparent that Frazer fell victim to many of the same methodological infelicities as later historians of sacred prostitution, a fact that is highlighted in his actual testimony on the subject. As will become evident in the following text, there is good reason that modern historians, among others, have looked to Frazer as the father of the sacred prostitution myth. It is not that he is the first to formulate the myth – far from it. Rather, it was he who put the myth into the form with which modern scholars are most familiar. It is with Frazer that we see the insufficiently critical assessment of the Classical scholars and Biblical texts; the close association with notions of fertility; and, perhaps just as important, the utter lacuna when it comes to seeing this institution practiced in the "West." It is no wonder that the sacred prostitution myth is embroiled in the Victorian construction of decadent Orientalism. According to Frazer,

> In Cyprus it appears that before marriage all women were formerly obliged by custom to prostitute themselves to strangers at the sanctuary of the goddess, whether she went by the name of Aphrodite, Astarte, or what not. Similar customs prevailed in many parts of Western Asia. Whatever its motive, the practice was clearly regarded, not as an orgy of lust, but as a solemn religious duty performed in the service of that great Mother Goddess of Western Asia whose name varied, while her type remained constant, from place to place. Thus at Babylon every woman, whether rich or poor, had once in her life to submit to the embraces of a stranger at the temple of Mylitta, that is, of Ishtar or Astarte, and to dedicate to the goddess the wages earned by this sanctified harlotry. The sacred precinct was crowded with women waiting to observe the custom. Some of them had to wait there for years. At Heliopolis of Baalbec in Syria, famous for the imposing grandeur of its ruined temples, the custom of the country required that every maiden should prostitute herself to a stranger at the temple of Astarte, and matrons as well as maids testified their devotion to the goddess in the same manner. The emperor Constantine abolished the custom, destroyed the temple, and built a church on its stead. In Phoenician temples women prostituted themselves for hire in the service of religion,

---

[36] Ackerman 2005: 271.

believing that by this conduct they propitiated the goddess and won her favour. At Byblus the people shaved their heads in the annual mourning for Adonis. Women who refused to sacrifice their hair had to give themselves up to strangers on a certain day of the festival, and the money which they thus earned was devoted to the goddess. This custom may have been a mitigation of an older rule which at Byblus as elsewhere formerly compelled every woman without exception to sacrifice her virtue in the service of religion, . . . We are told that in Lydia all girls were obliged to prostitute themselves in order to earn a dowry; but one may suspect that the real motive of the custom was devotion rather than economy. The suspicion is confirmed by a Greek inscription found at Tralles in Lydia, which proves that the practice of religious prostitution survived in that country as late as the second century of our era. It records of a certain women, Aurelia Aemilia by name, not only that she herself served the god in the capacity of a harlot at his express command, but that her mother and other female ancestors had done the same before her; and the publicity of the record, engraved on a marble column which supported a votive offering, shows that no stain attached to such a life and such a parentage. In Armenia the noblest families dedicated their daughters to the service of the goddess Anaitis in her temple at Acilisena, where the damsels acted as prostitutes for a long time before they were given in marriage. Nobody scrupled to take one of these girls to wife when her period of service was over. Again, the goddess Ma was served by a multitude of sacred harlots at Comana in Pontus, and crowds of men and women flocked to her sanctuary from the neighbouring cities and country to attend the biennial festivals or to pay their vows to the goddess.[37]

Even more famous than Frazer's description of ancient sacred prostitution, though, was his attachment of that institution to notions of fertility. As we have already seen, in this he very much follows Mannhardt (as he himself proclaimed). However, rather than linking the sacred prostitute necessarily with a "Corn-spirit," he legitimized, one might say, the sacred-sexual act by emphasizing its role in a kind of *hieros gamos*, and thus universal fertility:

In their licentious intercourse at the temples the women, whether maidens or matrons or professional harlots, imitated the licentious conduct of a great goddess of fertility for the purpose of ensuring the fruitfulness of fields and trees, of man and beast; and in discharging this sacred

---

[37] Frazer 1907: 32–34.

and important function the women were probably supposed, like their West African sisters, to be actually possessed by the goddess.[38]

Such is the evidence Frazer offered for pagan sacred prostitution. The reader will note that, contrary to earlier authors, there is no reference to either Corinth or Lokris in the text, thus, apparently, casting a thoroughly "Oriental" guise onto the institution. Furthermore, in other portions of *The Golden Bough* Frazer examined the role of the Biblical *qedešîm* and *qedešôt* in relation to his fertility theories. As such, he was the first scholar to pull together the data from the Classical *and* Biblical sources. It is to these "Oriental" data that we now turn.

FROM WEST TO EAST: THE RISE OF ASSYRIOLOGY

If there is any validity to the claim that the Victorians gave rise and form to the myth of sacred prostitution, a large part of that can be attributed to the fact that Assyriology was born in the nineteenth century. It was in the late 1830s that Rawlinson dangled himself in front of the Persian inscription at Behistun and thus allowed, finally, a translation of cuneiform. By the 1860s "Assyrian" language dictionaries were being published. The new materials influenced (and continue to influence) how the Bible is read and interpreted and how we understand the eastern *logoi* of the Classical authors.

Of course, as with any new discipline, logic dictates that one go from the known to the unknown, and in the late nineteenth and early twentieth centuries what was known was the Classical authors. As such, there was considerable interaction between the new cuneiform materials and what was expected to be found in them based on the works of, *inter alia*, Herodotos, Ktesias, and Strabo. It was this interaction that placed the stamp of approval on the theories of sacred prostitution. For in translating the cuneiform documents, nascent Assyriologists, predicated of course on the work of earlier Biblical scholars, used the myth of sacred prostitution to help them translate technical terms for which they had no parallels and could imagine no other options (the concept of, say, "liberated woman" was far beyond them).

As early as 1847 W. Gesenius, in his *Hebrew and Chaldee Lexicon to Old Testament Scriptures*, had this to say about the radicals קדש:

קָדֵשׁ m. — (1) a *sodomite*, pr. consecrated, sc. to Astarte or Venus, and prostituting himself in her honour, Deut. 23:18; 1 Ki. 14:24; 15:12;

---

[38] *Ibid*: 62.

22:47; Job 36:14. Fem. קדשה consecrated (to Venus), hence a *harlot*, Gen. 38:21, 22; Deu. 23:18; Hos. 4:14. As to the libidinous worship of Venus amongst the Babylonians, see Lucian, De Dea Syria; compare Nu. 25:1 sqq.[39]

Gesenius never does explain how the Roman goddess Venus figures into Canaanite religion, or why a woman consecrated to her would automatically be a *harlot*. Note also the reference to Babylon vis-à-vis Lucian. This, of course, should be Byblos.[40] The entry is not well thought out methodologically, and Gesenius offers no support for his translation other than a single, late Classical reference. Apparently this was not viewed as overly problematic.

What is especially important in this entry is the translations. In the process of accusing the Victorians of the creation of the sacred prostitution myth, some scholars, such as J. Assante and S. Hooks, have pointed to the fact that until 1927 the *qedešîm* and *qedešôt* were simply translated as sodomites and harlots respectively, with no reference to an apparently unknown meaning of sacred prostitute. As Gesenius shows, though, the words "sodomite" and "harlot" already had accrued to themselves the meanings of sacred prostitute. The semantics, then, flew faster than the vocabulary, with the concept of sacred prostitution being prevalent in Biblical studies well before the actual changeover in translation.

Like Gesenius, other scholars were just as willing to let the Classical authors speak for their eastern neighbors. Particularly guilty of this, with formidable consequences in the form of his protegé Frazer, was W. Robertson Smith. In the 1889 publication of his work *The Religion of the Semites* he was obviously perfectly content to let Herodotos do the talking:

> ... Herodotus himself tells us that among the Babylonians and Arabs every conjugal act was immediately followed, not only by an ablution, but by such fumigation as is still practiced in the Sudan (Herod. i. 198). This restriction is not directed against immorality, for it applies to spouses; nor does it spring from asceticism, for the temple of the Semitic deities were thronged with sacred prostitutes; who, however, were careful to retire with their partners outside the sacred precincts (Herod. i. 199, ἔξω τοῦ ἱροῦ; cf Hos. iv. 14).

[39] Gesenius 1847: DCCXXV. Italics in original.
[40] Or possibly Baalbek. It was definitely someplace beginning with B.

But not all early Semiticists were so blasé, and the rise of sacred prostitution in Assyriology was actually far more halting than the current situation would lead one to expect. A particularly enlightening testament of things not to come was issued by A. H. Sayce in a chapter on "The Family" in his 1899 book *Babylonians and Assyrians: Life and Customs*. Here, Sayce pointedly denies the description of sacred prostitution given by Herodotos:

> According to Herodotus, a gigantic system of public prostitution prevailed in Babylonia. Every unmarried woman was compelled to remain in the sacred enclosure of Mylitta – by which Ishtar is apparently meant – until some stranger had submitted to her embraces,[41] while the sums derived from the sale of their personal charms by the handsome and good-looking provided portions for the ugly. Of all this there is not a trace in the mass of native documents which we now possess. There were the devotees of Ishtar, certainly – the *ukhâtu* and *kharimâtu* – as well as public prostitutes, who were under the protection of the law; but they formed a class apart, and had nothing to do with the respectable women of the country.... The dowries provided for the ugly by the prostitution of the rich must be an invention of the Greeks.[42]

It is obvious that Sayce has here confused two separate chapters in the *Histories*, combining details from 1.196 – Marriage Auction – with 1.199 – Sacred Prostitution. Nevertheless, two details are worthy of note. On the one hand, Sayce gives no indication, as late as 1899, that sacred prostitution existed in Mesopotamia. He denies Herodotos' account, where, as Sayce sees it, the historian conflated the respectable women of Babylon with the public prostitutes, public prostitutes who are under the protection of the law, not a goddess. On the other hand, Sayce expresses skepticism as to the reliability of Greek authors writing about Babylon.

Sayce was the editor of another late nineteenth-century work that, in like fashion, makes no reference to sacred prostitution in ancient Mesopotamia. In this 1894 publication *The Dawn of Civiliztion: Egypt and Chaldea*, J. Maspero gave a narrative account of the then emerging *Epic of Gilgameš*. When it became necessary to civilize Enkidu, here called Eabani, the farmer bade his son to go to the city of Uruk, "and

---

[41] *He* had to submit to *her* embraces????
[42] Sayce 1899: 30–31.

to choose there from among the priestesses of Ishtar one of the most beautiful." Maspero then annotated this comment with

> The priestesses of Ishtar were young and beautiful women, devoted to the service of the goddess and her worshippers. Besides the title *qadishtu*, priestess, they bore various names . . . ;the priestess who accompanies Saîdu was an *ukhat*.[43]

The character Maspero is describing is the *harimtu* Šamhat. What is of particular interest here is the methodology used to determine Šamhat's identity. Although in the current literature Šamhat is generally understood to be a prostitute (frequently a sacred prostitute!), this notion is not yet established for Maspero. He sees her instead as a priestess of Ištar. The technical term he renders as *ukhat* is actually the word *šamhat*, the name of the *harimtu*, and not a cult title. Maspero's confusion on this is somewhat surprising in light of E. Norris' 1868 *Assyrian Dictionary*, where Norris takes UHT (Ú-ha-ti) as "samhati; agreeable, pleasant. Hebrew שמח."[44] Nevertheless, Maspero sees the woman not as a prostitute, but as a cult functionary. Granted, she has sexual intercourse as one of her duties, but this does not define her (at least yet) as a prostitute *per se*. The religion is there, the sex is there, but we do not yet quite have sacred prostitution.

It is, of course, eminently good scholarship not to accept foreign, possibly colored or distorted data as reliable evidence in and of themselves. Sayce was to be commended for his skepticism concerning ancient Greek evidence for Babylonian history. However, when Mesopotamian data started to emerge that seemed to corroborate the foreign accounts, change was in the wind.

This became apparent as early as 1898, in M. Jastrow's *Handbooks on the History of Religions*. Somewhat taking up where Maspero left off, Jastrow offered a "fuller" account of the role of Šamhat in the *Gilgameš Epic*.

> *Ukhatu* is a name for a harlot devoted to the worship of Ishtar. Other names for such devotees are *Kharimtu* and *Kizritu*. Elsewhere the city of Uruk is called "The dwelling of Anu and Ishtar, the city of the *Kizrêti*, *Ukhâti*, and *Kharimâti*," and in a subsequent tablet of the Gilgamesh epic these three classes of harlots are introduced as the attendants of Ishtar, obedient to her call. The conclusion is therefore justified that Uruk was one of the centers – perhaps the center – of the obscene rites to which

---

[43] Maspero 1894: 577.
[44] Norris 1868: Vol. 1, 287. On the term *šamhat* and the terminology of Mesopotamian female cult functionaries, see Chapter 2.

Herodotus has several references. Several other incidental allusions in cuneiform literature to the sacred prostitution carried on at Babylonian temples confirm Herodotus' statement in general, although the rite never assumed the large proportions that he reports.[45]

By 1902 Sayce had also completely changed his tune, not only identifying the concept of specifically sacred prostitution, but believing in it, and creating an entire sociology for it. In his work *The Religions of Ancient Egypt and Babylonia*, Sayce writes:

At Erech [Uruk], Istar was served by organized bands of unmarried maidens who prostituted themselves in honour of the goddess. The prostitution was strictly religious, as much so as the ceremonial cannibalism formerly prevalent among the South Sea Islanders. In return for the lives they led, the "handmaids of Istar" were independent and free from the control of men. They formed a religious community, the distinguishing feature of which was the power of indulging the passions of womanhood without the disabilities which amongst a Semitic population these would otherwise have brought. The "handmaid of Istar" owned allegiance only to the goddess she served. Her freedom was dependent on her priesthood, but in return for this freedom she had to give up all the pleasures of family life. It was a self-surrender which placed the priestess outside the restrictions of the family code, and was yet for the sake of a principle which made that family code possible, Baal, the lord of the Semitic family, claimed the firstborn as his right, and Istar or Ashtoreth similarly demanded the service of its daughters.

It was the same in Canaan as at Erech. Did the rites, and the beliefs on which the rites were based, migrate from Babylonia to the West along with Babylonian culture, or were they a common Semitic heritage in which Erech and Phoenicia shared alike? . . . [T]he rites with which Istar was worshipped were confined in Babylonia to Erech; it was there only that her "handmaids" and eunuch-priests were organized into communities, and that unspeakable abominations were practiced in her name. The Istar who was adored elsewhere was a chaste and passionless goddess, the mother of her people whom she had begotten, or their stern leader in war. It does not seem likely that a cult which was unable

---

[45] Jastrow 1898: 475–476. Later, in his 1915 edition of *The Civilization of Babylonia and Assyria*, Jastrow summarizes (pp. 272–273), "Some of these [priestesses] were 'sacred prostitutes,' and it is in connection with this class of priestesses that rites were practiced in the temples which, while probably regarded as purely symbolical to promote fertility among mankind and in the animal world, were unmistakably obscene, or at least degenerated into obscene rites."

to spread in Babylonia or Assyria should nevertheless have taken deep root in Phoenicia, had there not already been there a soil prepared to receive it.[46]

It is clear that Sayce still had some doubts. He strictly limits the practice of Babylonian sacred prostitution to Erech/Uruk and Phoenicia, both customs, apparently, deriving from a common Semitic ideology. Nevertheless, he also provides a detailed description of a socio-religious group that, three years earlier, he had not even recognized.

It is evident from the works of both Jastrow and Sayce that a new element had entered into the newly emergent sacred prostitution debate. Both scholars recognized that there were titled groups of females who were dedicated to and prostituted themselves for Ištar of Uruk. The texts they encountered are apparent especially in Jastrow. One was the passage in the *Erra Epic* (IV, 52–53) that reads,

> As for Uruk, dwelling of Anu and Ishtar, the city of *kezertu*'s, *šamhatu*'s and *harimtu*'s, whom Ishtar deprived of husbands and reckoned as her own.[47]

A similar list is found in the *Gilgameš Epic*, cited by both authors. At the death of the Bull of Heaven,

> Ishtar assmbled the *kezertu*'s, *šamhatu*'s and *harimtu*'s,
> over the Bull of Heaven's haunch she began the rites of mourning.[48]

With the initial translation of the Mesopotamian epics in the late nineteenth century, it began to appear that there was native Mesopotamian evidence for the prostitutes who until this point had remained within the confines of the Classical literature. The terms *kezertu*, *šamhatu/ukhatu*, and most certainly *harimtu* came to be translated as "(sacred) prostitute" due to their association with Ištar and their occasional sexual roles within the literature. D. G. Lyon (writing somewhat later) provides an interesting glimpse into the reasoning process:

> In the Gilgamesh Epic, for instance, Ishtar of Erech, the goddess of love . . . is attended by her maidens, the *harimâti* and the *šamhâti*, who are represented as lax in morals. In the same Epic the story how one of them, called both *harimtu* and *šamhat*, brought Eabani into Erech by her

---

[46] Sayce 1902: 341–342.

[47] Assante 1998: 40.

[48] George 1999: 53, adapted. George's original translation reads: "Ishtar assembled the courtesans, prostitutes, and harlots."

wiles, is related with much realistic detail. And when Gilgamesh and Eabani slew the bull of Anu, Ishtar gathered about her the *šamhâti* and the *harimâti* and set up lamentation over the bull. Erech is called "the city of *kizrêti*, the *šamhâti*, and the *harimâti*." These passages certainly indicate that there were excesses committed in connection with the worship of Ishtar of Erech.[49]

Although it is true that Šamhat did seduce Eabani/Enkidu "by her wiles," there is no evidence in the text itself that the *harimâti* and *šamhâti* were "lax in morals." This notion merely derives from their association with Ištar and the now-accepted translation of their titles as "harlot." If they are harlots, they must be lax in morals. If Ištar hangs out with them, then her cult must be typified by "excesses." The circular reasoning that has typified sacred prostitution studies is already present.

As Sayce noted, sacred prostitution existed in both Uruk and Phoenicia. Phoenicia, it turns out, is near where the Jews lived, and thus it was only a matter of (very little) time before Biblical scholars would harken back to Gesenius' definition of *qadeš/qedešâ* and find that it fit in perfectly with the Canaanite/Phoenician milieu of the Biblical texts. Already by 1901, H. Gunkel interpreted the story of Tamar and Judah in Genesis 38 in light of this new understanding of sacred prostitution:

> Religious prostitution (קדשה, Assyr. *qadištu*, > קדש, "to be holy") plays a great role since antiquity among the peoples of the Near East ... and was, as can be seen from this passage among others, also well known in ancient Israel. Israel may have learned these things from the Canaanites (Tamar is Canaanite, after all). They were only finally eradicated from Israel through the prophets' polemic.[50]

In his 1902 *Critical and Exegetical Commentary on Deuteronomy*, the Rev. S. R. Driver offered a less-than-restrained, one might even call it Victorian, analysis of the prohibition against the *qedešîm/qedešôt* in Deut. 23: 18–19:

> 18–19 (17–18). Against religious prostitution. – No Israelite, of either sex, is to become a temple-prostitute; nor is the gain derived from any kind of prostitution to be offered in payment of a vow. – Temple-prostitute] the allusion is to the immoral and repulsive custom, common

[49] Lyon 1912: 360. In a rebuttal to this description, Luckenbill in 1917 argued that while it was obvious that the *kadištum* was a prostitute, she should not be labeled as a "bad character," as her occupation "had the sanction of church and state" (Luckenbill 1917: 12).
[50] Gunkel 1997 [1901]: 401.

in Canaanitish and Phoenician cults, by which persons of both sexes prostituted themselves in the service of a deity. The law in v.[18] [(17)] is peculiar to Dt.; but Lev. 18[22] (cf. 20[13]), though general in its wording, is aimed probably at the same practice.

The renderings "harlot" and "sodomite" are both inadequate: in neither case is ordinary immorality intended, but immorality practiced in the worship of a deity, and in the immediate precincts of a temple: see Hdt. i. 199 (in Babylon); Ep. of Jeremy 43 (also in Babylon); Strabo, xii. 36; Ramsay, *Cities of Phrygia*, i. 94f, 115; Lucian, *Lucius*, §38; Athan. *c. Gentes*, p. 24 E; Ges. *Thes.s.v*; . . . *Kadesh* and *Kedeshah* are, respectively, the masc. and fem. of the same adj. (lit. *sacred*), which denotes a person dedicated to a deity for the purposes indicated. . . . The *kedeshim* (masc.) and *kedeshoth* (fem.) are frequently alluded to in the OT., especially in the period of the monarchy, when rites of foreign origin made their way into both Israel and Judah.[51]

It appears from Driver's wording that the recognition of the *qedešîm*/*qedešôt* as sacred prostitutes was still not entirely standard, as Driver must insist that the translations "sodomite" and "harlot" are "inadequate." It would take another 25 years before the *qedešîm* and *qedešôt* were translated as "male cult prostitute" and "cult prostitute," respectively,[52] but their new identities were already being well established.

By the first decade of the new century the identification of the Biblical *qedešâ* as a prostitute was established, and her role in religion was understood in light of the various theories prevalent on the topic for the previous 100 years. Matters pertaining both to fertility and to prenuptial rites flourished in the scholarship, and Herodotos, although still not regarded as infallible, was given far more credence. All of this is apparent in an extremely influential (to judge by the number of footnotes it appears in) article written by B. Luther in 1906. In discussing Judah, Tamar, and the *qedešôt* he wrote:

> Für die Propheten und das Deuteronomium sind allerdings Hure und Qedeše identisch. . . . Das Qedešenwesen ist hier noch eng mit dem Kultus verbunden.
>
> Aus diesen Stellen [referring back to a number of cited Biblical passages found here in Chapter 2] erhalten wir folgendes Bild. Mit den Festen, die an den Heiligtümern (Höhen) begangen werden, z. B. dem Erntefest, is Prostitution im Dienste der Gottheit verbunden. Die

---

[51] Driver 1902: 264–265.
[52] Assante 1998: 8, no. 8.

Geschenke, die die Qedešen erhalten, gehören (wenigstens zum Teil) der Gottheit. Die wichtigste Frage ist nun die: gab es berufsmäßige weibliche Qedešen, oder haben wir es uns änlich vorzustellen, wie Herodot I 199 aus Babylonien und Cypern erzält? Jedes Weib muß sich hier einmal in ihrem Leben . . . [the usual description of the Babylonian "sacrifice" appears here yet again]. Ein volles Verständnis für diese Sitte hat Herodot nicht gehabt. Ist es einerlei, wann diese Prostitution stattfindet, oder ist die an einem bestimmten Zeitpunkt gebunden? Einen tieferen Sinn hat die Sitte doch nur dann, wenn durch diesen Akt das Mädchen seine Jungfrauschaft der Göttin als Opfer darbringt. Die Institution steht vielleicht in gewisser Beziehung zur Beschneidung, und die ja ursprünglich erst an den Jünglingen vorgennomen wurde.

Nach den angeführten Stellen scheint es ausgeschlossen, daß es in Israel berufsmäßige Qedešen gegeben hat. Wahrscheinlich prostituierten sich vielmehr auch hier die Mädchen nur einmal, um dadurch der Gottheit geweiht zu sein. Die Sitte scheint ziemlich weit verbreitet gewesen zu sein (in Israel und Judah). Ob die Einrichtung ein Rudiment aus früherer Zeit is oder von außen importiert . . . wissen wir nicht.

In gewissen Volkskreisen hat man keinen Anstoß daran genommen, daß ein Mädchen Qedeše wurde, im Gegenteil es für ihre religiöse Pflicht gehalten.[53]

Likewise, F. V. M. Cumont, in his 1906 (1911 English translation) publication on Oriental religions in the Roman Empire gave what must be identified as a typically Victorian, pro-Roman-temperance, rather anti-Semitic view of the subject:

[I]mmorality was nowhere so flagrant as in the temple of Astarte, whose female servants honored the goddess with untiring ardor. In no country was sacred prostitution so developed as in Syria, and in the Occident it was to be found practically only where the Phoenicians had imported it, as on Mount Eryx. Those aberrations, that were kept up until the end of paganism, probably have their explanation in the primitive constitution of the Semitic tribe, and the religious custom must have been originally one of the forms of exogamy, which compelled the woman to unite herself first with a stranger.[54]

As a final nudge toward the increasing acceptance of sacred prostitution in the ancient Near East, the dictionaries began to define the

[53] Luther 1906: 177–179, excerpted.
[54] Cumont 1911: 118.

female cult functionaries as various types of sacred prostitutes, "hierodules," and general *femmes fatales*. In 1905 W. Muss-Arnolt published his *Concise Dictionary of the Assyrian Language*. According to him, the *qadištu* was, not surprisingly, "a temple-prostitute {Hierodule} *cf.* קדשה."[55] The *kazratu/kizritu* was, "*f.* servants & followers of *Ištar* of Erech; temple-slave, votary of Aphrodite {Hierodule, Aphroditedienerin, Dienerin der *Ištar* von Erech}."[56] The "*xarimtu*" [*harimtu*] was "the ensnaring" one who was known to have some connection with the šamkhatu and kazratu.[57] The *uxatu* [*ukhatu*]/*šamxatu* was, bizarrely enough, "one of the 3 classes of nymphs, mentioned in the Nimrod Epic, literally: a wailing woman." This, however, seems to be an odd translation of the German, which rendered, "eine der 3 Klassen von Hierodulen des Nimrod-Epos."[58] Only one term – *qadištu* – actually uses the word "prostitute" in its translation, no doubt based on the now-accepted translation of the Hebrew cognate *qedeśâ*. References to hierodules, though, as we have seen, tend to translate into modern minds as "sacred prostitute," especially when those hierodules are associated with Aphrodite or Ištar or Uruk. To one extent or another, then, the dictionaries helped to foster the sacred prostitution myth.

By the second decade of the twentieth century, the sacred prostitute was a permanent feature of the ancient religious landscape. Some scholars, such as S. Langdon in his 1914 *Tammuz and Ishtar* publication, found the entire practice quite embarrassing. Others, such as B. Meissner writing on *Babylonien und Assyrien* in 1925, took a more categorical and scientific approach. In 1911 a revised and expanded version of *The Golden Bough* was released, and Frazer's construction of the sacred prostitute went on to influence such literary minds as D. H. Lawrence and James Joyce.[59] By the late 1920s the terms *qadeś* and *qedeśâ* were being translated in the Bible as "cult prostitute." Although there were some continued debates as to the role(s) of these various characters in the religious rites – were they fertility functionaries? did they have other cultic service to perform? – the myth of sacred prostitution was firmly entrenched in modern scholarship.[60]

---

[55] Muss-Arnolt 1905: Vol. II, 910.
[56] *Ibid*: Vol. I, 376.
[57] *Ibid*: 337.
[58] *Ibid*: 31. I cannot quite fathom how Muss-Arnolt got "nymph" from "Hierodule."
[59] Vickery 1973: 303 and 373.
[60] For a survey of more recent sacred prostitution scholarship, especially since WWII, see Oden 1987: 138–140.

A Life of Its Own

One thing that is clear from the data given above is that sacred prostitution studies have been fairly constant for the past 200 years. The Classical scholars made use of the same data sets, which they shared for the most part with the Biblical scholars and Assyriologists. In all instances, there is a readily transparent rationale for why sacred prostitution was identified and understood as it was, even if, ultimately, these reasons proved wrong because of methodological problems.

In the twentieth century that changed, as scholars and other authors came to enhance the sacred prostitution myth. New data sets were created, adding to the vicious cycle, and methodologies became increasingly less transparent. This is not to say that all later twentieth-century scholarship on sacred prostitution is shoddy (although much of it is, obviously, inaccurate). Rather, the democratization and increasing ease of publication have made it easier to add far more to the myth than was ever the case previously. In many instances this occurs within academia itself.

One notable example is the creation, whole cloth, of a "tradition" of sacred prostitution at ancient Ephesos. It began innocently and typically enough. In 1915 P. Gardner wrote a book on *The Ephesian Gospel*. Here, syncretizing all ancient goddesses of the west into one prototypical "Asiatic Mother Goddess," he claimed that

> At Babylon and elsewhere her temple was a seat of prostitution. At Ephesus she appears in historic times, owing doubtless to Greek influence, in far less repulsive guise. She was served by a troop of virgin priestesses, called melissæ or bees, under the superintendence of a chief who was a eunuch, and who bore the Persian-sounding title of Megabyzus.... [T]he nature-goddess of Western Asia combined many attributes; and in her service the two extremes of sexual relation met. So although at Ephesus the priestesses of Artemis were virgins, yet there were doubtless elements of sexual impurity in her festivals.[61]

So far, so good; it sounds rather familiar, and we need not entirely complain that Gardner did not provided a single citation. Then in 1917 C. M. Cobern embellished this narrative a bit:

> The head of the temple hierarchy was the Megabyzus, or chief priest, who was probably a Persian. A multitude of priestesses, who came as

---

[61] Gardner 1916 [1915]: 4–6, excerpted.

virgins to the temple, were dedicated to prostitution in the temple's service. These vestals were presided over, at least in the early period, by a eunuch priest.[62]

Cobern offers no citations for his information save for Gardner, who, although admitting to a certain licentiousness in the Ephesian cult, also insisted that the priestesses were, and remained, virgins. Suddenly, then, with no ancient documentation whatsoever, there is sacred prostitution, *in honor of Artemis*, at Ephesos. This fact was then reaffirmed in 1991 in R. and C. Clark Kroeger's work *I Suffer Not a Woman*, wherein the authors mentioned that "Sacred prostitution was widely practiced in the temples of Asia Minor and also offered the worshipper a ritual union with the divine."[63]

The point of this book was to explain why Paul of Tarsus, in his *Letter to Timothy* (living at Ephesos), sternly demanded that no woman should be allowed to teach or to hold authority over a man. This notion was picked up with great abandon by S. H. Gritz in her work *Paul, Women Teachers, and the Mother Goddess at Ephesus*, published in 1991 (although still in time for Gritz to have access to the previously mentioned work, which appears in her footnotes). Speaking generally about the religious environment in which Paul wrote, Gritz claimed that

> In many parts of the Ancient Near East priestesses and female devo-tees of the Great Goddess (Ishtar, Cybele, Asherah, Aphrodite, Astarte, or whatever name used) lived in and around the temples dedicated to this deity. Scholars have sometimes described these women as "har-lots" or "ritual prostitutes." People in their own times and places called them "holy women." These women engaged in sacred rites that often included a free and active sexual life.... Although they took part in sacred sexual rites involving intercourse with men outside of marriage, the cults viewed this activity as sacred.... The sexual rites practiced by both priestesses and lay votaries possessed a widely acknowledged sanctity.... Male counterparts to these "holy women" also practiced the sacred sexual rites of the great goddesses. By the mid-Assyrian period and up to Greco-Roman rule, the temples of the Near East employed thousands of hierodules or slaves of both sexes for this purpose.[64]

[62] Cobern 1917: 465.
[63] Kroeger and Kroeger 1991: 98.
[64] Gritz 1991: 35–36.

Concerning the cult functionaries at Ephesus specifically, the cult Paul strove to counteract, she ponders:

> Did these priestesses function as temple prostitutes or did they retain their virginity? . . . The Mother Goddess did combine many contradictory attributes in her service, and that could have included extremes of sexual behavior. Even if the priestesses of Artemis were virgins, there existed elements of sexual impurity in her festivals. . . . As the Mother Goddess herself, priestesses could serve in temple rites without preserving their chastity and still be considered "virgins" or "sacred" simply because they had not married. . . . Contemporary writers would not have perceived temple harlotry as impure or immoral because it had an accepted sacred function. Some form of temple prostitution probably did exist in Ephesus. . . . [This] insured fertility of crops, secured children with divine sanction, or assimilated one to the deity.[65]

And so, without a single reference to ancient sources, the institution is established in ancient Ephesos, in a cult dedicated to a notoriously virgin goddess. The notion of sacred prostitution had become so readily believable that creating new examples of it was almost effortless, and then went on to furnish new understandings of scripture. S. M. Baugh, in his rather scathing review of Gritz's work, noted that

> . . . neither Strabo, Pliny the Elder, Dio Chrysostom, Pausanias, Xenophon of Ephesus, Achilles Tacitus, nor any other ancient author speaks explicitly or even hints at cult prostitution in either the narrow or broad sense in Ephesus of any period. Nor is it evidenced in the nearly 4,000 extant Greek and Latin inscriptions from Ephesus. This is an opinion found only in modern writers.[66]

The creation of new evidence for sacred prostitution was to become a hallmark of the later twentieth century.

DIVINE UNION: THE SACRED PROSTITUTE AS CONDUIT

If the invention of new data is one hallmark of the growth of the sacred prostitution myth in the later twentieth century, the other is definitely

---

[65] *Ibid*: 40–41.

[66] Baugh 1999: 449. It was this article that first clued me in to the notion that anyone associated sacred prostitution with either Ephesos or Artemis. At first I was fairly certain that I had misread the title and that the article was about Corinth.

a new understanding of the rite itself. As discussed above, there were two common understandings of ancient sacred prostitution in the early modern literature. The nineteenth century was primarily dominated by the not-mutually-exclusive notions of sacred prostitution as sacrifice of chastity in honor of a goddess of "free love," and sacred prostitution as a means of casting the dangers of defloration onto foreigners. These together might be called the prenuptial ideology. In the late nineteenth century a new theory emerged, by which sacred prostitution, as an aspect of sympathetic magic, was part of a fertility ritual, whereby the act reflected the *hieros gamos* of the earth goddess and her consort the vegetation god to promote earthy, animal, and human fertility.

More recently, sacred prostitution has taken on a new fascination. Rather than being *just* a fertility ritual of sorts (although this still exists in the literature), the supposed practice is venerated for its ability to link the world of the mundane with that of the deities, thus allowing the merger of humanity and divinity to occur through the auspices of the (typically female) body.

This notion is prevalent in modern scholarship. We saw it above in Gritz's understanding of the use and meaning of sacred prostitution, where it "insured fertility of crops, secured children with divine sanction, *or assimilated one to the deity.*"[67] H. Meenee notes how hierodules [sacred prostitutes], "in certain circles have inspired modern attempts to reconnect spirituality with sexuality ... the desire of human beings for union with the Divine."[68] B. MacLachlan, in her study of sacred prostitution, wrote that

> In the original understanding prostitution released the powers of Aphrodite with positive, not negative, force. In [the] Cypriot myths the women ... are surrogate Aphrodites who are generating fertility and prosperity for Cyprus as they embrace their lovers/fathers, priest-consorts.... The exchange of phalluses with the courtesan-goddess is a ritual affirmation of the need for and continuity of sexual power.[69]

Likewise, L. Kurke, in her 1996 study of "Pindar and the Prostitutes," analyzed the poet's discomfort vis-à-vis the Corinthian prostitutes insofar as "they are *temple* prostitutes, whose sacred status gives them a special

---

[67] Gritz 1991: 41. Emphasis mine.
[68] Meenee 2007.
[69] MacLachlan 1992: 153.

link to the goddess.... [T]hese women occupy an anomalous status – they sacrifice to Aphrodite, and they can intercede with her for public or private causes."[70]

This concept of sacred prostitution as a means of reaching divinity, specifically feminine divinity, has been the touchstone for what is now perhaps the most prolific generator of writings on the topic of sacred prostitution: the New Age Movement. For many Neo-Pagans, sacred prostitution is seen as the ultimate subversion of the monotheistic, anti-female, anti-material, anti-sexual "Religions of the Book" that dominate most of Western culture. The sacred prostitution myth, not seen as a myth, is a source of empowerment for women coming into touch with a new, feminine form of spirituality that values the powerful sexuality of the female body. While almost all of the New Age works on this topic are historiographic, methodological disasters, the sentiment is nevertheless well expressed. To give a few, typical examples:

N. Qualls-Corbett, a Jungian psychoanalyst, in her 1988 book *The Sacred Prostitute: Eternal Aspect of the Feminine*, claimed,

> In this union – the union of masculine and feminine, spiritual and physical – the personal was transcended and the divine entered in. As the embodiment of the goddess in the mystical union of the sacred marriage, the sacred prostitute aroused the male and was the receptacle for his passion. Her emotions and her creative, bodily energies were united with the suprapersonal. She touched basic regenerative powers, and thereby, as the goddess incarnate, assured the continuity of life and love. The sacred prostitute was the holy vessel wherein chthonic and spiritual forces united.[71]

M. Woodman, in the Foreword of the above-mentioned work, claimed that the sacred prostitute is

> ...the consecrated priestess in the temple, spiritually receptive to the feminine power flowing through her from the Goddess, and at the same time joyously aware of the beauty and passion in her human body. Surrendered to the cosmic energies of love, she magnifies the Goddess in physical delight and spiritual ecstasy. She opens the masculine to the potency of penetrating to the divine, and the feminine to the rapture of surrender to it.[72]

---

[70] Kurke 1996: 58.
[71] Qualls-Corbett 1988: 40.
[72] In Qualls-Corbett 1988: 8–9.

The ideology is most fully expressed by C. Fabian in her 1997 article "The Holy Whore: A Woman's Gateway to Power." Here she writes,

> The Holy Whore archetype derives from many stories such as this [Shamhat and Enkidu]. Sacred prostitute stories reveal an understanding of women as gateways to transformation. In them, women use combinations of sexual ecstasy, formal ritual, and informal teaching, and are seen to embody incarnations of their goddess, a goddess considered to be the source of kingship in prepatrilineal times. In Sumer, in the third millennium B.C.E., . . . the High Priestess bestowed kingship from her temple bed, to the young man whose sexual gifts proved him most worthy of royalty. Indeed, the *Hieros Gamos*, or "Sacred Marriage," was an important tie in most of the major religions of the western world, surviving even in Christianity's pogroms in rural areas of Europe into the last century.
>
> How refreshing to discover guiding religious metaphors . . . in which female sexuality *saves* rather than *damns* humankind. This is a marked departure from Christianity's representation of Eve and all her "daughters."[73]

A variation on this theme is presented by S. Bell in her 1994 work *Reading, Writing & Rewriting the Prostitute Body*, where the union is between fertility and sexual ecstasy:

> Embodied in the sacred prostitute, in practice and in representation, is the unity of womb and clitoris. The temples of sacred prostitution, the best known of which were the temples of Aphrodite in Corinth, were oriented simultaneously to clitoral, uterine, and spiritual purposes: sexuality, fertility, and spirituality were not radically distinguished. The temple prostitute was the embodiment of the sacred unity of the sexual and maternal bodies, which had by the classical age been split. . . . [74]

I believe that this understanding of sacred prostitution represents the final great myth in this inquiry. It is not because either sex or the female body is incompatible with religion or spirituality, but rather because the reconstruction(s) of the institution that typically leads to this understanding is flawed. What follows is two excerpted descriptions of the sacred prostitution ritual in what are two of the most popular (in all senses of the word) works on the topic. I believe that this description is how many people in the modern world who are familiar with the notion of sacred

---

[73] Fabian 1997: 48. Italics in original.
[74] Bell 1994: 24.

prostitution understand the practice. The first is from Qualls-Corbett's book, mentioned above.

> Imagine the sacred prostitute greeting the stranger, a world-weary man who has come to the temple to worship the goddess of love. No words are spoken; her outstretched arms and the soft, warm expression of her radiant eyes and face say what needs to be said. In her private chambers, the sacred love-room of the temple, filled with the fragrance of herbs and flowers, she bathes the stranger. . . . She tells him amusing stories of her training – how the temple priests and other ritual priestesses taught her the art of love-making. . . .
>
> She came to the temple, she tells him, in order to fulfill the law of the land, which every maiden must do. With reverence she speaks of her devotion to the goddess as she approaches the small marble image of Venus. In the near darkness, alone in her rapture, she performs the ritual of lighting the perfumed oil lamp, gently swaying and chanting softly in prayer of thanksgiving to the goddess. . . .
>
> The sacred prostitute leads the stranger to the couch prepared with white linens and aromatic myrtle leaves. She has rubbed sweet smelling wild thyme on her thighs. Her faint smile and glistening eyes tell the stranger that she is full of desire for him. The gentle touch of her embrace sparks a fiery response. . . . He is keenly aware of the passion within this votary to the goddess of love and fertility, and is fulfilled.
>
> The woman and stranger know that the consummation of the love act is consecrated by the deity through which they are renewed. . . . The sacred prostitute, now no longer a maiden, is initiated into the fullness of womanhood. . . . Her true feminine nature is awakened to life. The divine element of love resides within her.
>
> The stranger too is transformed . . . the image of the sacred prostitute is viable within him. . . . He makes no specific claims on the woman herself, but carries her image, the personification of love and sexual joy, into the world. His experience of the mysteries of sex and religion opens the door to the potential of on-going life; it accompanies the regeneration of the soul.[75]

Then, apparently, he leaves. There is no mention of payment, which is, of course, the *sine qua non* of prostitution.[76]

---

[75] Qualls-Corbett 1988: 22–24, excerpted from the chapter "The Goddess and Her Virgin."

[76] J. Hunter, in her 2004 book *Rites of Pleasure*, is to be commended for mentioning payment in the practice of sacred prostitution, although she qualifies this by stating that "Money was exchanged, but as an offering, which went to the temple, which in turn supported the priestesses" (Hunter 2004: 31).

The next description comes from Marion Zimmer Bradley's novel *The Mists of Avalon*. Although the rite described would more properly be called a *hieros gamos*, it sounds so similar to the preceding narrative that it is easy to see how this description would come to color notions of sacred prostitution in antiquity.

> Bathed naked in the moonlight, Morgaine felt the light of the Goddess streaming over, *through* her . . . she was Morgaine no more, she was nameless, priestess and maiden and mother . . . they strung a garland of crimson berries about her loins; . . . and she felt the full weight of virginity pouring and flooding though her like the spring tide. . . . All round her, on the walls, she could see the sacred symbols . . . , the swollen belly and full breasts of She Who Gives Life.
>
> . . .
>
> She lay there, feeling the life of the earth around her; she seemed to expand, to fill all the cave, the little scribbled drawings were painted on her breasts and her belly, and above her the great chalk figure, man or deer, strode with erect phallus . . . the invisible moon outside the cave flooding her body with light as the Goddess surged inside her, body and soul.
>
> . . .
>
> *Now it is the time for the Goddess to welcome the Horned One. . . .* She reached up to him, gripped his hands, drew him down to her, feeling the soft warmth and weight of his body. She had to guide him. I am the Great Mother who knows all things, who is maiden and mother and all-wise, guiding the virgin and her consort . . . dazed, terrified, exalted, only half-conscious, she felt the life force take them both, moving her body without violation, moving him too, guiding him fiercely into her, till . . . all the fierce fury of his young life burst and spurted into her womb. . . .
>
> Then slowly, tiredly, his breathing quieted to normal, and after a moment she knew that he slept in her arms. She kissed his hair and his soft cheek with a wild tenderness, and then she too slept.[77]

These descriptions are a far cry from what we saw of sacred prostitution throughout this study – the full population of Babylonian women being forced to wait outside the sanctuary of Mylitta for a random stranger, not

---

[77] Zimmer Bradley 1982: 177–179, excerpted. Everything became a lot less lovey-dovey when Morgaine found out that (a) her partner was her half-brother and (b) she was pregnant.

necessarily bathed, to throw any amount of coinage into their laps and demand access to their bodies; the joint humiliation of the unwilling rich and the rejected ugly; the "sacrifice" of dehumanized prostitutes to the lusts of drunken male revelers at the ancient equivalent of a frat party; the sacrifice of virgins in the hopes of preventing their wartime rapes. There has been little reason for the various "sacred prostitutes" in this study to offer "thanksgiving to the goddess."

But I believe this misunderstanding is an important reason that the myth of sacred prostitution endures. What is being honored and revered is not sacred prostitution *per se*, but some manner of sacred sexuality. In the efforts to find a spirituality that values the (female) body and its sexuality, members of the New Age movement (and others) have retrojected this desire onto what is apparently the only comparable ancient institution. And, in so doing, they have completely re-created the myth. Although this re-creation may serve positive psychological functions in modern times – several attestations do indicate this – it only serves to hamper study of the actual ancient evidence.

Antithesis

The final major development in the modern study of sacred prostitution is the suggestion that it never existed.[78] This development began slowly in the 1960s when some Classical scholars, notably Hans Conzelmann, began to doubt that sacred prostitution was actually practiced in the Greco-Roman world. Although Conzelmann was absolutely convinced that sacred prostitution was practiced in the Orient – "Daß es im Alten Orient sakrale Prostitution gab, wird nicht bezweifelt"[79] – he did not believe that there was sufficient evidence to suggest that this institution was passed on to the Greeks.[80] The presence of sacred prostitutes in Corinth, although nowhere else, has more recently been challenged by H. D. Saffrey in his 1985 article "Aphrodite à Corinth: Réflexions sur une idée reçue" and by V. Pirenne-Delforge in her 1994 book *L'Aphrodite grecque*.[81] Nevertheless, Pirenne-Delforge, although casting strong doubt on the presence of *Greek* sacred prostitutes – "Sacred prostitution in Greece is a historiographical myth"[82] – nevertheless accepts their

---

[78] I very much hope that this last one is not a myth.

[79] Conzelmann 1967: 260.

[80] See also Conzelmann 1975 in regard to the Corinth of Saint Paul.

[81] Saffrey 1985: 368 and 373–374; Pirenne-Delforge 1994: 125–126.

[82] Pirenne-Delforge 2007: 322.

existence in the east, using Herodotos' silence on the matter of Corinthian sacred prostitution in contrast with his frank discussion of it regards to Babylon as evidence for its absence in the civilized west.[83]

But sacred prostitution had always been in the domain of the "Orient"; if the myth was really going to be challenged, it had to be challenged on its own home turf. This began in earnest in the 1970s. In 1972, in a short presentation published by the Société Ernest-Renan, D. Arnaud took up the question going all the way back to Herodotos 1.199. Looking at different artistic representations and the vocabulary of sacred prostitution, Arnaud came to the conclusion that Herodotos and/or his Babylonian contacts had simply misunderstood the role of the women who worked around the temple. *La* <<*prostitution sacrée*>> he claimed, was purely <<*imaginaire*>>.[84]

In 1976 E. J. Fisher expanded upon this notion. Once again starting with the Bible and Herodotos and proceeding through the Mesopotamian vocabulary, Fisher determined that "Herodotus' account is lurid and almost too detailed to be convincing."[85] More importantly, though, he determined that in spite of the excellent detail offered by Herodotos, there was not a shred of corroborating evidence from Mesopotamia itself. If sacred prostitution were as important and prevalent as the historians claimed, "one would expect that the law codes, the records of temple administration, and the lists of temple personnel"[86] would make at least some mention of it. Amazingly, they did not. The problem with Fisher's argument was that it relied on negative evidence. Methodologically speaking, it was weak. Worse, there were many data which seemed to contradict his hypothesis. The cuneiform documents did refer to "sacred prostitutes" – the *qadištu*s and *harimtu*s, among others – and thus there remained the illusion that the presence of sacred prostitution was, in fact, corroborated by the indigenous sources.

A major breakthrough came in 1985, when S. Hooks completed his doctoral dissertation at Hebrew Union College – *Sacred Prostitution in Israel and the Ancient Near East*. Separately analyzing every word in the Biblical and Mesopotamian corpora that was taken to mean "sacred prostitute," Hooks determined that none of them, based on their descriptions and uses in the texts, suggested such a definition.

---

[83] *Ibid.*
[84] Arnaud 1973: 115.
[85] Fisher 1976: 226.
[86] *Ibid.*

In the absence of terminology, the Mesopotamian evidence ceased to exist.

Then, in 1987, R. A. Oden Jr. in his book *The Bible Without Theology*, took up the question from a different angle. Although he, too, reconsidered the identities of the various "sacred prostitutes" in the Mesopotamian corpus, more important for him were the actual sources of the evidence. Oden noted that all the evidence for this supposed institution came from outsider accounts – Herodotos writing about the Babylonians, Strabo writing about the Egyptians, Athanasius writing about the pagans. And so he formulated the hypothesis of accusation, whereby sacred prostitution was not necessarily an historical fact, but a myth used by one people to define themselves through the denigration of an "Other."

> Sacred prostitution *as accusation* played an important role in defining Israel and Israelite religion as something distinctive. So, too, similar accusations played the same role for Herodotus and other Greeks, and then for the early Church Fathers.[87]

This not only would account for the lack of indigenous evidence, but also coincided well with prevailing, contemporary notions of the western construction of the "decadent Orient." For many scholars who rejected the myth of sacred prostitution, Oden's thesis became the primary understanding of how the myth came into being. Many works negating the existence of sacred prostitution in the ancient Near East claim that it was Herodotos who deliberately invented the myth in full Hellenic chauvinism.[88]

Over the course of the 1990s the nonexistence of sacred prostitution in the ancient Near East became a commonplace in Biblical and Assyriological studies. As early as 1989 J. G. Westenholtz's "Tamar, Qedeša, Qadištu, and Sacred Prostitution in Mesopotamia" challenged the qedeša=qadištu=(sacred) prostitute tautology. Works such as P. Bird's "'To Play the Harlot': An Inquiry into an Old Testament Metaphor" and J. Assante's "The kar.kid / harimtu, Prostitute or Single Woman?" helped to hammer additional nails into the metaphorical coffin. The first explained the ancient Israelite rhetoric of whoring that so confused early studies of sacred prostitution; the second removed the word "prostitute" from the Mesopotamian vocabulary while shedding light on a previously unsuspected category of ancient Mesopotamian liberated

---

[87] Oden 1987: 153.
[88] See Chapter 5 for more on this notion.

female. These have been followed up respectively by C. Stark's 2006 book on the *Qedeschen der Hebräischen Bibel und das Motive der Hureriei* and (once again). J. Assante's article "From Whores to Hierodules: The Historiographic Invention of Mesopotamian Female Sex Professionals," which traces the nineteenth-century influences giving rise to the sacred prostitution debate in Assyriology.

This dismantling process has not been quite so popular in Classical studies, where eastern sacred prostitution still thrives. To date, very few publications have emerged that suggest that sacred prostitution did not exist at all (as opposed to not in Greece, but definitely in the east, as with Conzelmann above). Notable among them is Beard and Henderson's 1998 "With This Body I Thee Worship: Sacred Prostitution in Antiquity." Here the authors considered the secondary nature of the source materials, the storylike qualities of the accounts themselves, and the Victorian lens through which the whole myth was construed. As Beard and Henderson themselves put it:

> In what follows, we shall be exploring... both the classical 'testimonia' and its modern commentary; we shall be interrogating the certainties and uncertainties of the different accounts of sacred prostitution in the Greek world, which may or may not count as 'evidence' for the practice either in Greece or the Near East; examining its role in our own myth of the Orient *and* in a distinctively nineteenth-century version of the origins of human civilization. Temple prostitution remains a multiculturalist's scandal, writing obedience to law and proper conduct of religion on to gender and sexuality in a(n) (un)comfortable mix of stereotyping and demonization.[89]

Picking up from Beard and Henderson and considering the general absence of evidence for sacred prostitution in the ancient Near East as well, F. Glinister not only denied the presence of sacred prostitution in early Italy/Etruria, but argued that this was in fact further proof of the nonexistence of sacred prostitution at all in the ancient world. These two articles, though, and a few of my own publications are some of the very few voices to be heard among Classicists to deny the existence of ancient sacred prostitution in its entirety. It is to be hoped that this will soon change.

[89] Beard and Henderson 1998: 57.

BIBLIOGRAPHY

Ackerman, R. (ed.) 2005. *Selected Letters of Sir. J. G. Frazer*. Oxford University Press. Oxford.

———. 2002. *The Myth and Ritual School*. Routledge. New York.

Adams, C. D. [1917]. *The Speeches of Aeschines*. Harvard University Press. Cambridge, MA.

Adams, J. N. 1983. "Words for 'Prostitute' in Latin." *Rheinisches Museum für Philologie* 126: 321–358.

Amantini, L. S. 1984. "Ancora sulla prostituzione sacra a locri epizefirii." *MGR* IX: 39–62.

Ambaglio, D. 1988. "Strabone e la storiografia greca frammentaria." In E. Gabba (ed.), *Studi di Storia e Storiografia Antiche*. Edizioni New Press. Pavia, 73–84.

Arieti, J. A. 2002 [1997]. "Rape and Livy's View of Roman History." In S. Deacy and K. F. Pierce (eds.). *Rape in Antiquity*. Gerald Duckworth & Co. London, 209–229.

Arnaud, D. 1973. "La prostitution sacrée en Mésopotamie, un mythe historiographique?" *RHR* 183: 111–115.

Assante, J. 2003. "From Whores to Hierodules: The Historiographic Invention of Mesopotamian Female Sex Professionals." In A. A. Donohue and M. D. Fullerton (eds.), *Ancient Art and Its Historiography*. Cambridge University Press. Cambridge, UK, 13–47.

———. 1998. "The **kar.kid**/*harimtu*, Prostitute or Single Woman?" *UF* 30: 5–96.

Aubet, M. E. 2001. *The Phoenicians and the West: Politics, Colonies, and Trade*. Cambridge University Press. Cambridge, UK.

Bachofen, J. J. 1975 [1861]. *Das Mutterrecht*. Suhrkamp. Frankfurt am Main.

———. 1967. *Myth, Religion, and Mother Right: Selected Writings of J. J. Bachofen*. Routledge and Kegan Paul. London.

———. 1951 [1870]. *Die Sage von Tanaquil*. Benno Schwabe & Co. Verlag. Basel.

Bakker, E., I. de Jong, and H. van Wees (eds.). 2002. *Brill's Companion to Herodotos*. Brill Publishers. Leiden.

Barker, G., and T. Rasmussen. 1998. *The Etruscans*. Blackwell Publishers. Oxford.

Barnestone, W. 1988. *Sappho and the Greek Lyric Poets*. Schocken Books. New York.

Bassi, K. 2003. "The Semantics of Manliness in Ancient Greece." In R. M. Rosen and I. Sluiter (eds.) 2003, 25–58.

Batto, B. F. 1974. *Studies on Women at Mari*. Johns Hopkins University Press. Baltimore.

Baugh, S. M. 1999. "Cult Prostitution in New Testament Ephesus: A Reappraisal." *Journal of the Evangelical Theological Society* 42.3: 443–460.

Bean, G. E. 1960. "Notes and Inscriptions from Pisidia, Part II" *AS* 10: 43–82.

Beard, M., and J. Henderson. 1998. "With This Body I Thee Worship: Sacred Prostitution in Antiquity." In M. Wyke (ed.), *Gender and the Body in the Ancient Mediterranean*. Blackwell Publishers. Oxford, 56–79.

Bell, S. 1994. *Reading, Writing, and Rewriting the Prostitute Body*. Indiana University Press. Bloomington.

Berve, H. 1967. *Die Tyrannis bei den Griechen*. C. H. Beck'sche Verlagsbuchhandlung. Munich.

Bienkowski, P., and A. Millard (eds.). 2000. *Dictionary of the Ancient Near East*. University of Pennsylvania Press. Philadelphia.

Bird, P. 2006. "Prostitution in the Social World and the Religious Rhetoric of Ancient Israel." In C. A. Faraone and L. K. McClure (eds.) 2006, 40–58.

———. 1997. *Missing Persons and Mistaken Identities: Women and Gender in Ancient Israel*. Fortress Press. Minneapolis.

———. 1997a. "The end of the Male Cult Prostitute: A Literary-Historical and Sociological Analysis of Hebrew Qadeš-Qedešîm." In J. A. Emerton (ed.) *Congress Volume (1995)*. Brill. Leiden, 37–80.

Black, J., A. George, and N. Postgate (eds.). 2000. *A Concise Dictionary of Akkadian*. Harrassowitz Verlag. Wiesbaden.

Black, J., and A. Green. 1992. *Gods, Demons and Symbols of Ancient Mesopotamia*. Texas University Press. Austin.

Bloomer, W. M. 1993. "The Superlative *Nomoi* of Herodotus's *Histories*." *Classical Antiquity* 12: 30–50.

———. 1992. *Valerius Maximus and the Rhetoric of the New Nobility*. University of North Carolina Press. Chapel Hill.

Boas, M. 1905. *De Epigrammatis Simonideis*. J. B. Wolters. Groningen.

Boeckhius, A. 1821. *Pindari Opera Quae Supersunt*. J. A. Gottlob. Leipzig.

Boedeker, D. 1997. "Becoming Medea: Assimilation in Euripides." In Clauss and Johnston (eds.) 1997, 127–148.

Boedeker, D. (ed.). 1987. *Herodotus and the Invention of History*. Arethusa 20.

Boiy, T. 2004. *Late Achaemenid and Hellenistic Babylon*. Peeters. Leuven.

Bömer, F. 1960. *Untersuchungen über die Religion der Sklaven in Griechenland und Rom: zweiter Teil: Die sogenannte sakrale Freilassung in Griechenland und die (δοῦλοι)ἱεροί*. Akademie der Wissenschaften und der Literatur. Wiesbaden.

Bonfante, L. 2006. "Etruscan Inscriptions and Etruscan Religion." In Thomson de Grummond and Simon (eds.) 2006, 9–26.

Bonnet, C. 1996. *Astarté: Dossier documentaire et perspectives historiques*. Consiglio Nazionale delle Ricerche. Rome.

Boswell, J. 1980. *Christianity, Social Tolerance, and Homosexuality*. University of Chicago Press. Chicago.

Bowen, A., and P. Garnsey. 2003. *Lactantius: Divine Institutes*. Liverpool University Press. Liverpool.

Boyce, M. 1987 [1979]. *Zororastrians: Their Religious Beliefs and Practices*. Routledge & Kegan Paul. London.

Bradley, M. Zimmer. 1982. *The Mists of Avalon*. Alfred A. Knopf. New York.

Brenton, Sir L. C. L., 2005 [1851]. *The Septuagint with Apocrypha*. Hendrickson Publishers. Peabody, MA.

Brock, R. 2003. "Authorial Voice and Narrative Management in Herodotus." In Derrow and Parker (eds.) 2003, 3–16.

Brosius, M. 1998. "Artemis Persike and Artemis Anaitis." In M. Brosius and A. Kuhrt (eds.), *Studies in Persian History: Essays in Memory of David M. Lewis*. Nederlands Instituut voor het Nabije Oosten. Leiden, 227–238.

Brown, C. G. 1991. "The Prayers of the Corinthian Women (Simonides, *Ep.* 14 Page, *FGE*)." *Greek, Roman, and Byzantine Studies* 32: 5–14.

Brown, P. 1996 [1978]. *The Making of Late Antiquity*. Harvard University Press. Cambridge, MA.

Budin, S. L. 2008. "Simonides' Corinthian Epigram." *CP* 103.4.

———. 2006. "Sacred Prostitution in the First Person." In Faraone and McClure (eds.), 77–92.

———. 2004. "A Reconsideration of the Aphrodite-Ashtart–Syncretism." *Numen* 51.2: 95–145.

———. 2003a. "*Pallakai*, Prostitutes, and Prophetesses." *CP* 98: 148–159.

———. 2003b. *The Origin of Aphrodite*. CDL Press. Bethesda, MD.

Burkert, W. 1985. *Greek Religion: Archaic and Classical*. Harvard University Press. Cambridge, MA.

———. 1983. *Homo Necans: The Anthropology of Ancient Greek Sacrificial Ritual and Myth*. University of California Press. Berkeley.

Burns, J. B. 2000. "Devotee or Deviate: The 'Dog' (keleb) in Ancient Israel as a Symbol of Male Passivity and Perversion." *Journal of Religion & Society* 2: 1–10.

Calame, C. 1989. "Entre rapports de parenté et relations civiques: Aphrodite l'hétaire au banquet politique des hétairoi." In Françoise Thelamon (ed.), *Aux sources de la puissance: Sociabilité et parenté*. Université de Rouen. 101–111.

Cameron, A., and S. G. Hall. 1999. *Eusebius: Life of Constantine*. Clarendon Press. Oxford.

Carson, A. 1990. "Putting Her in Her Place: Women, Dirt and Desire." In D. M. Halperin, J. J. Winkler, and F. I. Zeitlin (eds.), *Before Sexuality: The*

Construction of Erotic Experience in the Ancient Greek World. Princeton University Press. Princeton, NJ, 135–170.

Chaumont, M.-L., 1965. "Le culte de la déesse Anahita (Anahit) dans la religion des monarques d'Iran et d'Arménie au 1ᵉʳ siècle de notre ère." *JA* 253: 167–181.

Clauss, J. J., and S. I. Johnston (eds.). 1997. *Medea: Essays on Medea in Myth, Literature, Philosophy, and Art*. Princeton University Press. Princeton, NJ.

Clemen, C. 1918. "Miszellen zu Lukians Schrift über die syrische Göttin. In W. Frankenberg and F. Küchler (eds.) *Abhandlungen zur Semitischen Religionskunde und Sprachwissenschaft (Festscrift für Wolf Wilhelm Grafen von Baudissin)*. Alfred Töpelmann Verlag. Giessen, 83–106.

Cobern, C. M. 1917. *The New Archaeological Discoveries*. Funk & Wagnalls Company. New York.

Cohen, E. 2006. "Free and Unfree Sexual Work: An Economic Analysis of Athenian Prostitution." In Faraone and McClure (eds.) 2006, 95–124.

———. 2002. "An Unprofitable Masculinity." In P. Cartledge, E. E. Cohen, and L. Foxhall (eds.), *Money, Labour and Land: Approaches to the Economies of Ancient Greece*. Routledge. London, 100–112.

Colbow, G. 2002. "Priestesses, either Married or Unmarried, and Spouses without Title: Their Seal Use Their Seals in Sippar at the Beginning of the Second Millennium." In Parpola and Whiting (eds.), 2002, 81–96.

Colonna, G. 1985. *Santuari d'Etruria*. Regione Toscana. Milan.

———. 1984–5. "Novità sui culti di Pyrgi." *Rend Pont*. LVII, 57–88.

Connelly, J. B. 2007. *Portrait of a Priestess: Women and Ritual in Ancient Greece*. Princeton University Press. Princeton, NJ.

Conzelmann, H. 1975. *A Commentary on the First Epistle to the Corinthians*. Fortress Press. Philadelphia.

———. 1967. "Corinth und die Mädchen der Aphrodite." *Göttingen Nachrichten*, 246–261.

Cooper, J. S. 2002. "Virginity in Ancient Mesopotamia." In Parpola and Whiting (eds.), 2002, 81–96.

———. 1993. "Sacred Marriage and Popular Cult in Early Mesopotamia." In E. Matsushima (ed.), *Official Cult and Popular Religion in the Ancient Near East*. Winter Heidelberg, 81–96.

———. 1973–1975. "Heilge Hochzeit. B. Archäologische." *RlA* 4: 259–269.

Cristofani, M. 1996. *Etruschi e Altre Genti nell'Italia Preromana: Mobilità in Età Arcaica*. Giorgio Bretschneider. Rome.

Cumont, F. V. M. 1911. *The Oriental Religions in Roman Paganism*. The Open Court Publishing Co. Chicago.

Dalley, S. 2003. "Why Did Herodotus Not Mention the Hanging Gardens of Babylon?" In P. Derrow and R. Parker (eds.) 2003, 171–189.

———. 1998 [1989]. *Myths from Mesopotamia: Creation, the Flood, Gilgamesh, and Others*. Oxford University Press. Oxford.

———. 1979. "ᴰNIN.LÍL = mul(l)is(s)u, the Treaty of Barga'yah, and Herodotus' Mylitta." *RA* 73: 177–178.

Darmezin, L. 1999. *Les affranchissements par consécration en Béotie et dans le monde grec hellénistique*. Études anciennes 22. De Boccard. Paris.

Davidson, J. N. 1997. *Courtesans and Fishcakes: The Consuming Passions of Classical Athens*. St. Martin's Press. New York.

Debord, P. 1982. *Aspects sociaux et économiques de la vie religieuse dans l'anatolie gréco-romaine*. E. J. Brill. Leiden.

———. 1972. "L'esclavage sacré: État de la question." In *Actes du Colloque 1971 sur l'Esclavage*. Centre de Recherches d'Histoire Ancienne. Paris. 135–150.

Delcor, M. 1979. "Le personnel du temple d'Astarté à Kition d'après une tablette phénicienne (CIS 86 A et B)." *UF* 11: 147–164.

Demand, N. 1994. *Birth, Death, and Motherhood in Classical Greece*. Johns Hopkins University Press. Baltimore.

Derrow, P., and R. Parker (eds.). 2003. *Herodotus and His World: Essays from a Conference in Memory of George Forrest*. Oxford University Press. Oxford.

De Sélincourt, A. 1972. *Herodotus: The Histories*. Penguin Books. London

Desmond, M. 1994. *Reading Dido: Gender, Textuality, and the Medieval Aeneid*. University of Minnesota Press. Minneapolis.

Detienne, M. 1994 [1977]. *The Gardens of Adonis: Spices in Greek Mythology*. Princeton University Press. Princeton, NJ.

Dewald, C. 1981. "Women and Culture in Herodotus' *Histories*." In H. Foley (ed.), *Reflections of Women in Antiquity*. Gordon and Breach Science Publishers. New York, 91–125.

Dillon, M. 2001. *Girls and Women in Classical Greek Religion*. Routledge. London.

Dirven, L. 1997. "The Author of *De Dea Syria* and His Cultural Heritage." *Numen* 44: 153–179.

Dods, M. 1952. *Augustine*. University of Chicago. Chicago.

Dover, K. J. 1978. *Greek Homosexuality*. Harvard University Press. Cambridge, MA.

Drake, H. A. 1975. *In Praise of Constantine: A Historical Study and New Translation of Eusebius' Tricennial Orations*. University of California Press. Berkeley.

Driver, S. R. 1902. *A Critical and Exegetical Commentary on Deuteronomy*. T. & T. Clark. Edinburgh.

Dueck, D. 2000. *Strabo of Amasia: A Greek Man of Letters in Augustan Rome*. Routledge. London.

Duichin, M. 1996. *Ieropornìa: Prostituzione Rituale e Sacrifici di Fanciulle nella Tradizione Classica, nelle Leggende e nei Racconti di Fiaba*. Il Mondo 3 Edizioni. Rome.

Edwards, M. 1999. "The Flowering of Latin Apologetic: Lactantius and Arnobius." In Edwards, Goodman, and Price (eds.) 1999, 197–221.

Edwards, M., M. Goodman, and S. Price (eds.). 1999. *Apologetics in the Roman Empire: Pagans, Jews, and Christians*. Oxford University Press. Oxford.

Ehrman, B. D. 2003. *Lost Christianities: The Battles for Scripture and the Faiths We Never Knew*. Oxford University Press. Oxford.

Eichert, O. 1967. *Vollständiges Wörterbuch zur Philippischen Geschicte des Justinus*. Georg Olms Verlag. Hildesheim.

Eppers, M., and H. Heinen. 1984. "Zu den <<Servi Venerii>> in Ciceros Verrinen." In V. Giuffrè (ed.), *Sodalitas: Scritti in onore di A. Guarino*. Editore Jovene. Naples, 219–232.

Fabian, C. 1997. "The Holy Whore: A Woman's Gateway to Power." In J. Nagle (ed.), *Whores and Other Feminists*. Routledge. New York, 44–54.

Faraone, C. A., and L. K. McClure (eds.). 2006. *Prostitutes and Courtesans of the Ancient World*. University of Wisconsin Press. Madison.

Fehling, D. 1989. *Herodotus and His 'Sources': Citation, Invention and Narrative Art*. University of Leeds. Leeds.

Ferguson, E. 1987. *Backgrounds of Early Christianity*. William B. Eerdmans Publishing Co. Grand Rapids, MI.

Fisher, E. J. 1976. "Cultic Prostitution: A Reassessment." *BTB* 6: 225–236.

Fisk, B. N. 1996. "Πορνεύειν as Body Violation: The Unique Nature of Sexual Sin in 1 Corinthians 6.18." *New Testament Studies* 42: 540–558.

Fornara, C. 1971. *Herodotus: An Interpretive Essay*. Oxford University Press. Oxford.

Foster, B. R. 1995. *From Distant Days: Myths, Tales, and Poetry of Ancient Mesopotamia*. CDL Press. Bestheda, MD.

———. 1993. *Before the Muses: An Anthology of Akkadian Literature*. CDL Press. Bethesda, MD.

Frayne, D. 1985. "Notes on the Sacred Marriage Rite." *Bibliotheca Orientalis* 42: 5–22.

Frazer, J. G. 1907. *Adonis, Attis, Osiris: Studies in the History of Oriental Religion*. MacMillan and Co. London.

Frymer-Kensky, T. 1992. *In the Wake of the Goddess: Women, Culture and the Biblical Transformation*. Fawcett Columbine. New York.

Gabrieli, F. 1989. *Arab Historians of the Crusades*. Dorset Press. New York.

Gaca, K. L. 2003. *The Making of Fornication*. University of California Press. Berkeley.

Gallery, M. L. 1980. "Service Obligations of the *kezertu*-Women." *Orientalia* N.S. 49: 333–338.

Gardner, J. F. 1986. *Women in Roman Law and Society*. Indiana University Press. Bloomington.

Gardner, P. 1916 [1915]. *The Ephesian Gospel*. Williams and Norgate. London.

Garlan, Y. 1988. *Slavery in Ancient Greece*. Cornell University Press. Ithaca, NY.

Garland, R. 1990. *The Greek Way of Life: From Conception to Old Age*. Cornell University Press. Ithaca, NY.

Garsoïan, N. G. 1989. *The Epic Histories Attributed to P'awstos Buzand (Buzandaran Patmut'iwnk')*. Harvard University Press. Cambridge, MA.

George, A. 1999. *The Epic of Gilgamesh: The Babylonian Epic Poem and Other Texts in Akkadian and Sumerian*. Penguin Books. London.

Gesenius, W. 1847. *Hebrew and Chaldee Lexicon to the Old Testament Scriptures*. Samuel Bagster and Sons. London.

Gkamas, D. 2000. "Banking." In G. Speake (ed.) *Encyclopedia of Greece and the Hellenic Tradition*. Fitzroy Dearborn Publishers. London, 214–216.

Glassner, J.-J. 2002. "Polygunie ou prostitution: Une approche comparative de la sexualité masculine." In Parpola and Whiting (eds.), 2002, 81–96.

Glinister, F. 2000. "The Rapino Bronze, the Touta Marouca, and Sacred Prostitution in Early Central Italy." In A. E. Cooley (ed.), *The Epigraphic Landscape of Roman Italy*. Institute of Classical Studies, University of London. London, 19–38.

Goff, B. 2004. *Citizen Bacchae: Women's Ritual Practice in Ancient Greece*. University of California Press. Berkeley.

Gould, J. 2000 [1989]. *Herodotus*. Bristol Classical Paperbacks. Gerald Duckworth & Co. London.

Graf, F. 1997. "Medea, the Enchantress from Afar: Remarks on a Well-Known Myth." In Clauss and Johnston (eds.) 1997, 21–43.

———. 1981. "Culti e Credenze Religiose della Magna Graecia." *Megale Hellas: Nome e immagine*. Istituto per la Storia e l'Archeologia della Magna Grecia. Taranto, 158–185.

Graves, R. 1979. *Suetonius: The Twelve Caesars*. Penguin Books. London.

Grenfell, B. P., and A. S. Hunt (eds.). 1903. *The Oxyrhyncus Papyri: Part III*. Egypt Exploration Fund. London.

Gressman, H., and A. Laminski. 1992. *Eusebius Werke: Die Theophanie*. Akademie Verlag. Leipzig.

Griffiths, A. 2001. "Kissing Cousins: Some Curious Cases of Adjacent Material in Herodotus." In Luraghi (ed.) 2001, 161–178.

Griffiths, E. 2006. *Medea*. Routledge. London.

Gritz, S. H. 1991. *Paul, Women Teachers, and the Mother Goddess at Ephesus*. University Press of America. Lanham, MD.

Gruber, M. I. 2005. "זונה וזנות בעולם המקרא." *Zmanîm* 90: 20–29.

———. 1986. "Hebrew Qedešah and Her Canaanite and Akkadian Cognates." *UF* 18: 133–148.

Gulick, C. B. 1927. *Athenaeus: The Deipnosophists*. Harvard University Press. Cambridge, MA.

Gunkel, H. 1997 [1901]. *Genesis*. Mercer University Press. Macon, GA.

Günther, W. 1970. "Eine neue didymeische Bauinschrift." *Istambuler Mitteilungen* 20: 237–247.

Haase, I. M. 1990. *Cult Prostitution in the Hebrew Bible?* Master's thesis, University of Ottawa.

Hajjar, Y. 1985. *La Triade d'Héliopolis-Baalbek: Iconographie, Théologie, Culte et Sanctuaires*. Université de Montréal. Montreal.

Hall, E. 2002 [1992]. "When Is a Myth Not a Myth? Bernal's 'Ancient Model.'" In T. Harrison (ed.) 2002, 133–152.

———. 1993. "Asia Unmanned: Images of Victory in Classical Athens." In J. Rich and G. Shipley (eds.), *War and Society in the Greek World*. Routledge. London, 108–133.

Hämeen-Anttila, J., and R. Rollinger. 2001. "Herodot und die Arabische Göttin 'Alilat.'" *JANER* 1.1: 84–99.

Hamilton, J. T. 2003. *Soliciting Darkness: Pindar, Obscurity, and the Classical Tradition*. Harvard University Press. Cambridge, MA.

Harper, R. P. 1967. "A Dedication to the Goddess Anaitis at Ortaköy, North of Aksaray, (Nitalis?)." *AS* 17: 193.

Harrell, S. E. 2003. "Marvelous *Andreia*: Politics, Geography, and Ethnicity in Herodotus' *Histories*." In R. M. Rosen and I. Sluiter (eds.), 2003, 77–94.

Harris, R. 1964. "The Naditu Woman." In *Studies Presented to A. Leo Oppenheim*. The Oriental Institute of the University of Chicago. Chicago, 106–135.

Harrison, T. 2003. "'Prophecy in Reverse'? Herodotus and the Origins of History." In Derrow and Parker (eds.) 2003, 237–255.

———. 2002 [1997]. "Herodotus and the Ancient Greek Idea of Rape." In S. Deacy and K. F. Pierce (eds.), *Rape in Antiquity*. Gerald Duckworth & Co. London, 185–208.

———. 2000. *Divinity and History: The Religion of Herodotus*. Clarendon Press. Oxford.

Harrison, T. (ed.). 2002. *Greeks and Barbarians*. Routledge. New York.

Hartog, F. 1988. *The Mirror of Herodotus: The Representation of the Other in the Writing of Herodotus*. University of California Press. Berkeley.

Harvey, A. E. 1955. "The Classification of Greek Lyric Poetry." *CQ* N.S. 5: 155–175.

Heltzer, M. 1987. "The *ger* in Phoenician Society." In E. Lipinski (ed.) *Phoenicia and the East Mediterranean in the First Millennium* B.C. Peeters. Leuven, 309–314.

Henderson, J. 1996. *Three Plays by Aristophanes: Staging Women*. Routledge. New York.

Hengel, M. 2001. "Judaism and Hellenism Revisted." In J. J. Collins and G. E. Sterling (eds.), *Hellenism in the Land of Israel*. University of Notre Dame Press. Notre Dame, IN, 6–37.

Henshaw, R. A. 1994. *Female and Male: The Cultic Personnel, The Bible and the Rest of the Ancient Near East*. Pickwick Publications. Allison Park, PA.

Héring, J. 1962. *The First Epistle of Saint Paul to the Corinthians*. Epworth Press. London.

Hertz, W. 1905. *Gesammelte Abhandlungen*. J. G. Cotta'sche Buchhandlung. Stuttgart.

Heyne, C. G. 1804. "De Babyloniorum Instituto Religioso, ut Mulieres ad Veneris Templum Prostarent." *Comentat. Soc. Reg. Götting.* XVI: 30–42.

Hooker, J. T. 1980. *Linear B: An Introduction.* Bristol Classical Press. Bristol.

Hooks, S. M. 1985. *Sacred Prostitution in Israel and the Ancient Near East.* Ph.D. dissertation, Hebrew Union College.

Hubbard, T. K. 1985. *The Pindaric Mind: A Study of Logical Structure in Early Greek Poetry.* E. J. Brill. Leiden.

Humphries, R. 1983. *Ovid: Metamorphoses.* Indiana University Press. Bloomington.

Hunter, J. 2004. *Rites of Pleasure: Sexuality in Wicca and NeoPaganism.* Citadel Press. New York.

Jacobs, F. 1837 [1811]. "Ueber eine Stelle beim Herodot." *Vermischte Schriften.* Leipzig, 23–53.

Jalabert, L. 1929. *Inscriptions grecques et latines de la Syrie* (IGLS). Paul Geuthner. Paris.

Jannot, J.-R. 2005. *Religion in Ancient Etruria.* University of Wisconsin Press. Madison.

Jastrow, M., Jr. 1915. *The Civilization of Babylonia and Assyria.* J. B. Lippincott. Philadelphia.

———. 1898. *The Religion of Babylonia and Assyria.* Ginn & Co. Boston.

Jeyes, U. 1983. "The *Nadītu* Women of Sippar." In A. Cameron and A. Kuhrt (eds.), *Images of Women in Antiquity.* Wayne State University Press. Detroit, MI, 260–272.

Johnson, D. O. 1997. *An English Translation of Claudius Aelianus'* Varia Historia. E. Mellen Press. Leviston, NY.

Johnston, S. I. 1997. "Corinthian Medea and the Cult of Hera Akraia." In Clauss and Johnston (eds.) 1997, 44–70.

Jones, H. L. 1917. *The Geography of Strabo.* Harvard University Press. Cambridge, MA.

Karageorghis, J. 2005. *Kypris: The Aphrodite of Cyprus: Ancient Sources and Archaeological Evidence.* A. G. Leventis Foundation. Nicosia.

Karageorghis, V. 1988. "Cyprus." In S. Moscati (ed.), *The Phoenicians.* Rizzoli Press. New York, 185–198 and bibliography 665.

Kass, L. R. 2003. *The Beginning of Wisdom: Reading Genesis.* Free Press. New York.

Keil, C. F. 2001. *Commentary on the Old Testament: Volume 1, the Pentateuch.* Hendrickson Publishers, Peabody, MA.

Kilian-Dirlmeier, I. 1985. "Fremde Weihungen in Griechischen Heiligtümern vom 8. zum Beginn des 7. Jahrhunderts v. Chr." *Jahrbuch des Römisch-Germanischen Zentralmuseums Mainz* 35, 215–254.

Kilmer, A. D. 1963. "The First Tablet of 'malku = šarru' Together with Its Explicit Version." *JAOS* 83: 420–446.

Kirchhoff, R. 1994. *Die Sünde gegen den eigenen Leib: Studien zu* πόρνη *und* πορνεία *in 1 Kor 6, 12–20 und dem sozio-kulturellen Kontext der paulinischen Adressaten.* Vandenhoeck & Ruprecht. Göttingen.

Knust, J. W. 2006. *Abandoned to Lust: Sexual Slander and Ancient Christianity.* Columbia University Press. New York.

Köpke, E. 1856. *De Chamaeleonte Peripatetico. Jahresbericht, Friedrichs-Gymnasium und Realschule,* 24–25.

Krevans, N. 1997. "Medea as Foundation Heroine." In Clauss and Johnston (eds.) 1997, 71–82.

Kroeger, R. C, and C. C. Kroeger. 1991. *I Suffer Not a Woman.* Baker Books. Grand Rapids, MI.

Kurke, L. 1999. *Coins, Bodies, Games, and Gold: The Politics of Meaning in Archaic Greece.* Princeton University Press. Princeton, NJ.

———. 1996. "Pindar and the Prostitutes, or Reassessing Ancient 'Pornography'." *ARION* 4.2: 49–75.

La Regina, A. 1997a. "La Tabula Rapinensis: Legge del popolo marrucino per l'istituzione della prostituzione sacra nel santuario di Giove padre nell'arce Tarincra (Rapino)." Accessed at http://xoomer.alice.it/davmonac/sanniti/rapino2.html

———. 1997b. "Lex populi Marrucini de ancillis Iouiis profanandis." In B. Magnusson et al. (eds.), *Vltra Terminvm Vagari: Scritti in onore di Carl Nylander.* Edizioni Quasar. Rome, 171–173.

Lambert, W. G. 1992. "Prostitution." *Xenia* 32: 127–157.

Langdon, S. 1914. *Tammuz and Ishtar: A Monograph upon Babylonian Religion and Theology.* Clarendon Press. Oxford.

Lapinkivi, L. 2004. *The Sumerian Sacred Marriage in Light of the Comparative Evidence.* State Archives of Assyria Project, Vol. XV. University of Helsinki. Helsinki.

Lasserre, F. 1975. *Strabon, Géographie, Tome VIII (Livre XI).* Société d'Édition <<Les Belles Lettres>>. Paris.

Lateiner, D. 1989. *The Historical Method of Herodotus.* University of Toronto Press. Toronto.

Latte, K. 1968. "Orakel" and "Promanteia." In *Kleine Schriften: Zu Religion, Recht, Literatur und Sprache der Griechen und Römer.* Munich.

———. 1940. The Coming of the Pythia. *Harvard Theological Review* 33: 9–18.

Laumonier, A. 1958. *Les Cultes indigènes en Carie.* E. de Boccard. Paris.

Lefkowitz, M. R. 1991. *First-Person Fictions: Pindar's Poetic 'I.'* Clarendon Press. Oxford.

Lefkowitz, M. R., and M. B. Fant (eds.) 1992. *Women's Life in Greece & Rome: A Source Book in Translation.* 2nd ed. Johns Hopkins University Press. Baltimore.

Leick, G. 1994. *Sex and Eroticism in Mesopotamian Literature.* Routledge. London.

Lerner, G. 1986. "The Origin of Prostitution in Ancient Mesopotamia." *Signs: Journal of Women in Culture and Society.* 11.2: 236–254.

Lesko, B. 2002. "Women and Religion in Ancient Egypt." In *Diotima* http://www.stoa.org/diotima/

Lewis, C. T. 1993 [1891]. *An Elementary Latin Dictionary.* Oxford University Press. Oxford.

Lightfoot, J. L. 2003. *Lucian on the Syrian Goddess.* Oxford University Press. Oxford.

Lipinski, E. 1995. *Dieux et déesses de l'univers phénicien et punique.* Peeters. Leuven.

Luckenbill, D. 1917. "The Temple Women of the Code of Hammurabi." *AJSL* 34: 1–12.

Luraghi, N. 2001. "Local Knowledge in Herodotus' *Histories.*" In Luraghi (ed.) 2001, 138–160.

Luraghi, N. (ed.). 2001. *The Historian's Craft in the Age of Herodotus.* Oxford University Press. Oxford.

Luther, B. 1906. "Die Nouvelle von Juda und Tamar und andere israelitische Novellen," in E. Meyer (ed.), *Die Israeliten und ihre Nachbarstamme.* Verlag von Max Niemeyer. Halle, 175–206.

Lyon, D. G. 1912. "The Consecrated Women of the Hammurabi Code." In D. G. Lyon and G. F. Moore (eds.), *Studies in the History of Religions Presented to Crawford Howell Toy.* The Macmillan Co. New York, 341–360.

McGinn, T. A. J. 1998. *Prostitution, Sexuality, and the Law in Ancient Rome.* Oxford University Press. Oxford.

MacGinnis, J. 1986. "Herodotus' Description of Babylon." *BICS* 33: 67–86.

MacLachlan B.. 1992. "Sacred Prostitution and Aphrodite." *Studies in Religion/Sciences Religieuses* 21.2: 145–162.

McNeal, R. A. 1988. "The Brides of Babylon: Herodotus 1.196." *Historia* 37: 54–71.

Mannhardt, W. 1905. *Wald- und Feldkulte.* Verlag von Gebrüder Borntraeger. Berlin.

Manniche, L. 1997. *Sexual Life in Ancient Egypt.* Kegan Paul International. London.

Manuel, F. E. 1959. *The Eighteenth Century Confronts the Gods.* Harvard University Press. Cambridge, MA.

Martínez-Pinna, J. 1998. "La Inscriptión Itálica de Rapino: Propuesta de Interpretación." *ZPE* 120: 203–214.

Maspero, G. 1894. *The Dawn of Civilization, Egypt and Chaldea.* D. Appleton and Co. New York.

Meeks, D., and C. Favard-Meeks. 1996. *Daily Life of the Egyptian Gods.* Cornell University Press. Ithaca, NY.

Meenee, H. 2007. "Sacred Prostitutes and Temple Slaves: The 'Sexual Priestesses' of Aphrodite." *Sacred History Magazine.* Accessed at http://www.ualhmeenee.com/1794/33201.html.

Meiggs, R., and D. Lewis. 1989. *A Selection of Greek Historical Inscriptions to the End of the Fifth Century B.C.* Clarendon Press. Oxford.

Meissner, B. 1925. *Babylonien und Assyrien.* Zweiter Band. Carl Winters Universitätsbuchhandlung. Heidelberg.

Mettinger, T. N. D. 2001. *The Riddle of Resurrection: "Dying and Rising Gods" in the Ancient Near East.* Almqvist & Wiksell International. Stockholm.

Metzger, B. M. 1963. *An Introduction to the Apocrypha.* Oxford University Press. New York.

Meyer, M. W. 1987. *The Ancient Mysteries: A Sourcebook.* University of Pennsylvania Press. Philadelphia.

Michaelides, D. 2002. "A Decorated Mirror from Nea Paphos." In D. Bolger and N. Serwint (eds.), *Engendering Aphrodite: Women and Society in Ancient Cyprus.* CAARI Monograph Vol. 3. ASOR. Boston, 351–364.

Michaelidou-Nicolaou, I. 1987. "Repercussions of the Phoenician Presence in Cyprus." In E. Lipinski (ed.), *Studia Phoenicia V: Phoenicia and the Eastern Mediterranean in the First Millennium B.C.* Uitgeverij Peeters. Leuven, 331–338.

Milgrom, J. 1990. *The JPS Torah Commentary: Numbers* במדבר. The Jewish Publication Society. Philadelphia.

Millar, F. 1993. *The Roman Near East: 31 BC – AD 337.* Harvard University Press. Cambridge, MA.

Miner, J. 2003. "Courtesan, Concubine, Whore: Apollodorus' Deliberate Use of Terms for Prostitutes." *AJPhil* 124: 19–37.

Momigliano, A. 1993 [1971]. *The Development of Greek Biography.* Expanded ed. Harvard University Press. Cambridge, MA.

Montero, S. 2004. "Mujeres extranjeras en la obra de Valerio Máximo." *Gerión Anejos* VIII, 45–56.

Montserrat, D. 1996. *Sex and Society in Græco-Roman Egypt.* Kegan Paul International. London.

Moore, C. A. 1977. *Daniel, Esther, and Jeremiah: The Additions.* Doubleday & Co. Garden City.

Muccioli, F. 1999. *Dionisio II: Storia e tradizione letteraria.* Coopertiva Libraria Universitaria Editrice Bologna. Bologna.

Müller-Kessler, C., and K. Kessler. 1999. "Spätbabylonische Gottheiten in spätantiken mandäischen Texten." *ZA* 89: 65–87.

Munson, R. V. 2001. *Telling Wonders: Ethnographic and Political Discourse in the Work of Herodotus.* University of Michigan Press. Ann Arbor.

Murnaghan, S. 1988. "How a Woman Can Be More like a Man: The Dialogue between Ischomachus and His Wife in Xenophon's *Oeconomicus.*" *Helios* 15: 9–22.

Murphy-O'Connor, J. 1983. *St. Paul's Corinth: Texts and Archaeology.* Liturgical Press. Collegeville.

Murray, O. 2001 [1987]. "Herodotus and Oral History." In Luraghi (ed.) 2001, 16–44.

———. 2001. "Herodotus and Oral History Reconsidered." In Luraghi (ed.) 2001, 314–325.

———. 1990. "Sympotic History." In Murray (ed.) 1990, 3–13.

Murray, O. (ed.). 1990. *Sympotica: A Symposium on the Symposion*. Clarendon Press. Oxford.

———. 1972. "Herodotus and Hellenistic Culture." *CQ* 22: 200–213.

Muss-Arnolt, W. 1905. *A Concise Dictionary of the Assyrian Language*. Reuther & Reichard. Berlin.

Nagy, G. 1990. *Pindar's Homer: The Lyric Possession of an Epic Past*. Johns Hopkins University Press. Baltimore.

Nickelsburg, G. W. E. 1981. *Jewish Literature between the Bible and the Mishnah: A Historical and Literary Introduction*. Fortress Press. Philadelphia.

Nicoli, R. 2001. "Strabone e la Campagna Partica di Antonio. Critica delle Fonti e Critica del Testo." In G. Traina (ed.), *Studi sull'XI Libro dei Geographika di Strabone*. Congedo Editore. Galatina, 95–126.

Nilsson, M. P. 1906. *Griechische Feste von Religiöser Bedeutung*. Teubner. Leipzig.

Nippel, W. 2002 [1996]. "The Construction of the 'Other'." In T. Harrison (ed.) 2002, 278–310.

Nixon, L. 1997. "The Cults of Demeter and Kore." In R. Hawley and B. Levick (eds.), *Women in Antiquity: New Assessments*. Routledge. New York, 75–96.

Norris, E. 1868. *Assyrian Dictionary*. Williams and Norgate. London.

Norwood, G. 1945. *Pindar*. University of California Press. Berkeley.

Oden, R. A., Jr. 1987. *The Bible without Theology*. University of Illinois Press. Urbana, IL.

———. 1977. *Studies in Lucian's De Syria Dea*. Scholars Press. Cambridge, MA.

Ogden, D. 1996. *Greek Bastardy: In the Classical and Hellenistic Periods*. Clarendon Press. Oxford.

Page, D. L. 1981. *Further Greek Epigrams*. Cambridge University Press. Cambridge, UK.

Palumbo Stracca, B. M. 1985. "Lettura Critica di Epigrammi Greci (I): 'Simonide' XIV Page." *Bollettino dei Classici* series 3, fasc. VI, 58–65.

Papageorgos, P. N. 1900. "Κυριας θεας Μας Ανικητου, Επηκοου Ναος εν Εδεσση τη Μακεδονικη (βοδενοις) και 14 Επιγραμματα." *Αθηνα* 12: 65–88.

Papazoglou, F. 1981. "Affranchissement par Consécration et Hiérodoulie." *Ž A* 31: 171–179.

Pardee, D. 2002. *Ritual and Cult at Ugarit*. Society of Biblical Literature. Atlanta.

Parker, R. 1996. *Miasma: Pollution and Purification in Early Greek Religion*. Clarendon Press. Oxford.

———. 1987. "Myths of Early Athens." In J. Bremmer (ed.), *Interpretations of Greek Mythology*. Croom Helm. London, 187–214.

Parpola, S. 1980. "The Murder of Sennacherib." In B. Alster (ed.), *Death in Mesopotamia*. Akademisk Forlag. Copenhagen, 171–182.

Parpola, S. and R. M. Whiting (eds.). 2002. *Sex and Gender in the Ancient Near East*. The Neo-Assyrian Text Corpus Project. Helsinki.

Paul, S. M. 2002. "The Shared Legacy of Sexual Metaphors and Euphemisms in Mesopotamian and Biblical Literature." In Parpola and Whiting (eds.), 2002, 81–96.

Pearson, L., and F. H. Sandbach. 1965. *Plutarch's Moralia*. Harvard University Press. Cambridge, MA.

Pellizer, E. 1990. "Outlines of a Morphology of Sympotic Entertainment." In Murray (ed.) (1996), 177–184.

Pembroke, S. 1970. "Locres et Tarante: Le rôle des femmes dans la fondation de deux colonies grecques." *Annales* 5: 1240–1270.

———. 1965. "Women in Charge: The Function of Alternatives in Early Greek Tradition and the Ancient Idea of Matriarchy." *Journal of the Warburg and Courtault Institute* 30: 1–35.

Peruzzi, E. 1976. "Sulla prostitutzione sacra nell'Italia antica." *Julian Huge Bonfante in Scritti in onore di Giuliano Bonfante*, Vol. I, Paideia. Brescia, 673–686.

Petit, T. 2004. "Herodotus and Amathus." In V. Karageorghis and I. Taifacos (eds.), *The World of Herodotus*. A. G. Leventis Foundation. Nicosia, 9–26.

Petsas, Ph. M., M. B. Hatzopoulos, L. Gounaropoulou, and P. Paschidis. 2000. *Inscriptions du Sanctuaire de la Mère des Dieux Autochtone de Leukopetra (Macédoine)*. De Boccard. Athens.

Pirenne-Delforge, V. 2007. "'Something to Do with Aphrodite?' *Ta Aphrodisia* and the Sacred." In A. Bendlin, P. Bonnechere, J. Bremmer, and D. Ogden (eds.) *A Companion to Greek Religion*. Blackwell. Malden, 311–323.

———. 1994. *L'Aphrodite grecque*. Kernos suppl. 4. Liège.

Ploss, H. H. 1887. *Das Weib in der Natur- und Völkerkunde*. Th. Grieben's Verlag. Leipzig.

Polanski, T. 1998. "Is It or Is It Not Lucian's: An Art Historian's Supplement to the Controversy over the Authorship of the 'Syrian Goddess.'" *Polska Akademia Umiejetnosci: Prace Komisji Filologii Klasycznej* 27: 161–184.

Poljakov, F. B. 1989. *Die Inschriften von Tralleis und Nysa: Teil I: Die Inschriften von Tralleis*. Habelt. Bonn.

Postgate, J. N. 1992. *Early Mesopotamia: Society and Economy at the Dawn of History*. Routledge. London.

Powell, J. E. 1977. *A Lexicon to Herodotus*. Georg Olms. Hildeshem.

Prandi, L. 1988. "La critica storica di Strabone alla geografia di Erodoto." In M. Sordi (ed.), *Geografia e storiografia nel mondo classico*. Università Cattolica del Sacro Cuore. Milan, 52–72.

———. 1985. *Callistene: Uno storico tra Aristotele e i re macedoni*. Jaca Book. Milan.

Price, S. 1999. "Latin Christian Apologetics: Minucius Felix, Tertullian, and Cyprian." In Edwards, Goodman, and Price (eds.) 1999, 105–129.

Pritchard, J. B. 1958. *The Ancient Near Eastern Texts: Volume I: An Anthology of Texts and Pictures*. Princeton University Press. Princeton, NJ.

Qualls-Corbett, N. 1988. *The Sacred Prostitute: Eternal Aspect of the Feminine.* Inner City Books. Toronto.

Race, W. H. 1997. *Pindar: Nemean Odes, Isthmian Odes, Fragments.* Harvard University Press. Cambridge, MA.

———. 1986. *Pindar.* Twayne Publishers. Boston.

Ramsay, W. M. 1975 [1895–1897]. *The Cities and Bishoprics of Phrygia.* Arno Press. New York.

———. 1883. "Unedited Inscriptions of Asia Minor." *BCH* 7: 276–277.

Reade, J. 1997. "Sumerian Origins." In I. L. Finkel and M. J. Geller (eds.), *Sumerian Gods and Their Representations.* Styx Publications. Groningen, 221–229.

Redfield, J. 2003. *The Locrian Maidens: Love and Death in Greek Italy.* Princeton University Press. Princeton, NJ.

———. 2002 [1985]. "Herodotus the Tourist." In T. Harrison (ed.) 2002, 24–49.

Renger, J. 1972–5. "Heilige Hochzeit. A. Philologisch." *RlA* 4: 251–259.

Robert, L. 1970 [1937]. *Études anatoliennes: Recherches sur les inscriptions grecques de l'Asie Mineure.* A. M. Hakkert. Amsterdam.

Robins, G. 1993. *Women in Ancient Egypt.* Harvard University Press. Cambridge, MA.

———. 1985. "The God's Wife of Amun in the 18th Dynasty in Egypt." In A. Cameron and A. Kuhrt (eds.), *Images of Women in Antiquity.* Wayne State University Press. Detroit, 65–78.

Romm, J. S. 1998. *Herodotus.* Yale University Press. New Haven, CT.

———. 1992. *The Edges of the Earth in Ancient Thought: Geography, Exploration, and Fiction.* Princeton University Press. Princeton, NJ.

Rosellini, M., and S. Saïd. 1978. "Usage de femmes et autres nomoi chez les 'sauvages' d'Herodote: Essai de lecture strucurale." *Annali Scuola Normale Superiore di Pisa,* ser. 3, 8, #3: 949–1005.

Rosen, R. M., and I. Sluiter (eds.). 2003. *Andreia: Studies in Manliness and Courage in Classical Antiquity.* Brill. Leiden.

Rosenbaum, J. 1901 [1838]. *The Plague of Lust, Being a History of Venereal Disease in Classical Antiquity.* Charles Carrington. Paris.

Rösler, W. 1990. "*Mnemosyne* in the Symposion." In Murray (ed.) 1990, 230–237.

Roth, M. T. 2006. "Marriage, Divorce, and the Prostitute in Ancient Mesopotamia." In Faraone and McClure (eds.) 2006, 21–39.

———. 1989. *Babylonian Marriage Agreements 7th–3rd Centuries B.C.* Verlag Butzon & Berker Kevelaer. Neukirchener Verlag Neukirchen-Vluyn.

———. 1988. "'She Will Die by the Iron Dagger:' Adultery and Neo-Babylonian Marriage." *JESHO* 31: 186–206.

———. 1983. "The Slave and the Scoundrel: CBS 20467, a Sumerian Morality Tale?" *JAOS* 103: 274–282.

Rouse, W. H. D. 1975. *Greek Votive Offerings.* New York.

Rutherford, I. 2001. *Pindar's Paeans: A Reading of the Fragments with a Survey of the Genre*. Oxford University Press. Oxford.

Saffrey, H. D. 1985. "Aphrodite à Corinthe: Réflexions sur une idée Reçue." *RB* 92: 359–374.

Salmon, J. B. 1997 [1984]. *Wealthy Corinth: A History of the City to 338 BC*. Clarendon Press. Oxford.

Sandys, J. 1915. *The Odes of Pindar*. Harvard University Press. Cambridge, MA.

Sauneron, S. 2000. *The Priests of Ancient Egypt*. Cornell University Press. Ithaca, NY.

Sayce, A. H. 1902. *The Religions of Ancient Egypt and Babylonia*. T. & T. Clark. Edinburgh.

———. 1899. *Babylonians and Assyrians: Life and Customs*. Charles Scribner's Sons. New York.

Scanlon, T. F. 1996. "Games for Girls." *Archaeology* July/August 1996: 32–33.

Schindler, R. K. 1998. *The Archaeology of Aphrodite in the Greek West: Ca. 650–480 BC*. Ph.D. dissertation, University of Michigan.

Schmitt-Pantel, P. 1990. "Sacrifical Meal and *Symposion*: Two Models of Civic Institution in the Archaic City?" In Murray (ed.) 1990, 14–33.

Schmitz, H. A. 1970. *Hypsos und Bios: Stilistische Untersuchungen zum Alltagsrealismus in der archaischen griechischen Chorlyrik*. H. Lang. Bern.

Schulze, W. 1904. *Geschichte lateinischer Eigennamen*. Berlin.

Scramuzza, V. 1936. "Were the *Venerii* in Sicily Serfs?" *AJPhil* 57: 326–330.

Serra Ridgway, F. R. 1990. "Etruscans, Greeks, Carthaginians: The Sanctuary at Pyrgi." In J.-P. Descudres (ed.), *Greek Colonists and Native Populations*. Clarendon Press. Oxford, 511–530.

Serrati, J. 2000. "Sicily from Pre-Greek Times to the Fourth Century." In C. Smith and J. Serrati (eds.), *Sicily from Aeneas to Augustus: New Approaches in Archaeology and History*. Edinburgh University Press. Edinburgh, 9–14.

Shaw, I., and P. Nicholson. 1995. *The Dictionary of Ancient Egypt*. Harry N. Abrams, Inc. New York.

Shrimpton, G. S. 1991. *Theopompus the Historian*. McGill–Queen's University Press. Montreal.

Simmons, M. B. 1995. *Arnobius of Sicca: Religious Conflict and Competition in the Age of Diocletian*. Clarendon Press. Oxford.

Sissa, G. 1990. "Maidenhood without Maidenhead: The Female Body in Ancient Greece." In D. M. Halperin, J. J. Winkler, and F. I. Zeitlin (eds.), *Before Sexuality: The Construction of Erotic Experience in the Ancient Greek World*. Princeton University Press. Princeton, NJ, 339–364.

Slater, W. J. 1969. *Lexicon to Pindar*. Walter de Gruyter & Co. Berlin.

Sluiter, I., and R. M. Rosen. 2003. "General Introduction." In R. M. Rosen and I. Sluiter (eds.) 2003, 1–24.

Sokolowski, F. 1954. "The Real Meaning of Sacral Manumission." *HTR* 47: 173–181.

Sourvinou-Inwood, C. 2003. "Herodotos (and Others) on Pelasgians: Some Perceptions of Ethnicity." In P. Derrow and R. Parker (eds.) 2003, 103–144.

———. 1997. "Medea at a Shifting Distance: Images and Euripidean Tragedy." In Clauss and Johnston (eds.) 1997, 253–296.

———. 1974. "The Votum of 477/6 B.C. and the Foundation Legend of Locri Epizephyrii." CQ 24: 186–198.

Spivey, N. and S. Stoddart. 1990. Etruscan Italy. B.T. Batsford. London.

Stark, C. 2006. <<Kultprostitution>> im Alten Testament? Die Qedeschen der Hebräischen Bibel und das Motiv der Hurerei. Acedemic Press Fribourg. Göttingen.

Steiner, D. 1986. The Crown of Song: Metaphor in Pindar. Oxford University Press. New York.

Stol, M. 1995. "Mulissu." In K. Van der Toom (ed.), The Dictionary of Deities and Demons in the Bible. Brill. Leiden. Columns 1138–1140.

Stoneman, R. 1997. Pindar: The Odes and Selected Fragments. Everyman. London.

Strong. R. A. 1997. The Most Shameful Practice: Temple Prostitution in the Ancient Greek World. Ph.D. dissertation, University of California, Los Angeles.

Stukey, J. H. 2005. "Sacred Prostitutes." Accessed at http://www.matrifocus.com/SAM05/spotlight.htm

Svenbro, J. 1976. La parole et le marbre: Aux origines de la poétique grecque. Lund.

Swanson, R. A. 1974. Pindar's Odes. Bobbs–Merrill. Indianapolis.

Teeter, E. 1999. "Temple Life." In J. Freeman et al. (ed.), Women of the Nile. Rosicrucian Egyptian Museum. San José, 25–26.

Thomas, R. 2000. Herodotus in Context: Ethnography, Science and the Art of Persuasion. Cambridge University Press. Cambridge, UK.

———. 1992. Literacy and Orality in Ancient Greece. Cambridge University Press. Cambridge, UK.

Thomson, R. W. 1976. Agathangelos: History of the Armenians. SUNY Press. Albany.

———. 1971. Athanasius: Contra Gentes and De Incarnatione. Clarendon Press. Oxford.

Thomson de Grummond, N., and E. Simon (eds.). 2006. The Religion of the Etruscans. University of Texas Press. Austin.

Tigay, J. H. 1996. The JPS Torah Commentary: Deuteronomy דברים. The Jewish Publication Society. Philadelphia.

Turano, C. 1952. "La prostituzione sacra a Locri Epizefiri," ArchClass, 4: 248–252.

Van Groningen, B. A. 1960. Pindare au Banquet. A. W. Sythoff. Leiden.

———. 1956. "Théopompe ou Chamaeléon? À propos de Simonide 137 B, 104 D." Mnemosyne 4.9.1: 11–22.

Van Nuffelen, P. 2004. Un Héritage de paix et de piété: Étude sur les histoires ecclésiastiques de Socrate et de Sozomène. Peeters. Leuven.

Vanoyeke, V. 1990. *La prostitution en Grèce et à Rome*. Les Belles Letters. Paris.

Verbrugghe, G. P., and J. M. Wickersham. 2000 [1996]. *Berossos and Manetho, Introduced and Translated: Native Traditions in Ancient Mesopotamia and Egypt.* University of Michigan Press. Ann Arbor.

Vickery, J. B. 1973. *The Literary Impact of The Golden Bough.* Princeton University Press. Princeton, NJ.

Walker, H. J. 2004. *Valerius Maximus: Memorable Deeds and Sayings: One Thousand Tales from Ancient Rome.* Hackett Publishing Company. Indianapolis.

Wallace, P. W. 1969. "Strabo on Acrocorinth." *Hesperia* 38.4: 495–499, Plate 124.

Wallace, R. E. 1984. *The Sabellian Languages.* Ph.D. dissertation, Ohio State University.

Walton, F. R. 1970. "Prostitution, Sacred." In *OCD²*. Oxford.

Wehrli, F. 1969. *Die Schule des Aristoteles: Texte und Kommentar.* Vol. 9. Schwabe & Co. Verlag. Basel.

Westenholz, J. G. 1995. "Heilige Hochzeit und kultische Prostitution im alten Mesopotamien." *Wort und Dienst (Jahrbuch der Kirchlichen Hochschule Bethel)* 23: 43–62.

———. 1989. "Tamar, Qedeša, Qadištu, and Sacred Prostitution in Mesopotamia." *HTR* 82.3: 245–265.

Westermann, W. L. 1945. "Between Slavery and Freedom." *AHR* 50.2: 213–227.

Wilamowitz-Moellendorff, U. von. 1889. *Commentariolum Grammaticum IV.* Ind. Schol. Hib. Göttingen, 3–28.

Wilhelm, G. 1990. "Marginalien zu Herodot Klio 199." In T. Abusch, J. Huehn-ergard, and P. Steinkeller (eds.), *Lingering Over Words: Studies in Ancient Near Eastern Literature in Honor of William L. Moran.* Scholars Press. Atlanta, 505–524.

Williams, C. K. II. 1986. "Corinth and the Cult of Aphrodite." In M. A. Del Chiaro (ed.), *Corinthiaca: Studies in Honor of Darrell A. Amyx.* University of Missouri Press. Columbia, 12–24.

Williams, F. 1987. *The Panarion of Epiphanius of Salamis.* E. J. Brill. Leiden.

Winkler J. J. 1990. *The Constraints of Desire: The Anthropology of Sex and Gender in Ancient Greece.* Routledge. New York.

Woodbury, L. 1978. "The Gratitude of the Locrian Maiden: Pindar, *Pyth.* 2.18–20." *TAPA* 108: 285–299.

———. 1968. "Pindar and the Mercenary Muse: *Isthm.* 2.1–13." *TAPA* 99: 527–542.

Yamauchi, E. M. 1973. "Cultic Prostitution: A Case Study in Cultural Diffu-sion." In H. A. Hoffner (ed.), *Orient and Occident: Essays Presented to Cyrus H. Gordon on the Occasion of his Sixty-Fifth Birthday.* Verlag Butzon & Bercker Kevelaer. Neukirchener Verlag. Neukirchen-Vluyn, 213–222.

Yardley, J. C., 2003. *Justin and Pompeius Trogus: A Study of the Language of Justin's Epitome of Trogus.* University of Toronto Press. Toronto.

Yardley, J. C., and R. Develin. 1994. *Justin: Epitome of the Phillipic History of Pompeius Trogus.* Scholar's Press. Atlanta.

Yardley, J. C., and W. Heckel. 1997. *Justin: Epiome of the Philippic History of Pompeius Trogus Books 11–12: Alexander the Great.* Clarendon Press. Oxford.

Zadok, R. 1980. "More Assyrians in Babylonian sources." *NABU* 1998–55. Accessed at http://www.achemenet.com/pdf/nabu/nabu1998-055.pdf

———. 1997. "A Group of Late-Babylonain Letter-Orders and Administrative Documents." *NABU* 1997–148. Accessed at http://www.achemenet.com/pdf/nabu/nabu1997-148.pdf

Zgoll, A. 1997. "Inanna als nugig." *ZA* 87: 181–195.

Zucca, R. 1988. "Venus *Erycina* tra Sicilia, Africa e Sardegna." *L'Africana Romana.* 6: 771–780.

INDEX

W. Mannhardt 311–312, 314
Mari 19, 24, 29, 30
Marriage Auction see Bride Auction
Martiales 187–188, 190
J. Maspero 317–318
Matriarchy 8
Medea 142, 144, 146–148
Memorable Deeds and Sayings 210, 232
meretrix 5, 43–44, 270, 289, 308
Mesopotamia 4, 14, 15, 17–33, 66, 108, 154, 162, 163, 287, 317
Minucius Felix 274
MÍ.SUHUR.LÁ 20, 29, 30
Mother Goddess 290, 301, 305, 306, 313, 325, 327
W. Muss-Arnoldt 324
Mutterrecht 300
Mylitta 6, 12, 51, 59, 60, 79, 82, 85, 91–92, 156, 228, 244, 293–294, 296–298, 300, 302–304, 306, 307, 311, 313, 317, 332

Naditu 20, 22–23, 25, 28, 29
M.P. Nilsson 307
NIN.DINGIR 20, 21–22
Nippur 22
nu'artu 31
NU.BAR 20
NU.GIG 20, 23–25, 26
Numbers 37

R.A. Oden 10, 11, 153, 209, 335
On the Malice of Herodotos (De malignitate Herodoti) 61, 141–142
Ovid 266

Palestine 15
pallakê/pallakis 7, 153, 191–198, 305
pallas 167, 191–198, 199
pallakeuô 191–198
Panarion 274–275
Paphos 122, 226, 267, 303, 307, 311
Paul of Tarsus (St. Paul) 260, 261–265, 273, 278, 326
Pausanias 131, 147, 237
Periandros 221–222, 228
Phoenicia(n) 14, 15, 16, 45–47, 190, 234, 236, 247, 260, 261, 277, 280, 283,

284, 294, 298, 302, 303, 306, 313, 319, 321
Pindar 5, 6, 7, 10, 12, 50, 94, 165, 177, 183, 226–227, 267, 284, 308–310
H.H. Ploss 306
Plutarch 61, 141, 143–145, 309, 310
Pompeius Trogus 7, 210, 220, 228, 239–240, 244
pornê/pornos 5, 43, 183, 260, 262, 264–265
porneia 260, 261–265, 276, 281
porneuô 5, 265
prostare 5
Prostibulatrix 258
prostituare 5
Pyrgi 247

Qadeš 16, 33–36, 42–45, 288, 289, 315–316, 321–322
Qedešâ 17, 23, 33–45, 288, 289, 292, 315, 316, 321–323, 335
Qadištu 20, 23–25, 26, 28, 29, 45, 110, 318, 324, 335
qdšm 45–46
quaestus 7, 229–230, 233, 238, 239, 241, 242
N. Qualls-Corbett 329, 331

W. Ramsay 292, 304–306
rape 82–83, 87, 205, 215–217, 218, 226, 237–238, 246, 284, 333
Rapino 247, 255–259
The Religion of the Semites 316
rhetoric 8, 16, 36, 62, 245, 286
W. Robertson Smith 312, 316
J. Rosenbaum 292, 298–300, 307

Sacred Bodies see *hiera sômata*
Sacred Marriage (*hieros gamos*) 4, 17, 21, 314, 328, 330
Saga von Tanaquil 302–304
Šamhat 30, 318
Šamhatu (ukhatu) 20, 23, 25, 27, 28, 29–31, 317, 318, 320–321, 324
J. Sandys 292, 310
A.H. Sayce 317, 319–320
scortum 4, 5, 44, 248, 250, 253, 254, 270
scortator 44
Septuagint 42–43
Sextus Aurelius Victor 223

INDEX LOCORUM

Primary Sources – Medieval